THE GUIDE
TO THE FOUNDATIONS
OF PUBLIC ADMINISTRATION

PUBLIC ADMINISTRATION AND PUBLIC POLICY

A Comprehensive Publication Program

Executive Editor

JACK RABIN
Professor of Public Administration and Public Policy
Division of Public Affairs
The Capital College
The Pennsylvania State University–Harrisburg
Middletown, Pennsylvania

Other volumes in preparation

THE GUIDE
TO THE FOUNDATIONS
OF PUBLIC ADMINISTRATION

DANIEL W. MARTIN
Public Administration Program
University of Baltimore
Baltimore, Maryland

MARCEL DEKKER, INC.   New York and Basel

Library of Congress Cataloging-in-Publication Data

Martin, Daniel
  The guide to the foundations of public administration.
  (Public administration and public policy ; 37)
  Includes indexes.
  1. Public administration—History—Bibliography.
  2. Public administration literature--History. I. Title.
  II. Series.
  Z7164.A2M27   1989 [JF1341]   016.35 89-11813
  ISBN 0-8247-8284-4 (alk. paper)

This book is printed on acid-free paper.

MARCEL DEKKER, INC.
270 Madison Avenue, New York, New York 10016

Current printing (last digit):
10 9 8 7 6 5 4 3 2 1

PRINTED IN THE UNITED STATES OF AMERICA

Preface

This is an annotated bibliographic guide to the development of the literature in public administration. It is organized into chapters on the basis of subject matters. Within each chapter, the literature is described as it developed chronologically, as it influenced later works, and as is has been remembered through subsequent summaries and citations.

For those seeking an individual author or work, an index of synopses immediately follows the text, and lists the numbered citation in which the work appears. For those researching subject matters that do not appear in the table of contents, a subject index follows the index of synopses.

Primarily, however, the text is designed to be read straight through. As is explained in the Introduction, one of the weaknesses in our approach to dated literature is that we normally approach it out of the context in which it was supposed to be judged. As a result, both its methodology and its concerns sometimes seem inappropriate or simplistic by modern standards.

It is easy to find literature for which such criticism is justified. Much of the dated literature, and much current literature, is inappropriate, simplistic, or worse. However, such judgments cannot be made fairly without considering the context that surrounded the work, and in which it was supposed to be applied. The running narrative of the annotations is designed to reintroduce some of that context.

Annotations do not substitute for reading the text in its original form. For that reason, the bibliographic information has been made as accurate as is practical, always using the publication data of the first known release of the work, and not of later reprints, excerpts, or summations.

At least three potential audiences come to mind for the book. First, it can be useful as a textbook to provide entering graduate-level students with exposure to the debates that have shaped their new field. Second--and it is for this audience that the book was first conceived--it provides a guide for students facing comprehensive examinations so that they can "glue together" some common heritage for arguments that are often taught from the most recently published literature on each subject. Finally, it can be a starting point for background literature searches for both faculty and students.

This book is largely an individual effort. Still, I would like to express my appreciation to graduate assistants Neil Cohen and Dave Juppé, each of whom worked on the project for brief periods. I would like to thank Larry Thomas for finding computer and printer support, and for keeping the voracious committee monsters from banging down the door. Also, the true magic that makes such a book possible is the computerized interlibrary-loan system. In that arena, I owe a great debt to Carol Vaeth, a librarian with a highly polished skill for deciphering incomplete and incorrect bibliographic citations.

Daniel W. Martin

Contents

PART II: THE INTERNAL OPERATION OF PUBLIC ADMINISTRATION

Introduction

Public Administration is a field with a surprisingly rich heritage. By popular definition, the formal study of the subject is barely more than a century old. However, during that century, governmental bureaucracies have grown large and mature. From its beginning, the discipline has also enjoyed extensive interaction between those who study the subject and those who practice it, allowing for more intensive experimentation than has been possible in some social sciences.

The wisdom that has been achieved in our short life is partially reflected in the practices and organizational structures that have evolved to make the governments of the past century possible. However, it is equally embodied in the analytical literature that proposed and helped shape that wisdom. That analytical record is the more far-reaching of the two, available across ages and cultures to be applied in circumstances never envisioned by the original authors, to solve problems that sometimes only recently developed. The summation of that record is the logical subject for annotated bibliographies.

Annotated bibliographies were common in this field in the late 1940s and early 1950s.[1] In more recent times, their popularity has waned, although three series with more limited objectives are still being published. Vance Bibliographies has compiled thousands of guides on very specific subjects with little annotation.[2] Garland Publishers has produced a series on subtopics of public administration, although the amount of annotation, if any, varies widely.[3] In addition, Sage Publications reviews most new releases on a monthly basis.[4]

Also, in 1972, Howard McCurdy published an alphabetized listing and brief synopsis of each of the 187 most cited literary works in the reading lists of Public Administration.[5] In 1986, he revised and updated his study to reflect the new literature that had been released in subsequent years.[6]

Annotated bibliographies can serve at least four potential uses for both new students and seasoned scholars approaching new subject areas. They can quickly identify the points in our spotted history that remain highly visible. They can also help bridge the chasm between the brief citations written into the context of newer works and the unwieldly lengths of the original documents. The works listed above have helped considerably on both counts.

However, there are at least two other potential uses for annotated bibliographies for which a different style of organization is more appropriate. For one, they can help beginning students understand the environment into which the original works were written. In doing so, they can also reinforce the notion that there is contemporary wisdom in our "classics" that still has potential use if considered in the appropriate context.

This work is designed specifically for these last two goals. It takes a developmental approach to the literature. More precisely, this is an annotated bibliography that is organized around two assumptions about our field that encourage a developmental perspective.

First, for better or for worse, most studies of Public Administration have about the same potential use today as they had when they were written. In fact, the utility of the dated works is often more obvious than for current research because, before the behavioral revolution, it was more fashionable for authors to reveal the biases that led them to the research.

However, we normally fail to appreciate the relevance of our heritage because we patronize it. We categorize it by the excesses that led each phase of it to be replaced, and then forgive it with the reassuring assumption that its successes, like its failures, must be applicable only to a simpler age.

The second assumption upon which this study is based is that it is impractical to understand the relevance of dated research outside of its own context. This may sound contradictory with the argument that the classical literature is still relevant, but it is not. The context is not just a time frame; in fact, it is not a time frame at all. It is a challenge to the author from the environment. The challenge may come from difficulties within the administrative world, or from debate within the academic profession. The challenge may disappear in time, especially if the proposed solution is effective, only to reappear later. However, without understanding the context in which the literature is written, it is impractical to understand the conditions under which the proposed solutions were supposed to be applied.

As a developmental study, this work sacrifices the first of the four goals of bibliographic studies--that of being a quick, alphabetized reference book. The difficulty is alleviated to a considerable degree by the index of authors that is included at the end. However, once the citations are located in this book, they are still written into the context of the surrounding authors.

Also, the literature that is reviewed here is selected for its value in the development of the field rather than for its current popularity. Most of it still appears on a wide variety of reading lists, although that is not the criterion by which it was chosen. On the other extreme, some of it has been all but forgotten.

More specifically, the literature is selected because it was frequently cited as "formative" by each generation of "formative" authors, preceding backwards until the trail fades into original sources. The selection has also been cross-checked with older textbooks and bibliographic histories in those cases in which they exist.

The strategy is subjective, as is explained later. However, it is utilized because it is particularly good at fulfilling the last three of the four goals of bibliographic studies. First, it provides students with a useful research bridge between the textbooks and the original sources in the field.

Public Administration abounds in textbooks, many of which contain excellent reviews of the literature. However, most texts are written to provide an introduction to the discipline, and not to the literature. Previous studies provide their data, not their subject. Their job is to edit that literature, encapsulating each consensus and disagreement so that our knowledge can be described for new students with more coherence than actually existed as our diverse field struggled for answers.

On the other side of the research bridge are the original sources. There comes a time in advanced education when textbooks do not provide enough detail on their subjects, and the students are expected to go to the original studies. However, as a tool of understanding, the tactic of reading the original works themselves presents its own set of burdens.

The first and least pedagogical problem is one of access. Except in extraordinarily complete academic libraries, many of the early works, and especially early editions, are simply not available. Before about 1930, only the truly major books are likely to exist in most collections. Even then, shelf space has become so costly, and outdated books on public management see so little use, that many have been discarded or sent into storage. Of course, these problems can be overcome with some time and help from interlibrary loans. But even then, as is documented later, our bibliographies often do not lead students to realize that the earlier works were ever written.

A second weakness in consulting the original texts for insights into our field's development is more problematical. Books, by definition, cannot explain their impact on, or their role in, the literature of the field. There is simply no way for the author to know the eventual impact of a work while it is still being written. Much of the literature is remembered for particular snippets of wisdom, or specific quips (or even "improved" misquotes) that had an impact on the rest of us. Whatever the author intended, subsequent generations effectively decide what the work said.

The third weakness of consulting the works directly is that they are too long. For beginning students facing their first research assignment, that first step beyond the textbooks can be frightening. It immerses the student in the full glory of the first few books that are located, hopefully wisely selected from a list of suggested readings, with little sense of where those books fit into the mainstream of academic thought.

The problem can be softened with a good annotated bibliography, or with reference sources such as the *International Encyclopedia of the Social Sciences*. But the difficulties are even more severe when the problem is not a lack of familiarity with the literature, but over-familiarity. When doctoral students attempt to read the entirety of all the books for which they are held responsible, they soon begin to forget who said what.

Chester Barnard once noted that he found it important to reread even the most influential books every few years.[7] If we neglect to do that, our memories become too fluid, and it becomes too difficult to distinguish what the authors actually said, and what we have grown to remember they said in support of our own arguments.

For the less significant works that comprise the bulk of the field, there is little time for these reviews. This field is awash in publications. Subscribing to all our regional and specialized journals would bankrupt a library. The sheer number of new books released annually is less convincing evidence of our wisdom than it is of our divergence, or perhaps even our awareness that publication has become a necessity for academic advancement.

In this environment, advanced students need quick references that give more detail and more citations than are appropriate in textbooks. Beginning students need such references as a transition into an overpowering array of literature with which they are not yet familiar. On this bridge between textbooks and texts, books such as McCurdy's and the *International Encyclopedia of the Social Sciences*, and series such as Garland's and Vance Bibliographies have been extremely useful.

But the bridge is fragile, and the weakness is best explained by the ultimate failure of either popularity-driven or alphabetized approaches to achieve the third potential promise of bibliographic studies. Despite their obvious emphasis on the content of the books, by definition they cannot integrate that content into the contexts for which the books were written.

It is unfair to judge social science literature outside of its environment, as if its milieu was irrelevant to its contribution, or as if its struggles will never reemerge. It would be equally sensible to ban controls for intervening variables from current publications, requiring all hypotheses to work under all conditions.

It is also an exercise in vanity to judge the value of books by the impact they have on today's scholars. Such an approach assumes that we are better judges of significance than were the original authors. However, as I hope becomes clear as this book proceeds, our understanding of our own heritage is embarrassingly incomplete, and often demonstrably incorrect.

Finally, it is proving dangerous to our literary heritage to rely on currently-popular works. Too often, the literature that has been eased off reading lists and out of footnotes has not been rediscovered once its relevance has been restored. With few exceptions, it has simply disappeared.

Others have noticed the same trend. After contending in the introductions to both editions that his methodology punished recent works and rewarded the classics, McCurdy noted in the opening chapter to his 1986 update that "[t]he books from the first fifty years of public administration dwindled in importance as the memory of the era of orthodoxy grew dim."[8]

The top of his list illustrated the same problem. When he measured the most frequent citations by the established scholars of the field, the most cited book on the 1972 survey, Cartwright and Zander's *Group Dynamics*, did not make the top twenty in 1985.[9]

We are not alone. Writers of business history lament the same lack of respect for their history.[10] However, the most disturbing measure of the scope of the problem may be the chronic publication data errors that plague the major bibliographic histories in both Public Administration and Management.[11] Correct placement of dated literature is simply not a priority in the social sciences.

Of course, it could be contended that dated literature deserves no special preservation, and that our lack of appreciation of our ancestry is no problem. In a field this forwardly focused and empirically motivated, one could argue that even our own history must demonstrate its merits for future American applications before deserving separate study.

However, problems are arising. If nothing else, our myopia is a burden for new students trying to grasp the focus of a field that continually bemoans its lack of focus. But beyond that, we have allowed the neglect of our heritage to develop to such extremes that even current studies are paying the costs.

First, we are missing the options that have already been studied, as if the debates of previous generations were founded in such antiquity, or perhaps naïveté, that they can no longer be of use to us. Those were simpler times. But it is only because we seldom read more than short excerpts from our classics that we no longer notice how many of them failed to dwell in the excesses by which we now sort them.

We have all but erased many of their struggles, and with them, the memory of the options that were not chosen. We are left with little sense of why we are here, and why we are not studying other subjects using other techniques. And yet, for all our disinterest in how we came to be here, we expend considerable anxiety trying to figure out where, as a field, we are. Our search for rediscovery is arduous, and not yet very successful.

We are doing something else that may ultimately prove to be even more painful for those who strive to make our advice useful. We are erasing much of the content even of the works that we still remember by name. As a simple example, techniques very similar to those developed in Scientific Management are still being used throughout government by position classification analysts. In the same vein, the Scientific Management advocates considered their knowledge of incentive plans to be one of their more impressive credentials.

Yet, almost no one in Public Administration has read enough Scientific Management literature to remember that serious and painful lessons were learned about what happens if the techniques of either subject are applied "incorrectly." We still vaguely remember that minor adjustments can turn MBO into a catastrophe, but few of us can tell personnelists anything about many similar lessons that Taylor, Gantt, and others already learned about job analysis and merit pay.

Most importantly, we are endangering what Waldo has labelled our self-awareness of our field. Few modern works discuss anything but the most recent works with an assumption that there is anything currently useful in them.[12] Instead, we pull our historical window along with us, only to discover that our heritage is dropping from sight. We find ourselves in identity crises, but it has fallen out of fashion to search for clues among those who defined the field in the first place.

It is not difficult to design a book to revive the heritage, but it needs three things. First, it requires a reintroduction of forgotten literature in sufficient quantities to set the scene for current research projects. It needs the literature that has been influential, not the literature that has been remembered. To do otherwise is to set up the authors for the same misjudgments that sometimes define our field.

Second, the book needs to tie that literature together, certainly by grouping it, but also by explaining the connections as they arise. Third, it needs to tie our heritage to current studies. It cannot defend our classics against the neglect of time if it treats modern works with the same neglect.

It can afford to assume that the student has a textbook-level exposure to the field. It can abbreviate explanations of the terms and labels of Public Administration, and concentrate with more detail than is normally appropriate on the literature itself. And it can search that literature for its continuing utility.

Those are the goals here. This book offers synopses. But, more importantly, it attempts to provide an opening focus and map to make it practical for students to find existing research in the listed areas with more speed, more detail, and a clearer sense of context than we have learned to anticipate.

Ultimately, this work is designed to reinforce the few bridges that already exist beyond textbooks to more detailed studies in the field. To help organize those studies, the literature of the field is bracketed into chapters around the subjects, experiments, or themes that generated a flurry of literature. Each chapter begins with a verbal description of the setting in which the issue became "publication worthy." It then contains summations of a representative sample of the authors and literature that evolved, including the works that are still considered most significant. When it is useful, there are also samples of other lesser-known authors who were working in the same field. Most notably, the book attempts to identify authors who were important in the development, and to the developers, but who have been lost in more recent summaries.

When the information is known, the reviews contain personal information about why the author was writing, and what he or she was trying to accomplish. The purpose is not to be anecdotal; in fact, interesting stories have often been bypassed because they seem more appropriate for other works. However, it is often surprisingly useful in understanding the author's purpose to know who knew each other, and who taught whom. Also, since this is the part for which students are held responsible, the reviews include the content for which the works are remembered, even if, as has happened on a few occasions, the author intended to say no such thing.

Finally, each chapter concludes with suggestions as to how the information that was discovered can be used. For the older sections, the use has sometimes already been made, and so the conclusions lead at least partially into other sections. However, the emphasis is on the content of what was there. It is not, as we too often find, a set of suggestions for future research that lays the older work aside.

There are some unavoidable limits to such an undertaking. Most obviously, it does justice to none of these works. The authors thought their ideas worthy of the number of words they used, not of one or a few paragraphs. In defense, this work is intended to provide a more detailed starting place than exists in textbooks, and to lead the students to the original works.

Secondly, the selection of works is reconstructed from a history that has a talent for erasing itself. As an adjustment, it is tempting to create a systematic, even a mathematical method for determining the books that should be included. It would not only give the list the façade of fairness, but it might even give some of the substance.

However, that approach has been tried, and from a developmental perspective, it seems to document the problem more than provide a solution. Instead, I have searched the bibliographies of textbooks, frequently cited works, and histories of the field to try to discover which works were cited as influential by those selected for review in each generation. The process begins with current studies and continues back in time until references to previous literature fade away. Older works are included when they have been located despite the lack of later references.

It is a subjective process, for the assessment of citations is qualitative rather than quantitative. In some chapters, notably those with a few established opinion leaders, it is easier than in the others. It is easier for older works; the pool of literature was smaller, and many authors still remembered the creation of their schools of thought.

On the other side, the most difficult sections by far to assess are the most recent, for they are dominated by literature about which we have yet to reach a consensus. For works that are too recent to be judged by the next generation, this review often resorts to a representative sample of literature, or to a subjective judgment that some works, whatever their quality, were attempting to steer the field in new directions.

Subjectivity is inevitable in the selection and description of the works in this book. The problem is partially alleviated by the availability of the books and articles to speak for themselves. It is helped even more by the existence of published reviews, some of which have the advantage or disadvantage of the perspective of time, and some of which were written while many of these literary struggles were in progress. But ultimately, this work should be judged by the degree to which the selections and summations lead in useful directions for current research, or strike a common chord in our struggle for self-awareness.

A FEW NOTES ON BIBLIOGRAPHIC CITATIONS

In searching for connections between our early works, one quickly becomes dismayed with our standard accepted practices of citing virtually any edition of a work as the first, or even worse, backdating later editions and new publishers to the "known" first date of publication. In addition, in a field that melds academic research and governmental studies, enough of our works are published by obscure or non-traditional sources that casual documentation formats can leave the researcher hopelessly confused.

In this work, a serious effort has been made to list the original publication information on each book, except in those cases such as Confucius or Aristotle in which the original date of publication was unrelated to the author's experience. If the book was never translated into English, an approximate translation follows the title in brackets. If the book has been translated, the English title is followed by the original publication data.

In all cases, quotations and page numbers are taken from the edition and printing that is cited. Also, if trade editions are known to have been published earlier as dissertations, both citations are given. In the case of simultaneous international publications, data are given for the release in the author's country, not for the "New York" publishers normally given in American citations. Finally, in those few cases in which complete citations are as baffling as brief ones (this happens in a few very old or unusual very new sources), endnotes are used to explain the publication data.

NOTES FOR THE INTRODUCTION

1. For a relatively complete listing, see Anthony E. Simpson, *Guide to Library Research in Public Administration* (New York: Center for Productive Public Management, John Jay College of Criminal Justice, 1976).

2. *Public Administration Series: Bibliography* (Montibello, IL: Vance Bibliographies, date varies).

3. The one of broadest scope is Gerald E. Caiden, Richard A. Loverd, Thomas J. Pavlek, Lynn F. Sipe, and Molly M. Wong, *American Public Administration: A Bibliographic Guide to the Literature* (New York: Garland Publishers, 1983). The book section, in chapter four, carries no annotation.

4. *Sage Public Administration Abstracts*, volume and date vary.

5. Howard E. McCurdy, *Public Administration: A Bibliography* (Washington, D.C.: College of Public Affairs, The American University, 1972).

6. Howard E. McCurdy, *Public Administration: A Bibliographic Guide to the Literature* (New York: Marcel Dekker, 1986).

7. Kenneth R. Andrews, "Introduction to the Anniversary Edition," in Chester I. Barnard, *Functions of the Executive* (Cambridge: Harvard University Press, 1968), p. xiii.

8. McCurdy, *Public Administration: A Bibliographic Guide to the Literature*, p. 6.

9. Both lists are in the 1986 version, pp. 4-5.

10. Daniel A. Wren, *The Evolution of Management Thought* (New York: Ronald Press, 1972), p. 4.

11. For Public Administration, the notable effort is McCurdy's. In Management, the closest equivalents are Claude George, Jr., *History of Management Thought* (Englewood Cliffs, NJ: Prentice-Hall, 1968); and Daniel Wren, *The Evolution of Management Thought*. While some errors are expected, and surely appear in this work as well, each of those works contains more than might have been expected. As one example among many, all three contain incorrect citations for Frederick Taylor, who published only two trade books, both of which are correctly listed in both the National Union and the Library of Congress catalogues.

12. One of the more successful exceptions is Howard McCurdy's *Public Administration: A Synthesis* (Menlo Park, CA: Cummings Publishing Co., 1977).

THE GUIDE
TO THE FOUNDATIONS
OF PUBLIC ADMINISTRATION

I
THE EMERGENCE AND
IMPACTS OF PUBLIC
ADMINISTRATION

1
The Histories of Public Administration

BACKGROUND

It may seem natural that a bibliographic history would start with the oldest known literature in the field. This book, however, begins with recent works about the oldest known administration. The reason is not that old or even ancient literature does not exist. It is a common oversimplification to contend that prior to the 1880s, almost nothing was written on public administration.

Quite to the contrary, older studies were profuse, even if they often focused on other topics or were in a form that we would not now find familiar. Selections from that literature are reviewed in chapter two.

Instead, this chapter begins with modern histories of public administration because the practice is older than the study. Perhaps it is more accurate to say that we can trace the practice further than we can trace the study, although Public Administration without public administration is difficult to imagine.

Public administration before Wilson is discussed in these next two chapters. This section is concerned with public administration (in small-case letters) as it evolved before Wilson or Weber described it. The dates on these studies are unimportant, and they are usually quite modern. The next chapter contains Public Administration (with capital letters) before Wilson, or the works that studied the subject in print before 1887. Chapter three describes Business Management before Taylor.

The separation between Public Administration and Business Management is sometimes artificial. However, the split between the two was clear enough by 1800 that this division is essential for clarity. The basis of that split, and the responsibilities that it creates, are the subject of chapters four through ten.

HISTORIES OF PRE-AMERICAN PUBLIC ADMINISTRATION

For organizational purposes, it is useful to think of administrative histories as falling upon a continuum that emphasizes descriptive details rather than conceptual models on one end, and conceptual explanations that use details mainly as data on the other. While the pattern is not universal, it fits closely enough to serve as a method of clustering the following works, beginning with those containing relatively more historical data.

1. E. N. Gladden, *A History of Public Administration*, 2 vol. (London: Frank Cass and Co., 1972).

This is an extremely detailed history of public administration that attempted to discuss the administrative practices of every major culture that has evolved in the history of our species. Since the history preceded the development of agriculture by ten thousand years, Gladden obviously speculated in early chapters on what must have existed. However, he used a tripartite division of scribes and clerks, middle managers, and top managers even in ancient times. He also convincingly demonstrated that, by Ancient Egypt, there were massive bureaucracies, red tape, and scandals over official corruption. (vol. 1, p. 62)

The book attempted to study administrative practices by separating them from politics, but found that the tactic was often unrealistic. (vol. 1, p. 103) For most of the history, the line was equally nebulous between private and public administration. (vol. 1, p. 252)

Gladden reviewed Oriental administration in a degree of detail seldom seen in Western works. He was briefer than Mumford, however, on the Dark Ages, and adjusted to the amount of available evidence so as to continue the broad brush-stroke approach as he approached modern times. He also did not try to compete with works such as Tout's when these more narrowly-focused histories existed.

For all eras, Gladden's approach was to describe the role and structure of administrative functions in the societies. He did not attempt to construct models or engage in conceptual analysis until the last few pages of volume two. The book has no bibliography, although the notes at the end of each chapter are helpful in locating additional sources.

2. Thomas F. Tout, *Chapters in the Administrative History of Mediaeval England*, 6 vol. (Manchester, England: University Press, Vol. 1 & 2 1920, vol. 3 & 4 1928, vol. 5 1930, vol. 6 1933). All reprinted with corrections 1937. Note that this work is usually misidentified as *Chapters in Mediaeval Administrative History* because it is so labelled on the spine of the reprintings.

Detailed administrative histories have been written for particular eras in such countries as England, France, and Italy. This is one of the more massive, and is used as an example here. This two volume work eventually grew to six volumes and had to be completed by the author's wife Mary Tout after his death. The entire work described England's national administrative machinery (local government was not included) in the Thirteenth and Fourteenth Centuries.

The topic is less esoteric than it might seem since this was the period during which the administrative machinery of England grew to maturity. Throughout, Tout maintained a strict distinction between political offices (the King's Council) and administrative machinery. While Roman practices on the treasury and administration of the census are better known and are much older, Tout noted that the "barbarian" tradition that shaped England and, by extension, the United States, spawned many of the same administrative solutions.

3.　　Lewis Mumford, *The City in History* (New York: Harcourt Brace and World, 1961).

Mumford used the city as his focus to explain the evolution of culture, people, and political institutions throughout history. While he paid little attention explicitly to public administration, he could not avoid using administrative functions to explain the relationship of people to their community.

Among points that stand out in the book, Mumford saw the genesis for modern democracy in the barbarian tribes that conquered Rome and introduced the concept that individuals had rights separate from the state. He also recorded that monarchs had to discontinue the practice of travelling to the taxpayers in mobile courts in England and France during the Fourteenth Century because the official records became too massive to move. (p. 353)

4.　　Gideon Sjoberg, *The Preindustrial City* (Glencoe, IL: The Free Press, 1960).

As is the case with Mumford, much of this work is not about administration. However, chapter VIII, on political structures, applied Weberian analysis to make a number of observations on administrative structures. Sjoberg noted that preindustrial bureaucrats had three important distinctions from their modern counterparts: 1) there was no clearly defined sphere of activity subject to impersonal rules; 2) no universal criteria governed appointments or promotions; and 3) there was no tenure or fixed salaries.

This helped Sjoberg explain why people with noble callings might have resorted to the abuses of their positions documented by Gladden. Sjoberg, who subtitled the book *Past and Present*, then used modern examples to explain the pre-Weberian bureaucracies that still operate in the developing world. For these purposes, Sjoberg's notes at the end of the chapter are particularly useful to modern researchers.

5.   Arnold Toynbee, *The Study of History*, 12 vol. (London: Oxford University Press 1934-61). 2 vol. version of vols. 1-10 abridged by D. C. Somervell (London: Oxford University Press, 1947 and 1957).

Histories that include administration as a logical component of society's development vary from such works as Sjoberg's, which has a separate chapter on the subject, to those in which administrative topics are virtually nonexistent. The latter are not included here. However, some with only passing references have original suggestions or perspectives that often cause them to be cited in public administration histories. Mumford's is an example. So are Toynbee's and the Durants'.

Toynbee's twelve volume work traced the development and decline of twenty-six civilizations to document his belief that moral and religious crises have been more significant to the life of societies than the environmental challenges that they have faced. That thesis did not permit him to place much respect or permanence in institutions, such as bureaucracies, that exist to serve the state. In making his point, he noted the wide variations that have existed in administrative machinery, from bureaucracies that heavily influenced the sovereign to those that were populated by slaves.

6.   William (and Ariel) Durant, *The Story of Civilization*, 11 vol. (New York: Simon and Schuster, 1935-1975). The last five volumes list joint authorship.

This is the other massive and even more popular world history that has often been used as a source in administrative histories. It was designed as a five part project that would meld economic, political, religious, and social history through the development of world cultures. In his opening volume, Durant set his theme with "a nation is born stoic, and dies epicurean." (p. 259). Durant saw little permanence to political institutions. "Man is not willingly a political animal" (p. 21). Governmental machinery, therefore, is a dependent variable with no established moral purpose, and it has often been a vehicle for "epicurean" waste.

7.   Gerald D. Nash, *Perspectives on Administration: The Vistas of History* (Berkeley: Institute of Governmental Studies, March 1969). Offset publication.

This short book (77 pages) that formed part of Dwight Waldo's series on "Perspectives on Administration," was an attempt to summarize both the development of administration throughout history, and the perspectives that historians now use to study it. The review is understandably shorter on details than is Gladden's. However, the general trends are well documented.

The book is notable for the degree to which it uncovers administrative explanations to many historical events. It notes, for instance, the decline in Roman administrative efficiency while the Byzantine culture was better adapted to Roman-style administration. However, the most beneficial aspect of the book may be its bibliography, which is now dated, but which was designed to bracket and explain the significance of other historical works on bureaucracy.

8.   Henry Jacoby, *The Bureaucratization of the World*, trans. by Eveline L. Kanes (Berkeley: University of California Press, 1973). Originally *Die Bürokratisierung der Welt: Ein Beitrag zur Problemgeschichte* (Neuwied: Hermann Luchterhand Verlag BmbH, 1969).

This is an extraordinarily useful summation of the rise of centralist administration from mediaeval Europe to modern times. Throughout, Jacoby's focus is on the struggle between the forces of central governmental control and those (be they feudal lords or modern individuals) who have been the subjects of control.

Jacoby's perspective on the rise of public administration from feudal states is insightful, and sometimes unique. For instance, he felt that the evolutionary history from the feudal system to absolute monarchs hid the rift caused by the rise of the middle class. He also offered an explanation for the notable differences in the bureaucracies that arose in Prussia and France. The book also contains an extensive bibliography, with English translations noted.

9.   Ernest Barker, *The Development of Public Services in Western Europe 1660-1930* (London: Oxford University Press, 1944).

Barker's goal was to explain the evolution of England, France, and Germany from the pre-Absolutist states of the Seventeenth Century into their more modern bureaucratic forms. (He ignored the state of affairs in 1944 as a historical aberration). He argued that, in the 1600s, governments were not separate entities in the social structure, but were extensions of the Family, Property, and the Society. These governments needed little bureaucracy since they did little on their own. The dual developments of Absolutism and then national sovereignty gave the state a separate identity and need to compete.

The book is short and it offers almost no references. However, the framework provides an alternate explanation to Jacoby on many points, and is particularly useful in conjunction with the following work.

10.   S. N. Eisenstadt, *The Political Systems of Empires: The Rise and Fall of Historical Bureaucratic Societies* (New York: Free Press of Glencoe, 1963).

Eisenstadt applied sociological analysis to the rise of Historical Bureaucratic Empires in 27 cases. Abandoning the strict politics/administration dichotomy used by Barker, he hypothesized that bureaucratic empires arise only under conditions of autonomy in the political sphere and the differentiation of "free-floating" institutions in society. By abandoning the dichotomy, he was able to explain the possibility of bureaucratic withering based on the designs of the political ruler. In the modern state, he saw totalitarianism as having more potential for existence than before, but not as being inevitable.

11.   Michael T. Dalby and Michael S. Werthman, eds., *Bureaucracy in Historical Perspective* (Glenview, IL: Scott Foresman, 1971).

This is a set of 21 readings based in an historical, cross-cultural approach to bureaucracy. The articles are grouped under five subjects with a brief introduction to tie each section together. The sections include the role of bureaucracy in society, personnel, bureaucratic behavior, control of bureaucracy, and the impact of bureaucracy on society.

The topic is broad enough that the articles serve as windows into various aspects of bureaucratic history. Examples of the historical approach include Gladden on Ottoman slave-bureaucrats, Balazs and Kracke on Imperial China, and Rosenberg on Prussia. The bureaucratic perspective is also well represented with two readings by Weber, and several more that use his model.

Many of these readings are available in greater length elsewhere, although this concentration of readings helps illustrate the breadth of historical approaches to bureaucracy. Each article is necessarily brief, however, and the documentation was often edited out for this edition.

HISTORIES OF AMERICAN PUBLIC ADMINISTRATION

12.   Leonard D. White, *The Federalists* (New York: Macmillan, 1948).

The following four books by White may be viewed as separate volumes of one large work that described the American administrative experience from 1789 to 1901. Unlike most administrative histories, White's work integrated administrative and political developments to explain the evolution of governmental machinery. As he explained in *The Jacksonians*, political and constitutional issues often dictated our willingness to concentrate on administrative concerns. (pp. 550-51)

In this opening volume, White described the creation and maturation of executive authority and the cabinet departments under "Hamilton [who] was the administrative architect of the new government, balanced by Washington's common-sense judgments on official relationships." (p. 127)

They struggled to create administrative wisdom without significant help from the private sector (pp. 471-72) or the available literature (pp. 476-77). Despite obvious failures in the U.S. Mint and the Post Office, most executive offices flourished in competence and integrity, even if they were too small to have any real administrative theory. The triumph of competence was most notable in Treasury, which housed the vast majority of executive employees at the time.

13. Leonard D. White, *The Jeffersonians* (New York: Macmillan, 1951).

White set the tone for this second volume on the era 1801-1829 by noting "(t)he Jeffersonian era in the field of administration was in many respects a projection of Federalists ideas and practice." (p. vii) Accordingly, moral standards were high. However, most agencies were so small that there was no administrative theory.

Still, with growth and experience, some theory emerged. Most notably, there were massive reorganizations after the War of 1812. Also, congress became more involved in administration through investigations and the Tenure of Office Act of 1820.

14. Leonard D. White, *The Jacksonians* (New York: Macmillan, 1954).

Continuing his history through the period 1829-1861, White chronicled the rise in importance of state and local governments, the general decline in public service morality, and the diversification of administrative structure to meet the increasing size of government. He theorized that these occurred because of three factors that affected the public business: magnitude, facility for communication, and democracy. However, office management techniques felt little pressure, and remained completely unchanged from 1800 to 1860. (p. 548)

15. Leonard D. White, *The Republican Era* (New York: Macmillan, 1958).

This final entry in White's series brought his administrative history up to 1901. He concentrated on the two great administrative issues of reviving the presidency after Johnson and Grant, and civil service reform. Due to the time frame of this volume, he was able to take both causes through their times of crises, and well into the recovery process.

16. Alexis (Charles Henri Clerel) de Tocqueville, *Democracy in America*, first published as *De la démocratie en Amérique;* 4 vol (Paris: Charles Gosselin, 1835 (vols.
1 & 2) and 1840 (vols. 3 & 4). Published in U.S., trans. by Henry Reeve, Part I
(New York: Dearborn, 1838) and Part II (New York: Langley, 1840).

Stated simply, these were the observations of a French official who toured the U.S. for nine months in 1831-32 for the purpose of writing a report on American prisons. However, the work (or at least the first half of it) has been recognized since publication as one of the more profound theoretical works on the evolution of democratic institutions.

On administration, de Tocqueville was struck by our relative lack of it, and the decentralization of what we had. He argued that such a practice was part of an overall societal plan that promoted popular participation in government and, thereby, protected our democracy. He also predicted that democracy would eventually push us toward industrialization rather than farming. On the weak side, he was led by the

Jacksonian era into believing that the federal sector would continue to lose ground to state and local administration.

De Tocqueville's writings have been particularly useful for advocates of public choice theory and democratic administration, such as Ostrom (discussed below).

17.   Lynton Caldwell, *The Administrative Theories of Hamilton and Jefferson* (Chicago: University of Chicago Press, 1944).

At Leonard White's (who wrote the introduction) encouragement, Caldwell set out to describe the divergent theories and objectives of these two founders, whose still-unresolved struggle shaped our political and administrative institutions. Hamilton was concerned that the natural tendency of both the few and the masses to try to tyrannize each other could be controlled only through stable and centralized political institutions. Jefferson "...was a realistic politician whereas Hamilton remained a confirmed idealist." (p. 111) Jefferson's belief that the morality of man was likely to improve with time allowed him to experiment, and a tendency toward decentralized administrative power was his great contribution to our political tradition.

18.   Matthew A. Crenson, *The Federal Machine: Beginnings of Bureaucracy in Jacksonian American* (Baltimore: Johns Hopkins University Press, 1975).

Crenson's argument was that the United States evolved from a pre-bureaucratic to a bureaucratic government during the administration of Andrew Jackson. By tracing history and demographic data, he attempted to show that in this time frame informal procedures became formalized and generalists became specialized.

Jackson's administration proceeded with few principles, and part of their difficulty was that their organizational style mimicked Hamilton's, which they could not profess to admire. Also, their efforts to depersonalize offices were not very successful. Nevertheless, they did achieve simplification and formalization of procedures. Ironically, much of their formalization was in rules to ensure moral conduct in a morally declining society, something for which their administration is hardly known today.

19.   Vincent Ostrom, *The Intellectual Crisis in American Public Administration* (University: University of Alabama Press, 1973).

The purpose of this book was not history. However, writing during a period of particular "turbulence" and reexamination in Public Administration, Ostrom suggested that our difficulty was that the field took a wrong turn when it followed Wilson and, by extension, Hobbes, Bryce, and Weber into a centralized, professional bureaucratic state. As an option, Ostrom used the perspective of "public choice" theory that has become popular in policy analysis (see chapters six and nineteen in this book) to define the administrative model that we left behind in the 1880s.

Ostrom advocated that we return to an updated version of the administrative theories of our founders. He suggested that "overlapping jurisdictions and fragmentation of authority can facilitate the production of a heterogeneous mix of public service goods in a public service economy." (chapter 4) He leaned heavily on de Tocqueville, Madison, Jefferson, and even Hamilton to describe an experiment that went awry because theorists followed Hobbes' lead without appreciating that Hobbes was writing for a polity in a recurrent state of war.

20.   Carl Fish, *The Civil Service and the Patronage* (Cambridge: Harvard University Press, 1904).

This was the first of two books that developed our administrative history through the perspective of personnel. Because of the publication date, this work obviously concluded when the merit system was in its infancy. However, that also placed Fish closer to the sources and emotions of the time.

Fish distinguished rotation in office, which was common, from the more recent practice of spoils. He also argued that civil service reform efforts before 1860 suffered from the two flaws that they wanted to hinder removals rather than control appointments and that they wanted to shift the burden of merit from the President to the Senate, thereby dividing the responsibility. Particularly on his first flaw, the perspective of the ages has changed.

21.   Paul Van Riper, *History of the United States Civil Service* (Evanston, IL: Row, Peterson and Co., 1958).

The second of the histories specifically describing personnel, this book was a logical complement to Fish in that it concentrated on the era of personnel merit and issues that arose after the publication of Fish's work. It is also instructive how Van Riper could see centralization in the same Federalist-period administrative theories that Ostrom viewed as decentralized.

Van Riper's theme was that personnel was a massive, if sometimes unexciting, weapon for political power. For a book that went into considerable administrative detail and viewed personnel as politically interesting and currently relevant, it has also worn fairly well over thirty years. For instance, even though he concluded with concerns about representative bureaucracy rather than personnel management, the foundations of both were firmly laid in this book.

CONTINUING CONCERNS

In reviewing the histories of public administration that have been published to date, it appears that either the causal model that can explain the rise and form of bureaucratic states has not been developed, or the field has not yet reached a consensus on it.

Several models exist, and they collectively hold some important assumptions. For instance, most authors appreciate that bureaucracies did not rise singularly, but were instead part of the differentiation in society that led to the rise of both bureaucracy and the modern state. Most agree that bureaucratic forms are very ancient (the data on this is overwhelming).

However, the disagreements are equally impressive. The most important may be between those who are public administration historians, who tend to view the bureaucracy as both important and relatively inevitable, and more general historians, who tend to treat the subject as one of the images that float through the grander cycles of societal change.

Even within this discipline, there is no continuity in the literature on such basic questions as whether there was one cause for the rise of the modern bureaucratic state (with local variations), or whether separate causal models are needed for each European state. Much of the literature ignores all except the modern European experience in collecting data. But there is also some disagreement, even in Europe, on whether bureaucracy or absolute monarchy arose first.

There is a trend in this literature that is hardly profound, but that is particularly relevant here. While there is little disagreement over the historical data, which are plentiful and precise, they can be used to document dramatically different models with no particular difficulty. Those models include ones that place bureaucracy in some type of linear progression, and those that see its demise as inevitable.

In short, our historians have reached no consensus, and are not likely to do so, on whether the basic structure of bureaucracy can be altered. That leaves the question in the hands of modern authors on bureaucratic dysfunctions and futurism, both of whom operate with no particular historical perspective, and both of whom are discussed later.

2
Public Administration Before Wilson

BACKGROUND

As noted in the introduction to chapter one, one often hears the argument that prior to the 1880s, almost no written materials existed on management or public administration. To some extent, the argument is only postdated, for one can easily support the more limited statement that prior to the Industrial Revolution, almost no works extensively and explicitly discussed the practice of public or private administration.

All that changed with the advent of industrialization, as is documented in these next two chapters. But before that, even if we have some difficulty identifying them, there have almost always been some analyses of public administration, and a few works in the area predate the technology to publish them by more than two millennia. The reason we overlook them now is that they were either so foreign to our current approach to the field as to make the relevant literature essentially invisible, or so concerned with other subjects as to make the administrative sections difficult to find when we look for our roots.

Until recent history, public administration at the managerial level was an exercise in civic or divine responsibility. The mechanics were so simplistic and the responsibilities so lofty that the most appropriate training for the trade was political or religious, depending on the sovereign for which one worked. Of course, such a definition turns almost everything into Public Administration and makes a literature search senseless.

However, the evidence that specific literature is there is easy to find, and it also helps identify what is being sought. For strictly governmental applications, White and then Ostrom popularized the search for explicit administrative choices in what would otherwise be considered Political Science literature.[1] But more easily, by the mid-1800s, both personnel reformers and French academics were engaged in studies that look surprisingly like modern Public Administration research.

For business applications, the route is different but equally well defined, and is reviewed in chapter three. Of course, there were also more technical skills for which some degree of job training was essential. These responsibilities fell upon the clerks, who existed long before anyone except sovereigns and priests assumed the role of "manager." Some of their training manuals and records survive, and are truly ancient. Unfortunately, they often are not in a form that we would consider "published," and they are mentioned here through secondary sources (the history texts in chapter one) only.

The works in this chapter vary from those in the previous one in that they are attempts to study Public Administration in the present tense. As such, they do not feel themselves to be removed by time or passion from their topic.

Such a standard could be met by few Public Administration studies today, and so it may be a poor standard for division. However, our surgical objectivity is a recent creation, much more recent than the creation of our field, as becomes clearer as this bibliographical study proceeds. Of course, as Hobbes and any number of others discovered, theoretical works could cause societal reactions far worse than those likely to be encountered today. But for whatever reason, these works share a characteristic with those that dominate the literature of management and Public Administration from their "beginnings" in the 1880s until the 1940s--they felt committed to and affected by their findings.

22.   Confucius (circa 551-479 B.C.).

There are nine core books of Confucian thought, one of which, *Spring and Autumn Annuals*, may actually have been written by Confucius. The most relevant to Public Administration is *Lun Yu* or *Analects*, which was compiled from his thoughts by his later disciples. To Confucius, who was an extraordinarily effective teacher and Minister of Crime for the State of Lu, the overriding principle of good administration was the morality of the public servant. The ruler and his servants had paternalistic control over respectful subjects, and therefore had to approach perfect morality to set an example for those being ruled.

His goal for administration was, in the modern pejorative sense, good manners. That makes it difficult to advocate his system today without risking ridicule. In his defense, he was extremely detailed in defining good manners, and it is not patently obvious that, if everyone treated everyone else with dignity, many of our administrative or even political structures would be needed.

NOTE: The following several books, except *The Domesday Book*, are works in political philosophy, not administration. However, they often mention administrative practices, or have administrative significance, and are mentioned in that context. Some familiarity with the political significance of the works is assumed.

23. Plato, *The Laws* (348 or 347 B.C.).

In one of his last works, Plato described and defended the legal system considered ideal by the Greeks. In Book Six, he offered one of the longer descriptions of
Greek administrative practices that still exists, although he adopted the occasional
Greek approach of assuming that the sheer beauty of the description should suffice as
its justification. Plato distinguished three branches of administration: the wardens of
the city; the wardens of the agora; and the wardens of the temples.

Unlike most ancient works, he assumed the existence of minor officers, down to
the keepers of the animals. He described in some detail their numbers, their methods
of selection (some by lot, some by election), their duties, and their punishments for
malfeasance. None of his description, however, was analytical.

24. Aristotle, *Politics* and *On the Athenian Constitution* (dates uncertain).

In books four and six of *Politics* and chapter 54 (modern rendering) of *On the
Athenian Constitution*, Aristotle continued Plato's descriptive style of minor administrative offices in the Greek city-state. Aristotle described the offices in less detail,
but included the category of wardens for the countryside. He also paid more attention to the methods of selecting officials (often by lot, to give the Gods a voice in
the process).

25. *Domesday Book* (Compiled 1086); officially published Abraham Farley, ed., *Seu
liber censualis Willelmi Primi regis Anglia*, 2 vol. (London: Record Commission,
1783).[2]

After the fall of Greece, administrative writings almost disappeared in the West.
The Romans created a remarkable bureaucracy, but seldom discussed it. The Catholic
Church had higher callings than describing its operating structure.

The evidence that the technology lived on, however, is reflected in the histories
already listed, and eventually in the *Domesday Book*. This book was not about administration; it was administration. As the Normans attempted to consolidate their
control over England, William I ordered a comprehensive list (a census) of who owned
taxable property in the new kingdom.

Censuses were well known to the Romans, as is recorded in the New Testament.
However, the size, accuracy, and comprehensive nature of this document in England at
such an early age are worthy of note. It virtually created the local governmental
jurisdictions of England by its categorization. The book has been used in English
common law for centuries to settle claims and genealogy disputes. Duplicate census
takers, or "legati," were used to insure the accuracy of the final product.

26. Niccolò Machiavelli, *The Prince*. Manuscript completed 1513. Papal permission to
publish granted August 23, 1531. First published *Il Principe* (Rome: Antonio Blado
d'Asola, January 4, 1532).

In the Sixteenth Century, administrative theory began its slow ascent with Machiavelli, although the ascent was uneven and often painfully slow. While both Machiavelli and his father served as minor officials in Florence, his writings to the prince concentrated on the clearly more exciting princely "advisors." In chapters 22 and 23, he identified the significance of these servants, noting that particularly talented ones could inflate the image of an inferior prince if only that prince had the capacity to recognize and reward the advisor's good deeds.

At times, Machiavelli seemed almost humanist in his realization that praising one's servants leads to greater productivity. It should not be overlooked, however, that the goal of the praise was to keep the servants honest, productive, and dependent, and was not anchored in any concern for human development.

27. Thomas Hobbes, *The Leviathan* (London: Printed for Andrew Ckooke (sic) [Crooke], 1651).

Hobbes' work on the origins and rights of the state is a classic example of pre-administrative Political Science. In one short chapter (#23), he offered a distinction between general-purpose and specific-purpose ministers, and tied all authority to the degree that the ministers represented the sovereign. He ignored minor officials except to the extent that the same rules of authority would apply. In short, even on the eve of mercantilistic bureaucracies, Hobbes continued the view that administration could be ignored in describing the newly-emerging polity.

28. Charles de Secondat, Baron de Montesquieu, *The Spirit of Laws*, originally *De l'esprit des lois* (Geneva: Chez Barillot & fils, 1748).

It is with the French that the study of administration came alive. Montesquieu touched only briefly on the subject, although unlike Hobbes, he made a distinction that emphasized the difference between the legal system and administration. Describing the roles of police and judges in book 26, chapter 24, he noted that police must deal with routinized, trifling matters. The law does not become relevant to the police unless matters must be taken before the magistrate. For police in their daily administrative functions, therefore, the operating guidelines are properly termed regulations, not laws. This recognition, that administrative functions work with a different set of rules than would be used to describe the political output of the state, is still sometimes cited in our literature, and eventually made the politics/administration dichotomy possible.

29. Jean Jacques Rousseau, *The Social Contract, or Principles of Political Right*, originally *Du contrat social; ou, Principes du droit politique* (Amsterdam: Chez M. Rey, 1762).

Rousseau's short section on administration in book two, chapter nine represented a critical challenge that goaded the French to study the impact of administration on

the political entity. Rousseau argued that, as states expand, the burden of administration upon the polity grows because of the necessity to tax the local residents to
support ever-increasing levels of administrators. The central coordinating offices
become removed from the problems at the local levels. In those offices, "(t)alent is
buried, virtue unknown and vice unpunished, among such a multitude of men who do
not know one another, gathered together in one place at the seat of the central
administration. The leaders, overwhelmed with business, see nothing for themselves;
the State is governed by clerks."

30.   "Publius" [John Jay, Alexander Hamilton, James Madison], *The Federalist Papers*
       (Appeared in various U.S. newspapers, October 1787-April 1788).

Deciding what the Federalist Papers said about administration has become an
enterprise that generates some controversy.[3] The papers said little, but implied as
much as one chooses to read into them. With certainty, papers 72 and 77 by Hamilton suggested that minor administrative officers should not be automatically rotated
upon the rise of new chief executives. William Crawford's and Andrew Jackson's later
arguments were therefore attacked, even if Hamilton's real target was more likely the
then-current practice of rotation without spoils. Papers 17 and 36, also by Hamilton,
argued that state governments were in a better position to regulate local affairs than
would be a federal administrative structure. Beyond these points, there were so few
administrators in the Confederation that the issue was dwarfed by the larger questions
that dominated this debate.

31.   Charles-Jean Baptiste Bonnin, *Principes d'administration publique*, 3 vol. (3rd ed.,
       Paris: Chez Renaudiére, 1812).[4]

Books entitled *Principles of Public Administration*, such as Willoughby's, are
supposed to be a vestige of the 1920s. This one predates Willoughby by over a century, but it was never translated into English, it is listed as being in the collections
of only five libraries in the United States, and it is therefore almost entirely unknown
to the current field.[5]
Public Administration became a more pressing subject in France than in the
English-speaking world at this time because Napoleon's administrative revolution had
extended the state's reach more completely into society's business. Bonnin had begun
in 1808 to draft an administrative code for these new responsibilities. When the
proposed code needed annual updating, he decided to propose some general principles
of public administration by which the code would be kept current.
This three volume work contained both his proposed code (in 708 sections) and
68 principles of public administration. They were derived from a mixture of administrative law, politics, and the social responsibilities of government. Most of the
principles, however, were specific to French administration.
For future training, Bonnin argued that we needed to develop a science of administration. It would go beyond politics and administrative law by combining several

disciplines, especially the statistics that would be needed for administration's special role in implementing the laws among the population.

Bonnin also felt that administrators needed a school for in-service training. There were such schools for politics, but "politics is a science, administration is a science and an art." Arts were more difficult to learn, and it was critical that we train administrators because the dual "principles of the gradual march" to progress required the competent use of administrative techniques and the moral sense that administrators were serving the state.

See also Pierre Escoube, "Charles-Jean Bonnin, précurseur de la Science administrative," *Revue administrative*, vol. 11 (January/February 1958): 15-18, or Daniel Martin, "Déjà vu: French Antecedents to American Public Administration," *Public Administration Review*, 47, (July/August 1987): 297-303.

32. Georg Wilhelm Friedrich Hegel, *The Philosophy of Right*, originally *Grundlinien der Philosophie des Rechts* (Berlin: In der Nicolaischen Buchhandlung, 1821).

Unlike the French who had already isolated the subject of Public Administration, the Germans continued the tradition of analyzing the subject as a subset of Political Science. As a logical extension of the democratization movement that swept much of Europe and the United States in the Eighteenth Century, Hegel contended that the civil service could act as a buffer against tyranny. The paragraphs numbered 287-297 concerned the role of the executive. In his additions to paragraph 290, he noted that the executive logically divided functions, but that the divided functions of government joined at both the top (the chief executive) and at the bottom (implementation on the street). However, his basic protection against political abuse was pluralism. In particular, in paragraph 297 and its additions, he expressed a faith that in countries with a large middle class (the U.S., but not Russia, for instance), that group could populate the civil service and keep the corruptible rulers in check.

33. U.S. Senate Report 88, Senate Miscellaneous Documents, 19th Congress, 2nd Session (May 4, 1826), 149 pp.

In the United States, serious studies on the impacts of personnel regulations began in congressional investigations long before they could be found in other sub-fields of Public Administration. In this report, following the "Corrupt Bargain of 1825," a special Senate committee was assigned to evaluate six bills attempting to reduce presidential patronage in limited areas.

Unlike later patronage reform studies, this one was rather primitive, and was concerned with the implications of patronage as a tool for political power. As the reporting committee noted, "(p)ower over a man's support, has always been held and admitted to be power over his will." (p. 7) They felt that, by dispersing the patronage, they would keep the power of the presidency in check.

34.   Andrew Jackson, "First Annual Message," in *A Compilation of the Messages and Papers of the Presidents: 1789-1897,* vol. 2, ed. by James D. Richardson (Washington, D.C.: Government Printing Office, 1896), pp. 442-462. Relevant section is on p. 449. The speech was delivered December 8, 1829.

In a more practical application of the rise of Hegel's middle class into the civil service, Jackson noted that "(t)he duties of all public officers are, or at least admit of being made, so plain and simple that men of intelligence may readily qualify themselves for their performance...." He argued that long tenures lead to indifference, and that artificial rotation (he favored extending the Four Years Law of 1820) would destroy the growing sentiment that government offices were a matter of property right. The congressional reform effort of 1826 noted above had, for the time, been quelled.

35.   *La revue administrative* [*Administrative Review*]. Paris: April 1839-1849.

Students of French public administration, who had been publishing in *Revue française* or *Revue de législation et de jurisprudence* until this time, created their own journal in 1839. While Bibliotheque Nationale holds the complete run of ten years, the only collection that could be located in the U.S. is missing the final two years.[6]

In the opening issue, the journal editor announced that they were not interested in general politics nor in the literature of commerce or industry. They were interested in the implementation of the laws, or "Public Administration." As the French still largely believe, however, political discussions are largely meaningless except as they relate to administration. Therefore, they regularly tackled the administrative implications of the biggest political issues of the day. In the end, the publishers' opposition to forced reorganization and their subsequent involvement in revolutionary politics caused the journal's demise.

The journal published some political economy studies, especially in the early years. It also kept the members informed on recent legal and personal developments, as the *Public Administration Times* might do in the U.S. today. It contained historical studies, and contemporary analyses of administrative questions. It also contained extensive bibliographies of both regulations and Public Administration literature.

It was never widely circulated, reaching a subscription rate of about 150. Many of those, however, were shipped to foreign addresses. In the end, the journal was too small and too politically belligerent to survive the political crisis of 1848-1849.

See also Jean-Emile Reymond, "La Revue Administrative...de 1839 à 1849," *La revue administrative,* 5, (1952): 359-67, or Martin, "Déjà vu."

36.   Edouard Laboulaye, "Education and the Administrative System of Probation in Germany," (1843); reprinted in U.S. House Report 8, 39th Congress, 2nd Session, January 3, 1867, pp. 14-29. Originally "De l'enseignement et du noviciat administratif en Allemagne," *Revue de législation et du jurisprudence,* XVIII, pp. 513-611. Reprinted 1843 by Paris: rue Bergere, 21.

In 1840, Laboulaye was sent by the French Minister of Public Instruction to study German public education. Laboulaye reported that German liberal arts emphasized both political and administrative instruction, and that the result was both a more informed citizenry and a more efficient governmental administration.

Laboulaye argued that "(w)e have recovered equally from the doctrine put forth by M. Say and his disciples, that government is an ulcer on the body politic, and M. de Tocqueville has long since cured us of our admiration for the self-government of the Americans." Still, Laboulaye would be an advocate of what Mosher would later call the Barnard-Appleby-Bailey Construct, that society is best protected by administrators trained in the liberal arts.

37.   Sir Stafford Northcote and Sir Charles Trevelyan, "The Organization of the Permanent Civil Service," (Report signed November 23, 1853; submitted to Parliament February 1854). The report, without supporting documentation was reprinted in *Public Administration* (England), 32, (Spring 1954): 1-16.

This report to Parliament advocated and led to the creation of the class-oriented merit system in Britain. They complained that the spoils system was creating low efficiency and public estimation of the service. As a remedy, they wanted a civil service commission (established in May 1855) that would offer standardized entrance exams (first offered in June 1855).

For position classification, they advocated dividing governmental positions into clerk positions that involved routine work and administrative positions that required intellectual work. The latter would be reserved for university graduates. They also wanted merit-based promotions and annual salary increases.

Despite heavy opposition, Parliament followed the basic tenets of the report and, within a short period of time, the full system was operational. However, while Northcote, Trevelyan, and John Stuart Mill corresponded regularly with such American reformers as Dorman Eaton, Thomas Jenckes, and George William Curtis, the Americans were never able to accept the class distinctions of the Northcote-Trevelyan approach that often had little to do with the difficulty of the work being performed.

For more information, see Edward Hughes, "Civil Service Reform 1853-5," *Public Administration* (England), 32, (Spring 1954): 17-51; or Dorman Eaton listed below.

38.   [Alexandre Francois Auguste] Vivien, *Études administratives*, [*Administrative Studies*] 2 vol., 3rd ed. (Paris: Librarie de Guillaumin & Cie, 1859).[7]

By mid-century, the French Institute had developed the study of Public Administration to a level that was not to be seen in the U.S. until the Brownlow Committee. There is no better evidence for this than Vivien's two volume textbook on the subject, which is still sometimes cited (in the third edition) in France, but which has yet to be translated into English.

To begin, Vivien established the politics/administration dichotomy as the basis of his study. "The executive power itself is divided into two branches: the political,

which is the moral direction of the general interests of the nation, and the administrative, which consists principally in the performance of the public services" (my
translation, vol. 1, pp. 3-4). Similarly, "the political power is the head, the administration is the arms." (p. 30)

Unlike the American tradition, however, the French saw administration as the
original and normal state of government. (p. 12) Politics arose as a protection once
administration became capricious. This view partially explains why administrative
studies evolved so early in political writings in France, while other cultures continued
to study political economy.

Subsequent chapters discussed the relationship of administration to the judiciary
and legislature; the need for and the forms of hierarchy; committees and commissions
vs. single-headed administration; techniques for financial accountability; the special
problems of administrative tribunals; and personnel placement and promotion policies.
Volume two discussed local administration and intergovernmental administrative relations.

39.   John Stuart Mill, *On Liberty* (London: J. W. Parker and Son, 1859); also *Consid-
      erations on Representative Government* (London: Parker, son, and Bourn, 1861).

Mill feared public administration, and saw fit to close his work *On Liberty* with
a warning about the need to restrict the governmental interference in local and
personal affairs that is a logical consequence of bureaucratic expansion. Providing an
opposite viewpoint to both civil service reformers and eventually to Wilson, he was
concerned that the new use of civil service exams in Britain would create a bureaucracy so talented that the population would be helpless to protect itself. He was
much more impressed with the American experience of allowing local governments to
spring up virtually everywhere for the expression of the popular will.

In *Representative Government*, he expanded on his belief that the legislators
should control the administrators, but that they could do so only by selecting honest
and honorable men for the positions. They could not hope to monitor the actual
content of administrative regulations. One of the clearer statements of his distrust
appeared in chapter six, in which he argued "that the only governments, not representative, in which high political skill and ability have been other than exceptional,
whether under monarchical or aristocratic forms, have been essentially bureaucracies."

40.   Thomas Jenckes, "Civil Service of the United States," House Report 8, 39th
      Congress, 2nd Session (January 31, 1867); also "Civil Service of the United
      States," House Report 47, 40th Congress, 2nd Session (May 25, 1868), 220 pp.

These two reports, especially the second, mirror the best and the worst of both
governmental reports and personnel research. On the weak side, they were extraordinarily disjointed and sometimes sensationalist in style. "Terror, meanwhile, reigned
in Washington. No man knew what the rule was upon which removals were made."
(1868, p. 9) At best, they were the most sophisticated historical studies of the merit

system written to date. They detailed personnel practices in Britain, France, Prussia, Russia, China, and others. The history of U.S. personnel is rivalled today only by Fish and Van Riper.

To Representative Jenckes, the spoils system was a problem of morality. The insecurity it created sapped the moral fibre of the republic, and could only be repaired by a merit system.

The documents contain extensive appendices of countless interviews with revenue agents supporting reform, and personnel documents from other countries. The transitions and titles are unnecessarily confusing, however, and at times it is almost impossible to determine what one is reading.

41.   Dorman B. Eaton, *Civil Service in Great Britain* (New York: Harper and Brothers, 1879).

This history, by the man who would become the first chair of the U.S. Civil Service Commission, is still one of the more sophisticated works on this subject. Eaton studied British administration from a period well before the Norman conquest through the time he was writing in 1879.

As a civil service reformer, Eaton's purpose helped shape the book. Specifically, while his history was well researched and reasonably objective, it covered the merit system at more length than would be expected in such a study. Eaton argued that nothing was more remarkable in Great Britain in the last century than the effort to reform the civil service.

Three things also help tie the book to the U.S. reform movement: the Introduction by reformer George William Curtis; chapter 28 which compared the British changes to the U.S. system; and a letter from Trevelyan to Eaton favoring U.S. reform, that was reprinted in an appendix.

42.   Chester Arthur, "First Annual Message," in *A Compilation of the Messages and Papers of the Presidents: 1789-1897*, vol. 8, ed. by James D. Richardson (Washington, D.C.: Government Printing Office, December 6, 1881), pp. 37-65. Relevant pages are 60-63.

This is part of the general movement after Garfield's assassination that eventually led to the Civil Service Act of 1883. Arthur, a recent convert to both the merit system and morality in government, argued for a bottom-entry, promotion-based merit system. However, he was concerned that literacy alone was not sufficient as a test, and in describing moral responsibilities, made one of the first published references to the need for government to operate according to good business principles. After elaborating on the details of his proposal, he assailed those who attacked the honesty, competence, and efficiency of the average civil servant, arguing that most were doing a good job.

CONTINUING CONCERNS

In some context, the existence of bureaucracy has been acknowledged by political philosophers for some time. However, the institution was not seen as a separate power base until so late in its development that the proposals for its control were shaped by the crisis that neglect had helped create.

There was no Western equivalent to Confucius and, as a result, our impressions since the time of Rousseau have been reactive to an administrative system that had already grown large. Our two reactions, both stated in Rousseau, may be stated as the themes that still define almost all of the academic discipline of Public Administration.

First, bureaucracy has been seen by a substantial portion of our heritage as a subversion of the delicate balance of political power in the state. Beginning with Montesquieu, we have appreciated that administrators operate under a different set of rules, as powerful as laws, but different from them. They are not easily controlled by constitution building. However, except for a scattering of efforts (the 1826 congressional hearings, for instance), we did not seem to know how to begin controlling them.

The second theme begins with Rousseau. Uncontrolled bureaucratic growth does nothing to insure the morality or dignity of its administrators. Since the beginning of national sovereignty, our best minds have struggled with ways to constrain the abuses of the chief executive while maintaining executive dignity. We have nurtured the integrity of our chief executives by forcing them to be neither tyrants nor immature, ineffectual clerks.

With the bureaucracy, however, we have attempted no such balance. Growing unchecked, we often allowed the bureaucracy to become a force to be feared, while individual bureaucrats were justifiably afraid for their jobs.

The rise of the merit system reformers may be seen as a late start on correcting the neglect. Alternately, one could argue that their efforts were an admission of defeat, for nothing in the original personnel reform proposals tried to develop the dignity of the administrators. Rather, as moral crusaders, the reformers believed dignity to be inherent in the species. Like many later social psychologists, they were merely attempting to remove the abuses of a repressive environment.

Personnel has long since abandoned the single-minded purpose of its early reformers, and has sought structural tools to develop its employees. (See chapter 16 on staffing.) On the first theme, of placing the bureaucracy within the power-balance of the state, see chapter 10 and further references throughout Part I of this book.

However, on both themes, we missed the opportunity that constitution writers had to shape the institution from the beginning. It grew on its own, and ever since, we have been reacting and attempting to regulate its impact.

NOTES FOR CHAPTER TWO

1. Leonard White and Vincent Ostrom published descriptions of American administrative thought as it existed at the beginning of the republic, and their works are are discussed later in this section.

2. There is a partial, unofficial publication that was compiled while the full document was being prepared. See Treadway Nash, ed. *Domesday Book*, 2 vol. (London: Printed by J. Nichols, 1781 & 1782). This version, however, has no legal standing.

3. For nearly opposite viewpoints, see Vincent Ostrom, *The Intellectual Crisis in American Public Administration* (University: University of Alabama Press, 1973), and Dwight Waldo, *The Enterprise of Public Administration* (Novato, CA: Chandler & Sharp, 1980).

4. The third edition is the one being described here. The second edition, in one volume and correspondingly less detail, was published Paris: Clament frères, 1809. The first edition, hardly more than a booklet, was published 1808. However, there is considerable confusion over the title. In the third edition, Bonnin lists it as *Considerations sur la nécessité d'un code administratif*. However, no title that could be interpreted as a first edition appears in *Catalogue général* of Bibliothèque Nationale. The U.S. National Union Catalogue lists only *De l'importance et de la nécessité d'un code administratif* for 1808 with no publisher and 70 pages, and this may be the same book.

5. These lists do not include privately held copies or those in libraries that did not enter them into the OCLC lists, or the *National Union Catalogue*. Still, copies of Nineteenth Century French administrative literature are rare in the United States.

6. In France, Bibliothèque Nationale has the entire run of the journal plus advertising précis from the original publishers. In the USA, the University of Illinois at Urbana holds the volumes for years 1839-1847. The missing two years in the U.S. collection, however, are described in the article in the current *Revue administrative* cited in the review.

7. Once again, the third edition is the one that had the most impact. The second edition, by the same publisher in 1852, is less complete. The first edition, in one volume, was published in 1845.

3
Management Before Taylor

BACKGROUND

Even though the literature of the Nineteenth Century included several works on administrative topics, it could not compete with the explosion of studies that were soon to follow. This transformation occurred first in the business sector through the efforts of the Scientific Management advocates in the American Society of Mechanical Engineers. This chapter lays the groundwork from which they evolved. The next seven chapters review the implications of the split between the public and private sectors in the study of management. Chapter eleven reviews the Scientific Management reformers themselves.

Prior to Scientific Management, two themes dominated the attention of those who studied the workings of the industrial revolution. First, Political Economists popularized factory studies in the Nineteenth Century, including some detail on the workings of management, but even more emphasis on the economic theories that explained the emergence of factories. These books are very developmental in their approach to the topic, and are often in the form of historical interpretations.

However, while some business owners may have read some of these works, there is little reason to believe that the foremen in the factories would have done the same. Instead, it seems more likely that they were the market for an entirely different variety of literature which emerged in the early 1800s, and which contained suggestions for good business practices. These works generally had a moralistic tone, although one strain of them eventually evolved directly into the "principles" approach to management.

Representative samples of each of the two types of literature are reviewed in this chapter. In addition, the chapter includes histories written after Taylor's era on the rise of the factory system before Scientific Management. In all three cases, the selection is limited by the appreciation that business management is not the thrust of this bibliography.

POLITICAL ECONOMICS

These books are significant in the development of Public Administration in that they are the academic precursors to Scientific Management, and its competitors as a method of analyzing the factory. Their scope is production, or sometimes generic management. However, the works are equally different from the works that follow in this chapter, and that focus more narrowly on the environment of the manager.

These reviews begin with some of the classic works that helped shape business' sense of its own purpose in society. These are followed by some more recent examples that tie the histories to more current practices.

43. Adam Smith, *An Inquiry into the Nature and Causes of the Wealth of Nations*, 2 vol. (London: W. Strahan and T. Cadell, 1776).

This is the first of several books in economic theory that slowly transformed that field from believing that only land and labor were factors of production, into accepting management as a factor that was worthy of academic study.

To begin, Smith's recommendations on the politics of governmental noninterference (not laissez faire, which he never used in this book) are too well known to be reviewed here.[1] While his ideas leaned heavily on François Quesnay and other Physiocrats, he popularized the notion that wealth is created, not just by the traditional means of rent and wages, but also by capital. However, his approach also legitimized the study of manufacturing and political economy as subjects that were separate from political science.

One can overstate the role of Smith in studying the process of manufacturing. To land and labor, he added capital as a means of production. Therefore, whether he was discussing industrialization, trade, or governmental services, his emphasis was on the impact of investment and finance. Before management could become the focus of political economy, Say had to add it to the list of the factors of production.

44. Jean-Baptiste Say, *A Treatise on Political Economy*, 1st American ed., trans. from 4th French edition by C. R. Prinsep (Boston: Wells and Lilly, 1821). Originally published as *Traité d'économie politique* (Paris: Deterville, 1803). Note that Say continued to revise the French and English versions until his death in the 1830s.

For the purposes of manufacturing, Say took Smith to his logical conclusion. He attacked the Eighteenth Century economic belief that went back to Plato, which said that the only true production was production of raw materials. Say argued that there are four factors of production--land, labor, capital, and the "adventurer" or manager.

He recognized that certain people, who may or may not own the means of production, nevertheless bring resources together in combinations that create wealth that would not otherwise exist. While he did not distinguish the entrepreneur from the manager, he helped bring the value of "organizing" into the legitimate study of economics.

45. Charles Babbage, *On the Economy of Machinery and Manufactures* (London: Charles Knight, 1832).

Babbage is today best known for the creation of his "differential machine," or mechanical calculator that was a forerunner of modern computers. Unfortunately, this overshadows his role as the first advocate of Scientific Management.

As a mathematician and scientist, Babbage approached manufacturing as a cooperative effort between human and mechanical machines. Like Adam Smith, he concentrated on the division of labor. However, like Taylor forty years later, he advocated subdividing the work so that it could be timed to determine a fair rate of pay. As an early cost accountant, he also wanted to determine the cost of each facet of the work, and he advocated paying bonuses (essentially a profit sharing plan) to workers who produced more than the expected amount.

Modern reviewers sometimes overrate the sophistication of Babbage's work. The concepts of Scientific Management were all there. However, unlike Taylor, Babbage was content to observe techniques used by others. For instance, he was particularly fond of a profit sharing scheme that was implemented in the Flintshire lead mines by, ironically, a Mr. Taylor (chapter 26).

Nevertheless, Babbage's work was extremely popular, despite boycotts from both publishers and booksellers. In the book, he had calculated their excess profits from his work, and even Babbage was unable to buy a copy of his own book. Also, the concepts were modern enough that some Taylor advocates have felt obligated to argue that Taylor had not heard of Babbage and, therefore, could not have plagiarized his ideas. Still, the 1830s were too early for this approach; the 1890s were not.

46. James Montgomery, *The Carding and Spinning Masters' Assistant: or the Theory and Practice of Cotton Spinning* (Glasgow: J. Niven, Jr., 1832); also *A Practical Detail on the Cotton Manufacture of the United States of America* (Glasgow: J. Niven, Jr., 1840).

While the second book listed above is far better known, the first book is sometimes cited as the first book to discuss management practices explicitly. Montgomery limited his concern to cotton manufacturing, and the book might be considered "consciousness-raising" only in that he bemoaned the lack of attention to management without offering much concrete analysis of his own. Still, he gave useful advice on dealing with employees, and described the role of the manager in controlling the flow of work. While the first printings appeared semi-anonymously with his initials "JM" only, his identity was quickly discovered as his reputation grew. His visit to the

U.S., where he was particularly well received, led to the publication of the second book.

See James Baughman (ed), "James Montgomery on Factory Management, 1832," *Business History Review*, 42, (Summer 1968): 219-26.

47.   Andrew Ure, *Philosophy of Manufacturers* (London: Charles Knight, 1835).

Many of these books bring something from their cultural background, be it Frederick Taylor's reference to "niggers" or Charles Babbage's attack on shoddy Jewish workmanship, that no longer sits comfortably with most readers. Ure is a classic example.

In the tradition of Montgomery, Ure attempted to analyze the factors of textile manufacturing in Great Britain. He argued that there were three economies to the factory--scientific, moral, and commercial. The scientific economy occupied much of the book, telling us more about fibers and machines than anyone except those designing such factories would need to know. The commercial economy is self-explanatory and beyond the scope of this bibliography.

The moral economy, however, was the condition of personnel in the plant. In an often outrageous defense of child labor (one girl learned to play the organ, so how bad could deformities and diseases be?) and other conditions of factory life, he discredited his opposition as being uninformed, atheistic, alcoholic, and sexually deviant. The fact that he was often partially correct, about both factory conditions and the critics he identified, does not change his lack of credibility in describing the "promised land" of factory living.

Still, Ure was influential in his day, and his argument that factory life was infinitely safer and more comfortable than work in cottage industries may well have been valid.

48.   William Stanley Jevons, *The Theory of Political Economy* (London: Macmillan and Co., 1871). Note that this is not *Political Economy*, also by Jevons.

Within a few years of Taylor's beginning at Midvale, it could be expected that similar questions would occur to others. Jevons duplicated Taylor's concerns in two areas, although his answers and approaches were somewhat different. First, Jevons was fascinated with fatigue studies, and he hit upon one of the same examples that Taylor later made famous when he questioned which size shovel would be appropriate to each job.

He also was extremely interested in incentive plans and, more generally, in the entire area of labor-management relations. Jevons was trained in political economics, however, and investigated solutions such as profit sharing and even joint ownership that Taylor would have found irresponsible.

The biggest difference between Jevons and Taylor, however, was the same as the difference between Babbage and Taylor. Jevons had scientific training, but as a political economist. He observed the tests done by others. Taylor was a mechanical engineer. That allowed him to test his ideas in the plant. It also put Taylor on the winning side in a war for control of the factory that was just then beginning to erupt.

HISTORIES OF THE FACTORY SYSTEM

49.   R. Whately Cooke Taylor, *Introduction to a History of the Factory System* (London: Richard Bentley & Son, 1886).

Cooke Taylor lamented that he wanted to write *The History of the Factory System*, but decided that he could not because there was no literary tradition and insufficient sources on which to build. (p. v) Instead, he wrote a book that read like two works stuck together. First, he borrowed economic theory to justify the use of machines as adding value to the resources of the land. Then he gave an extensive description of manufacturing throughout history.

He noted that the term factory did not take on its current meaning until about 1802. (p. 4) Nevertheless, mill-factories developed in Bologna, Italy in the Fifteenth Century, and first blossomed in England in the Eighteenth Century. (pp. 353-54) He also issued a critique of the dehumanizing and disrupting effects of industrialization. (pp. 428-29)

50.   Max Weber, *The Protestant Ethic and the Spirit of Capitalism*, trans. by Talcott Parsons (New York: Scribners, 1930), originally published as *Die Protestantische Ethik und der Geist des Kapitalismus* (undated reprint from *Archiv für Sozialwissenschaft u. Sozialpolitik*, II, 1904).

Max Weber, a Prussian sociologist who is best known to us for his later description of bureaucracy, attempted in this unrelated work to refute Marx's interpretation that capitalism, or any other economic system, arose inevitably from economic causes alone. Using historical reinterpretation, he attempted to tie the rise of capitalism to changes in the religious and moral fabric of Protestant societies. The work has been subject to considerable criticism in more recent times, based largely on questions about the accuracy of Weber's claim that Protestantism predated the essential conditions of capitalism.

51.   Lewis Mumford, *Technics and Civilization* (New York: Harcourt, Brace and Co, 1934).

Unlike the economic theorists who dominate this field, Mumford chose to concentrate on the social relationship between man and his tools through the past millennium, with the sociologist's perspective that little is economically inevitable. He argued that the relationship of man and machines had developed through three phases in this era. The first, the eotechnic, evolved in the Tenth Century, and involved artisans using the elements of nature in an attempt to achieve order through means that were external to the moral and social difficulties of the time.

The second phase, the paleotechnic, began in the mid-1700s in England and the mid-1800s in the U.S. It attempted to impose order through mass production and regimentation of workers as the tools of the machines. Mumford's book was finally optimistic, however. He saw us beginning a neotechnic age, in which people would assimilate the values of the machine, including objectivity, impersonality, and neutrality, and would therefore be able to shrink the role of machines back into being the tools of man.

Mumford saw Frederick Taylor as a vestige of the paleotechnic age (pp. 384-85), but saw hope for progress in the then-new neotechnic experiments at Hawthorne. (pp. 385-86) While the book's findings were controversial, it provided an alternate approach to economic determinism. Its bibliography is superb (although dated) for additional research.

52.   J. Leander Bishop, *History of American Manufacturers From 1608 to 1860*, 2 vol. (Philadelphia: Edward Young & Co., 1861); also

53.   Victor S. Clark, *History of Manufactures in the United States 1607-1860* (New York: McGraw-Hill for the Carnegie Institution of Washington, 1916). Revised and expanded to 3 volumes, 1929. Volume 2 covers 1860-1893; volume 3 covers 1893-1928.

With these two early works, one could argue that the study of American manufacturing matured before manufacturing itself. Both were solely economic histories. As Clark stated, his work was true to its title "in the strict sense of the word. It does not deal with technology or mechanics." (vol. 1, p. v) Both discussed the development of economic protectionism of domestic industries in our new republic, and Bishop included the role of patent policy in manufacturing. Clark also explained our delayed development of a factory system. However, both dismissed the role of management as being too narrow a concern for their massive tasks. As a result, Clark described both Midvale and Bethlehem Steel Corporations during Taylor's tenure without mentioning Taylor or Scientific Management.

54.   Sidney Pollard, *The Genesis of Modern Management: A Study of the Industrial Revolution in Great Britain* (Cambridge: Harvard University Press, 1965).

Pollard's book was about the development of management techniques as a response to the common challenges of the industrial revolution: labor recruitment and training; discipline; control over production; accountancy and accountability. He noted that the entrepreneur and the manager were usually the same person until the second or third generation of the industrial revolution. After that, the managers forced a change in public education to include more technical, and less academic, subjects.

He argued that the best documented case "of conscious thought on management and the attempts to systemize it" was the Boulton and Watt partnership in the 1770s. Through a series of surviving letters, they planned and introduced regularity, delegation, and the division of functions into their factories.

Pollard also studied the conditions of the workers, noting that managers had to shape their lives to fit the requirements of the machines. Stable workers were worth more than skilled workers, and owners did little to keep the factories from looking like prisons.

55. Claude S. George, Jr., *The History of Management Thought* (Englewood Cliffs, NJ: Prentice-Hall, 1968). Second edition, 1972.

This is the closest that Business Management has come to a bibliographic history of their field. The book offers a detailed listing of both the practices and authors that shaped management, and uncovered the first use of therapy interviews (the Egyptians in 2700 B.C.) and numerous other such practices that we presume are of recent origin.

The book proceeds to current times, although not with as broad a scope once the proliferation of literature began in the 1900s. George also attempts to construct a composite model (composed largely of abstract mathematical formulas) near the end to summarize what we have learned about management. Briefly, the model combines the behaviorists and Fayol to argue that managers need to be generalists.

56. Daniel Wren, *Evolution of Management Thought* (New York: Ronald Press, 1972).

This is one of the more popular modern histories written from the perspective of the modern study of business management. The first five chapters of this book discuss the topic of this review in as much detail as may be needed for most purposes, sometimes overlapping Gladden, but in a more abbreviated form.

The emphasis early in the book is on the search for the roots of business management in public affairs. However, in that goal, the review is sometimes unexpectedly brief, discounting the role of merchant activity until the Crusades. (pp. 20-21) The review, particularly on management thought, is more detailed after the onset of industrialization. Chapter six and beyond discuss topics too recent to be included in this chapter.

57. Daniel Nelson, *Managers and Workers* (Madison: University of Wisconsin Press, 1975); also *Frederick W. Taylor and the Rise of Scientific Management* (Madison: University of Wisconsin Press, 1980).

Nelson's two books (especially the first) are particularly helpful in explaining the rise of the first factory system (pre-Taylor) in the United States. Nelson contends that the first factory system began in the U.S. in Waltham and Lowell in the 1810s and 1820s, and was common throughout the country by the 1860s. In that system, the foreman (not the entrepreneur) was the manufacturer, and the machines were run by an inordinate number of skilled craftsmen.

The precise relationship of the foreman to the higher-level supervisor depended on the technology. Supervisors did better in factories in which the work was "the fabrication of a multitude of distinct parts." By the end of the period, work was becoming more divided because of the advanced machinery, and engineers began to find their way into managerial positions.

BOOKS ON GOOD BUSINESS AND MANAGEMENT PRACTICES

Apart from the grander economic concerns that dominated the business literature of the Nineteenth Century, some authors occasionally offered suggestions on how managers could perform more effectively. Overwhelmingly, their advice fit into two categories--organizational principles similar to those eventually popularized by Fayol; or personal traits for good management.

The literature ranges from asides in highly respectable political economy texts to books that are so oriented toward "good citizenship" that they are indistinguishable from religious tracts. The latter are sampled only very briefly here, although dismissing them entirely would lead to the false impression that they were not widely read and respected.

The trait approach to business has remained with us, as is discussed in chapter 14 on leadership. Through most of the 1800s, that type constituted much of what would be identified as management literature. A century before that, it was written for young men of responsibility, but did not label itself as managerial at all.

The literature is arranged chronologically. However, it has already been noted that management often filled a minor role in many of the earlier books, and the summations below are sometimes appropriately brief.[2]

58. Anne Robert Jacques Turgot, Baron de l'Aulne, *Reflections on the Formulation and Distribution of Riches*, originally *Réflexions sur la formation et la distribution des richesses*, see note for publication details.[3]

As soon as factories began to rise in the industrial revolution, some of the more famous authors began speculating on how to operate them. Adam Smith considered manufacturers to be "unproductive," and therefore unworthy of study except in their role as investors. Turgot and Say, however, both saw a separate managerial role for manufacturers.

Turgot, a liberal economist and later Comptroller General, wrote his *Reflections* for the benefit of two Chinese students who were returning to China, so that they could better explain France's approach to political economy. In it, he struggled with the questions of direction and control of the workers, feeling that this duty was so critical that it could not be delegated by the entrepreneur to paid managers (p. 18 of

1898 Macmillan Co. translation), thereby making the development of a separate study of management impossible.

59.   Jean-Baptiste Say, *Catechism of Political Economy*, originally *Catéchisme d'économie politique* (Paris: Impr. de Crapelet, 1815).

After his more academically oriented *Treatise,* Say produced this "elementary" book for entrepreneurs, and advertised it accordingly. "This work does not pretend to furnish the means of becoming rich; it professes only to point them out." He then argued that all manufacturing was a matter of planning and organizing resources. This talent for planning distinguished the entrepreneur from the workman. Say continued to muddle the distinction between managerial and ownership functions, however, and so was unable to distinguish managerial planning from financial planning.

60.   Charles Dupin, *Discours sur le sort des ouvriers* [*Discourse on the State of Workers*] (Paris: Bachelier, Libraire, 1831).

Dupin could easily be labelled the first Western humanist, and his suggestions (although not his style) are reminiscent of Confucius. He was technically skilled, but using the results of a study of the English navy's management practices, he suggested that the manager's role was to put his own house into order so that he could command respect and treat his workers with dignity. On the mundane level, he advocated that managers pay their debts promptly and keep their appointments. The purpose, however, was to inspire confidence and esprit de corps in the subordinates.

61.   Samuel P. Newman, *Elements of Political Economy* (Andover: Gould and Newman, 1835).

Newman created the first full-blown list of the traits of a good manager. He suggested that such a person would have foresight, calculation, perseverance, constancy of purpose, discretion, decision of character, and technical competence. Where one would find this manager was not clear, and training techniques were not mentioned.

62.   Freeman Hunt, *Worth and Wealth: Maxims for Merchants and Men of Business* (New York: Stringer & Townsend, 1856). Note: this is the shortened title used on the spine.

By this date, much administrative literature was literally forcing itself into popular circulation by the lack of guidance that was available for the growing managerial class. These were mass market books, not academic tomes. There are far too many of them, and they are generally too poorly written to be reviewed here. However, this is one of the better, or at least better known, examples.

Hunt was editor of *Merchant's Magazine,* a periodical for people with small enough businesses that they had to perform administrative as well as the financial duties. He compiled this book of short articles from his magazine and other newspapers.

Like Dupin, human fulfillment ranked heavily with Hunt, although that is largely explained by the dual roles of the reader as manager and laborer. It is also explained by the heavy role that religious inspiration played in these works and in that audience. This book and this entire strain of literature leaned heavily on such good personality traits as honesty, perspective, goodwill, and trust of customers and employees. Once the religion is removed, however, it sounds much like the "excellence" literature of today.

63.   Francis Bowen, *American Political Economy* (New York: Charles Scribner and Co., 1870).

Bowen was another political economist who had little concern for traits, since all the traits that were needed could seldom be found in one individual. Nevertheless, the growing trend toward decision-making committees was even more harmful. "(O)ne executive head, and a very able one, is an essential prerequisite of success in any large undertaking." (p. 124)

64.   Emile Louis Victor de Laveleye, *The Elements of Political Economy*, trans. by Alfred W. Pollard (New York: G.P. Putnam's Sons, 1884). Originally *Les éléments de l'économie politique* (Paris: Hachette, 1882).

Laveleye was a political economist who felt that studies of production were incomplete without explaining the moral, political, and religious aspects of worker motivation. He was also representative of a growing concern in the late 1800s that there was inadequate training for the new managerial role in business. While France had excellent institutions to train political scientists, he was concerned that there was no similar school for "good industrial managers." "Nothing contributes more to increase the productiveness of labour than the application to it of science, that is to say of observation of the facts and laws of nature." (p. 74) If there were well trained managers, they could then pass on effective practices to the workmen.

65.   J. Lawrence Laughlin, *Elements of Political Economy* (New York: American Book Co., 1896).

This book is mentioned because the author was well respected, and because it is indicative of a trap that was built into Political Economy that made it increasingly irrelevant to concerns within the factory. This is an excellent book on political economy that tried to get specific, but that continually merged the managerial and entrepreneurial roles of the manufacturer, even though different people had long since been performing the two functions in factory settings. Eventually, political economics would have to adjust by creating a separate study of microeconomics. However, even then, the adjustment would be imprecise. Besides, by the 1890s, the engineers had already seized the initiative for control of management studies.

CONTINUING CONCERNS

By the late 1880s, factory studies in the industrialized world had reached a crossroads with which they were not prepared to deal. The authors were trained as economists, and felt obligated to analyze factories within that light. As political economists, they could explore the regulation and evolution of factories as an institution. It was not in their training, however, to adjust to the specificity that managers needed to do their jobs.

The adjustment came in the form of an invasion of experts with training in mechanical engineering. The invasion was successful--perhaps too successful. We have adjusted so completely to applied research within institutions that we have abandoned much of the cultural awareness that was the whole point of political economics.

This approach was abandoned by managers because it failed to meet pressing needs within the factory. It did not fail to meet the needs of those who try to understand the evolution of the factory system, however, and it seems uniquely qualified to continue to fulfill that role.

NOTES ON CHAPTER THREE

1. Despite popular opinion, Smith used the "invisible hand" analogy once, in passing, in his book and did not use the term "laissez faire" at all. The invisible hand comment had nothing to do with it current usage. Instead, it was part of an argument on international trade that assumed that balance of payment problems would not occur because people would prefer to invest their money in domestic markets.

2. For the more scholarly literature, the list is derived heavily from chapter four of Claude George, Jr., *History of Management Thought*, 2nd ed. (Englewood Cliffs, NJ: Prentice-Hall, 1972).

3. Text dated November 1766. Published under original title with author listed as "Mr. X" in *Ephemerides du citoyen*, XI & XII, (December 1769 and January 1770), although these issues were not released until January-April 1770. The journal version contained several unauthorized deletions and additions, and Turgot insisted

that the editor arrange for a private printing (n. p.: n.d. [1770]). Of the original 100 or 150 copies, one still exists. Most reprints have been of the incorrect version, which is altered to argue the positions of the physiocratic editors.

4

"Government Is Different"

BACKGROUND[1]

The debate over the appropriate relationship between the governmental and private sectors is older than either academic discipline that now studies the subject. However, the subject seems to lie relatively dormant until a crisis arises in the interactions of the two. Such crises occurred at the beginning of mercantilism, in the midst of the industrial revolution, in the regulatory fervor of Progressive politics, in the societal calamities of the 1930s-1940s, and again today with privatization of public services.

New insights have been gained on each occasion. However, the new insights did not replace the old ones; they merely supplemented the old, and were more appropriate to the issue of the moment.

These next seven chapters discuss several themes in the literature relating to the interactions of, and differences between the two sectors. This chapter introduces the general literature on the subject, including early recognitions that the sectors were performing different roles, and the more recent literature on the continued growth of government. The next chapter reviews the growth of governmental regulation over the private sector.

Chapter six discusses the delivery of goods and services by the government through its own employees or through contracts to the private sector. Chapters seven and eight discuss the literature on bureaucratic politics that evolved from government production, and chapters nine and ten review citizen controls over, and demands for these services.

Rather artificially, these six chapters do not discuss the impacts of these issues on the internal mechanics of public administration. The reason, quite simply, is that there is a need to bracket this enormous proliferation of literature into manageable segments. This study is written with the assumption that one cannot recommend internal structures for government without understanding the mission of each sector, and how it relates to the mission of the other.

Therefore, these chapters review the "black box" literature that discusses the interface between the sectors without looking inside each. Part II of this bibliography, beginning with chapter eleven, uses the internal perspective to discuss the impacts of this interface within the bureaucracy itself.

In this chapter, the historical selections are brief since this is one case in which the older literature was describing a world that no longer operates with the same assumptions. However, the regulatory, the New Deal, and the 1970s-1980s privatization literature are extensive, and are still relevant enough to be reviewed in considerable detail.

EARLY BEGINNINGS--MERCANTILISM

66. Barthelemy Laffemas, *Reiglement général pour dresser les manufactures en ce royaume* [roughly, *General Regulations to Set Up Manufacturing Within the Realm*] (Paris: C. de Monstroeil, 1597).

This is one of the earliest books advocating mercantilistic policies. Laffemas, who was Minister of Commerce under Henry IV, defined the role of private enterprise as a servant to the state. Among other things, he wanted to restrict foreign products that hurt the local economy, and he suggested that manufacturing bureaus (bureaux de manufactures) be established to provide technical advice and arbitrate disputes in the basic industries.

67. Antoyne de Montchrétien (sic) [Antoine de Montchrétien], *Traicte de l'oeconomie politique, dédié av Roy et à la Reyne mère dv Roy* [*Tract on Political Economy, Dedicated to the King and the Queen Mother*] (Roven [Rouen]: Iean [Jean] Osmont, 1615).

This is generally accepted as the first textbook of Political Economy. While it was written and printed for the King of France, he never read it (he was fourteen at the time), and the book was soon forgotten. It is a classic statement of the mercantile policies of an absolutist state that were to evolve before the book was rediscovered. Montchrétien concentrated on the need for accurate economic information, and went into considerable detail on the statistical techniques that would be needed to accomplish this. He also strongly suggested that the king develop a more equitable system of taxation to avert rebellion by narrowing the gap between the extremely poor and the extremely rich.

68. Thomas Hobbes, *The Leviathan* (London: Printed for Andrew Ckooke (sic) [Crooke]: 1651); also, *Behemoth* (London: Printed for William Crooke, 1680).

Hobbes made one of the strongest statements of the need for the absolutist state to control all commerce. Viewing the state as the deliverance of humanity from the chaos of nature, Hobbes subjected everything, including commerce and even religion, to that cause. He understood the conflict that was inevitable because the merchant mentality was based on selfish interest. He especially attacked the greed and self-centered approach of merchants in *Behemoth*. However, since the state was the embodiment of all the people, it had the right and the obligation to tell all of them, including the economic producers, what to do.

THE INDUSTRIAL REVOLUTION

69. Arnold Toynbee, *Lectures on the Industrial Revolution of the 18th Century in England* (London: Rivingtons, 1884). Note: This is the political economist, and not the more commonly known Arnold Toynbee (historian) who wrote in the Twentieth Century.

Countless works (notably Adam Smith and John Stuart Mill) recited the orthodox view that the industrial revolution was possible because of a governmental policy of laissez faire. This one is mentioned because it is one of the more orthodox, because it generated considerable academic respect at the time, because it is relatively recent, and because it is still frequently cited in business histories.

Toynbee was a man of uneven talents--denied entry as a student at Oxford, but offered a job as a tutor because he was too valuable to lose. He became an extremely talented speaker and guest lecturer before his untimely death. In this set of posthumously published lectures at Balliol College, Oxford, Toynbee gave a general theoretical history of the industrial revolution. He argued the traditional laissez faire case that governmental noninterference was essential for industrial growth. Specifically, he stated that Adam Smith's economics and James Watt's steam engine combined to destroy the old England, and that we were clearly in better shape because of it.

70. Karl Polanyi, *The Great Transformation* (New York: Farrar and Rinehart, 1944). Republished with expanded last chapter as *Origins of Our Time* (London: Gollancz, 1945).

Toynbee's interpretation of industrialization is seldom accepted today, and the disagreement begins here. Polanyi's classic economic history of our times rejected laissez faire as a natural state of affairs. Instead, he argued that the market economy was possible only because of governmental planning, administration, and protection. Eventually, Polanyi suggested, the price of maintaining the artificial world of a free market place became too heavy, and the system collapsed, leaving behind the governmental regulations that had made them possible in the first place.

71.   Phyllis Deane, *The First Industrial Revolution* (London: Cambridge University
      Press, 1965).

   In one of the more popular current histories of England's industrial revolution,
Deane followed Polanyi's lead in tackling Toynbee and other laissez faire historians.
She argued that we have been misled by noting the steady removal of regulations
from 1750 to 1850. Instead, she said, entrepreneurs never wanted freedom from
government, but only from ineffective government. In fact, the role of government in
English society grew dramatically during this period.
   Government was left with a new set of responsibilities in the upheaval that led
to industrialization. Eventually, these new responsibilities led the Board of Trade to
adopt merit-based entrance examinations. "This was another departure from the
eighteenth-century pattern where government officials had characteristically been the
lackeys of the landed aristocracy. It was the beginning of a new kind of bureaucracy, an officialdom from which today's professional civil service can trace direct
descent." (p. 213)

PROGRESSIVE ERA--THE CALL FOR MORE GOVERNMENT

   By the late 1800s, the first industrial revolution was well established, even in the
United States where the changes had begun much later than in Europe. As we had
time to reflect, an increasing number of people came to believe that the revolution
had been incomplete. It had changed society in ways that could not be retracted, but
it had also created new problems that could not be ignored.
   The Progressive movement had several aspects. It was a moral movement, complete with literature that is mostly beyond the scope of this study. Three exceptions
that affect administration are the Scientific Management reformers considered in
chapter eleven, the Administrative Scientists discussed in chapter twelve, and the
budgetary reformers reviewed in chapter eighteen. Progressivism was also a political
movement, but that aspect is not discussed here at all.
   However, another set of literature arose from this movement that was read by
Public Administration students, and that led their activity through the next forty
years. It began with adherents to, and defectors from, the Fabian Socialists in
England, but quickly became integrated into the mainstream of administrative literature.
   Most of the early theoreticians knew each other and fed off each other's ideas.
Therefore, the precise dates of their publications were less important than their
personal reputations for determining who helped shape the movement. These reviews
begin with two classic statements of opposition to governmental intervention during
the late industrial revolution. They are then followed by the reformer who would
give the progressive movement one of its more famous labels.

72. Herbert Spencer, *Essays Scientific, Political, and Speculative*, 3 vol. (London: Longman, Brown, Green, Longmans and Roberts, 1857 [vol. 1] and London: Williams and Norgate, 1863 [vol. 2] and 1874 [vol. 3]); also *Man Versus the State* (London: Williams and Norgate, 1884).

Spencer was a Social Darwinist who was praised by industrialists as one of the great thinkers of the day, while being shunned by philosophers as a shallow thinker and a charlatan. His opposition to governmental interference into social lives was intense, and justified by two sets of arguments. First, as a Social Darwinist, he felt that society was best served by those who rose to the top through competition. The winners, in short, were superior competitors ordained by nature to lead. Second, he felt that government was capable of all manner of evil. In his essay on over-legislation, he defined "officialdom" as habitually slow, stupid, extravagant, unadaptive, and corrupt. Industrialists found a "philosophical" justification to their position in Spencer, and his books circulated even more widely in the United States than in his native England.

73. William Graham Sumner, *What Social Classes Owe To Each Other* (New York: Harper and Brothers, 1883); also *Collected Essays in Political and Social Science* (New York: Henry Holt, 1885).

Sumner was the major Social Darwinist in the United States, following the lead of the better-known Spencer. Reacting against then-current German theories of the benevolent state, he belligerently defended the superiority of the rich, and argued that governmental interference was creating a system in which it made more sense to be intentionally poor.

His faith in industrialists was absolute. He assumed that they would create one-on-one charity for the truly needy. Government, however, was the embodiment of evil. In the *Essays*, he argued that civil service reform made no sense without fixing the hopelessly corrupt presidential election system that caused panic in the business community every four years.

74. Graham Wallas, *The Great Society: A Psychological Analysis* (London: Macmillan, 1914); also *Our Social Heritage* (London: Allen and Unwin, 1921); also *The Art of Thought* (London: [Jonathan] Cape, 1926).

"The Great Society," a label that became identified with the progressive reform effort, came from "The Great Industry" movement of Spencer's day and before. Looking at Wallas' works, it may be difficult now to understand their impact on Public Administration. They were published later than other books of this genre, and they were essentially studies in psychology.

What they did, however, was popularize the arguments that material production does not equal human happiness, and that a combination of property (individualism), the democratic state (socialism), and non-local association (syndicalism) were necessary to maintain the human spirit.

Wallas had begun as a Fabian Socialist, and sought ways to make the industrial world livable. He lamented the impersonalization and crowd psychology of modern society that had made happiness almost impossible. He had lost faith in industrial democracy, and saw both unionism and Scientific Management as diversions because both sought resources, not happiness. As a Fabian defector, he encouraged individualism, and even capitalism. However, the forces of capitalism were well entrenched, and needed little protection. The forces needing development were the democratic state (in *Social Heritage*) for social reconstruction and particularly public education (in *The Art of Thought*). With a wide range of resources, people could develop in individual ways toward their potentials and, thereby, achieve happiness.

Wallas taught at the London School of Economics, and was highly respected by Lippmann (to whom he addressed *The Great Society*), Laski, and others who were publishing at the same time, and who sometimes came up with more administrative recommendations to achieve the same goals.

75.   Herbert Croly, *The Promise of American Life* (New York: Macmillan, 1909).

This was one of the earliest academic books in the area, although it owes much of its inspiration to the political movement that was well formed by this point. Croly argued that wealth combined with freedom was insufficient to carry society through the industrial age. The wealth did not get evenly disbursed, and the freedom that encouraged capital investment lacked the planning that was necessary to ensure that all segments of society received what they really needed.

Croly felt that our problems were systemic, and that government had an obligation to step in and assure an acceptable distribution of wealth. Unlike many of the muckrakers, however, he did not feel that the solution was to break up the holdings of evil industrialists. Instead, he was devoted to controlled, centralized power as the tool of social reform. To the extent that industries and political machines had already achieved centralization, they were of more use if controlled than divested. He also advocated governmental assistance to unions as a method of worker coordination.

76.   Walter Weyl, *The New Democracy* (New York: Macmillan, 1912).

Walter Lippmann described Weyl, who had a Ph.D. from the Wharton School, as "by far the best trained economist of the progressive movement," and *The New Democracy* was at least partially a reaction to the unsophisticated literature that had dominated both the progressive movement and Weyl's earlier writings.

Weyl described our economic history as a "shadow democracy," because the economic elites, or the "the plutocracy," had always ruled. He rejected individualism and the frontier spirit because they had created the greed that drove industrialists to their extremes. The path to reform, however, was not with the revolt of the downtrodden masses, for they were at too low a "level of democratic striving." Reform would come with the rise of the middle class that had retained enough power and morality to make a difference.

Weyl felt governmental ownership to be inevitable in several industries. However, unlike Croly, he advocated a mixture of solutions (ownership, regulation, political reform) that did not all lead to centralized control.

77.   Frederick A. Cleveland, *Organized Democracy* (New York: Longmans, Green and Co., 1913).

Cleveland's book takes a more global view of political reform while maintaining the basic faith in progressive principles. Having recently chaired the United States Commission on Economy and Efficiency, he noted that we had long stated the belief that government existed for the purpose of serving the public. However, we were now engaged in "(o)ne of the most inspiring movements in human history" in which that service was now becoming possible. Through an administration trained in the techniques of efficient and economical organization and, equally importantly, through an enlightened population, it would be possible to expand the responsibilities of government while maintaining the "organized democracy" for which the book was named.

78.   Walter Lippmann, *A Preface to Politics* (New York: Mitchell Kennerley, 1913).

In the Wallas tradition, Lippmann argued that we had written a constitution under the mechanical assumptions of Newton and Montesquieu, and we were left with a government that kept trying to improve its operations with little memory of its purposes. "When politics revolves mechanically it ceases to use the real energies of a nation. Government is then at once irrelevant and mischievous."

Lippmann saw the problem as a general societal moral decay. The evil industrialists had been produced by a societal ethic of greed and an apathy that allowed the industrialists to operate without interference. Lippmann argued that the solution rested in a heightened state of moral concern.

Like Wallas, Lippmann made few administrative recommendations. However, he felt it critical that we use government as a tool, and stop worrying about perpetuating traditions and rights that had lost their meaning.

79.   William F. Ogburn, *Social Change* (New York: B.W. Huebsch, 1922).

Ogburn brought the Sociological perspective to Progressive reform, and achieved some notoriety in his day. The book leaned heavily on the tradition of Wallas and the French Sociologist Auguste Compte, however, and his Sociology looked very similar to their Psychology. In attempting to correlate social change to adaptive strategies, Ogburn identified technological innovation as one of the most significant causes of change, and government and unions as strategies of correcting social maladjustments. His description of the cultural lag in social maladjustments is quite similar to Toffler's later *Future Shock*.

Ogburn's book was not driven by ideology in the manner of several that have been mentioned, and he apologized that his presentation was "less emphatic" than those found elsewhere. However, he helped reflect a cross-disciplinary academic belief at the time that the movement toward an increased role for government was driven by technology, and demanded by society.

80.   Harold Laski, *A Grammar of Politics* (New Haven: Yale University Press, 1925).

Laski's book is a study in contrasts, for his political philosophy partially changed while the book was being written. It was mainstream Progressive, psychological literature. It argued that political democracy was meaningless unless it lead to economic democracy. Government was "the fundamental instrument of society" and must be used to achieve economic democracy.

Unlike Croly and some others, however, Laski could not bring himself to trust popular government as the change agent. He distrusted concentrated power, and advocated decentralization, legal restraints, and consultation with competing groups as a way of protecting society from its institutions.

As one of the last books that might be labelled Progressive, some differences from the earlier literature are notable. It has already been mentioned that Laski trusted government much less than his cohorts. The book is also much more structural. Laski said that "(a) working theory of the State must, in fact, be conceived in administrative terms," and this book goes into far more detail than the others on governmental structure and public administration, even to the extent of evaluating the contribution of the merit system to democratic theory.

THE NEW DEAL

In *The Administrative State*, Waldo argued that Progressivism died as a political movement in 1917 because the War "diverted our attention from realizing the Promise of American Life to the much narrower goal of preserving America."[2] By this time, Scientific Management had already risen to the national scene in public administration, as described in chapter eleven. Similarly, the growth of government had left administrators with unresolved problems that dominated the attention of Administrative Scientists in the 1920s, as is discussed in chapter twelve.

The progressive-style literature never completely faded away. Once the War and Coolidge prosperity were behind us, it rose again as the call for governmental intervention into society began anew.

This time, the literature was far more mixed. Government was larger now, and opposition to further expansion came from sources other than sensationalist journalists and industrial lobbyists. In fact, a more useful way to look at this resurgence may be that, as had happened with Progressive literature, the works opposing big government had roots in the earlier prosperity, but were overtaken by hard times, and the subsequent literature suggested that government once again could join society's battles.

81. John Maynard Keynes, *The General Theory of Employment, Interest, and Money* (London: Macmillan, 1936).

Like Wallas, this is not an early book on New Deal idealism; it is instead the book that finally gave the movement its precise definition and sense of momentum. Keynes, an English economist, had tried to explain business cycles in his earlier *A Treatise on Money* (1930). However, he could not explain extended depressions because the theory of the day insisted that savings would pile up in a depression and be invested, thereby correcting the problem. *The General Theory* tackled this problem anew, arguing that stagnant savings did not automatically get invested. Those investments instead came from a number of other factors, such as technological advances or new markets. While the economy was not self-correcting on investments, government's fiscal policies could help either stimulate or repress economic activities, whichever was required.

Progressive literature had been basically moralistic, and its "science" was a nonquantitative approach to psychology. Keynes reversed all that, giving governmental interventionists a scientific and quantitative justification. As such, in the middle of a world calamity for which governmental activity seemed essential, Keynes' theory was quickly adopted by the governments in both Great Britain and the United States.

82. Lord Chief Justice Gordon Hewart, Baron of Bury, *The New Despotism* (London: Ernest Benn, 1929).

Using his legal background, Lord Hewart attacked the encroachment of administrative adjudication and rule-making into the area of individual rights. He lamented that the public had recently begun to defer to the expertise of "ardent bureaucrats," "placing a large and increasing field of departmental authority and activity beyond the reach of the ordinary law." (p. 5) He was also concerned that the sovereignty of Parliament and the rules of law were generally seen as obstacles to good administration.

While much of the book was well-written, its blind faith in "the ordinary law" seemed at times undefended. Still, the book had a sizable circulation in both England and the United States, and was widely cited in subsequent Public Administration works.

83. James M. Beck, *Our Wonderland of Bureaucracy* (New York: Macmillan, 1932).

Well before Keynes or even the "New Deal," attacks on the increasing role of government were common in the popular press, although most of the articles were political propaganda of such poor quality as not to deserve review here. Hewart was an exception of some quality in England. This one, of less quality, was one of the earlier American efforts, written by a former congressman and Solicitor General of the U.S..

Beck argued that bureaucracy was growing because we had surrendered our sense of constitutional morality to expediency. He documented the growth in size. In 1800, the federal government's records were moved from New York to Philadelphia in seven large and five small boxes. He attacked the constitutional problems of administrative law, governmental corporations, and the practice of agencies drafting legislation. As seems to be a major theme in this set of literature, he cited numerous examples of silly governmental publications.

The book was widely circulated at the time. However, regardless of where one stands on the issues, the methodology of this book and most of its contemporary genre was primitive and unfair. Beck intentionally used examples of governmental waste and pointless publications out of context. As such, the book was more a popular nuisance than a serious argument to New Dealers.

84.   Charles Merriam, *Political Power* (New York: McGraw-Hill, 1934).

Merriam was, of course, a Political Scientist, and not a Public Administrator. However, in this eclectic field that borrows from any useful source, Merriam's book was cited by much of the Public Administration literature that followed for some time thereafter. Merriam's "purpose is to set forth what role political power plays in the process of social control." (p. 4) He followed the historical rise of such institutions as government, the state, and capitalist enterprises to note that only government avoided narrow interests, and retained its role as the representative of the society as a whole. Even in outlaw societies, he noted, there is a tendency for the governmental function to arise.

Since government is the representative of society, it is obligated to regulate groups that have narrower interests. Merriam acknowledged that governments could become dictatorial, but that the solution was to return to democracy, and not to abandon governmental control.

85.   Herbert Hoover, *American Individualism* (New York: Doubleday Page, & Co., 1922); also *The Challenge to Liberty* (New York: Charles Scribner's Sons, 1934).

Because of his presidency, little attention is now paid to Hoover's extensive career as an author and director of relief programs. In recalling that career, it is probably most useful here to notice the degree to which even the conservative approach in the early part of this century had abandoned any pretense that laissez faire had ever existed, or would be desirable.

"We have learned that the impulse to production can only be maintained at a high pitch if there is a fair division of the product. We have also learned that fair division can only be obtained by certain restrictions on the strong and the dominant." (*American*, p. 11) Alternately, "(i)ndividualism cannot be maintained as the foundation of a society if it looks to only legalistic justice based upon contracts, property, and political equality." (*American*, pp. 10-11)

The basic program of conservatism, however, was a balancing of mistrust of both the capitalists and the socialistic tendencies of bureaucracy. (*Challenge*, p. 6) Playing the middle road had been the basic platform of conservatives from John Stuart Mill to Hoover.

86. Stuart Chase, *Government in Business* (New York: Macmillan, 1935).

This is evidence that even liberal economists and New Dealers could appeal to the mass market of publications that had been the haven of the opposition. Chase accepted George Bernard Shaw's contention that all revolutionary movements are attacks on private property, but argued that private property is a bundle of rights, not a set of objects. He said that, despite the poor press government receives, we all agree with Adam Smith that government must perform the functions that the private sector cannot.

He reviewed a number of functions that he felt were public business, including the control of natural resources as among the most important. He said that public business was expanding with the need for coordination caused by advancing technology. He then argued that government ownership of corporations (a recent concept at the time; see chapter six) was superior to shared control and not inferior to private ownership in many industries.

By comparison to Beck, this work was academically sophisticated. However, it was a popular appeal, and contained no bibliography because of Chase's unexplainable contention that there was no literature on the subject.

87. E(dward) Pendleton Herring, *Public Administration and the Public Interest* (New York: McGraw-Hill, 1936); also *The Politics of Democracy* (New York: W. W. Norton and Co., 1940).

Herring was concerned that "the public interest" was a fiction in our political system. We had become such an accumulation of special interests that no one represented the public as a whole. The public was too diverse. Congress was divided by its need to represent. Even the bureaucracy was impotent.

The president alone had the positional advantage to represent the public interest. To do so, however, he needed a strong, centralized, responsive bureaucracy. Through a set of recommendations that were largely reflected in the Brownlow Committee, government would be in a position to expand its control in the public interest.

88. Lawrence Sullivan, *The Dead Hand of Bureaucracy* (Indianapolis: Bobbs-Merrill, 1940).

This was one of the more widely circulated but poorly argued attacks by a newspaper and business-magazine correspondent on a government that had now become quite large. The most convincing part of the book is the statistics. In the 1940 budget, half the agencies listed had been created since 1933. Since 1800, the population had expanded 25 times while federal civilian personnel had expanded 17,950 times.

He attacked the increase in patronage appointments under FDR, and the impossibility of following all the new federal regulations. The wording throughout was sensationalist enough, however, to overshadow some good points. He also had a chapter on Communists in government. It was irresponsible red-baiting at its worst, and it is difficult to read it now within its own context, and without thinking of it as a harbinger of the early 1950s.

89. Joseph Alois Schumpeter, *Capitalism, Socialism, and Democracy* (New York: Harper and Brothers, 1942).

We have a tendency now to discount the degree to which socialism and Marxism were serious avenues of discussion among reformers of the period, at least partially because we now have a clearer perspective on Stalin, and we no longer see the effects of unregulated robber barons on society. However, while most of the socialists cited in this section assumed that their approach would be applied within strict limits, some did not.

Schumpeter was a socialist who used Marxist ideology to explain the causes of social change. He used sophisticated economic analysis, although the ideology that drove it was never left in doubt. "Can capitalism survive? No. I do not think it can." "Can socialism work? Of course it can."

Schumpeter saw the inevitable socialistic bureaucracy as large and centralized. That concerned him because large bureaucracies have a tendency to stifle personal initiative. However, for the believer, the price was worth the benefit to society.

90. Ludwig Von Mises, *Bureaucracy* (New Haven: Yale University Press, 1944).

Von Mises and Hayek, who follows, are the logical opposites to Schumpeter, both using the degeneration of Germany's socialism as evidence to question the path of social reform and the abandonment of individualism that was then reflected in American politics. Von Mises presented us with puzzles. First, is it democracy if the people vote to give away their own rights? Second, if private bureaucracy is so abusive, why is public bureaucracy so trustworthy? Third, what governmental control is as effective as bankruptcy for punishing a bureaucracy that fails to operate in the public interest?

The answers are in the questions. Von Mises also documented the tendency of government bureaucrats to institutionalize themselves in Europe, and he ended with a call for "profit management."

91. Friedrich Hayek, *The Road to Serfdom* (Chicago: University of Chicago Press, 1944).

If Hayek is the opposite of Schumpeter, which is a reasonable assessment, he also helps illustrate the image of moderation in New-Deal-era conservative beliefs by comparison to those of modern libertarians. As John Chamberlain stated in the Foreword, "Hayek is no devotee of laissez faire; he believes in a design for an enterprise system." Having spread his life between Austria, England, and the United States, however, he had become convinced that many of the factors that destroyed Germany were at work here.

He was concerned that socialism had replaced liberalism as the doctrine of the progressives, and that democratic socialism was impossible. He cited the "totalitarian" Compte's definition of civilization as "the perennial Western malady, the revolt of the individual against the species." He felt that property was essential to freedom, and that National Socialism was not just a revolt against reason, but a logical culmination of the socialist movement. Like Schumpeter, Hayek did little to hide his colors. However, the book had an enormous impact in the reading lists of Public Administration because like Schumpeter, it is surprisingly well written for a book with such obvious political motives.

92.   Herman Finer, *The Road to Reaction* (Boston: Little, Brown and Co., 1945).

This may be the most convincing illustration of why Hayek was well received. Finer's point was simple--planning and liberty were compatible. However, his book was such an angry and vicious attack on Hayek's "most sinister offensive against democracy to emerge from a democratic country for many decades" that it distracted from the point. To Finer, if you loved your country, you must see that the alternative to dictatorship was not individualism and competition, but democracy.

He documented the corporate abuses that had led to progressive reforms. He also established that economists since Adam Smith had expected governmental planning and protection. He argued that such planning, democratically decided, helped production. But mainly, he attacked Hayek relentlessly, and quite possibly helped popularize Hayek in the process.

POST-WAR REFLECTIONS

After the War, there was a subtle but significant shift in both the policies and the literature of public-private separation. Stated simply, as illustrated by the Full Employment Act of 1946, we rediscovered Progressive politics in a bigger way. The sense of national emergency we had held in the Depression became a sense of national mission. The literature justifying government as an agent of social justice began instead to justify government as an agent of social equity.

That debate was extensive, and is reflected in some of the questions raised on social equity in chapter ten. However, there was also a continuation of more reflective literature on the general difference between public and private roles. It continued for several years until diverging into the directions of either policy issues, or public service ethics, both of which are reviewed in later chapters. The post-War literature is among our most quoted, however, and needs to be attached to its own heritage in this chapter.

93.   Paul H. Appleby, *Big Democracy* (New York: Alfred A. Knopf, 1945).

In one of the better books ever written on the subject, Appleby addressed the issue of the differences between the public and private sectors. The most commonly cited portion of the book is the chapter "Government is Different," in which Appleby defined the difference between the sectors as being that they serve different clients. Business serves its own interests (or the interests of those they are hired to represent) while government serves the public interests.

In a subject that is often dominated by cheap moralizing, Appleby wrote books about ethics with little preaching. He accepted the legitimacy of both interests, and tried to suggest ways they could work together. In the chapter "Working With People," he noted that while business people complain that government does not understand them, they seldom try to understand the "governmental attitude" either.

In "Size," he noted that government is difficult to understand because departments have become so big and diverse. However, he was an optimist on governmental control of the bureaucracy (in the chapter "Big Democracy") so long as bureaucracy accepted its political role by allowing people access and by treating citizens as individuals.

94.   Robert McIver, *The Web of Government* (New York: Macmillan, 1947).

The attacks on large government, of course, continued. This one, however, was considerably more reserved and sophisticated than most. McIver was a professor of Sociology at Columbia University, and wrote his book from the perspective of the impact of the government on the social community. While he saw a substantial useful role for government, he was concerned that we treat governmental decision-making as if it is scientific. There is no science of government, he argued; it is an art. In particular, we run into difficulty when we allow government the reign over the cultural life of the community, and he borrowed heavily from the recent fascist states for examples.

95.   Fritz Morstein Marx, ed., *Elements of Public Administration* (New York: Prentice-Hall, 1946); also

96.   Dwight Waldo, *The Administrative State* (New York: Ronald Press, 1948).

Occasionally, it is useful to step back and determine where we are by recounting where we have been. These are two of the first books to do that. As early general reflections on our roots, the books applied to various subjects throughout Public

Administration. For this chapter, they summarized the common themes in the literature to that date.

Morstein Marx's reader was a compilation of articles written for that book by
fourteen authors, including some of the more prominent names in the field. The first
two chapters gave particularly good histories, and have been used heavily to identify
sources for this bibliographic study.

Waldo's summations have been more widely cited, however, and they give a better overall perspective of the field. According to Waldo, administrative reformers of
the Twentieth Century virtually all believed in democracy as their goal. However,
they also believed democracy to be unobtainable unless government could produce
usable results. (p. 74) That true democracy and true efficiency were reconcilable "is
so fundamental that, by definition, it could hardly be denied by an American writer
on public administration." (p. 207) However, he expected the post-War environment to
pull us in both directions, toward centralization to meet world problems, and toward
decentralized democracy if the problems could be alleviated. In either case, however,
the dissolution of the politics-administration dichotomy was going to force administration to recognize its reliance upon the community.

97.   Adolph A. Berle, Jr., *The 20th Century Capitalist Revolution* (New York: Har-
       court, Brace & Co., 1954); also *Power Without Property: A New Development in
       American Political Economy* (New York: Harcourt, Brace & Co., 1959).

One of the reasons that Public Administrators accepted the safety of expanded
government may have been that virtually everyone, including most conservatives,
distrusted unregulated capitalists. However, the memory of robber barons eventually
grew dim, and some observers began to notice that industrialists no longer acted as
they had in the Nineteenth Century.

Berle argued that governmental regulations had little effect on industrialists.
Similarly, the "owners" of industry no longer had significant control over the operators. Instead, presaging Galbraith, Berle argued that corporate power had become
aggregated into interdependent "concentrates" that extended well outside the corporation itself.

The net effect was to break down the distinction between government and corporations, as the leaders of each became indoctrinated into a "corporate consciousness" that forced industrialists to take on some welfare functions to insure their own
survival. The consciousness was reinforced and enforced by laws, but it was equally
enforced by the evolving nature of our political economy that no longer permitted
isolation.

98.   Peter Blau, *Bureaucracy in Modern Society* (New York: Random House, 1956).

Blau's short book on bureaucracy used a sociological perspective to note that
bureaucracy and democracy have conflicting goals--efficiency vs. the freedom of
dissent. However, he felt that these could be reconciled so long as the political

system reigned supreme. The difficulty came with agencies that were responsible for both determining public goals and implementing them. This circumstance arose most regularly in political parties and corporations.

In both cases, Blau advocated a permanent opposition "party" within the organization. While he was uneasy with the solution, he felt that we had no choice since bureaucracies provided more services than risks, and were likely to continue.

99. Roscoe Martin, ed., *Public Administration and Democracy* (Syracuse, NY: Syracuse University Press, 1965).

This is a book of readings by sixteen authors that was designed to commemorate Paul Appleby's life and concerns. While the articles tied into Appleby's works to differing extents, most were on topics that are relevant here. One general theme, most directly stated in Dwight Waldo's article, was that we now live in an administrative culture. We therefore no longer have a choice of abandoning or controlling administration. Emmette Redford noted the increasingly fuzzy distinction between public and private concerns. Bailey and Egger suggested techniques for controlling the bureaucracy by internal means. Several other articles related to other aspects of Appleby's works, and the book contains an essay compiled from Appleby's papers that was not published elsewhere.

100. Andrew Shonfield, *Modern Capitalism* (London: Oxford University Press, 1965).

Shonfield, a British Economist, studied the post-War economic development of six "capitalist" countries. While he considered the historical accidents of governmental structure to be extremely important in understanding the operations of these countries, he felt there were certain common characteristics that defined "modern capitalism" and the role of public administration in it. These included an active role for administration, and an emphasis on long-range, and not just Keynesian short-range planning.

To accomplish this without totalitarian results, three safeguards were required: the visible and audible exercise of administrative power; technically trained monitoring of administration; and an explicit and open intimate relationship between the public and private sectors.

Public Administration students may find the book too economically oriented for their training, and the examples are increasingly dated. However, the book is impressively documented, and its implications are directly relevant to public-private relationships.

101. John Kenneth Galbraith, *American Capitalism* (Boston: Houghton Mifflin, 1952); also *The Affluent Society* (Boston: Houghton Mifflin Co., 1958); also *The New Industrial State* (Boston: Houghton Mifflin, 1967).

Galbraith's popular approach to Economics has added significantly to the vocabulary of private-public relations. In *The Affluent Society*, which contains an excellent review of much of the literature listed in this chapter, he argued that we have artificially emphasized production to the point that we are privately rich, but publicly poor. In *American Capitalism* he developed a theory of countervailing powers, in which he argued that our industrial society was clustered into power groups, and that the protection for the public was that none of the power groups could prevail on its own. Government existed largely to insure the balance of these groups. Finally, in *The New Industrial State*, he studied the group decision-making process within the "technostructure" that our interdependent society had created.

102.　E. S. Schumacher, *Small is Beautiful* (London: Blond and Briggs, 1973).

These last two entries are of relatively current works that have taken entirely new approaches to argue for small government. Schumacher's is the least familiar to Western observers. Following the lessons of Mohandas Ghandi, Schumacher developed what he called Buddhist Economics, and disagreed with just about everything in Western Economics since before the time of Adam Smith.

Schumacher said that we are stifled by three traditions: unity; large size; and the economy of scale. The traditions exist in government and business, and are harmful to both. Instead, he said, we need to break our culture into smaller units that can be economically self-sufficient. To do that, we need "appropriate technologies," not large technologies.

Schumacher's recommendations are revolutionary in that they advocate the disruption of not just our economic organization, but of our entire approach to knowledge. However, they are appropriate as warnings against accepting large-scale operations by tradition, without adequate reason to believe that they are necessary.

103.　Milton and Rose Friedman, *Free to Choose* (New York: Harcourt Brace Jovanovich, 1980); also *Capitalism and Freedom* (Chicago: University of Chicago Press, 1962).

Any number of books could be chosen to represent the relatively recent libertarian school of thought. A far more representative sample is presented in the privatization literature in chapter six, where it is more appropriate to review the mechanics of their beliefs. However the Friedman's, while not the creators of the school, have grabbed the attention of the academic world and the popular press, and they are used here.

The Friedmans accept that Adam Smith's "capitalism" was not a system of laissez faire. However, they define our economic miracle as the joint acceptance of Smith and the Declaration of Independence, to create both economic and human freedom. Since then, the residual governmental role has led to the abuses in the industrial revolution, and the artificial creation of monopolies.

The Friedmans are particularly harsh on the competence of government to accomplish its missions, citing Max Gammon's "Theory of Bureaucratic Displacement" that increases in expenditure are matched by decreases in production. They wish to eliminate many government functions and place competition back into the rest. Even public education, for instance, would be funded by vouchers that taxpayers could take to the schools of their choice.

CONTINUING CONCERNS

Through most of our early history, the rise of government from mercantilism was a two-way street. The wealth and concentrated power of the private sector rose, but not at the expense of government. Instead, using economic theories that were well developed by Adam Smith's day, power was the big winner in the concentration and the planned interdependence of capital. There was plenty of power to go around. The private sector rose to unprecedented wealth and control within society while government kept pace by accepting new responsibilities that had not previously been possible.

In more recent times, however, the distinction between the sectors has become muddled. Power and wealth have become so concentrated that they require the cooperation of increasingly large sectors of society to keep them running.

Public Administration literature, for the most part, does not accept the notion that the distinction between the sectors is disappearing. Instead, government exists to represent a different clientele--the public interest. It measures its success by political means and not by profits. As such, it puts special obligations on public servants, and those are the subject of the public ethics and democratic control portions of chapter ten.

NOTES FOR CHAPTER FOUR

1. On mercantile policies and other early developments between the sectors, a strong reference source is Henry Jacoby, *The Bureaucratization of the World*, trans. by Eveline Kanes (Berkeley: University of California Press, 1973). On progressive and New Deal literature, a good brief introduction is found in Dwight Waldo, *The Administrative State* (New York: Ronald Press, 1948). Stephen Skowronek has provided a book-length introduction in *Building a New American State: The Expansion of National Administrative Capacities, 1877-1920* (Cambridge: Cambridge University Press, 1982).

2. Waldo, *The Administrative State*, p. 10.

5
The Rise of
Governmental Regulation

BACKGROUND

By the late Nineteenth Century, the two new Behemoths of government and industry clashed. The first arena was government regulation of corporate abuses, introduced in this chapter. A second clash was in the direct delivery of services by the government, and that is the subject of chapter six. The impacts of the new administrative machinery on government are discussed in chapters seven and eight, while democratic controls are the subject of chapters nine and ten.

This chapter discusses the literature that helped Public Administration shape its approach to governmental regulation. It is not a history of that regulation. Neither is it an attempt to duplicate the case law and legislative analysis of textbooks and classroom instruction. Instead, keeping within the theme of this study, this chapter is an attempt to follow the debate on the basic rules that have evolved to define the relationship between the regulators and the regulated.

Some of that debate first appeared in legislation or judicial opinions. The rest was published in scholarly texts or governmental reports. In integrating the sectors, however, the general roles, and not the mechanics, remain the focus.

THE TWO BASIC GOALS OF REGULATION[1]

As is reflected later in this chapter, we have had a tendency in recent years to define regulation according to any number of possible approaches. These are often just subsets, however, of the two forces that have struggled for control of the regulatory movement since its formative years. The first, reacting to imperfect competition and the abuses of the trusts, has seen regulation as a tool to outlaw disruptions

in the market place. That movement began at the state level but was crippled by the
Supreme Court in *Wabash, St. Louis & Pacific Railroad Co. v Illinois*,
118 U.S. 557 (1886). Reform soon shifted to the Federal level with the Interstate
Commerce Act (24 Stat. 379 (1887)) and the Sherman Anti-Trust Act (26 Stat. 209
(1890)).

The second force, embodied in the Progressive Movement, was an attempt to
foster, but also to regulate vigorously, concentrated economic power toward the
fulfillment of public purposes. The struggle between these two philosophies dominated the early literature of the field.

104.   Henry Demarest Lloyd, "The Story of a Great Monopoly," *Atlantic
        Monthly*, XLVII, (March 1881): 317-34.

Public interest in trusts and their eventual regulation grew during the 1870s,
fed by sensationalist features in newspapers and magazines, and by a few governmental hearings that received little circulation at the time. Lloyd's article, however,
thrust the sophisticated study of the subject into a national issue.

Lloyd used data from the Hepburn committee investigation in the New York
legislature in 1879 to write an expose on the railroad rebate practices of the
Standard Oil Company. He ended with recommendations that railroad rates must be
publicly known, stable, reasonable, and equal. The railroads must perform a public
function, and must be regulated by a national board to hear citizen and railroad
complaints. (p. 333)

The article, rushed into publication without some of its documentation, became
a sensation. The magazine went through seven editions, and led to a flurry of
literature and state regulations for railroads before the Supreme Court crippled
state efforts in 1886.

105.   William Wilson Cook, "Trusts," [pamphlet] (New York: L.K. Strouse and Co.,
        1888); also *The Corporation Problem* (New York: G.P. Putnam's
        Sons, 1891).

Once the federal government entered the regulatory arena, the first book to
become something of a classic in the area advocated publicity as one of the best
defenses against abuses by the trusts. Cook's book was strongest in attacking the
trusts, those "efficient instruments of fraud, speculation, plunder and illegal
gain." (p. 81) His suggestions for improvement were somewhat less detailed, reflecting an age in which the ICC and the Sherman Anti-Trust Act were still new.
Cook sought some government agency that could publicize the abuses of the trusts,
believing that their behavior was tolerated only because of the secrecy they had
built around themselves.

106.   *Chicago Conference on Trusts* (Chicago: Civic Federation of Chicago,
        1899); also

107.   U.S. Bureau of Corporations, *Report of the Commissioner of Corpor-ations, 1904* (Washington, D.C.: USGPO, 1904).

More specific proposals for regulation arose in these two works, both of which were written long enough after the ICC Act to have some perspective on additional needed changes. The Chicago Conference, consisting of invited legislators, govern-ors, attorneys general, lawyers, and representatives of both trades associations and labor, reflected so many viewpoints that the Committee on Resolutions voted not to present recommendations.

However, William Jennings Bryan attended the meeting, and proposed new legislation that was largely echoed by the Commissioner of Corporations in 1904. Bryan recognized that state corporation charters were ineffective as regulatory devices. However, he proposed that any corporation wishing to do interstate busi-ness be required to obtain a federal charter, granted by a new agency to be created for the purpose. (pp. 584 & 626) The charter would be granted if 1) the stock was not "watered"; 2) the corporation was not trying to monopolize any market; and 3) there was full publicity of corporate affairs.

108.   John Bates Clark, *The Control of Trusts* (New York: Macmillan, 1902).[2] The more popular version is the revised and expanded John Bates Clark and John Maurice Clark, *The Control of Trusts* (New York: Macmillan, 1912).

This is still one of the more frequently cited statements of the anti-trust ap-proach to regulation. In the first edition, Clark extolled the virtues of competi-tion, arguing that it was still the most effective means for protecting the public from corporate abuses. He said that the monopolistic trusts were an accident of the times, not a logical result of survival of the fittest.

While competition was virtuous, however, it was unstable and subject to the accidents that create monopolies. Specifically, in the survival of the fittest, the conditions of the struggle help determine the type of fitness that is needed. Therefore, competition must be controlled by governmental agencies with the power to set the rules of competition.

The second edition was more subdued, and more clearly in accord with the Wil-sonian approach to regulation described below. The coauthors no longer found dif-ficulties in the concentration of wealth, but only in monopoly and unfair prac-tices, both of which needed to be controlled.

109.   Bruce Wyman, *Control of the Market: A Legal Solution of the Trust Problem* (New York: Moffat, Yard and Co., 1911).

While the Progressives arose after the trust-busters, they soon dominated the literature. Much of the appeal of this new movement was in its optimism. Unlike those who wanted to destroy the evil system of trusts, the Progressives wanted to turn this concentration of wealth to benevolent purposes.

This argument can be traced to Herbert Croly, whose 1909 work is discussed in the previous chapter. Soon, however, authors such as Wyman began focusing more specifically on the economic implications of this regulation. Wyman argued that "regulation--not destruction--will soon be shown to be the policy of the twentieth century." (p. 260) Like political economists, he felt the concentration of wealth to be essential to economic development, so that all would lose in divestiture. However, Wyman did not get as specific about the administrative implications of the regulation as did those who soon followed.

110.   Charles R. Van Hise, *Concentration and Control: A Solution of the Trust Problem in the United States* (New York: Macmillan, 1912).

By the 1912 election campaign, three different factions were calling for new legislation on the trusts. Taft, the conservative, wanted a federal commission to regulate antitrust provisions more efficiently; Wilson, the moderate progressive, wanted an agency to allow the concentration of wealth, but to regulate competitive practices; Roosevelt, the more extreme progressive, wanted an agency to encourage concentration, but also to regulate all interstate corporations for the public good. Van Hise provided what is often used as the classic statement of Roosevelt's more intense form of progressive regulation.

"This book is one of opportunism. Its aim is to present an outline picture of the situation regarding concentration of industry in the United States, and to suggest a way to gain its economic advantages and at the same time to guard the interests of the public." (p. v) Van Hise openly opposed trust-busting. Instead, he proposed allowing businesses to expand and consolidate so as to take advantage of economies of scale. Once competition failed, however, the industries would become subject to the commission form of regulation. This regulation, Van Hise argued, would protect the population against unfair practices and high prices, and would help conserve and protect natural resources.

111.   Woodrow Wilson, *The New Freedom* (New York: Doubleday, Page & Co., 1913).

This compilation from several of Wilson's campaign speeches is one of the better statements of Wilson's approach to regulatory reform. This approach, which finally prevailed in the Clayton (38 Stat. 730 (1914)) and Federal Trade Commission (38 Stat. 717 (1914)) Acts, was spelled out in his chapter "Monopoly, or Opportunity?" In it, Wilson distinguished free competition from the illicit competition that allowed the big corporations to crush the little. However, "I am not jealous of any process of growth, no matter how huge the result, provided the result was indeed obtained by the processes of wholesome development, which are the processes of efficiency, of economy, of intelligence, and of invention." (p. 191)

112.   William Howard Taft, *The Anti-Trust Act and the Supreme Court*
(New York: Harper and Brothers, 1914).

Taft, writing as Chief Justice of the Supreme Court, warned of the dangers that
conservatives saw in the progressive legislation then being considered. He felt
that the existing anti-trust regulations were based in sufficient common-law analogies so that they could provide ample guidance to judges in meeting the needs of
the changing world. He argued that the proposed legislation was unnecessary, and
even potentially harmful in its expansion of governmental influence into the private sector.

113.   Rinehart John Swenson, *The National Government and Business*
(New York: Century Co., 1924); also

114.   Earl Willis Crecraft, *Government and Business* (Yonkers-on-Hudson,
NY: World Publishing Co., 1928).

In a more general statement of progressive principles, Swenson noted that most
governments throughout recent history have been controlled by the same people who
control business. Regulation is just a logical extension of the subsidies that have
always been a part of the relationship. Both authors documented that most early
regulation was for the purpose of helping merchants. Both saw regulation as a conservative option to the radical proposals of public ownership.
Neither book is cluttered with mechanical details or constitutional issues.
Unlike authors in the next part of this chapter, Swenson saw few problems in the
expansion of regulatory power. "(T)he power to regulate is legislative and administrative, not judicial." (p. 157) For research purposes, it should also be noted
that while Crecraft's book lists few details, Swenson's history is extensive and
the bibliographies at the end of each chapter are massive.

115.   John Maurice Clark, *Social Control of Business* (Chicago: University
of Chicago Press, 1926).

Clark had been active in this issue virtually since its inception, and had
coauthored the revised edition of *The Social Control of Trusts* described
earlier. He was the cynic who tempered the enthusiasm of the second edition of
that book, and he carried his moderation into this book. Clark had limited faith
in both trusts and government's ability to regulate them. In 1912, he actually
opposed the creation of new regulatory commissions as a futile exercise. This
book, however, is more cautiously optimistic, admitting more success in the regulation of competition than he had earlier believed possible.

116.   Edgar L. Heermance, *The Ethics of Business* (New York: Harper
        and Brothers, 1926); also *Can Business Govern Itself?* (New
        York: Harper and Brothers, 1933).

Heermance stands out in the literature, not because his arguments are unique,
but because others of his field were generally ignored by public administration
authors. While government was tackling the problems of abuses by the trusts, some
members of trades associations were doing the same thing from within the private
sector. Heermance believed that many of the problems could be solved by industry
without governmental interference. He felt that business motives were too complex
to be defined by the profit motive, and that they were shaped by social standards.
When social standards changed, peer pressure forced business people to adjust their
behavior accordingly.

117.   Henry R. Seager and Charles A. Gulick, Jr., *Trusts and Corporation
        Problems* (New York: Harper and Brothers, 1929).

Seager and Gulick provided one of the more detailed histories and descriptions
of trust regulations that has been published. At 671 pages, these economists were
able to demonstrate on an industry-by-industry basis that regulation was neither
new nor static. Instead, trusts evolved through six distinct types in order to
work around legal barriers.
        As points of interest, they noted that government prohibitions of restraint of
trade were centuries old in English common law. They also argued that trusts
evolved as a solution to the problem of overproduction that industry believed had
caused the Panic of 1873. Since then, industry had learned to use government to
its own purposes. "Laissez-faire is moribund; strangled by the hands of those who
are the most determined opponents of any kind of collectivism." (p. 628)
        As advocates, their solution was proudly rooted in a prior age. They believed
in the Bryan tradition that forced governmental accounting would solve many problems. Specifically, they wanted all corporations except rails that were capital-
ized over $10 million to make annual detailed financial reports to the FTC.

118.   Dexter Merriam Keezer and Stacy May, *The Public Control of
        Business* (New York: Harper and Brothers, 1930).

This book, reflecting Herbert Hoover's conservative approach to regulation, was
one of the first attempts since Taft's work (see above) to refute the progressive
philosophy on regulation. Like Hoover, Keezer and May were activists for regulation. However, they wanted to return to a balance between regulation for effective
competition, and regulation of services within public utilities. Keezer and May
also considered the possibility of governmental ownership but, like Hoover, wished
to keep it at a minimum.

The book contains an extensive history of regulation, although its point is polemic, not academic. Keezer and May were concerned that we had been misled by a political system that regulated only those industries that had organized opponents. They were particularly perplexed by such practices as the courts restricting the regulation of property rights, but allowing local governments to compete directly with those same businesses. They were also concerned that regulation was doomed to failure unless we created personnel practices to staff commissions with the best possible people.

In short, the conservative approach represented here was to return to pre-progressive values--to shore up the regulatory process and to restore a balance in regulation by reemphasizing the protection of competition.

119.   John D. Clark, *The Federal Trust Policy* [dissertation] (Baltimore: Johns Hopkins Press, 1931); also

120.   Thomas C. Blaisdell, Jr., *The Federal Trade Commission* (New York: Columbia University Press, 1932).

Once the depression hit, it was obvious to most observers that our regulatory policies had failed to stop a complete collapse of the economic system. While many looked for new solutions, these are two of the last to suggest that the old policies would still work if we did not abandon them. Clark rejected the argument that regulation of competition had caused the depression. Instead, in reviewing the Sherman Act, he found that "it lives because it exemplifies the American theory of individualism."

Blaisdell weighed the goals of the FTC, "to maintain competition and make more certain the results which competition supposedly produces," against the results which had been produced. He was concerned that the FTC had lost its ability to perform its work, especially in the area of publicizing unfair trade practices. The FTC "has been little more than a body for the regulation of the trade practices of 'small business.'" (p. 259) Partially, the cause was that the FTC was unable to coordinate its efforts with the Attorney General.

More importantly, however, the country in the 1920s had turned away from progressive causes, and expected government to be controlled by big business, not by the farming and small business interests that had previously held sway. As an indication of the turmoil, Blaisdell reported that by 1930, no FTC commissioner had been reappointed, and most had not served a full term. It should also be mentioned that Clark's work, written as a dissertation, contains what may still be the most extensive literature review of this subject ever published.

121.   Benjamin A. Javits, *Business and the Public Interest* (New York: Macmillan, 1932).

During the campaign of 1932, most proposals for reform were more radical than Blaisdell's. One of the proposals that eventually led to the NIRA was the Swope plan, named for Gerald Swope, the president of General Electric. The plan and the arguments for its adoption were spelled out in this book.

The plan was very detailed, and a model contract was given in Appendix A and the necessary legislative changes were spelled out in Appendix D of Javits' book. However, the basic concept was that trade associations would be formed in cooperation with the government to assure the financial survival of American industry. These trade associations would create uniform cost accounting and planning procedures, would conduct joint research and share knowledge on efficient operations, and would enforce fair practices among themselves and with the public.

122. *National Industrial Recovery Act*, 48 Stat. 195 (1933).

The NIRA was the crowning achievement of the Progressive approach to business regulation. The Act established the National Recovery Administration to administer and approve the industrial codes of fair competition that would protect both industry and workers under the umbrella of governmental protection.

The Act is described in numerous textbooks, and it is detailed enough that it is impractical to summarize all its provisions here. However, within the context of this review, it was an attempt to combine Heermance's optimism that the industries could derive their own codes of conduct with Swope's belief that government's role was to enforce these codes against uncooperative businesses. While the Act was largely dismantled by the courts in 1935 (see later), many of the labor provisions live on in the National Labor Relations Act (49 Stat. 449 (1935)).

123.   Ford Poulton Hall, *Government and Business* (New York: McGraw-Hill, 1934).

One final entry in the relatively optimistic approach to regulation was this one, written with the help of both Crecraft and Swenson. Hall was concerned about the recent attacks on expanding government. He felt that a better perspective would be gained if the study of government dropped its emphasis on individual rights and governmental organization, and put more emphasis on the services that government provides.

THE FIRST CONSTITUTIONAL ISSUE--DELEGATION OF POWER

By the 1930s, the regulatory function grew so complex that serious constitutional issues arose as to its effect on the separation of powers within the government. Some of these issues had been resolved much earlier, but took on new meaning in the regulatory environment of the New Deal.

124. Chief Justice John Marshall, *Scott v Negro Ben*, 6 Cranch 3, 7 (U.S. 1810); also *Wayman v Southard*, 10 Wheaton 1, 43 (U.S. 1825).

In defining the early role for regulation, Chief Justice Marshall seemed to set constitutional questions at rest. The 1810 case noted that the collectors of customs fulfilled a partially judicial function, but that such powers were necessary for the proper execution of their jobs. The second case permitted the legislature to delegate rule-making discretion to the executive branch. While neither case was profound by the standards of the progressive era, they helped reinforce a sense of judicial non-interference that lingered for some time.

125. Albert Venn Dicey, *Lectures Introductory to the Study of the Law of the Constitution* (London: Macmillan, 1885). Subsequent editions entitled *Introduction to the Study of the Law of the Constitution*.

The English jurist Dicey wrote one of the more widely-read texts of his era with arguments on administrative law that were so commonly accepted by American legal scholars that the effect backfired on him. Dicey argued that administrative law was a French invention. In fact, his openly hostile chapter on the subject "Rule of Law Compared with *Droit Administratif*" kept most of the legal terms in French because of his contention that there were no English equivalents.

Ultimately, the impact of his work was not to arrest the growth of administrative law, but to discourage us from studying it as it evolved on its own. Once the subject could no longer be ignored, Emlyn C.S. Wade notes in the Preface to the Ninth Edition (1939), Dicey's definition of administrative law had become so narrow as to be irrelevant to the issues at hand.

126. Roscoe Pound, "Justice According to Law," *Columbia Law Review*, 13, (December 1913): 696-713, continued 14 (January 1914): 1-26, and (February 1914): 103-21; also *The Spirit of the Common Law* (Boston: Marshall Jones Co., 1921).

In the United States, Pound was probably the most widely-read opponent of administrative law. It was "one of those reversions to justice without law," like the special English courts in the sixteenth century, that was evolving now only because the courts had been unable to adjust to recent societal demands for regulation.

The solution was not to abandon judicial justice, for the costs of executive justice to constitutional liberties were too high. Instead, he wanted to adjust the judicial process to handle regulatory adjudication with the speed, sensitivity, and expertise that the public demanded.

127. Adoph A. Berle, Jr., "The Expansion of American Administrative Law," *Harvard Law Review*, 30, (March 1917): 430-48.

Berle acknowledged the shift in political powers, but saw no cause for alarm in it since administrative law was the transmission of the will of the state. It involved the powers of all three branches in ways that could not be differentiated. Therefore, it was necessary to create "special instruments," regulatory commissions, that exercised all three powers while excluding the general machinery of government from their fields.

128.   Elihu Root, *Addresses on Citizenship and Government* (1916); and "Public Service by the Bar," (Presidential Address), 41 ABA Rep. 359, 368 ([August 30] 1916); also

129.   Felix Frankfurter, "The Task of Administrative Law," *University of Pennsylvania Law Review*, 75, (May 1927): 614-21; and "Foreword," *Columbia Law Review*, 41, (April 1941): 585-88.

Not all observers were content with ignoring constitutional problems, and appropriately, justices were also among the first to question the implications of the new regulatory structures. While the courts were unwilling to overrule the powers of the new agencies at first, jurists such as Root were concerned that "the old doctrine prohibiting the delegation of legislative power has virtually retired from the field, and given up the fight." (*Addresses*, p. 534) Such addresses and articles were early-warning-signs that the judicial establishment wanted a new set of "administrative laws" to establish the boundaries around the growing powers of regulatory agencies.

130.   Ernst Freund, *Administrative Powers Over Persons and Property* (Chicago: University of Chicago Press, 1928).

Not everyone agreed that the delegation of power was increasing. This massive study of administrative power in the United States, New York, Great Britain, and pre-war Prussia, underwritten by the Commonwealth Fund's Special Committee on Administrative Law, noted that administrative power was increasing everywhere. However, Freund also reported a trend toward legislatures granting less discretion to administrative agencies. As a result, the behavior of administrators was increasingly dictated by statutes.

131.   Felix Frankfurter and J. Forrester Davison, *Cases and Materials on Administrative Law* (Chicago: Foundation Press, 1932).

Most jurists, however, were quite concerned about the deteriorating barriers among the branches of government, as shown in this first legal textbook on administrative law. Roughly two-thirds of the pages in the 1932 edition are devoted to questions of separation of powers and delegation. Concerns with the internal procedures of regulation, that later would dominate the field, come in a distant third.

132. Frederick Blachly and Miriam Oatman, *Administrative Legislation and Adjudication* (Washington, D.C.: Brookings Institution, 1934).

Heeding the call of the justices, this is one of the first academic studies of the area to call openly for new legislation. Blachly and Oatman noted that the change of relationships between constitutional law, statutory law, common law, and the newer administrative law had been haphazard, leading to confusion and to the danger "that the legislature may practically surrender to the administration its own functions of determining general lines of policy." (p. 47)

They felt that administrative rule-making was both inevitable and beneficial. Therefore, they advocated that congress pass a law to define the new relationship.

Much of the book is devoted to details on their proposed law. Unfortunately, they summarized their ideas in three places, and each summary varies considerably. Their simplest synopsis was that all general rules and regulations would be a) in specified form, openly published, with reference to their legal authority; b) issued in the name of the president; c) prepared for promulgation by a bureau of the presidency; and d) subject to review by the Supreme Court for constitutional issues and by administrative courts for questions of law. (pp. 89-90)

133. Charles C. Rohlfing, Edward W. Carter, Bradford W. West, and John G. Hervey, *Business and Government* (Chicago: Foundation Press, 1934).

Once the NIRA was passed, even textbooks with no political agenda felt compelled to notice that constitutional questions in regulation had become critical. "Congress has apparently adopted the axiom of 'when in doubt use the commerce power' with the corollary 'when the commerce power will not work try the tax clause.'" (p. 5) However, "(c)areful students of constitutional law entertain serious doubts as to the legality of some of the legislation enacted in the special session of the Seventy-third Congress." (p. 8)

While much of the text is about the relations of government and business generally, the portions on regulation are quite detailed. The authors called for administrative courts that could issue advisory opinions to make regulation more workable. (pp. 146-50) Also, the chapter on NIRA had the unusual perspective of being written after the passage of the act, but before the Supreme Court ruled on it. After a chapter of discussion, the authors (one abstained) decided that the NIRA was probably constitutional because of the economic crisis. (p. 689)

THE SECOND CONSTITUTIONAL ISSUE--PROCEDURAL QUESTIONS

134.   Gerald C. Henderson, *The Federal Trade Commission: A Study in Administrative Law and Procedure* (New Haven: Yale University Press, 1924).

Much as was the case with delegation of power, lawyers were among the first to question the legality of procedures used within regulatory agencies. In 1920, the Commonwealth Fund set up a Special Committee on Administrative Law (Ernst Freund, Walter Fisher, Felix Frankfurter, and Frank Goodnow) to sponsor legal research into the area.

Henderson's work, the first product of the Fund, complained that the FTC was ill-equipped to perform its job adequately. It was unable to separate its prosecuting from its judicial role. It was also too slow. Henderson proposed several changes, including that the FTC should issue interlocutory orders or citations, not complaints. On the hearing day, the FTC would behave in a judicial fashion, allowing evidence to be presented by others. The FTC would then issue narrative reports and signed opinions, not the legalistic "findings" that were often poorly documented.

135.   Isaiah Leo Sharfman, *The Interstate Commerce Commission: A Study in Administrative Law and Procedure*, 4 parts, 5 vol. (New York: Commonwealth Fund, 1931-1937).[3]

This most massive project of the Commonwealth Fund took the opposite view from Henderson's when studying the ICC. In an extraordinarily detailed and favorable review, Sharfman felt that the ICC had used its procedural flexibility to adjust to political pressure well. It worked so well, in fact, that the ICC had become a "dumping ground" for all marginally related governmental functions. Legislatures, on the other hand, were driven by political influence, and were unable to balance private rights and public interests. (Part II, p. 478) In short, the ICC had protected and promoted the public interest through administrative policy dominated by realism and restraint, and the flexibility of its procedures needed to be maintained.

136.   U.S. Supreme Court, *Panama Refining Co. v Ryan*, 293 U.S. 388 (1935); also *Schecter Poultry Co. v U.S.*, 295 U.S. 495 (1935); also "The Morgan Cases": *Morgan v U.S.*, 298 U.S. 468 (1936); *Morgan v U.S.*, 304 U.S. 1 (1938); *U.S. v Morgan*, 307 U.S. 183 (1939); and *U.S. v Morgan*, 313 U.S. 409 (1941).

Although the courts decided several cases in the late 1930s on the basic issues described here, these six cases illustrate the complete shift in judicial attitudes toward regulation that occurred in a very short time frame. The opening problem, addressed in *Panama* and *Schecter*, was that the NIRA had gone too far in delegating congressional power to administrative agencies. In doing so, agencies had been left with almost complete autonomy in determining the limits of their own behavior.

The issue could have been left as a question of delegation. In the Morgan cases, however, the court began for the first time to tackle questions of administrative procedure. Whatever powers the administrative agencies were given, there were certain procedural guarantees that could not be violated in carrying them out.

The precise answers offered in the Morgan cases are not as important as the questions, which both the courts and governmental commissions proved unable to resolve, and which eventually required the passage of the Administrative Procedures Act.

137.   Robert E. Cushman, *The Problem of the Independent Regulatory Commissions*, number III in *The President's Committee on Administrative Management* [The Brownlow Committee] (Washington, D.C.: USGPO, 1937); also *The Independent Regulatory Commissions* (New York: Oxford University Press, 1941).

When the Brownlow Committee was established in 1936, the legal difficulties of Independent Regulatory Commissions were a popular topic for discussion. Cushman was retained to write a special background report which he later expanded into the book listed above. His recommendations were also incorporated into the report of the committee to the president.

Cushman was concerned with a basic structural conflict between the administrative side of regulation, which should be answerable to political authorities, and the judicial side, which should not. While he noted that the Supreme Court had little difficulty in mixing legislative, executive, and judicial functions within one agency (1941, p. 423), the result was haphazard.

In the Brownlow report, Cushman advocated placing commissions within executive departments, but also insulating the limited judicial role from the larger administrative/political role. By 1941, with the Brownlow recommendations rejected, Cushman lightened the proposal to increased executive control and coordination with increased separation of judicial and legislative functions. In both cases, he reinforced Brownlow's desire to increase the power of presidential management while protecting judicial due process.

138.   James M. Landis, *The Administrative Process* (New Haven: Yale University Press, 1938).

If the regulatory commissions were a problem to Cushman and the Brownlow committee, the Brownlow committee was a problem to observers such as Landis. He actively attacked Brownlow's "somewhat hysterical" concern about a fourth branch of government, wondering what made three branches so sacred in political theory. "In terms of political theory, the administrative process springs from the inadequacy of a simple tripartite form of government to deal with modern problems." (p. 1) He found judicial precedents to be an equally unsatisfactory way to adjust to changing needs.

Landis called for new developments in the study and regulation of administrative law. He gave few details because of his concern that doctrinaire approaches are too inflexible. However, his approach included a recognition that experts needed to play an increasing role in regulation, and that restrictions on regulations should be based in observations about the way the world operated at that time.

139. Walter Gellhorn, *Administrative Law: Cases and Comments* (Chicago: Foundation Press, 1940). Note: later editions coauthored with Clark Byse.

Frankfurter's administrative law text in 1932 reflected the concerns of the field when it concentrated on the issues of separation of powers and delegation. This text, published in 1940, shows how fundamentally the field had changed. The 1940 edition was the first textbook to be dominated by questions of fair administrative procedures. By the third edition in 1954, Gellhorn and Byse adjusted their focus to questions of informal procedures. By the fourth edition in 1960, questions of informal procedures were so pervasive that the authors repudiated the argument that a single set of rules would work for all agencies.

140. Attorney General's Committee on Administrative Procedure, *Final Report*, Senate Document 8, 77th Cong., 1st sess. (1941).

A partial effort to answer procedural questions came from a special committee convened by the Attorney General. The report is lengthy and detailed, encompassing sixty pages of specific recommendations for twenty-five agencies, and a bill for legislative consideration. A later Department of Justice publication gave it credit for starting the process toward the APA of 1946.[4]

The committee wanted to utilize the growing expertise within regulatory agencies, and saw considerable benefit from having informal and formal procedures within the same agencies. They recommended increasing the caliber, independence, and significance of hearing examiners, while delegating more internal management chores to the agencies.

A minority report by three members includes a "Code of Standards of Fair Administrative Procedure," although the constrictive tone of the code is not consistent with the majority report.

141. *Administrative Procedures Act*, 60 Stat. 237 (1946).

The APA cannot be said to have laid the issue of administrative procedures to rest. However, it was the goal toward which a substantial number of jurists and lawyers had been working, and its longevity is testimony to the degree to which it addressed the principle issues in question.

The content of the law is extensively addressed in most texts. Briefly, the law divided agencies actions into orders and rules. Orders require formal proceedings with a hearing examiner (changed to administrative law judge in 1972) holding quasi-judicial hearings. These requirements mirror the recommendations made by the ABA Committee on Administrative Law as early as 1933. Rules require informal proceedings, but can be set aside judicially if they are arbitrary and capricious, unsupported by substantial evidence, or unwarranted by facts that are subject to trial. In short, the APA attempted to split the difference, satisfying the advocates of both administrative efficiency and due process.

142. *Report of the Conference on Administrative Procedure Called by the President of the United States* (Washington, D.C.: USGPO, April 29, 1953).

Of course, satisfying everyone on such a controversial issue was not practical. In 1953, a presidentially-called conference on administrative procedure opened the agenda by noting that the process had become too formalized and burdensome. To help alleviate the load and speed the process, they recommended prehearing and other conferences for "simplification, clarification, and disposition of issues."

143. Commission on Organization of the Executive Branch of Government Task Force, *Report on Legal Services and Procedures* (Washington, D.C.: USGPO, 1955).

A far more biting attack came from the other side, however, in the Second Hoover Commission report. Taking the traditional stand of the ABA, they argued that administrative procedures were indispensible to administrative justice. Therefore, the procedures of regulation must be increasingly formalized. They must copy much of the formal judicial process, or else due process would be sacrificed.

144. Peter Woll, *Administrative Law: The Informal Process* (Berkeley: University of California Press, 1963).

The Second Hoover Commission was not heeded, however, and formalization did not occur. By 1963, Woll was able to argue the "the hypothesis which this book is going to investigate is that requirements of public policy, *expertise*, and speed have rendered administrative adjudication today primarily informal in nature." (p. 2, italics in original) He noted that the ICC had discovered that the use of formal processes increased litigation, whereas purely administrative processes were often delegated to subordinate staff, making judicial review impractical.

Woll also defended the practice of having the formulation of policy in the same agency as adjudication since the two were adjuncts of the same process.

THE POLITICAL INDEPENDENCE OF REGULATORY AGENCIES

145.   Earl Latham, *The Politics of Railroad Coordination 1933-1936* (Cambridge: Harvard University Press, 1959).

In the post-war environment, an increasing number of observers began to reverse earlier questions. Instead of asking whether regulatory commissions had become too strong, they wondered aloud whether the commissions had become captives of the political process. Latham described the older model of commissioner independence which by then had passed from the scene.

This book is a delayed eulogy to Joseph Eastman, former chair of the ICC and the Office of Defense Transportation. Latham openly admired Eastman's style and treated the man as a hero. Eastman believed firmly in the politics/administration dichotomy. He defended the independence of regulatory commissions against all forms of political pressure, and used consultation, conciliation, and compromise in resolving industrial disputes.

As the book noted, Eastman was unique even within his day. By the time this book was written, Latham noted, Eastman's style had completely disappeared.

146.   Commission on Organization of Executive Branch of the Government, *Task Force Report on Regulatory Commissions* (Washington, D.C.: USGPO, 1949).

The First Hoover Commission report, reassessing the structure of regulatory commissions in the wake of the APA, praised the ability of the commission format to provide expertness, deliberation, impartiality, and continuity. The more controversial part of the report, however, dealt with the separation of powers, not from the legislature or judiciary, but from the executive. Specifically, the Hoover Commission listed a number of executive functions in the ICC that should be turned over to the Department of Commerce. More generally, the Commission wanted to increase the political responsiveness of the agencies by centralizing their power under commissioners appointed by the President.

147.   Victor A. Thompson, *The Regulatory Process in OPA Rationing* (New York: King's Crown Press, Columbia University, 1950).

In his dissertation, Thompson introduced a new perspective for studying the politics of the regulatory process. He argued that regulation is an exercise in applied social psychology. The failure to realize that has resulted in the "light switch theory" under which the regulators blindly expect their orders to "turn on" certain behaviors in the regulated industries.

Thompson noted that many rules of decision-making seemed reversed in the object of his study, the Office of Price Administration. High officials obeyed lower official rulings more than the reverse occurred; the staff usually gave more commands than did line personnel.

His most lasting contribution may be in his perspective that the most interesting interplay of politics and psychology occurs between regulator and regulated, not regulator and other branches of government. This perspective became the basis of Huntington's article, which followed shortly.

148.   Samuel P. Huntington, "The Marasmus of the ICC: The Commission, The Railroads, and the Public Interest," *Yale Law Journal*, 61, (April 1952): 467-509.

The rejection of the NIRA by the courts in the 1930s had seemed to lay to rest Progressive hopes of industry-government cooperation. In 1952, however, Huntington introduced the argument that what had been abandoned in theory had not necessarily been lost in practice.

Huntington's case study of the Interstate Commerce Commission offered the hypothesis that regulatory agencies (the ICC specifically) have a tendency to become trapped as servants of the very interest groups they are designed to regulate. Since 1935, he noted, the railroads have supported the ICC, opposing efforts to reorganize it into a more effective body.

To Huntington, the public suffered because of this relationship. If the regulator's independence was lost, as he argued it had been in this case, then the need to subordinate the ICC to politics was more obvious.

149.   Louis L. Jaffe, "The Effective Limits of the Administrative Process: A Reevaluation," *Harvard Law Review*, 67, (May 1954): 1105-35.

Jaffe went somewhat further in describing the growing relationship between the regulators and the regulated, but with more optimistic results. He felt that the planning mentality of the 1930s had given too little weight to the dynamism of the industrial system. "Administration was a branch of geriatrics." Instead, we needed to use strategic control, with the least regulation that was absolutely essential to meet our urgent needs. The ability of regulated groups to gain power, combined with staffing difficulties of regulatory agencies, leads to a counterbalancing of the administrator's natural bias toward regulation.

150.   Marver Bernstein, *Regulating Business by Independent Commission* (Princeton, N.J.: Princeton University Press, 1955); also

151.   Anthony Downs, *Inside Bureaucracy* (Boston: Little, Brown, and Co., 1967).

    Bernstein took the political model to a more general conclusion. In his book, he offered a life cycle theory of all regulatory agencies, based in the political science theory of pluralism that policies are made as a response to the political subgroups that try to influence them. He argued that the regulated industry is the only stable subgroup in the agency's environment, and that the industry will eventually and inevitably "capture" the policy-making discretion of the agency.

    While several authors have repeated and further developed Bernstein's arguments, Downs' approach is unique. Using a style of argumentation earlier popularized in *An Economic Theory of Democracy*, he developed arguments from assumptions stated at the beginning of his work, and concluded that Bernstein's "capture" theory is inevitable.

152.   Emmette Redford, "The President and the Regulatory Commissions," unprinted report of November 17, 1960, filed at the Bureau of the Budget, described pp. 307-09 below; also "The President and the Regulatory Commissions," *Texas Law Review*, 44, (December 1965): 288-321.

    With Redford, an increasing amount of literature on the regulatory commissions began to switch to the issue of presidential control. Redford proposed five rules that should define this relationship. The president should avoid *ex parte* statements on particular concerns; he should propose legislation in the area when needed; he should insure that commissioners have competence and integrity; he should insure efficient management; he should lead commissions in developing policies.

153.   James M. Landis, *Report on Regulatory Agencies to the President-Elect*, Submitted by the Chairman of the Subcommittee on Administrative Practice and Procedure to the Committee on the Judiciary, U.S. Senate, 82nd Cong., 2nd sess., (December, 1960).

    Continuing the concerns of effective management through presidential control, Landis proposed that a number of routine procedures be delegated within the agencies and made more informal. He called for an administrative conference, which was held and which resulted in the reorganization plans of 1961. He also proposed that the president appoint commission chairs, who would coordinate policies and serve at the president's pleasure. Finally, he wanted three offices in the Executive Office to coordinate policies as well as an Office for the Oversight of Regulatory Commissions.

154.　H. J. Friendly, *The Federal Administrative Agencies: The Need for Better Definition of Standards* (Cambridge: Harvard University Press, 1962).

To Judge Friendly, the difficulty is not a lack of presidential leadership; it is an unwillingness of agencies to create standards or "make laws" that are sufficiently definite that decisions will be predictable and that the reasons will be understood. Friendly longed for the days of independent commissioners, such as Eastman. However, lacking that, he did feel that the president could force the agencies to adopt such standards.

155.　William L. Cary, *Politics and the Regulatory Agencies* (New York: McGraw-Hill, 1967).

These lecture reprints are one of the purest statements of the case for presidential leadership on broad policies, and informal processes for more narrow issues. Cary liked the premise of having authority and responsibility in the same hands by mixing rule-making with adjudication. He did not favor congressional interference since that would introduce more political control by industry than already existed.

156.　Paul A. Sabatier, "Regulatory Policy-Making: Toward a Framework of Analysis," *National Resources Journal*, 17, (July 1977): 415-60.

In a more conceptual work, Sabatier designed a flow-diagram model of regulatory decision-making based on a number of variables. These include six sets of resource and/or attitudinal variables, consisting of legal resources; technical, monetary and personnel resources; personal preferences and leadership ability; the attitudes and resources of the agency's sovereigns; constituency groups; and other agencies. Five situation variables include socio-economic factors, political culture, the state of technological development, public opinion, and the perceived nature of the problem calling for regulation.

157.　Kenneth J. Meier and John P. Plumlee, "Regulatory Administration and Organizational Rigidity," *Western Political Quarterly*, 31, (March 1978): 80-95.

Downs and others created hypotheses from theoretical models without empirically testing them. To Meier and Plumlee, the problem with that approach is that, in this case, the hypotheses make predictions that are not correct.

Specifically, several activities, including airline safety, banking, and pharmaceuticals, are heavily regulated by government agencies even though no effective opposition to the industry position exists in those cases. Meier and Plumlee offered a counter-explanation, which is that the pluralist model of subgovernments is mitigated by both internal and external pressures, often leading to strict regulation where it would not otherwise have been predicted.

FRUITFUL COLLABORATION--JUDICIAL INTERVENTION AFTER 1971

158.   Kenneth Davis, *Administrative Law Treatise* (St. Paul: West Publishing, 1958); also *Discretionary Justice: A Preliminary Inquiry* (Baton Rouge: LSU Press, 1969); also

159.   Louis L. Jaffe, *Judicial Control of Administrative Action* (Boston: Little, Brown and Co., 1965).

The APA was a compromise. It permitted considerable agency discretion, but it did not obliterate judicial oversight as convincingly as some of the later literature contended. Instead, the "traditional model" stayed alive in some of the literature.

Davis is a case in point. While he wanted to eliminate only unnecessary discretion so as to maintain flexibility, he felt that discretion leads to injustice. To balance the needs of flexibility and justice, he emphasized the need for judicially mandated standards to be created through rigorous rule-making in the agencies.

Jaffe was even more direct. "It is the central thesis of this book that agencies and courts are in a partnership of lawmaking and lawapplying." While the "delegation of power to administration is the dynamo of the modern social service state," he felt that judicial review should be balanced by its appropriateness against the harm of denying relief.

160.   U.S. Circuit Court of Appeals, *Environmental Defense Fund v Ruckelshaus* 439 F.2d 589, 597 (D.C. Cir. 1971).

In ruling that administrators must initiate proceedings to ban the use of DDT, Chief Judge David Bazelon of the D.C. Circuit Court of Appeals added another phrase to the vocabulary of the "partnership" described by Jaffe when he acknowledged "a new era in the long and fruitful collaboration of administrative agencies and reviewing courts."

161.   Abraham D. Sofaer, "Judicial Control of Informal Discretionary Adjudication and Enforcement," *Columbia Law Review*, 72, (December 1972): 1293-1375.

Adding to the arguments for a partnership, Sofaer complained that the APA made administrative disclosure the exception rather than the rule. However, he contended that wide discretion leads to inconsistency, arbitrariness, and inefficiency. As a counterproposal, he suggested that agencies should have to develop standards, but through adjudication procedures rather than rules. Their standards should be made public. If their actions deviate from the standards, they should be overruled. Discretion should be allowed only for the purposes that are legislated.

162.   J. Skelly Wright, "The Courts and the Rulemaking Process: The Limits of Judicial Review," *Cornell Law Review*, 59, (March 1974): 375-97; also

163.   William F. Pederson, "Formal Records and Informal Rule-Making," *Yale Law Review*, 85, (November 1975): 38-88; also

164.   Richard B. Stewart, "The Reformation of American Administrative Law," *Harvard Law Review*, 88, (June 1975): 1667-1813; also

165.   David H. Rosenbloom, *Public Administration and the Law: Bench v. Bureau in the United States* (New York: Marcel Dekker, 1983).

Each of these authors attempted to describe the new spirit of judicial activism. All four saw this spirit arising from the unacceptably confusing and poorly-defined standards operating within the agencies. Stewart in particular felt that the judicial phase arose from necessity, but is not really based in a coherent model of democratic regulation.

Rosenbloom was more optimistic about these "reforms," arguing that the courts are intervening in many areas of administrative abuse, especially in defense of institutionalized persons.

Pederson suggested new rules that would improve the rule-making function without reimposing adjudicatory hearings. He proposed that agencies have a rule-making docket that would be published in the *Federal Register*. All documents and responses would be placed in a public file, and the final rule would have to discuss the contents of the file. The entire file would be used for judicial review.

166.   U.S. Supreme Court, *INS v Chadha*, 462 U.S. 919, 952 (1983); also *Bowsher v Synar*, 106 S.Ct. 3181, 3187 (1986).

Two of the more active decisions of the courts in the 1980s increased the isolation of administrative discretion from easy "tricks" of congressional control. *Chadha* declared the legislative veto to be unconstitutional while *Bowsher* similarly disallowed sections of the Gramm-Rudman-Hollings Act that permitted the

Comptroller General to control executive spending levels. Both decisions are described in more detail in chapter seven.

167.   Phillip J. Cooper, "Conflict or Constructive Tension: The Changing Relationship of Judges and Administrators," *Public Administration Review*, 45, (November 1985) [Special Issue]: 643-52.

This review ends on a note of moderation. After recounting recent decisions, Cooper argued that the phase of judicial activism has not been as extreme as many administrators have felt. He tried to demonstrate that the courts are aware of the need for administrative discretion, and that they have been pulling back from intervention to accomplish this. The one exception, however, which is the one that led to the phrase "fruitful collaboration," is that the courts remain actively involved when administrators neglect to use the discretion they have been given.

CONTINUING CONCERNS

The debate over administrative regulation can be framed within two central questions: to what extent should government regulate the private sector; and who should be responsible for the regulations?

Both of these questions have been addressed within the larger context of an increasingly interdependent economy, and government has been adjusting to the interdependence in ways that make regulation easier, but that have almost certainly made the interdependence more profound. In fact, a few free-market economists blame government for the interdependence in the first place, claiming that trusts could never have arisen in the 1800s without governmental sponsorship and regulation.

The argument in its purest form has few followers outside of economics, although movements in that direction have enjoyed some political popularity. In public administration, few have seemed enthusiastic about creating an unregulated economy to see if the scale of industry collapses and interdependence dissolves.

As Dwight Waldo noted in *The Administrative State*, Public Administration is built upon progressive principles. It believes that a partnership between government and business is so beneficial that the only interesting questions are ones of implementation.

However, the answer to neither of the two questions above is set in stone. As free-market economists begin to reintroduce some of the basic questions, we are vulnerable because we have largely forgotten that regulatory options other that progressive partnerships have already been devised and investigated.

And even within progressive principles, the field has seldom agreed for long on who should regulate. With the increasingly fuzzy distinction between the sectors and their roles, it is not as clear that only government speaks for the public, or who in government should do the talking.

Government and business share an interdependence that the constitution long ago created among the branches of government. Like the branches of government, the marriage is one of shifting needs and shifting jealousies. In the continuing contest, it is reasonable to suspect that each of the solutions tried so far may live to see another day.

NOTES FOR CHAPTER FIVE

1. For those desiring more detail on the legislative and judicial debates on early regulation, see Robert E. Cushman, *The Independent Regulatory Commissions* (New York: Oxford University Press, 1941); or *Report of the Attorney General's Committee*, Senate Document 8, 77th Cong., 1st sess. (1941).

2. The book received a copyright and was probably released in 1901, but is dated 1902.

3. For reasons that are not clear, this citation is almost always listed with two errors. There are five volumes, not four. Part Three of four is contained in two sizable volumes, marked "A" and "B". Also, the publication dates are normally listed as 1931-1936, even though Part Four was copyrighted and published in December 1937.

4. United States Department of Justice, *Attorney General's Manual on the Administrative Procedure Act* (Washington, D.C.: USGPO, 1947).

6

The Government as Entrepreneur

BACKGROUND

A frequent theme in the literature of the previous chapter is that its proposals were preferable to the alternative of direct governmental ownership and delivery of products and/or services. Government ownership, or "socialism" in the almost-universally accepted parlance, has been a pariah in most of the political literature of the twentieth century.

Of course, government has been producing and delivering some products and services for millennia. In fact, all that government does may be viewed that way. In that environment, some definition is needed to distinguish the activities that are legitimately government's from those that clearly are not.

This chapter is about that definition. Unfortunately, while there is no shortage of proposed definitions, there is also no consensus. As a result, the precise governmental programs that are included in this chapter are selected more for their historical ability to generate public debate than for their utility in defining public and private business.

There is a second difficulty with organizing this chapter. Governmental production has been a subject for study in the literature in its own right. Some of those production facilities, however, also provided the laboratories that literally created the study of intergovernmental relations, and that helped shape the study of public personnel administration.

This chapter begins with the opening debate on governmental ownership and delivery of products, followed by a selection of literature on the specific industries that have helped shape the controversy, and ending with the more recent literature on contracting, governmental competition, and privatization. The literature of intergovernmental relations, which sprang from studies of governmental corporations, is extensive enough to be reviewed separately in chapter eight.

UTILITIES AND RAILWAYS--THE OPENING DEBATE

Public production is not new. At least one historian dates government-owned corporations from the time of Emperor Augustus.[1] In the United States, the town of Boston was operating a public water system as early as 1652.[2] However, three forces arose in the late 1800s to make the topic a renewed subject of controversy. First, private industry was developing by leaps and bounds, often making the option of large private utilities physically possible for the first time. Second, Eastern cities were growing at a sizable rate, creating new demands for such services. In such an environment, the debate over public ownership of the utilities took on new urgency.

The third force was the railway crisis that led to the reforms described in the previous chapter. At first, however, it was not clear that regulation was the answer; both proponents and foes noted that exclusively private ownership of the railways was unique to the United States.[3] As such, rails served as an ideal source of comparative data for both sides.

168. Arthur T. Hadley, *Railroad Transportation: Its History and Laws* (New York: G.P. Putnam's Sons, 1885).

Henry Demarest Lloyd and the states set the regulatory theme described in the previous chapter that eventually provided the solution to the railway crisis. At first, however, their's was not the only option considered.

Hadley investigated the same history and abuses of the railways that were familiar to other reformers. However, he felt that the abuses were going to be more difficult to correct than most people believed. He was also more impressed with European experiments in governmental ownership. Sensing a "strong popular feeling" in favor of governmental ownership here, he argued that it was the only option that could achieve the desired efficiency.

169. M. J. Francisco, "Municipal Ownership, Its Fallacy," [pamphlet] (Rutland, Vermont: self-published, 1895); also "Municipal Light Plants," *City Government*, 4, (April 1898): 131-32; also

170. John R. Commons, "Municipal Electric Lighting," *Municipal Affairs*, 1, (December 1897): 631-73.

The Interstate Commerce Act of 1887 gave the upper hand in the debate over governmental ownership to those who favored the private sector. However, the debate raged on, especially for public utilities. In the private sector, Francisco helped publicize a study by the Massachusetts Gas and Electric Light Commission ("Municipal Ownership versus Private Corporations") on the relative efficiency of publicly and privately owned utilities. Opponents labelled their massive public education campaigns "propaganda." Professor Commons, who taught the first course in the

United States on public utility economics, was the best known public-ownership advocate in the early years.[4]

Both sides used extensive cost comparisons, although not always honestly, and the tones were often vicious, personal, and moralistic. Francisco, a utility operator, considered all government to be corrupt while Commons, writing in the official organ of the New York Reform Club, argued "...that nine-tenths of the existing municipal corruption and inefficiency results from the policy of leaving municipal functions to private parties...." (p. 668) The December 1897 issue of *Municipal Affairs* also offered an extensive pro-government bibliography on p. 790.

171.   Edward W. Bemis, ed., *Municipal Monopolies* (New York: Thomas Y. Crowell & Co., 1899).

For utilities, if not railroads, the advocates of public ownership quickly regrouped from the Interstate Commerce Act. In this book of readings by various scholars and industry experts, historical and statistical cases were made for the economy and effectiveness of public ownership of water supplies, electric power supply, telephones, natural gas, and street railways.

Professor Frank Parsons cited the judicial precedents for public ownership. However, both Parsons and Bemis proposed improvements in the process. Parsons thought state interference was a mistake, and made an impassioned plea for municipal home rule. Bemis suggested that municipal franchises to utility companies should be publicly known, regulated to prevent overcapitalization, and broad enough to cover the entire city.

The passion of the debate, however, was not completely lost. After a book whose approach was quite rigorous, Bemis ended with a quotation that was carefully misconstrued to make public ownership sound patriotic, and to accuse its opponents of betraying those who shed their blood at Santiago.

172.   Samuel O. Dunn, *Government Ownership of Railways* (New York: D. Appleton and Co., 1914); also *Regulation of Railways* (New York: D. Appleton & Co., 1918).

The battle for public ownership of the railways was going poorly, as indicated by these widely-read books written during the regulatory crisis of the 1910s. Like Hadley in 1885, Dunn used the European and Canadian experiences to document his points. Hadley's methodology was far more sophisticated, however, and he measured the railways' economy, adequacy and quality of service, rates, and financial impacts on the public, as well as the influence of politics.

Dunn concluded that "the preponderance of evidence does not indicate that, under existing conditions, at least, the adoption of government ownership in the United States would be beneficial to the public." (1914, p. 378) Instead, he advocated further development and improvement in the system of public regulation.

173. Albert May Todd, *Municipal Ownership* (Chicago: Public Ownership League of America, September 1, 1918).

In 1918, Albert Todd formed the Public Ownership League based on two principles of public ownership--political justice and social justice. This book, which contained both the credo and the constitution of the league, was designed "to promote the public ownership, efficient management and democratic control of public utilities and natural resources--municipal, state and national--as rapidly and as far as may be practical and consistent with the public welfare." (p. 119) The League supported numerous publications in the area, and this one was not copyrighted, so as to encourage its duplication and circulation.

174. Carl D. Thompson, *Ownership of Railways* (Chicago: Public Ownership League, 1919); also *Public Ownership* (New York: Thomas Y. Crowell Co., 1925).

Demonstrating that both sides could use statistics to appear more objective, Thompson claimed in 1925 not to argue the case for public ownership, but only to present the facts. Both books stressed the railway issue, and emphasized the degree to which the U.S. approach of strictly-private ownership was unique. In the second book, Thompson also "considered" each of the standard objections to public ownership, finding cause to reject each.

175. Herbert Hoover, "Government Ownership," unpublished address, Washington, D.C., September 29, 1924. Printed and distributed by several sources, especially (New York: National Electric Light Association, n.d.).

This was one of the more concise summations of the arguments of the field. The speech took on special significance since it was delivered by President Coolidge's Secretary of Commerce. For that reason, it was distributed widely at the time by industrial lobbyists whose propaganda campaign continued to heat up. Hoover cited the standard examples of gross inefficiency in such places as the Canadian railroad and municipal utilities. He also summarized the arguments against public ownership, including inefficiency and the inevitable abuse of the spoils system in staffing.

176. Lewis C. Sorrell, *Government Ownership and Operation of Railways for the United States* (New York: Prentice Hall, 1937).

The next time the question of ownership arose for railroads, it came from the opposite direction; during the Great Depression, governmental ownership was reconsidered in some circles because the railways were financially too weak to survive, not too strong to be controlled. However, there was little sentiment for the change. Sorrell, who advised a 1935 transportation conference on the issue, argued that ownership might help special interests, but would be harmful to the public interest. Therefore, public ownership was "neither necessary nor inevitable."

REGULATING THE UTILITIES

177.   National Civic Federation, *Commission Regulation of Public Utilities* (New
        York: National Civic Federation, 1913); also

178.   Morris L. Cooke, *Public Utility Regulation* (New York: Ronald Press, 1924);
        also

179.   John Bauer, *Effective Regulation of Public Utilities* (New York: Macmillan,
        1925); also

180.   Martin Glaeser, *Outlines of Public Utility Economics* (New York: Macmillan,
        1927).

Regulation and government ownership of public utilities were often considered together as options in the larger debate over the "public interest." The literature was among the most technical and detailed reviewed in this text as such diverse issues as rate determination, public safety, and ownership were analyzed as problems in comparative economics.

The National Civic Federation opened the debate with a 1229 page survey of utility regulation by the federal government and the 43 states that had a regulatory commission. The exhaustive work was cross-referenced and indexed by sections and subjects.

Cooke's book of readings by Felix Frankfurter, John Bauer, Charles Merriam, Harold Lasswell, and others, extended scientific investigation from utility rates to the measurement of public opinion. Like Bauer, Cooke felt that regulatory problems could be overcome without an expansion in the public ownership that already existed.

Glaeser's 753 page treatise is generally considered to be the first textbook on the subject. Glaeser noted that private ownership of public utilities was a vestige of eighteenth-century liberalism. While it often worked, Glaeser was concerned that franchising policies should never surrender the ability of the government to reclaim utilities should they be abused.

181.   Federal Trade Commission, "Investigation of Utility Companies," Senate Doc-
        ument 92, 70th Cong., 1st sess., February 17, 1928, parts 1-84, and reports, parts
        1-16.

In 1928-1929, the Federal Trade Commission intensified the debate with another massive study. The early parts concentrated on the utilities' propaganda activities that resulted in what the FTC called a systematic manipulation of public opinion by the utilities. Later parts and the reports studied the financial transactions of each of the major utilities that were suspected of operating outside the public interest.

182.   Hilmar S. Raushenbush and Harry W. Laidler, *Power Control* (New York: New Republic, 1928); also

183.   Hilmar S. Raushenbush, *The Power Fight* (New York: New Republic, 1932).

Similarly, Raushenbush wrote these intense but well-documented exposés of abuses by the utility companies, and their manipulation of public opinion. He charged that the commissions and courts were being packed by the power companies. He also documented numerous cases of utility financial improprieties.

While he applauded government ownership of utilities, he recognized in 1928 that it would be politically easier to control utility investment practices. By 1932, he lost faith in regulation, and called for a "power fight."

184.   William E. Mosher, ed., *Electrical Utilities, the Crisis in Public Control* (New York: Harper and Brothers, 1929)[5]; also

185.   William E. Mosher and Finla Crawford, *Public Utility Regulation* (New York: Harper and Brothers, 1933).

Also following the lead of the FTC, these multidisciplinary studies by the staff of Syracuse University's Maxwell School compared several options including improved regulation, competition from government, and national ownership as solutions to the recent changes and expansions in public utilities.

The approach was incremental. "Rarely in the history of either government or industry does one single considered decision of policy determine the road for the future." (1929, p. 178) They noted that the commission form of regulation had become pervasive, so that "regulation rises or falls with the efficacy of the public service commission." (1933, p. 562)

They were concerned about the massive "educational" propaganda campaigns being conducted by the utilities, and they were strong advocates of public officials acting in the public interest. To overcome interest politics, they suggested that commissioners be chosen on the basis of experience and dedication, that the commissions be adequately funded, and that their jurisdiction be as broad as the industry's which they regulated. They also suggested that the commissions needed more planning, and that utilities should subordinate the profit motive to public needs.

GOVERNMENT CORPORATIONS BEFORE 1945

The issues raised by the FTC were never satisfactorily resolved. Eventually, they led into the broader-scoped literature on the capture of regulatory agencies, that is reviewed in the previous chapter. However, a form of government ownership became popular in the first World War, and it had even greater implications for public-private sector relations. The new form was the proprietary government corporation.

186.   William F. Willoughby, "The National Government as a Holding Corporation: A Question of Subsidiary Budgets," *Political Science Quarterly*, 32, (December 1917): 505-21; also *Principles of Public Administration* (Washington, D.C.: Brookings Institution, 1927).

While Willoughby's book was more widely read and cited by later generations, his 1917 article appears to be the first and most purely stated defense of the holding corporation as a new form of governmental organization. He saw the holding (or subsidiary) corporation as an adjustment to the massive workloads of both the executive and legislative branches. He did not feel that such a form was appropriate for all governmental functions. However, in those areas in which it was appropriate, the holding corporation relieved congress from details, simplified the national budget into a net budget by creating subsidiary budgets, and helped develop esprit de corps among the workers.

Willoughby was not specific in defining holding corporations, and included examples from regulatory commissions in his article. This lack of precision was the subject of later attacks.

187.   Harold A. Van Dorn, *Government Owned Corporations* (New York: Alfred A. Knopf, 1926).

Van Dorn wrote a detailed and generally favorable review of government corporations, describing the development and role of each in separate chapters. He was particularly impressed with the Federal Land Banks and the U.S. Grain Corporation, which he credited with stopping war speculation in grains. Similarly, he praised the role of the U.S. Shipping Board Emergency Fleet Corporation for its role in the war. From an administrative standpoint, he noted the increased simplicity in dealing with government-owned producers.

188.   Marshall Dimock, *Government-Operated Enterprises in the Panama Canal Zone* (Chicago: University of Chicago Press, 1934); also *Developing America's Waterways* (Cambridge: Harvard University Press, 1935).

Dimock, perhaps the most prolific writer on the subject, was also impressed with the government corporations, but suggested several improvements. He felt that the Panama Railroad Company, which was superbly run, should be combined with The Panama Canal, and that the combined operations should be delegated more operational discretion. Similarly, the Inland Waterways Corporation should be given a more simplified hierarchy, and should be moved from Washington D.C. to give it more managerial discretion.

189. John A. McIntire, "Government Corporations as Administrative Agencies: An Approach," *George Washington Law Review*, 4, (January 1936): 161-210.

By the 1930s, government corporations were so diverse in function and structure that it was becoming less clear what the concept meant. McIntire, attacking the subject from a legal standpoint, tried to argue that the confusion was unimportant. While there was confusion over the distinction of "public" and "proprietary" corporations, he noted that corporations themselves could not be defined accurately and exclusively. Instead, he felt, government corporations held enough advantages that we should be satisfied with an "organic theory" of the corporation.

190. John Thurston, *Government Proprietary Corporations in the English-Speaking Countries* (Cambridge: Harvard University Press, 1937); also

191. John McDiarmid, *Government Corporations and Federal Funds* (Chicago: University of Chicago Press, 1938).

What Dimock did for the specific corporations he studied, Thurston and McDiarmid attempted to do for government corporations as a class. Working under a Brookings Institution grant, Thurston used history to document his prescriptive, administrative study. In general, he and McDiarmid agreed with Dimock that the corporations needed simplified hierarchies, more autonomy and self-sufficiency, and a greater management focus.

McDiarmid responded more directly to some of the suggested reforms of the day, arguing for instance that these corporations should be audited by Department of Treasury personnel, not GAO personnel. It should also be noted the McDiarmid's book contained one of the more extensive bibliographies published on this topic.

192. The President's Committee on Administrative Management, *Report of the President's Committee, Administrative Management in the Government of the United States* (Washington, D.C.: USGPO, January 1937), pp. 38-41.

Suggested reforms were diverse, however, as shown by the Brownlow Committee report. In an attempt to increase the importance of presidential leadership, they recommended less autonomy for corporations, not more. Specifically, each corporation would be housed within a particular department, to which it would answer for its budget and general direction. Actual management of the corporation would become the responsibility of a president or general manager, not the board of directors as was then often the case.

193. David E. Lilienthal and Robert H. Marquis, "The Conduct of Business Enterprises by the Federal Government," *Harvard Law Review*, 54, (February 1941): 545-601.

The Brownlow Committee recommendations worked against the general flow of the literature, which generally wanted more rather than less autonomy. No one spoke as clearly for increased corporate autonomy as TVA Director David Lilienthal, who was concerned that reforms might "strangle the best devices for efficiency." He was also concerned that government audits should be used only to ensure honesty and business efficiency, and should not include political considerations.

194.   C. Herman Pritchett, "The Paradox of the Government Corporation," *Public Administration Review*, 1, (Summer 1941): 381-89.

By the 1940s, dissatisfaction with the growing number and diverse forms of governmental corporations was widespread enough that basic government-wide reorganizations were often proposed. This is one of the first and more concise statements of the problem.

Pritchett noted that, as an organizational form, "the corporation was used not wisely but too well," often being adopted because it was easy to get through congress. However, governmental corporations were now so diverse in structure that they had lost their unique identity. "The paradox is that government corporations remain and even increase in number while *the* government corporation is passing away." (p. 381)

195.   Lewis Corey, *The Unfinished Task: Economic Reconstruction for Democracy* (New York: Viking Press, 1942).

Rounding out the diverse literature on corporate forms before 1945, Corey used Marxist analysis to determine how the transformation of the capitalist system could be completed without resorting to the totalitarianism of Hitler or Stalin. Government corporations provided a valuable resource for insuring the separation of economic and political power, but only so long as they operated with relative autonomy. In opposition to the Brownlow Committee recommendations, Corey felt that the lack of direction and accountability of these corporations served as a protection against both corporate and governmental monopolies of power.

THE TVA: REGIONALISM AND INTERGOVERNMENTAL RELATIONS

No government corporation was to have the impact of the Tennessee Valley Authority. Not only was it unprecedented in size, but the autonomy and the experimental nature of its early leadership led to fundamental changes in the ways public administrators viewed intergovernmental relations.

196.   Arthur DeWitt Frank, *Development of the Federal Program of Flood Control on the Mississippi River* [dissertation] (New York: Columbia University Press, 1930); also

197. Judson King, *The Legislative History of Muscle Shoals* (Knoxville: Tennessee Valley Authority, 1936).

These two histories, especially the first, were used extensively by the later authors on the TVA. Both documented our nation's historical reluctance in developing water resources. For instance, while federal legislation dated at least to 1824's "Act to improve the navigation of the Ohio and Mississippi Rivers," the emphasis was strictly on navigational improvements, and was restricted almost exclusively to maintenance of levees within the commerce clause, largely ignoring such obvious benefits as flood control or power generation.

The Federal Water Power Act of 1920 marked a change in strategy. In giving the federal government control over the development of water sites in the public domain, it ushered in an unanticipated era of federal-state cooperation on resource development. This cooperation blossomed in the case of the TVA.

198. Clarence Lewis Hodge, *The Tennessee Valley Authority: A National Experiment in Regionalism* (Washington, D.C.: American University Press, 1938).

Hodge was among the first to publish the claim that the TVA was more significant for its governmental innovations than for its resource development. While he made some suggestions for administrative simplification, his major concern was that "regionalism is a trend the importance of which has been inadequately recognized by students in the field of government." (p. vii) "The creation of the Tennessee Valley Authority is thus in a way an exploration in methods of government." (p. 229) He briefly discussed some of the TVA's strategies in regional cooperation, but was equally interested in the more abstract literature suggesting that states should be replaced by regional governments.

199. Ellis F. Hartford, *Our Common Mooring* (Athens: University of Georgia Press, 1941); also

200. Joseph Sirera Rausmeier, *The Tennessee Valley Authority: A Case Study in the Economics of Multiple Purpose Stream Planning* [dissertation for Columbia University] (Nashville: Vanderbilt University Press, 1942).

These books repeated the theme that comprehensive plans for water control benefitted all sectors of the regional economy. Hartford, who was hired by the TVA to spell out Board Chairman Harcourt Morgan's views, argued that southerners needed balanced farming practices, with decentralized industrial development, and that education was a social force to accomplish these goals.

To Rausmeier, the economy of multiple use planning had influenced the growth in water resource policy. As a dissertation, Rausmeier's book offered extensive documentation on the history of both water management and the Tennessee Valley. On the negative side, his approach was occasionally obtuse, especially in his Euclidean and non-Euclidean models of resource allocation.

Rausmeier concluded that "the planning and administration of federal water policy has failed to keep pace with the evolution of multiple purpose technology." (p. 422) Therefore, the U.S. should coordinate a national water plan, much like the one used for the TVA.

201.   C. Herman Pritchett, *The Tennessee Valley Authority* (Chapel Hill: University of North Carolina Press, 1943).

Pritchett, who had earlier written on the nature of government corporations (see earlier this chapter), applied his analysis here more directly to the TVA. The book was openly pro-TVA and written from within a camp of supporters publishing on the subject. (Pritchett had been an employee at TVA, and an earlier doctoral student under Marshall Dimock).

Pritchett's main research interests were the questions raised by government corporations. He noted that "(t)he T.V.A. certainly had not achieved 'the essential freedom and elasticity of a private business corporation'," but that "that is, in fact, a goal to which a government agency cannot and should not aspire, for it is not consonant with the claims of public responsibility." (p. 266) More generally, he saw the New Deal as a giant retooling job, to make governmental machinery adequate for the requirements of the 1930s.

202.   David E. Lilienthal, *TVA: Democracy on the March* (New York: Harper and Brothers, 1944).

Lilienthal, writing as one of the TVA's first directors, marked a shift in the literature of the TVA. Instead of concentrating on the advantages of regional planning, Lilienthal noted that some of the most useful lessons were in the areas of decentralization and intergovernmental relations. He argued that "*a task cannot be done democratically if the method chosen for doing it is bureaucratic.*" (p. 169, italics in original) On a personal level, he dismissed the inevitability of exploitative management styles. On an institutional level, the TVA used no written plan because Lilienthal felt that planning could not be separated from action.

Instead, the TVA tried to develop "extensive and close relations with state and local agencies" to achieve "*centralized large-scale production combined with decentralized, grass-roots local responsibility.*" (p. 134, italics in original) The term we now use for this, cooptation, was introduced later by Selznick.

Occasionally, Lilienthal reported, the effort took unusual forms. For example, rather than establish separate libraries for dam construction workers, the TVA contributed to local library systems. Another example is contained in the following review.

203. [Roscoe C. Martin, ed.], *New Horizons in Public Administration: A Symposium* (University: University of Alabama Press, 1945). The book itself lists no author or editor.

This book is the first publication by the University of Alabama Press, an enterprise created through a study funded by the TVA. Most of the articles, by Leonard White, Marshall Dimock, Donald Stone, John Millett, and Arthur Macmahon, were on general administrative topics. The one article on the TVA was one of the first published by Gordon Clapp, General Manager of the TVA.

204. Philip Selznick, "Foundations of the Theory of Organization," *American Sociological Review*, XIII, (February 1948): 25-35; also *TVA and the Grass Roots* [dissertation and trade editions] (Berkeley: University of California Press, 1949).

Selznick was an early organizational sociologist who was responsible for introducing the term "cooptation" to define the process of *"absorbing new elements into the leadership or policy-determining structure of an organization as a means of averting threats to its stability or existence."* (*TVA*, p. 13, italics in original)

Selznick's major concern in the *ASR* article was the impact of delegation of power, as expressed through changes in the informal systems. Much of this is reviewed separately in a later chapter. In the *TVA* book, he was particularly interested in cooptation as an adaptive mechanism within the organization's informal "action system." In the TVA, it took two forms. Formal cooptation, aimed at providing accessibility to power, involved relationships between the TVA and specially-organized voluntary associations. Informal cooptation, aimed at sharing power, involved relationships between the TVA and existing organizations (and governments).

Cooptation was possible at the regional level. Above that, however, Selznick felt that society's differences became too great for effective coordination to occur.

205. James W. Fesler, *Area and Administration* (University: University of Alabama Press, 1949).

This was one of the last of the pre-Lilienthal-style studies of regional coordination. In a series of lectures at the University of Alabama, Fesler attempted to describe in general concepts the inevitable clashes that occurred between central and areal (field) offices. Part of the difficulty arose because central administration was usually most efficiently organized along functional lines while field offices were small enough that they were usually organized along areal lines. Fesler argued that greater coordination could be sought between the two by redesigning areas and by improving horizontal and vertical cooperation.

206. Robert S. Avery, *Experiment in Management: Personnel Decentralization in the Tennessee Valley Authority* (Knoxville: University of Tennessee Press, 1954).

The TVA was such an unprecedented experiment for government that much of its literature leads into questions asked in other chapters. The intergovernmental relations literature that is described in chapter eight, for instance, was given a large boost by studies of the regionalism and shared responsibility of the TVA. Lilienthal also contributed to the literature on leadership styles. TVA's personnel structure was also unique within the federal government, and that is the subject of Avery's book.

TVA was not subject to the Civil Service Commission, but was obligated to run a system that was free of political influence, and that was based on "merit and efficiency." To Avery, TVA adopted personnel policies that reflected the philosophy of decentralized administration of centralized authority.

In general, he concluded that the goal had been successfully accomplished, and that both supervisors and workers had been integrated into the process. He also suggested some improvements, however, especially in the area of supervisory training on personnel, and in overall coordination.

207.   Roscoe C. Martin, ed., *TVA: The First Twenty Years* (Knoxville: University of Alabama Press and University of Tennessee Press, 1956)[6]; also

208.   John R. Moore, ed., *The Economic Impact of TVA* (Knoxville: University of Tennessee Press, 1967); also

209.   Steven M. Neuse, "TVA at Age Fifty--Reflections and Retrospect," *Public Administration Review*, 43, (November/December 1983): 491-99; also

210.   Michael R. Fitzgerald and Steven M. Neuse, "TVA: The Second Fifty Years--a Symposium," *Public Administration Quarterly* [formerly *Southern Review of Public Administration*], 8, (Summer 1984): 138-41, extends to 259.

In more recent times, TVA has continued to generate the volume of literature that would be expected from such a sizable agency. In general, the TVA continues to enjoy the favorable press that has enveloped it from the beginning. The trend of the literature, however, is best reflected in the steadily more restrained enthusiasm of these "anniversary" retrospectives. By 1984, titles such as Welborn's "Persistent Dilemmas: TVA as a Problem in Organizational Governance," were not uncommon.

In 1983, Neuse concluded with three lessons. First, even the more capable agencies are faced with intractable problems. Second, even anti-bureaucratic agencies pick up pathologies of bureaucracy as they mature. Third, the TVA serves as the perfect object lesson that we cannot live with or without bureaucracy.

GOVERNMENT CORPORATIONS SINCE 1945

211. *Government Corporation Control Act*; 59 Stat. 597 (1945); also

212. C. Herman Pritchett, "The Government Corporation Control Act of 1945," *American Political Science Review*, 40, (June 1946): 495-509; also

213. V. O. Key, Jr., "Government Corporations," in Fritz Morstein Marx, ed., *Elements of Public Administration* (New York: Prentice-Hall, 1946), pp. 236-63.

In 1945, congress attempted to set some basic guidelines that would define all government corporations. Among its provisions, all such corporations had to be organized through legislation. All were required to have business-like budgets submitted through the Bureau of the Budget to congress. All needed to estimate returns on capital and to submit to General Accounting Office audits. All accounts over $50,000 had to be kept with the Department of Treasury.

The impacts of the legislation were unclear at first, as shown by the two articles cited above. To Pritchett, so much discretion had been removed from government corporations that "American experience with autonomous public corporations is substantially at an end." (p. 509) To V. O. Key, however, enough autonomy remained to keep corporations viable, especially in times of emergency.

214. Commission on Organization of the Executive Branch of the Government, *Reorganization of Federal Business Enterprises*, (March); also *Task Force Report on Revolving Funds and Business Enterprises of the Government* [Appendix J], (January); also *Task Force Report on Lending Agencies* [Appendix R], (January) (Washington, D.C.: USGPO, 1949).

While the various Hoover Commission task force reports that touched on the subject were not entirely consistent, the general theme was to support both the recent standardization and the degree of business-like autonomy that remained. The first report listed above featured a classic defense of the argument that corporations encourage sound business practices, not the political decision-making that permeates the rest of government. The Revolving Fund Task Force tended to support as much autonomy as was consistent with the position of the overall commission, while the Lending Agency Task Force was far more negative.

215. Marshall Dimock, "Government Corporations: A Focus of Policy and Administration, I," *American Political Science Review*, XLIII, (October 1949): 899-921; also "Government Corporations: A Focus of Policy and Administration, II," *American Political Science Review*, XLIII, (December 1949): 1145-64.

Dimock, in one of the better summations of the issues that is available, was concerned by 1949 that reforms had removed so much discretion that government corporations might be disappearing as a recognizable form. To satisfy those who wanted standardization while protecting corporate autonomy, he suggested that groups of related corporations be organized into holding companies. These holding companies would have a "relation" with the secretary of a relevant department, and the secretary would be kept informed on corporation plans, and serve as a liaison to the rest of government.

216.   Harold Seidman, "The Theory of the Autonomous Government Corporation: A Critical Appraisal," *Public Administration Review*, 12, (Spring 1952): 89-96.

Among those advocating more control, Seidman was concerned that Willoughby's original concept of "holding corporations" left out the president as the chief policy-maker. As a result, "unless Willoughby's interpretation of the President's role is accepted, the theory of the autonomous corporation cannot be reconciled with the American constitutional system." (p. 95)

217.   Annemarie Hauck Walsh, *The Public's Business: The Politics and Practice of Government Corporations* (Cambridge: MIT Press, 1978).

Governmental corporations continued to grow, however, as documented by this 1978 study sponsored by the Twentieth Century Fund. "Public enterprise has thrived in the United States because, with few exceptions, it has proved satisfactory--indeed profitable--for particular segments of business and government." (p. 332)

Walsh was not content with the excess of managerial discretion, however, that often places corporate managers outside the reach of elected officials. Therefore, she advocated several reforms, including that corporate budgets be integrated with overall governmental budgets, that the leadership be made responsive to elected officials, and that there be more performance controls and administrative decentralization within government corporations.

218.   Harold Orlans, ed., *Government-Sponsored Nonprofits* (Washington, D.C.: National Academy of Public Administration, November 1978).

On June 8, 1978, NAPA held a conference on the government sponsorship of nonprofit organizations. This is a reprint of the papers presented, with summations of the discussions that accompanied the presentations. As is the case in any conference, the themes depended on the presenter. There was a general agreement that nonprofits allowed quick demonstration projects outside the boundaries of congressional hesitancy and regulation. Harold Seidman also noted that it created "twilight zone" agencies that allowed the president and congress to play "shell games" with the budget.

However, these demonstration projects were not the "real thing," in that they were pilot projects and they were able to avoid the rules by which normal projects live or die.

PRIVATIZATION VS. CONTRACTING OUT

In the years following the New Deal, government ownership slipped quietly from the list of hot topics that dominated public administration literature. There are three likely reasons why. Between the 1930s and the 1960s, the corporate form stopped being adopted as frequently as it had in earlier years. Second, the Government Corporation Control Act had narrowed the options for potential abuse. Finally, the behavioral revolution took hold in public administration and squeezed out older agenda.

The Department of Defense and other highly technological agencies kept the subject alive under the general title of contracting out. However, most of that literature related to a specialized policy area that primarily concerned the federal level (except for a few studies in technology transfer). Of more interest here are the studies that finally merged with government ownership literature in the 1970s under the label of privatization.

As is discussed below, the definition(s) of privatization depend upon who is being asked. However, whereas contracting is an economic arrangement in a market of multiple potential suppliers with government as a single consumer, privatization is both an economic and a political arrangement that is promoted as giving each citizen some choice as to both goods and suppliers. In this way, effective economic competition, and its benefits, are hopefully restored to government services.

219.   Michael D. Reagan, *The Managed Economy* (New York: Oxford University Press, 1963).

This book was a prelude--an indicator of the kinds of questions asked about contracting before the privatization literature began in earnest. Reagan's central point was that the distinction between the public and private sectors died in 1929. Stated more theoretically, the distinction between economic and political power that provided a basis of the constitution no longer made sense. Instead, with the sectors mixed, more societal control over business was required.

On the issue of contracting, Reagan saw the issue as another device for mixing the sectors. In what Don Price has called "federalism by contract," Reagan noted the way in which defense and space contracts have been used to redistribute resources at the local level. He cited concerns of regulatory capture and conflict of interest within advisory bodies, and insisted that contracting, like big business in general, needs to be recognized as a form of political power.

220.   Mancur Olson, *Logic of Collective Action* (Cambridge: Harvard University Press, 1965); also

221.   Gordon Tullock, *The Politics of Bureaucracy* (Washington, D.C.: The Public Affairs Press, 1965); also editor of *Papers on Non-Market Decision Making*, 1, (Spring 1968) [later renamed *Public Choice*]; also *Private Wants, Public Means* (New York: Basic Books, 1970); also

222.   Vincent and Elinor Ostrom, "Public Choice: A Different Approach to the Study of Public Administration," *Public Administration Review*, 31, (March/April 1971): 203-16; also

223.   William A. Niskanen, Jr., *Bureaucracy and Representative Government* (Chicago: Aldine Publishers, 1971).

In Public Administration, however, privatization literature began less in political economy and more in political theory, under the general rubric of "public choice."

It is a field that developed through the interaction of a relatively small group of scholars, and these are among the works that are most frequently cited as being formative. Olson, in describing the conditions under which coalitions are built, noted that large voluntary associations arise to pursue public goods only when substantial private rewards are expected. Tullock described the high social costs of decision-making that he expects in governmental bureaucracies as ambitious public employees distort information to enhance their own careers.

The solution to the high social costs of unified decision-making, as described by the Ostroms and several articles in *Public Choice*, is given the name "public choice." Niskanen, who was introduced to the arguments by Tullock, suggested several procedural changes to increase competition within the federal government. More generally, the proponents argued, citizen-consumers need to be offered competing organizations through "overlapping jurisdictions" for the delivery of services. This will force high performance and efficient operations in an environment that does not otherwise require it.

224.   Peter F. Drucker, *The Age of Discontinuity* (New York: Harper and Row, 1969).

One of the first statements on privatization by name did not come from Public Administration or Political Economy.[7] Drucker, who was concerned with world-wide societal changes, devoted one section of his book to the evolving roles of organizations. In Chapter 8, he noted the "new pluralism" that has faded the public-private distinction. Most importantly, in Chapter 10, he suggested that government cannot be managed, and is not designed to be efficient. Instead, through a process he called "reprivatization," he suggested that government should be the decision-maker while the private sector should compete for the delivery of the selected goods.

225.   Robert L. Bish and Robert Warren, "Scale and Monopoly Problems in Urban Government Services, *Urban Affairs Quarterly*, 8, (September 1972): 97-122.

Privatization came into its own, however, at the level of urban service delivery. Bish and Warren used examples of education by contract, private fire protection, the "Lakewood Plan," and intergovernmental subcontracting in Southern California to demonstrate that problems of scale and monopoly must be considered together. In many cases, centralization is inappropriate, and privatization can result in a selection of service delivery options for diverse political subdivisions, and in increased efficiency as public authorities are put under nonpolitical incentives.

226.   Bruce L. R. Smith, ed., *The New Political Economy: The Public Use of the Private Sector* (London: Macmillan Press, Ltd., 1975).[8]

This study, sponsored as part of the Carnegie Corporation's series on accountability in the "new political economy," was designed as "an exercise in political theory." Following Drucker's lead, it was based in a belief that a new public sector has emerged which gains much of its energy from outside the government. These new sources are not just in the private sector, but in sectors which defy classification.
Several authors, including Staats, Seidman, [Michael] Reagan, and Sharkansky developed different aspects of the study, which Smith categorized as broad views, case studies, and devices and instrumentalities. While the book carries no theme, it concentrates near the end on the way in which the new interdependence has made it possible for agency independence and accountability to increase at the same time.

227.   Daniel Guttman and Barry Willner, *The Shadow Government* (New York: Pantheon Books, 1976); also

228.   Ira Sharkansky, "Policy Making and Service Delivery on the Margins of Government: The Case of Contractors," *Public Administration Review*, 40, (March/April 1980): 116-23.

Of course, not all scholars are as enthusiastic, as is reflected in these works. Guttman and Willner's book, which carries an introduction by Ralph Nader, openly attacks "The Shadow Government" for promising too much and delivering too little. Case by case, the authors retold the stories of such respected accomplishments as PPBS, MBO, PERT, and incentive contracts to argue that they do not perform well or have been misused. More disturbingly, they described numerous cases of flagrant rule violations and conflicts of interest.
Sharkansky, noting some estimates that more people work under contract to the federal government than work *for* the government, and noting the general lack of consensus on the forms and purposes of contracting, expressed his concern that political theory could be rendered obsolete by a workforce that does not answer to

the traditional political controls. Like Guttman and Willner, he felt that government agencies have abandoned their responsibilities through excessive contracting.

229.   Emanuel S. Savas, ed., *Alternatives for Delivering Public Services* (Boulder, CO: Westview Press, 1977); also *Privatizing the Public Sector* (Chatham, NJ: Chatham House Publishers, 1982).

Obviously, Savas did not invent the arguments of public choice or of privatization. However, he can reasonably be credited with bringing the two together. He divided public services into private goods, common pool goods, toll goods, and collective goods based on their divisibility and barriers of access. Comparing each type to existing delivery systems, he proposed four reforms for government: the reduction of some government subsidies; increased private participation in some service delivery; user charges; and increased governmental competition.

230.   Donald Fisk, Herbert Kiesling, and Thomas Muller, *Private Provision of Public Services: An Overview* [Report URI 18300] (Washington, D.C.: The Urban Institute, 1978).

This study, funded by the National Commission on Productivity, attempted to provide an overview of ten areas of contracting, and offered a set of recommendations for the future. The study members found that the most common form of contracting is still the performance contract. In general, they recommended that local governments continue to survey the efficacy of private contracts, and that state and local governments reduce restrictions and provide technical assistance so that such contracts can expand when appropriate.

231.   Patricia S. Florestano and Stephen B. Gordon, "Public vs. Private: Small Government Contracting With the Private Sector," *Public Administration Review*, 40, (January/February 1980): 29-34.

Unlike many statistical studies in this area, which try to show which option is cheaper, this survey of 89 municipalities measured the extent and purposes of contracting-out. The authors discovered that most services are still delivered in-house, although small size and geography (North Central states) increase the practice of contracting. Those services under contract are most often of a professional or housekeeping nature.

232.   Jeffrey D. Straussman, "More Bang for Fewer Bucks? Or How Local Governments Can Rediscover the Potentials (and Pitfalls) of the Market," *Public Administration Review*, 41, (January 1981) [Special Issue]: 150-58.

Straussman advocated privatization and contracting as part of a larger phenomenon--the return to "first principles" as a result of fiscal stress. "These first principles are deceptively simple. Market mechanisms--price, choice, and competition-- should be used both to curb expenditure growth and to stimulate improved public sector performance." (p. 150) He discussed contracting, user fees, privatization, public sector-private sector competition, and competitive bureaus, as possible tactics to accomplish these ends. While he acknowledged that there are good traditional arguments against these tactics, he felt that there was a case for experimentation.

233. Thomas Borcherding, Werner W. Pommerehne, and Freidrich Schneider, "Comparing the Efficiency of Public and Private Production: The Evidence From Five Countries," *Zeitschrift für Nationalökonomie: Journal of Economics*, Supplement 2 (1982): 127-56;[9] also

234. Thomas Borcherding, "Toward a Positive Theory of Public Sector Supply Arrangements," in J. Robert S. Prichard (ed.), *Crown Corporations in Canada: The Calculus of Instrument Choice* (Toronto: Butterworth & Co., Ltd., 1983), pp. 99-184.

Recent literature is filled with surveys and case studies attempting to demonstrate that either governmental production or contracting is the more attractive alternative, and it would go beyond the scope of this work to describe more than an inadequate sampling of them. However, at a seminar in public economics held in Bonn in 1981 (1982 publication date), these economists reviewed more than 50 studies covering such conventional targets of contracting as utilities, refuse collection, and hospitals. Overwhelmingly (40 to 3), the studies found private-sector delivery to be less expensive. An additional five found no difference or mixed results. The authors also noted that costs between the sectors became closer as public-sector competition for delivery of the service increased.

In 1983, Borcherding reviewed two centuries of literature to build a theoretical framework to explain why private production of public goods would be cheaper. His argument, which he warned provided only a "vision of a model," leaned heavily on the reasoning of Niskanen in explaining the behavior of those put in charge of production decisions.

235. Stuart Butler, *Privatizing Public Spending: A Strategy to Eliminate the Deficit* (Washington, D.C.: Heritage Foundation, 1985).

Tying privatization to the goals of the Reagan administration, Butler argued that the budget could not be cut by supply-side measures alone. Instead, conservatives also had to attack the demand-side of coalition politics. Butler recommended three strategies used by Prime Minister Thatcher in Britain: contracting out; deregulation of statutory monopolies and licensing barriers; and denationalization.

236.   Dick Netzer, "Privatization," in Charles Brecher and Raymond D. Horton,
        eds., *Setting Municipal Priorities, 1984* (New York: New York University Press,
        1983), pp. 158-87.[10]

Reviewing the standard arguments for privatization in terms of their applicabil-
ity to New York City, Netzer found that many could be dismissed. Volunteerism was
falling off. He found little support that the private sector is cheaper or more efficient, except in one study of solid waste removal conducted by Savas. Usually, small
towns contract out (and provide data for the concept's proponents) because they
cannot provide the service, and not because of any analysis.

Netzer was not anti-privatization, however. He claimed there were two lessons
to be learned from the record. First, privatization is more efficient when quantifiable
products are needed in geographically dispersed areas. Second, governments are often
able to overcome many of the traps often described by opponents of contracting. In
short, decisions on contracting should be highly specific to the agency and the service.

237.   Ted Kolderie, "The Two Different Concepts of Privatization," *Public Adminis-
        tration Review*, 46, (July/August 1986): 285-91.

Stating a concern similar to that of Sharkansky's, Kolderie pointed out the dangers in confusing the different forms of privatization. To Kolderie, government
performs two potential functions: the decision to provide the service and the production of the service. Contracting out the second, he suggested, carries all the potential benefits of reduced cost and added efficiency. Contracting out the first, which
Butler called "complete privatization," would abandon government's role as a force
for social equity unless additional income subsidies are guaranteed.

CONTINUING CONCERNS

Government ownership of public utilities has come full circle in the last century.
In the 1880s, corporate advances made it possible for the first time for the private
sector to provide many of the services that had previously been the responsibility of
government. The major arguments for private development of utilities and other
services were efficiency and the control of corruption. The major arguments for
governmental development were social equity and the control of corruption.

In the interim, both sides won. Government corporations and private utilities
both developed beyond the goals they originally set. By 1945, both government regulation and government ownership worked within legislated rules, and the issue seemed
to be put to rest.

In recent years, however, there has been a slow reemergence of the issue using
arguments that are surprisingly similiar to those of the previous century. The litera-

ture is not as technical, and it is often stated in more political, and less economic, terms. It has a new name--privatization--and this time it faces no Progressive coalition demanding new regulations.

The arguments, however, are approximately the same. Within obvious constraints, we stand again at the old fork in the road, and have the opportunity to reassess our earlier decision.

NOTES FOR CHAPTER SIX

1. Max Radin, *The Legislation of the Greeks and Romans on Corporations* (New York: Columbia University Press, 1909), pp. 92-97.

2. See Edward Bemis (p. 19) reviewed in this section.

3. Perhaps because it muddied the example, the debates of the time almost always ignored the Panama Railroad Company, which the United States government acquired in 1904.

4. The course was taught at the University of Wisconsin in 1907. See Richard T. Ely, "Editor's Introduction," in Martin Glaeser, *Outlines of Public Utility Economics* (New York: Macmillan, 1927), p. xi.

5. In addition to William Mosher as editor, the book lists Finla G. Crawford, Ralph E. Himstead, Maurice R. Scharff, A. Blair Knapp, Richard L. Schank, and Louis Mitchell as coauthors.

6. This was a joint release by the two publishing houses.

7. The origin of the term is obscure, but dates at least to Carl J. Friedrich and Taylor Cole, *Responsible Bureaucracy: A Study of the Swiss Civil Service* (Cambridge: Harvard University Press, 1932), p. 86.

8. The book was published first in London. However, since it consisted primarily of American authors describing the American experience, it was soon released as (New York: John Wiley and Sons, 1975).

9. This English-language journal, published by Springer-Verlag in New York, is printed in Austria. The supplements are issued occasionally, and are not given volume numbers.

10. This source is not rare. However, of all the works reviewed here, this may be the one that gives the cataloguing systems of American libraries the most trouble. There was a set of these books published annually, obviously with the year changed in each title. While they look like books, they are normally classified as an irregular journal. OCLC's listing is so misleading as to be unidentifiable. The Library of Congress call number is HJ9289/ N4S47.

7
The Agency's Political Milieu

BACKGROUND

Since their creations, governmental agencies have dealt with each other and with other political organizations through carefully prescribed rules. However, by most accounts, the crisis of the Great Depression intensified the need for mutual cooperation, and permanently reshaped the importance of the relationships.

The next four chapters are devoted to the external political environment of executive-branch agencies. This chapter concentrates on interactions between the agencies and their chief executives, the legislatures, and the courts. It also includes writings on the constitutional legitimacy and role of the bureaucracy in a system of separation of powers.

Chapter eight discusses federalism in the context of relations between executive agencies and their counterparts at other levels of government. Chapter nine discusses agency relations with the public and the press, while chapter ten reviews questions of democratic control.

It is important to note that the artificial divisions between the topics that are used to organize these three chapters are often not reflected in the literature. More specialized but overlapping literature can be found in the chapters on decision-making (expertise), regulation, staffing, and budgeting, as well as under related headings within these four chapters.

THE AGENCY AS A POLITICAL ACTOR

238. E(ward) Pendleton Herring, *Public Administration and the Public Interest* (New York: McGraw Hill, 1936); also *The Politics of Democracy* (New York: W. W. Norton and Co., 1940).

Herring's works, which are described separately in chapter four, were groundbreaking in their appreciation of the political role of both governmental regulation and administration. As then constituted, Herring did not see the administration as being very powerful. However, he felt that the legitimate role of the bureaucracy was "the burden of reconciling group differences and making effective and workable the economic and social compromises arrived at through the legislative process." (1936, p. 7) In his acceptance of bureaucracy's political role during the era of the politics-administration dichotomy, Herring's perspective was ahead of its time.

239. Norton E. Long, "Power and Administration," *Public Administration Review*, 9, (Autumn 1949): 257-64.

It was Long's article, however, which is now credited with popularizing the argument that "the lifeblood of administration is power." Following Herring's lead, Long stated that administration could not be explained in entirely rational terms because its components represent an assortment of political interests and pressure groups. For Public Administration to progress, he felt, it must dedicate itself to studying the nature of political power in bureaucracy.

240. Paul Appleby, *Policy and Administration* (University: University of Alabama Press, 1949).

Similarly, Appleby argued that administrators are in the business of making policy, through both rule-making and decisions, and through direct lobbying. "The great distinction between government and other organized undertakings is to be found in the wholly political character of government. The great distinction between public administration and other administration is likewise to be found in the political character of public administration." (p. 12) Accordingly, he offered an eightfold classification of government agencies based on their responsiveness to political controls.

241. Herbert Kaufman, "Emerging Conflicts in the Doctrines of Public Administration," *American Political Science Review*, 50, (December 1956): 1057-73.

Kaufman argued that the goals of administrative reformers have not been permanent, but have evolved through a succession of three political values: representativeness, politically neutral competence, and executive leadership. The value dominating at any one time would determine the nature and purposes of political-administrative relationships.

At first, reformers of the second and third types were allies, although in more recent times, "the tendencies toward division reinforce each other." Kaufman speculated, obviously incorrectly, that neutral competence would eventually become the focus of the American Society for Public Administration while executive leadership forces would become clustered in the American Political Science Association.

242.   Marver H. Bernstein, *The Job of the Federal Executive* (Washington, D.C.: Brookings Institution, 1958).

Bernstein summarized the results of a set of roundtable discussions chaired by Wallace Sayre in 1957 on the roles of political and career executives in the top ranks of the federal government. While some of the themes go beyond the scope of this section, the panel agreed that, above about GS-13, virtually all career executives are involved in policy-making. Also, career positions are varied, and differ from each other more than from political positions.

"The impact of presidential staffs upon departmental staffs is likely to be only as great as the secretary and under secretary permit." (p. 71) Interagency rivalries are often intense. Congressional relations are even "more complex, more subtle, and more detailed." Political parties are far less influential than interest groups. The group also included suggestions for both career and political executives on how to work with each other.

243.   Peter Woll, *American Bureaucracy* (New York: W. W. Norton and Co., 1963).

"American bureaucracy is deeply involved in the political process, a fact all too often overlooked or underplayed in the literature of political science." Woll considered the political role of bureaucracy in several different respects. He noted the constitutional and democratic questions that are raised by the administrative state, and analyzed bureaucracy's political relations with both congress and the chief executive. The constitutional questions are discussed separately later in this chapter.

As a general theme, he concluded that the bureaucracy serves as a balancing agent, too legislatively important to be controlled by the president and more representative than the congress. Bureaucratic politics, therefore, is a force that helps protect the democratic system.

244.   Matthew Holden, "'Imperialism' in Bureaucracy," *American Political Science Review*, 60, (December 1966): 943-51.

Holden contended that bureaucratic imperialism is inevitable because the first necessity of the administrative politician is to gather sufficient resources for his or her agency. The strategies of imperialism, however, vary according to such factors as the agency disposition, the occasions for allocation decisions, and the modes of resolution.

245.   Harvey Sherman, *It All Depends* (University: University of Alabama Press, 1966).

Like Holden, Sherman felt that appropriate bureaucratic strategies in the political world are variable. However, Sherman developed the point more forcefully by arguing that even variable principles would not work since "organizing is still more an art than a science." While his book is about internal organization more than bureaucratic politics, he felt that both problems are dominated by complexity ("what's 'true' in one case is often not 'true' in another") and dynamics ("what's 'true' today is not 'true' tomorrow").

246.   Anthony Downs, *Inside Bureaucracy* (Boston: Little, Brown and Co., 1967).

Downs agreed with the general theme of the literature in his central hypothesis that bureaucrats are motivated by self-interest. However, whereas Sherman felt that the forms of that motivation are too varied to be usably described, Downs felt they could be differentiated into five categories of bureaucrats: climbers, conservers, zealots, advocates, and statesmen. Further development of each of these types, he argued, could lead to predictions on the forms of bureaucratic politics that would be practiced.

247.   Theodore J. Lowi, *The End of Liberalism* (New York: W. W. Norton and Co., 1969).

To at least one observer, bargaining within the bureaucracy is dangerous for the political system, because it is the lifeblood of interest-group liberalism. Lowi attacked such liberalism because it corrupts democratic government by rewriting formal policies during implementation, by rendering government incapable of planning, by making it impossible to achieve justice, and by weakening the ability to live by democratic formalisms. His solution was to recentralize representativeness into the policy-making machinery of the constitution, and to insist that the bureaucracy implement the formalisms enacted there.

248.   Francis E. Rourke, *Bureaucracy, Politics, and Public Policy* (Boston: Little, Brown, and Co., 1969).

Most of the literature, however, chose to study bureaucratic politics as a fact of life, rather than to try to eliminate it. As Rourke explained in a book that was often used as a text, "it is the role of bureaucracy in the policy process which is at the center of concern in this book." (p. vii) Throughout Rourke's study, bureaucracy was treated as one of the political forces that has arisen to help formulate public policy.

It is not the dominant force, except in the way that many policy forces control certain decisions over which they have a structural advantage. However, Rourke felt that the bureaucracy's role in policy formulation has become too fundamental to be ignored.

249.   Harold Seidman, *Politics, Position, and Power: The Dynamics of Federal Organization* (New York: Oxford University Press, 1970).

Seidman continued the theme that "organizational arrangements are not neutral" (p. 14), especially in regard to reorganization, which has "become almost a religion in Washington." (p. 3)[1] He attacked the organizational orthodoxy that he felt continues to dominate government and its reformers. Instead, he described the roles of organizational culture, the president, and congress in administrative processes. He also described in separate chapters the ways in which agencies can operate effectively in influencing each of the other political actors.

250.   Douglas M. Fox, *The Politics of City and State Bureaucracy* (Pacific Palisades, CA: Goodyear Publishing, 1974).

At the local level, Fox similarly found that "neglect of bureaucratic politics is especially notable in the literature on urban and state politics." (p. 1) In his exploratory book on the subject, he described the degree to which the power of local bureaucracies has grown through structural fragmentation, weak executives and legislatures, and agency ties to interest groups and advisory boards. All of these, he felt, make the subject worthy of further study.

EXECUTIVE RELATIONS

The books above are among those most frequently cited on the general subject of bureaucratic politics. It has been a popular subject, and more could be cited. From the beginning, however, most of the literature on bureaucratic politics has not been so broadly focused. Rather, the literature is often limited to contacts between bureaucratic agencies and one of the other political institutions to such an extent that the other political institution often seems to be the subject of the research. In this review, considerable arbitrary judgment has been used to separate those works that focus on interagency relations from other, often more important classics on the executive, legislature, and judiciary, but whose interest in the bureaucracy is too marginal to be relevant here.

251.   James Bryce, *The American Commonwealth*, 2 vol. (London: Macmillan and Co., 1888).

Questions of executive control of the "administration" became a popular topic in the political literature of the 1880s as reflected by Bryce and, of course, Woodrow Wilson. In the chapter on the cabinet of Bryce's classic work, he noted that "(i)n America the Administration does not work as a whole. It is not a whole. It is a group of persons, each individually dependent upon and answerable to the President, but with no joint policy, no collective responsibility." He also detailed the way in which appointments often went to those to whom the president owed his office, rather than vice versa.

252.   Leonard D. White, *Trends in Public Administration* (New York: McGraw-Hill, 1933).

During FDR's administration, literature concentrated on the increasing and desirable control of the bureaucracy by the president. As White summarized in a book whose theme was the centralization of government, "the departments have lost their independent and uncoordinated position and have been coordinated into a single national administrative machine." (p. 174)

253.   The President's Committee on Administrative Management, *Report of the President's Committee, Administrative Management in the Government of the United States* (Washington, D.C.: USGPO, January 1937).

For relations between the bureaucracy and chief executives, the Brownlow committee report long stood as orthodoxy. Like almost all works before Norton Long's, the power relationship spelled out in Brownlow was unidirectional. "Stated in simple terms these canons of efficiency require the establishment of a responsible and effective chief executive as the center of energy, direction, and administrative management; the systematic organization of all activities in the hands of a qualified personnel under the direction of the chief executive; and to aid him in this, the establishment of appropriate managerial and staff agencies." (p. 2)

The approach was orthodox, but hardly naïve. The committee's approach greatly appreciated the policy-making ability of the bureaucracy, but considered the power of the subordinates to be an usurpation of the potential that could be accomplished by a unified executive.

254.   Arthur W. Macmahon and John D. Millett, *Federal Administrators* (New York: Columbia University Press, 1939).

Macmahon and Millett used the biographical method to determine what federal administrators did, based on their belief that practice often precedes theory. By examining recent secretaries, and every assistant and undersecretary who ever served, they concluded that departments had neither political nor administrative coherence.

At the top level, secretaries had three tasks: dealing with policy determination and execution; promoting coordination within and without the department; and liberating the energies of the operating units. To perform these functions, they needed separate contacts and staffs for their administrative roles and for their advisory roles. They needed to be accessible. However, to be useful advisors to the president, they also needed to be freed from administrative details.

255. Norman M. Pearson, "The Budget Bureau: From Routine Business to General Staff," *Public Administration Review*, 3, (Spring 1943): 126-49; also

256. Fritz Morstein Marx, "The Bureau of the Budget: Its Evolution and Present Rôle, I," *American Political Science Review*, 39, (August 1945): 653-84; also "The Bureau of the Budget: Its Evolution and Present Rôle, II," *American Political Science Review*, 39, (October 1945): 869-98.

Both authors described the evolution of the Bureau of the Budget from the advocate of business management that it became under its first director Charles Dawes "into a broader instrument of management" in the 1930s and 1940s. Marx was somewhat more impressed with the management philosophy in the original Budget and Accounting Act (42 Stat. 20 (1921)). However, both agreed that particularly under Harold D. Smith, the Bureau became an active presidential adviser that laid its stress "on the connection between budgeting and executive management."

257. Marshall E(dward) Dimock, *The Executive in Action* (New York: Harper and Brothers, 1945).

New Deal-era literature was largely united in the need for presidential coordination of unified bureaucracy. However, different scholars often looked for tools to accomplish the coordination in different places. Based on his experience in the Recruitment and Manning Organization of the War Shipping Administration, Dimock argued that "there are few faults of bureaucracy more serious than lack of co-ordination." However, as he looked at the available resources for his program to emphasize leadership, coordination, and structural antidotes to bureaucracy, he decided that "there is no alternative but to make the President's Cabinet the means to that end." (p. 242)

258. Louis Brownlow, *The President and the Presidency* (Chicago: Public Administration Service, 1949).

In this reprint of a set of lectures delivered in 1947, Brownlow reassessed the needs of the president after the changes of the Roosevelt administration. Brownlow still believed that the president's job is "top management," or the shaping of opinions among the highest policy leaders. To get the "authority" to do his job, Brownlow felt, the president needed a number of administrative changes, including a consolidation of top advisors into a manageable number, and an open-ended reorganization act that would allow the president to keep his advisory machinery up-to-date.

259.   Herbert Emmerich, *Essays on Federal Reorganization* (University: University of
        Alabama Press, 1950).

Emmerich found the answer to administrative control in the continuing process
of governmental reorganization. He felt that the test of any reorganization plan is
its ability to make the bureaucracy more responsive to the general interests of the
country, and to strengthen the president's ability to execute the laws faithfully.
        He felt that "(t)here is a persistent, universal drive in the executive establish-
ment for freedom from managerial controls and policy direction." (p. 33) He then
gave one of the more informative insider accounts of the drafting of the Brownlow
and first Hoover reports, concentrating on the presidential management concerns of
both. He concluded with "unfinished business," consisting largely of reforms not yet
implemented six months after the release of the Hoover reports.

260.   Herbert A. Simon, Donald W. Smithburg, and Victor A. Thompson, *Public Ad-
        ministration* (New York: Alfred A. Knopf, 1950).

By 1950, there were skeptics who felt that staff agencies (called overhead agencies) would lead to organizational confusion and a more diverse bureaucracy. In
chapter 13, the authors attacked the myths that staff agencies do not exercise authority, and that they are closer to the executive than are the line agencies.

261.   Richard F. Fenno, Jr., *The President's Cabinet: An Analysis in the Period From
        Wilson to Eisenhower* (Cambridge: Harvard University Press, 1959).

Unlike Dimock, most scholars saw little hope for bureaucratic coordination in
the cabinet. As Fenno contended, the cabinet officers represent constituencies that
are too diverse in a society that runs on pluralistic interests. He argued that reformers who look to the cabinet for help often underestimate the opposition and overes-
timate the unity of the institution of the cabinet.

262.   Richard E. Neustadt, *Presidential Power* (New York: John Wiley and Sons,
        1960).

Neustadt's work was one among many during this era that described presidential
difficulties in controlling the bureaucracy. Neustadt stood alone, however, in arguing
that presidential control over the administration was exercised mainly through persuasion.
        Using case studies as evidence, Neustadt concluded that relatively few presiden-
tial orders are self-executing. In those few cases, Neustadt found that the source of
the order is clear, the message is clear, the message has the necessary publicity, the
resources are available, and the authority to give the order is clear. However, those
circumstances happen "not very often and not very much." Beyond those circumstances, persuasion is the main presidential weapon.

263. Louis W. Koenig, *The Chief Executive* (New York: Harcourt, Brace & World, Inc., 1964); also

264. Dean E. Mann and Jameson W. Doig, *The Assistant Secretaries* (Washington, D.C.: Brookings Institution, 1965).

These authors reflected the growing sentiment in the mid-1960s that the bureaucracy was being pulled beyond presidential control by pluralistic pressures. "The executive branch has not one but two managers--the President and his rival, Congress." (Koenig, p. 160) Koenig suggested that the president needs "a dual organization" of formal machinery and personal staff to maintain coordination.

Mann and Doig studied the "second level" appointees, noting that the appointment process is "highly decentralized and personalized." While incoming administrations avoid those identified with the previous president, the vast majority of appointments have already served in the federal government, and carry or quickly pick up institutional loyalties.

265. Herbert Kaufman, "Administrative Decentralization and Political Power," *Public Administration Review*, 29, (January/February 1969): 3-15; also *Administrative Feedback* (Washington, D.C.: Brookings Institution, 1973); also *Are Government Organizations Immortal?* (Washington, D.C.: Brookings Institution, 1976).

Kaufman was generally an optimist on the ability of the president to control the bureaucracy. His 1969 article acknowledged that "the champions of executive leadership and the evangelists of expanded representativeness have many obstacles to overcome before they have their respective ways." However, he believed that an emerging coalition of chief executives would become an attractive ally for interest groups, and that in the continual cycle of change, executives would be able to establish a stronger power base.

In 1973, he continued to develop a strategy for executives to control the bureaucracy. He found that five strategies--reports, inspections, the "grapevine," investigations, and centralized administrative services--work well. Clients, the media, and disgruntled employees are not reliable sources of information. The biggest problem, however, is not a lack of feedback; it is in finding incentives to encourage agency leaders to use their information.

In 1976, he described in more detail the powers that agencies can use to fight accountability, although he argued that the agencies are losing the battle over time.

266. I. M. Destler, *Presidents, Bureaucrats, and Foreign Policy* (Princeton: Princeton University Press, 1972); also

267. Donald P. Warwick, *A Theory of Public Bureaucracy* (Cambridge, Mass: Harvard University Press, 1975).

In a book about "how the government should be organized for *purposive* and *coherent* foreign policy," Destler ran into largely the same problem that "the bureaucratic politics view of government suggests considerable modesty about just how much coherence and central purpose can be brought to foreign policy." He found that presidents since Franklin Roosevelt have responded to the bureaucracy of the State Department by increasing the role of the White House staff. The State Department employees, on the other hand, have seen the president as "a transient meddler in their business."

Destler suggested that the president attempt to emphasize the importance of the Secretary of State as advisor, and that the Secretary be backed up by several levels of appointments in the State Department from the president's team.

Warwick also tackled the State Department bureaucracy, based on an analysis after the 1965 "simplifying" reorganization. He felt that reform from the top will never work, and that the only hope for reduced bureaucracy will come by convincing those at the bottom that reforms work in their favor.

It should be noted that both books were written before Kissinger was appointed Secretary of State, and his tenure would have provided interesting data for both cases.

268.   Richard P. Nathan, *The Plot that Failed: Nixon and the Administrative Presidency* (New York: John Wiley and Sons, 1975); later revised as *The Administrative Presidency* (New York: John Wiley and Sons, 1983).

From his experience in OMB during Nixon's first term, Nathan catalogued Nixon's experience in finding himself at odds with his cabinet advisors, and in trying in 1973 to adopt an "administrative presidency" strategy to gain control of his own bureaucracy. The strategy, simply defined, involved placing his own people in the line agencies instead of in White House staff offices. He also reorganized functions and issued new regulations.

Nathan was somewhat sympathetic to the concepts of the Administrative Presidency, even though he realized that Nixon had crippled such efforts for a while by surrounding himself with unprincipled advisors.

269.   Dwight Ink, "The President as Manager," *Public Administration Review*, 36, (September/October 1976): 508-15.

As the presidency began its recovery from Watergate, Ink saw continued potential for presidential management despite the long-term challenges to presidential authority of greater state and local power, the blurred separation of powers, and the tendency of programs to cross agency borders. Ink suggested nine strategies to increase presidential managerial power, based primarily in attempts to solicit the help of bureaucrats and other political actors. He ended with the challenge that only the president is in a position to make government manageable.

270.   Richard Rose, *Managing Presidential Objectives* (London: Collier Macmillan, 1976).[2]

In 1974 Nixon, acting through budget officials Roy Ash and Fred Malek, attempted to implement Management by Objectives into government for presidential objectives. Shortly thereafter, Rose used 72 interviews and numerous other sources to try to determine whether it is possible to manage presidential objectives, or whether such objectives even exist. He noted that it is a relatively new concept (by British standards) for U.S. presidents to lead the government, and he recited the limited administrative controls available to the president.

Rose concluded that the original attempt in 1974 was clouded by agency rivalries, hostility, and confusion. However, he was convinced that the effort, particularly in its reduced scale, was useful for identifying some objectives of government, and was probably helpful in implementing nonpolitical objectives.

271.   National Academy of Public Administration, *The President and Executive Management: Summary of a Symposium* (Washington, D.C.: National Academy of Public Administration, 1976).

During the 1976 presidential campaign, 25 members of the Academy participated in a symposium on presidential management, summarized in this report. The participants still shared some of the concerns of Watergate, and they concentrated on the problem that, with the cabinet having no real role as a viable institution, presidents tend to allow White House staffs to grow too large and too diverse to be useful as a management device.

Staffs were considered still to be crucial to presidential management, and the report detailed several options that might improve their utility. In the end, however, the participants reached no consensus.

272.   Hugh Heclo, *A Government of Strangers: Executive Politics in Washington* (Washington, D.C.: Brookings Institution, 1977); also

273.   Thomas P. Murphy, Donald E. Nuechterlein, and Ronald J. Stupak, *The Presidents' Program Directors: The Assistant Secretaries* (Charlottesville, VA: Federal Executive Institute [USGPO], 1977); also *Inside the Bureaucracy: The View from the Assistant Secretary's Desk* (Boulder, CO: Westview, 1978).[3]

Heclo concentrated on another weak link in executive leadership--relations between career bureaucrats and the president's appointees who direct them. The political leaders, whose role Heclo defined as direction-setting and heat-taking, face a proliferating, permeable, interdependent bureaucracy with it own momentum, while "the single most obvious characteristic of Washington's political appointees is their transience."

Managing the bureaucracy, Heclo concluded, could be partially accomplished only through "conditional cooperative behavior," or coalition building and mutual supports between the two groups. He also proposed changes in the higher civil service in the spirit that was later implemented in the Senior Executive Service.

Murphy reported on the findings of a symposium held at the Federal Executive Institute in December 1976. The first publication above is a transcript of the symposium. The second includes summations that describe the powers of assistant secretaries to evade presidential accountability, and it agrees with Heclo's point that career officials are becoming more political while political appointees are becoming more bureaucratic.

274.   Martha Wagner Weinberg, *Managing the State* (Cambridge: M.I.T. Press, 1977).

Weinberg saw many of the same problems of executive control at the state level. Based on her experiences in the governments of Massachusetts and Illinois, Weinberg concluded that traditional models of public-sector management and decision-making do not describe the modern governor. Rather, governors resort to crisis management, driven by incidents as well as issues. Most intervention in the business of agencies is short-termed. At other times, authority is delegated to lower officials, even though the governor frequently has to "intervene" to reaffirm that delegation. The end result is a governor with too many responsibilities to be a "manager" in the private-sector sense.

275.   Frank Kessler, *The Dilemmas of Presidential Leadership: Of Caretakers and Kings* (Englewood Cliffs, NJ: Prentice-Hall, 1982).

Kessler's book was intended as a text for courses on the presidency. In it, he detailed the limits of the presidential staffs, selected by the BUGAT (Bunch uh guys around the table) system. He described the conflicting roles, interagency rivalries, excessive numbers, and personal ambitions of presidential advisors. Combined with all that, the president is caught in the trap that the public expects both leadership and accountability, causing Kessler to wonder why anyone would want the job.

276.   Bert A. Rockman, *The Leadership Question: The Presidency and the American System* (New York: Praeger Publishing Co., 1984).

Rockman expanded the list of constraints on presidential power beyond those listed in Kessler. Rockman considered leadership to be the ability "to impart and sustain direction," effectiveness, and acceptance. He found personal characteristics of the president to be less important in determining leadership than luck and opportunity as constrained by parties, elections, media, public opinion, the constitution, history, and the political culture. For a book that is often cited in public administration sources, however, he spent surprisingly little time discussing presidential relations with the bureaucracy.

277.   Lester M. Salamon and Michael S. Lund, eds., *The Reagan Presidency and the Governing of America* (Washington, D.C.: The Urban Institute, 1984).

This set of edited papers came from a conference called by the Urban Institute in December 1983 on "Governance in the Reagan Era." The papers of most interest here, of course, are the ones that analyze the relationship of the presidency to the bureaucracy. James Ceaser described the simplification of management through the cutting of government's agenda. Lowi noticed, however, that the agenda have been changed more than cut. Edie Goldenberg described the centralization of decision-making in the White House, and the packing of line positions with political appointees. Laurence Lynn analyzed the experiences of five such appointees to show that it is possible for appointees to gain control of their agencies.

278.   James P. Pfiffner, "Political Appointees and Career Executives: The Democracy-Bureaucracy Nexus in the Third Century," *Public Administration Review*, 47, (January/February 1987): 57-64.

Pfiffner argued that the distrust that incoming presidents have felt toward career bureaucrats in recent times has often been misplaced, and that there has usually been a cycle of accommodation between the two. More importantly, the increase in political appointees that has been created in that mistrust has caused the government to operate less efficiently and effectively than would have been the case with fewer inexperienced appointees.

LEGISLATIVE RELATIONS

279.   Woodrow Wilson, *Congressional Government* (Boston: Houghton, Mifflin and Co.: 1885).

The classic statement on legislative-agency relations was, of course, Woodrow Wilson's. "Accordingly [congress] has entered more and more into the details of administration, until it has virtually taken into its own hands all the substantial powers of government." (p. 45) Wilson considered the president to be the executive in theory, but the secretaries to be the executive in fact. That was important since the congress used the budget and other oversight powers to make the secretaries its "humble servants."

280.   Henry Campbell Black, *The Relation of the Executive Power to Legislation* (Princeton: Princeton University Press, 1919); also

281.   Robert Luce, *Legislative Problems* (Boston: Houghton Mifflin, 1935).

While Wilson considered the congress to be dominant, congress itself long worried about executive intrusions into the legislative process. Their major concern was legislation that was proposed and/or drafted by the heads of executive departments. As Luce recalled in his legislative history, this conflict appeared as early as the first congress, when there was considerable concern over legislation drafted by the Secretary of the Treasury. By the end of the Jackson administration, one member of the Ways and Means Committee complained that all their legislation was drafted within the Treasury Department.

Black was still concerned about such practices in 1919, complaining that some were trying to "vest a monopoly of legislative initiative in the executive," (p. 73) and to abandon our principles for parliamentary-style control by the executive over both administration and legislation.

282.   Edwin E. Witte, "The Preparation of Proposed Legislative Measures by Administrative Departments," in *The Exercise of Rule-Making Power and the Preparation of Proposed Legislative Measures by Administrative Departments*, report number V of The President's Committee on Administrative Management [The Brownlow Committee] (Washington, D.C.: USGPO, 1937), pp. 49-65.

In a staff report for the Brownlow Committee, Witte expressed a different concern about the same practice. He feared that the common practice of drafting bills within executive departments was helping to usurp the president's control over the executive branch. Therefore, in implementing the sixteen principles which he felt should govern these activities, he proposed that drafting remain within the departments, but that all drafts be cleared by the Bureau of the Budget, and that the president be given a Legislative Counsel or Secretary to help coordinate executive-legislative activities.

283.   Ernest S. Griffith, *The Impasse of Democracy* (New York: Harrison-Hilton Books, 1939); also *Congress: Its Contemporary Role* (New York: New York University Press, 1951).

Griffith approached the subject from a far more theoretical perspective. He searched the general political trends of industrialized states in the 1930s to determine whether democracy was still a viable form of government. In that investigation, he helped popularize the interest-group approach to government as reflected in congressional politics. Policies were determined by "whirlpools or centers of activity focusing on particular problems." These whirlpools included several participants. "Some are civil servants, some are active members of the appropriate committees in the House and Senate, some are lobbyists, some are unofficial research authorities...or even entirely private individuals." (p. 182)

By 1951, Griffith was less convinced that interest groups dominated congressional activity, even though their presence was pervasive. The book is primarily remembered, however, for its admiration of congress' role in controlling the bureaucracy. Griffith argued that congress not only has the right to become involved in implementation, but that its contribution is essential to honesty, efficiency, and accountability.

284.   Arthur Macmahon, "Congressional Oversight of Administration: The Power of the Purse I," *Political Science Quarterly*, 58, (June 1943): 161-90; also "Congressional Oversight of Administration: The Power of the Purse--II," *Political Science Quarterly*, 58, (September 1943): 380-414.

Macmahon described the change in congressional emphasis over time. Rather than give broad directions, "the legislative body itself seeks to be continuously a participant in guiding administrative conduct and the exercise of discretion." (p. 162) Macmahon also described the power of congressional staffs and appropriations hearings as oversight tools, and appropriations committee reports as means of control.

285.   Lawrence H. Chamberlain, *The President, Congress, and Legislation* (New York: Columbia University Press, 1946).

Nominally, Chamberlain's purpose in studying the legislative history of 90 statutes was to document his conclusion that congress was more important and the president was less important in framing legislation than was commonly believed to be the case. Even when the president appeared to be strong, however, he noted that the leadership often came from the agencies. "The administrative official's interest in and promotion of proposed legislation frequently anticipates presidential action by months and even years." (p. 24) Specifically, in the presidential stronghold of conservation legislation, he repeatedly noted the importance of bureaucrats "working hand-in-hand with members of Congress on the one side and the representatives of private interests on the other." (p. 460)

286.   Arthur Maass, *Muddy Waters: The Army Engineers and the Nation's Rivers* (Cambridge: Harvard University Press, 1951); also

287.   David B. Truman, *The Governmental Process* (New York: Alfred A. Knopf, 1951).

These two works followed Chamberlain's theme on water resources and are now best remembered for expanding the participation in agency-congressional relations into a tripartite relationship. "These devices produce a variety of continuing contacts among legislators--particularly committee chairmen--the administrators and interest groups." (Truman, p. 423)

Both authors used the Army Corps of Engineers to illustrate their points. Truman found it interesting that the Corps' formal (vertical) authority came from the president while its actual (horizontal) authority came from congress. Maass, and particularly Harold Ickes in his Foreword, were more direct. The Army Corps of

Engineers was using a coalition of congressional supporters and private lobbyists to defy presidential orders. The result was a water-use policy that was narrowly defined toward those interests, and not in the public's best interest.

Note: On interest-group politics, see also chapter nine.

288. J(ohn) Leiper Freeman, *The Political Process: Executive Bureau-Legislative Committee Relations* (Garden City: Doubleday, 1955)[4]; also

289. Douglass Cater, *Power in Washington* (New York: Random House, 1964).

Freeman continued the study of the "political subsystems" of the executive bureaus (which are semi-autonomous from the president), the legislative committees (which are semi-autonomous from the congress), and the interest groups (which are semi-autonomous from the political parties). He noted that an increasing amount of legislation was left to these secondary levels, and his book offered a number of propositions on the operations of both bureau chiefs and members of congressional committees.

Almost ten years later, Cater also defined presidential and congressional power as being dispersed, and the real power as residing in the "subgovernments" that dominated decision-making on their particular issues.

290. Joseph P. Harris, *Congressional Control of Administration* (Washington, D.C.: Brookings Institution, 1964).

Harris described the relationship of congress to administration by making a clear distinction between control, which he felt was being overemphasized, and oversight, which he felt could be improved. Oversight implies administrative accountability for implementing congressional actions. Such oversight tools as the audit, he felt, were used ineffectively. Control, however, is applied before or during implementation, and eliminates too much administrative discretion that is needed to get the job done. Harris used Great Britain as an example of a political system that achieved more effective oversight.

291. Richard F. Fenno, *The Power of the Purse* (Boston: Little, Brown, and Co., 1966).

Fenno's book went into detail on the precise structure of the legislative budgetary/oversight process, and the relationships of the agencies to it. Fenno argued that appropriations committees responded to expectations of both the full bodies and the agencies. In questioning agency heads, they would "shake 'em up once in a while," to satisfy oversight needs. However, Fenno argued that it was very important that the committees and the agency heads learn to trust each other, and that the committees serve agency needs as well.

292.   A. Lee Fritschler, *Smoking and Politics* (Englewood Cliffs, NJ: Prentice Hall, 1969).

An example of what happens when the trust between congress and the agency collapses was the subject of Fritschler's *Smoking and Politics*. Reviewing the Federal Trade Commission's attempt to regulate cigarette advertising without giving congress adequate notice, Fritschler was far less enthusiastic about the wisdom with which governmental subsystems control policy-making. By his second edition in 1975, the balance between agency, committee, and interest groups was somewhat restored. However, Fritschler was still ambivalent about the process, and not very impressed with the power of administrative agencies to operate within a subsystem environment.

293.   Morris S. Ogul, *Congress Oversees the Bureaucracy* (Pittsburgh: University of Pittsburgh Press, 1976); also

294.   Edgar Crane, *Legislative Review of Government Programs* (New York: Praeger Publishers, 1977).

These two studies are far more empirical than most in this field. Ogul studied three committees and subcommittees over three years to test his hypothesis that the likelihood of oversight is related to the number of "opportunity factors" that are present. Crane's goal was to review mechanisms then being adopted for legislative overview and program control as state legislatures increasingly absorbed program control responsibilities from the executives.

Both researchers expressed concerns that their data bases were too small and temporal to draw many conclusions. However, Ogul was able to suggest some improvements, including a closer matching of member priorities with committee structures. Crane was also able to draw some preliminary conclusions, and he encouraged additional developments of program review techniques.

295.   Hugh Heclo, "Issue Networks and the Executive Establishment," in Anthony King, ed., *The New American Political System* (Washington, D.C.: American Enterprise Institute for Public Policy Research, 1978), pp. 102-05.

On a more conceptual level, Heclo decided that the permanence reflected in the traditional model of subsystem politics no longer described the workings of interest-group influence over congressional decisions. Rather, he identified "issue networks," consisting of fluid groupings of individuals in and out of government that flow together to try to influence individual policies. These are "shared knowledge" groups that congeal into organized existence only when the issue area arises in the political arena.

296.   Lawrence C. Dodd and Richard L. Schott, *Congress and the Administrative State* (New York: Wiley and Sons, 1979).

Dodd and Schott compared the development of congress and the bureaucracy to argue that congress' shift from committee government (early 1900s-1960s) to sub-committee government (1960s-present) has hindered congress' ability to oversee administration. Increased oversight activity does not result in enhanced surveillance of policy implementation because the subsystem politics has grown too complicated while the bureaucracy has become more autonomous. The solution is not in executive reorganization, but in changing the dynamics of congress.

297.   William Lyons and Larry W. Thomas, "Legislator Attitudes Toward the Feas-
        ibility of Sunset Legislation," *Midwest Review of Public Administration*, 14,
        (March 1980): 3-14; also "Oversight in State Legislatures: Structural-Attitudinal
        Interaction," *American Politics Quarterly*, 10, (January 1982): 117-33; also

298.   William M. Pearson and Van A. Wigginton, "Effectiveness of Administrative
        Controls: Some Perceptions of State Legislators," *Public Administration Re-
        view*, 46, (July/August 1986): 328-31.

Based on legislator surveys conducted in Florida, Missouri, and Tennessee, Lyons and Thomas investigated the ways in which the form of oversight structures affect legislative attitudes on the subject. In 1980, they found that minimal sunset legislation leads to complaints about time and staff problems, whereas more formal structures lead to political intervention. In 1982, they reported that when oversight structures do not exist, the use of oversight is determined by legislator norms. Weak structures lead to partisan uses of oversight, while strong structures lead to partisan and constituency interest uses of oversight.

Pearson and Wigginton surveyed legislators in eight states to discover that, while the legislators do not feel that any methods are overly successful in monitoring the operations of the administrative state, they do put more trust in legislative than in executive means. Most notably, they favor such traditional methods as legislative oversight committees.

299.   U.S. Supreme Court, *INS v Chadha, et al.*, 462 U.S. 919 (1983); also *Bowsher v
        Synar*, 106 S.Ct. 3181 (1986); also

300.   Louis Fisher, "The Administrative World of *Chadha* and *Bowsher*," *Public Ad-
        ministration Review*, 47, (May/June 1987): 213-19.

During the 1980s, the Supreme Court intervened to disallow some forms of congressional control of implementation. *Chadha* declared legislative vetoes, or decisions to overrule administrative decisions by something other than new legislation, to be a violation of constitutional separation of powers. In *Bowsher*, the section of the Gramm-Rudman-Hollings bill that allowed the Comptroller General (an agent of congress) to intervene in spending decisions was similarly struck down. The court declared in 1986 that the constitution "does not contemplate an active role for Congress

in the supervision of officers charged with the execution of the laws it enacts."
Instead, "once Congress makes its choice in enacting legislation, its participation ends.
Congress can thereafter control the execution of its enactment only indirectly--by
passing new legislation."

Fisher, from the Congressional Research Service, offered a constitutional history
of the topic to argue that "the Court presented a highly formalistic model of the
relationship between Congress and the President" that "will not serve the interest of
Congress, the agencies, or government generally."

301.   Allan W. Lerner and John Wanat, "Fuzziness and Bureaucracy," *Public Administration Review*, 43, (November/December 1983): 500-09.

Lerner and Wanat investigated the complaint that bureaucracy often fails to
implement programs correctly by introducing the concepts of "fuzzy" versus "crisp"
mandates from congress. The authors argued that agencies that continually receive
crisp mandates logically develop an emphasis on efficiency and due process, while
agencies with fuzzy mandates logically emphasize effectiveness and high levels of
discussions. Furthermore, the authors felt that both congress and agencies sometimes
intentionally misinterpret fuzzy mandates as crisp and vice versa.

302.   Richard C. Elling, "State Legislative Influence in the Administrative Process:
Consequences and Constraints," *Public Administration Quarterly*, 7, (Winter
1984): 457-81.

Elling tried to determine whether the primary constraints on legislative oversight of administration are institutional or personal. Using surveys of senators and
administrators in Minnesota and Kentucky, he concluded that most legislators feel increasing pressure to perform oversight and program evaluation. However, the available resources in many states are inadequate, and only senior legislators have the
political security and the experience to know how to perform oversight effectively.

JUDICIAL RELATIONS: CONSTITUTIONAL TORTS

Most issues that have arisen in judicial-bureaucratic relations involve government regulations, and that set of literature is discussed in chapter five. However,
two separate issues have occasionally arisen that do not properly fit into the legality
of regulation: to what extent should administrators be legally liable for their actions;
and how effectively can the courts monitor the administration of court-mandated
actions? These two issues are the subject here.

303.   U.S. Supreme Court, *U.S. v Lee,* 106 U.S. 196 (1882); also *Spalding v Vilas*, 161
U.S. 483 (1896); also *Barr v Matteo*, 360 U.S. 564 (1959).

Sovereign immunity for public officials is based in English common law, and was carried over without debate into the American system. As the Supreme Court stated in 1882, "while the exemption of the United States and of the several states from being subjected as defendants from ordinary actions in the courts has...repeatedly been asserted here, the principle has never been discussed or the reasons for it given, but it has always been treated as an established doctrine." (p. 207)

In *Spalding v Vilas*, the court clarified that they meant to protect federal department heads with absolute immunity from being sued. "It would seriously cripple the proper and effective administration of public affairs as entrusted to the executive branch of the government, if he were subject to any such restraint." (p. 498) By a much less convincing consensus, the same concept was carried over into the modern era for a minor official in *Barr v Matteo*.

304. *Federal Tort Claims Act*, 60 Stat. 842 (1946).

The first breach in the concept of immunity came in 1946. The Federal Tort Claims Act gave citizens standing to sue for common law torts (negligent or wrongful acts or omissions) that are committed by federal employees within the scope of their employment. It was important for later developments, however, that the Act did not extend standing to issues of constitutional violations, nor to suits against individual administrators for damages.

305.   U.S. Supreme Court, *Bivens v Six Unknown Named Agents of the Federal Bureau of Narcotics*, 403 U.S. 388 (1971); also *Scheuer v Rhodes*, 416 U.S. 232 (1974); also *Wood v Strickland*, 420 U.S. 308 (1975); also *Smith v Wade*, 461 U.S. 30 (1983).

In 1971, the Supreme Court took a large step towards reversing the concept of absolute immunity for administrators. In a case involving the constitutional rights of a wrongfully arrested person, the court recognized that the ability to act in the name of the federal government gave exceptional powers to do harm. In the Court of Appeals case that followed, and in the other two cases listed above, the courts adopted a limited immunity that did not cover acts of an administrator "if he knew or reasonably should have known that the action he took within his sphere of official responsibility would violate the constitutional rights...or if he took the action with the malicious intention to cause a deprivation of constitutional rights or other injury...." (*Wood*, p. 322) The strongest statement of liability came in *Smith v Wade*, in which the court rejected the need to demonstrate "wrongful intent" as the grounds for collecting damages, arguing instead that "reckless indifference" was sufficient.

306.   Robert G. Vaughn, "The Personal Accountability of Public Employees," *American University Law Review*, 25, (Fall 1975): 85-130.

Vaughn applauded the increasing liability for administrators, except that he felt that it had not gone far enough. He felt that tort acts, which have been permitted for some time, are risk-sharing for all taxpayers; the removal of immunity would be risk-shifting to those causing the blame. He argued that we should have citizen-initiated sanctions against employee misconduct.

307. "Developments in the Law--Section 1983 and Federalism," *Harvard Law Review*, 90, (April 1977): 1133-1361.

This "Note," written anonymously for the *Review*, provided an exhaustive summation of the increased use of 42 U.S.C. 1983, first passed in the Civil Rights Act of 1871 (17 Stat. 13), and revived in the modern era in *Monroe v Pape*, 365 U.S. 167 (1961). The section said:

> Every person who, under color of any statute,
> ordinance, regulation, custom, or usage, of any
> state or territory, subjects or causes to be sub-
> jected, any citizen of the United States or other
> person within the jurisdiction thereof to the
> deprivation of any rights, privileges, or immunities
> secured by the constitution and laws, shall be
> liable to the party injured in an action at law, suit
> in equity or other proper proceeding for redress.

Monroe disallowed a good-faith defense since the penalties were civil, not criminal. While the "Note" supported the new use of the law, it acknowledged the increased judicial restrictions on its use in the 1980s.

308. David H. Rosenbloom, "Public Administrators' Official Immunity and the Supreme Court: Developments During the 1970s," *Public Administration Review*, 40, (March/April 1980): 166-73.

In a particularly concise and useful lay review of the evolving role of official immunity during the 1970s, Rosenbloom described the declining immunity of administrators, but presented the trend as a reasonable attempt by the courts to redress the balance between discretion and individual rights that had been lost in the rise of the administrative state. The harm that was documented in some of the cases of the 1970s, he felt, simply could not have been done in simpler times. Adjustments were needed, and were being made.

309. James D. Carroll, "The New Juridical Federalism and the Alienation of Public Policy and Administration," *American Review of Public Administration*, 16, (Spring 1982): 89-105.

Carroll described the new "juridical federalism" as being adaptive to two other developments in American federalism--the increasing distrust of government, and the "intergovernmental mess." The three components of "juridical federalism" were grants law, administrator liability, and judicial supervision of institutions.

310.   Charles R. Wise, "Suits Against Federal Employees for Constitutional Viola-
        tions: A Search for Reasonableness," *Public Administration Review*, 45,
        (November/December 1985): 845-56.

Wise investigated a sample of Justice Department case files on constitutional torts to argue that the Supreme Court in *Bevins* had created a method for protecting individual rights that had unintended consequences, and that the Department had been trying since then to adjust those consequences. Specifically, suits against federal officials had grown into the thousands, usually against multiple defendants, who usually were found innocent. In a number of cases, most notably *Harlow v Fitzgerald*, 457 U.S. 807 (1982), Wise argued that the court was wrestling with redressing a balance in immunity toward the "good faith" defense.

JUDICIAL RELATIONS: COURT MANDATED ADMINISTRATION

311.   Martin Shapiro, *The Supreme Court and Administrative Agencies* (New York:
        Free Press, 1968).

This book was typical of those published before court mandated administration became an issue of high concern to administrators. Shapiro noted that both courts and agencies are involved in supplemental law-making as they serve as intermediaries between the statutes and individual cases. In 1968, they each worked as advocates of themselves, however, rather than as opponents of the other side. The chief role of the courts was to "legitimate" agency decisions. While there was some friction, described in the book through case studies, there were equal instances of judicial restraint on administrative discretion.

312.   "The Wyatt Case: Implementation of a Judicial Decree Ordering Institutional
        Change," *Yale Law Journal*, 84, (May 1975): 1338-79; also

313.   Abram Chayes, "The Role of the Judge in Public Law Litigation," *Harvard
        Law Review*, 89, (May 1976): 1281-1316.

These two articles described the new role then developing out of the *Wyatt v Aderholt*, 503 F.2d 1305 (5th Cir. 1974) case, in which a federal judge ordered changes in the treatment of mentally impaired persons confined in Alabama. He rejected "lack of funds" as a "legally insufficient reason" for the state's failing to meet its constitutional obligations. Chayes' article, not explicitly about *Wyatt*, described the new process of on-going affirmative decrees. He felt that there were problems to be worked out, but that the new role was workable and inevitable in our regulated society.

314.   Donald L. Horowitz, *The Courts and Social Policy* (Washington, D.C.: Brookings Institution, 1977).

Horowitz documented the intrusion of judicial rulings into administrative decisions over the previous two decades with some concern. The difficulty was that the tools of adjudication that have been honed to decide individual cases are not always well-adapted to making general policy. He was concerned that the cases are plaintiff-driven, piecemeal, and focused on the complaint rather than the systemic problem. Methods of gathering evidence, including fact-finding, are not general enough to include the impacts of general changes in policies. As a result, broadly-sweeping policies are delivered within narrow frameworks.

Horowitz suggested several improvements that could make the judicial process more effective in its new role, including the expanded use of social science research in its arguments. He also cautioned that restraint should be used by the courts in these broad decisions.

315.   Richard Neely, *How Courts Govern America* (New Haven: Yale University Press, 1981).

Neely, an appellate judge, wrote an interesting and lively defense from the "inside." His principle thesis is that American courts are the central institution that make American democracy work. They have had no consistent philosophy over time, but have adjusted "to supply corrective balance to institutional weaknesses," even when they have had to label their concerns as "procedural due process."

Neely had little faith in administrative accountability, noting that only two officers in the three-million-member executive branch are elected, and that those two cannot control the rest. In the past, independent boards and commissions have been created to pass unpalatable legislation and reduce corruption. The courts, Neely felt, are also available to step in when the political system cannot do what needs to be done.

316.   David H. Rosenbloom, "Public Administrators and the Judiciary: The 'New Partnership'," *Public Administration Review*, 47, (January/February 1987): 75-83.

As discussed in chapter five, Rosenbloom felt at first that many of the judicial interventions into policy-making were beneficial because they improved areas needing reform, such as the treatment of prisoners. By 1987, however, he was far more concerned about the tensions that have been raised by the new judicial activism. He described five possible reactions that might develop, including coping, convergence, judicial withdrawal, expansion of judicial intervention, or the evolution of a new administrative culture. However, he hazarded no guess as to which might be adopted.

THE CONSTITUTIONAL ROLE OF THE BUREAUCRACY

In recent years, a new perspective has arisen that reflects lingering concerns on such issues as bureaucratic politics, the politics-administration dichotomy, and the rise of the administrative state. That perspective is that the role of bureaucracy in our constitutional system may have been misunderstood by much of the field, or alternatively may have changed to fill a function left vacant as the relative power and purposes of the original branches of government have shifted. In either case, the administrative state can be used to fulfill some of the original purposes of the constitution in different forms.

317.   Joseph Story, *Commentaries on the Constitution of the United States,* 3 vol. (Boston: Hilliard, Gray and Co., 1833); also

318.   Charles M. Wiltse, "The Representative Function of Bureaucracy," *American Political Science Review,* 35, (June 1941): 510-16; also

319.   Norton E. Long, "Bureaucracy and Constitutionalism," *American Political Science Review,* 46, (September 1952): 808-18.

No work can be clearly labelled as the beginning of this literature since there is no way to differentiate the strictly "political science" questions of separation of powers from ones relevant to public administration. Justice Story fit between the two approaches in his concern that we do not allow members of the executive branch to be members of congress. As a result, we require the executive to resort to subterfuge to get its measures introduced into congress. Should we change, he speculated that joint members would have to possess enough talent that they could defend their positions in open debate.

Both Wiltse and Long advanced the more recent argument that the bureaucracy is able to substitute for the representative role of congress which, according to Wiltse, collapsed with the rise of modern technology. Long encouraged the use of personnel recruitment and other tactics to develop an even more representative bureaucracy to supplement congress' limited success.

320.   Peter Woll, *American Bureaucracy* (New York: W. W. Norton and Co., 1963).

A second variation on the argument, that the bureaucracy is not solely part of the executive, was popularized by Woll. "Although technical constitutional norms prevail, the constitutional system to limit governmental power through the separation of powers no longer functions in the manner or to the degree thought necessary by the framers of the Constitution." (p. 12) Woll noted the constitutional provisions that involve a sharing of control over the bureaucracy. He justified such developments as administrative adjudication as an extension of the legislature and the judiciary, and he cited arguments on the representative value of the administrative machinery.

321.   Vincent Ostrom, *The Intellectual Crisis in American Public Administration* (University: University of Alabama Press, 1973).

A different approach to the profound impact of the bureaucracy on the constitution was taken by Ostrom. To Ostrom, Woodrow Wilson and his ideological compatriots created a problem in that they had abandoned an earlier philosophy of constitutionally fragmented authority for a centralized, bureaucratic state. The solution was not in more representativeness, but in a return to the fragmentation and increased choices of the earlier era.

322.   Don K. Price, *America's Unwritten Constitution: Science, Religion, and Political Responsibility* (Baton Rouge: LSU Press, 1983).

Taking the opposite stand, Price felt that fragmentation and increased choices have caused a loss of confidence in our system because it leads to a fixation with practical concerns, but no really coherent overall policies. Stated differently, our unwritten constitution, defined by our fixed political customs, troubles us more than our written constitution. Our distrust of authority and lack of faith in perfectability has led to a system of individualized rights and powers, for bureaucrats as well as for citizens. Unlike the British, we believe discretion and accountability to be opposites, so we tie the hands of all potential leaders.

The answer is to change attitudes, not the constitution. The public needs to loosen the immediate accountability that it demands from legislators, so that congress can grant the executive the flexibility it needs for effective management.

323.   James Sundquist, *Constitutional Reform and Effective Government* (Washington, D.C.: Brookings Institution, 1986).

Sundquist noted a general uneasiness with our stalemated form of government, and he examined five problems that have led to proposals for reform. These include divided partisan control of the legislature and presidency, the shortness of terms leading to perennial campaigning, the inability to remove a failed government in a timely fashion, the lack of collaboration between the branches, and numerous difficulties in the mechanics of checks and balances.

Sundquist then described nine "ideal" amendments to the constitution, including team political tickets, extended congressional terms, special elections, dual officeholding, limited item veto, restoration of the legislative veto, a war powers amendment, approval of treaties by both houses, and national referendums.

324.   John A. Rohr, *To Run a Constitution: The Legitimacy of the Administrative State* (Lawrence: University Press of Kansas, 1986).

In one of the more forceful statements of constitutional roles, Rohr summarized his argument in three steps. First, the separation of powers in the constitutional debates was not rigid, and is not violated by the mixture of powers in administrative agencies. Second, high ranking civil servants fulfill the balancing function originally assigned to the Senate. Third, the career civil servants fulfill the representation goal that was present but inadequately addressed by the constitution.

Rohr felt that a sizable "public administration" was mandated by the constitution. Wilson and the administrative scientists rewrote their justifications to abandon many of the constitutional principles. However, the New Dealers, who installed the administrative state, attempted in their writings and actions to restore the constitutional sense of balance to governmental affairs.

CONTINUING CONCERNS

The theme of bureaucratic politics is not bureaucratic politics; it is the constitution. One cannot begin to describe the operations or tactics of political maneuvering without making some, perhaps unstated, assumptions about the legitimacy of the entire process.

The literature of the field began exactly when it should have been expected--in the era of the New Deal. Administrative structures grew precipitously in that era, and increased political interaction was an inevitable result. But the political culture also made a fundamental choice in that era. Progressive doctrine was institutionalized. It was not the moderate Progressive philosophy of Wilson, in which the major concerns were regulation and political independence. It was a belligerent Progressive doctrine which demanded that government agents actively seek out the means of material progress. Bureaucratic politics was a result of more than size; it was a result of purpose.

In the intervening years, the purpose remained largely unchallenged, and the literature grew more comfortable in describing the mechanics of the interactions without discussing the underlying assumptions. However, in more recent times, the underlying assumptions are being questioned again.

The defense of bureaucratic politics flows in two unrelated directions. One defense is that the products of the administrative state are demanded by the population. A sampling of that literature appears in chapter nine. The other defense, which concluded this chapter, is that the bureaucracy has taken on a new constitutional role unrelated to its products.

The attack is in Lowi, and "public choice theory," and in the Reagan presidency. It is also in the "New Public Administration," described later. One can also argue that the attack is new and still forming. Whether it succeeds or not, however, it has already reawakened old concerns.

NOTES FOR CHAPTER SEVEN

1. For an extensive review of executive reorganization efforts in Washington, see Peri E. Arnold, *Making the Managerial Presidency: Comprehensive Reorganization Planning 1905-1980* (Princeton: Princeton University Press, 1986).

2. Released in the United States by (New York: Free Press, 1976).

3. The three names are listed as editors on the first report, and authors on the second.

4. Soon after publication in the Doubleday Short Series on Political Science (SSPS), the contract was purchased by Random House, which published all future printings. For this reason, Random House is almost always listed as the publisher.

8
Federalism and Intergovernmental Relations

BACKGROUND

Long before bureaucratic politics or even public administration was a popular topic in the literature, there were massive debates on the subject of federalism. It is a topic, however, which is both much older and much newer than the study of public administration, for the study of federalism evolved in fundamental ways during the New Deal, and the literature eventually picked up the more descriptive title of intergovernmental relations.

DUAL FEDERALISM

325. Johannes Althusius, *Politica methodice digeste* [roughly, *Politics Methodically Considered*] (Herborn, Prussia: publisher unknown, 1603). Third edition (1614), in Latin, edited by Carl Friedrich.[1]

Sophisticated studies on federalism began surprisingly early. In 1603, for instance, Althusius used the concept of shared sovereignty extensively in an attempt to update classical political theory to the realities of his Calvinist world. Althusius tried to argue that one organization could not provide for all the needs of people's lives. Instead, people belonged to groups that were largely responsible for their protection. As a result, of course, his emphasis was on the separation of powers, and not on the modern public administration interest in the reintegration of them.

326. *Land Ordinance*, (1785); also *Morrill Act*, 12 Stat. 503 (1862); also *Hatch Act*, 24 Stat. 440 (1887); also *Morrill Act*, 43 Stat. 970 (1890).

The emphasis during the early years of the American republic was on the fundamental issue of the separation of powers between the sovereign levels of government.[2] Long before the relationship was recognized as significant, however, some degree of fiscal transfer began to emerge. As early as the Land Ordinance, a tract of land was set aside for the maintenance of local schools in each township carved out of federal land. The Morrill Act expanded the land grants for state-level education to endow, support, and maintain colleges of agriculture and the mechanical arts. The Hatch Act appropriated $15,000 per state per year for agricultural experimental stations. While the Hatch Act required annual reporting by the states, the second Morrill Act (1890) added serious provisions for enforcement, allowing the federal government to monitor the funds, and withdraw them if they were misspent.

327.   John W. Burgess, "The American Commonwealth," *Political Science Quarterly*, 1, (March 1886): 9-35; also

328.   Simon N. Patten, "The Decay of State and Local Governments," *Annals of the American Academy of Political and Social Science*, 1, (July 1890): 26-42.

As becomes clear by the end of this chapter, we still debate the instability of federalism. The debates are restrained, however, and it is easy to forget that twice in the last century, serious scholars who were within the mainstream of American political thought considered the possibility that the federal system might have to be abolished.

The first period of doubt was the American industrial revolution, during which the regulatory debates described in chapter five began. In that era, these were two of the more widely noted works to suggest that state and local governments might have to be restructured. Burgess took the more theoretical approach, arguing that sovereignty had been placed in the people, and that the immutability of the states was a fiction and a misreading of the constitutional debates. Patten's concerns were more practical. He saw few problems with the concept of sovereign local governments. However, the old boundaries were outdated and dysfunctional, and should never have been made so difficult to change to meet evolving cultural migrations.

329.   Sidney Webb [Baron Sidney James Webb Passfield], *Grants in Aid: A Critique and a Proposal* (London: Longmans, Green and Co., 1911); also

330.   John A. Lapp, "Legislative Notes and Reviews: Federal Grants in Aid," *American Political Science Review*, 10, (November 1916): 738-43; also

331.   Ben A. Arneson, "American Government and Politics: Federal Aid to the States," *American Political Science Review*, 16, (August 1922): 443-54; also

332. Committee on Federal Aid to the States of the National Municipal League,
      "Federal Aid to the States," *National Municipal Review*, 17, (October 1928):
      [supplement] 619-59.

Some of the pessimism on federalism may have been related to weak national
financing of critical state programs. At least, optimism rose with increased federal
funding. One encouraging sign cited by Lapp was the publication of Webb's *Grants in
Aid* in England in 1911. While the national-local structures of the two countries had
little in common, Webb claimed that the more generous grants in England revitalized
both levels of government. It gave local governments needed expertise and resources,
while "buying" for the central government the rights of inspection, audit, supervision,
initiative, criticism, and control.

Lapp and Arneson were also impressed by the Smith-Lever Act of 1914 (38 Stat.
372), which had created the mechanism of matching grants. Both described it in
language similar to Webb's, and both predicted that it was a positive incentive that
would lead to greater cooperation between the levels of government. The National
Municipal League study, written by Austin MacDonald, felt that grants changed with
the Weeks Act (36 Stat. 961) of 1911, in which the government required state plans
and held inspections. MacDonald warned, however, that "(i)n plain words, some
federal bureaus are doing their task of administration--of inspection and supervision--
more carefully and more completely than others." (p. 658)

333. Harold J. Laski, *Studies in the Problems of Sovereignty* (New Haven: Yale Uni-
      versity Press, 1917); also

334. Max Hildebert Boehm, "Federalism," *Encyclopedia of the Social Sciences* (New
      York: Macmillan, 1931), vol. 6, pp. 169-72; also

335. Edward S. Corwin, *The Twilight of the Supreme Court* (New Haven: Yale
      University Press, 1934).

For a while, purely theoretical works on federalism continued to enjoy popularity among Public Administration readers. Laski saw federalism as a useful way to
adjust to a world in which central governments could not provide all of people's
needs. The necessary cooperation, however, seemed elusive. "No kind of working
compromise has been reached between the States on the one hand, and the Federal
Government on the other. Each has gone its way often almost wilfully duplicating the
work of the other... The possibility of co-operation is not considered. The lines of
demarcation are never made plain." (p. 280)

Boehm saw federalism as a reflection of a pluralistic society. Federalism could be
either unifying or divisive, however, depending on the needs of society. In continen-
tal Europe, it had been divisive (centrifugal) in dividing the unitarian states. In the
British Empire, it had been unifying (centripetal) in guaranteeing the union of separate states.

In chapter one of his classic work on the constitutional crises of the Supreme Court, Corwin laid out one of the last pure statements of split federalism, which he labelled "dual federalism." (pp. 47-48) He argued that the tenth amendment to the constitution had created a fixed and immutable distribution of powers between two sovereign and equal powers, that the relationship was meant to be one of tension, not collaboration, and that the federal government had enumerated powers only, while reserved powers rested with the lower levels.

336.   Leonard D. White, *Trends in Public Administration* (New York: McGraw-Hill, 1933); also

337.   Luther Gulick, "Reorganization of the State," *Civil Engineering*, 3, (August 1933): 420-22; also

338.   Harold J. Laski, "The Obsolescence of Federalism," *The New Republic*, 98, (May 3, 1939): 367-69.

The theoretical literature, however, soon became swamped by the second great constitutional crisis of federalism. The Great Depression brought with it a crisis in federal relations because it became painfully obvious that many state governments lacked the talent and/or the integrity to help their own citizens. In response, the literature and politics changed dramatically.

As an immediate solution, the federal government simply stepped into roles that the states would not or could not perform adequately. As White noted, "(t)he general effect of this shift has been to transfer power and responsibility from local government to the state, from the state to the federal authorities." (p. 15) The mechanisms were both legalistic, through interpretations of the commerce clause, and fiscal, through grants-in-aid. Centralization of power did not mean a decline in the activities of the states, however, which were still growing.

Other highly responsible observers felt that centralized federalism was not enough to fight the crisis. Gulick felt that the effect of the New Deal had been to destroy the federal form of government. "The American State is finished. I do not predict that the States will go, but affirm that they have gone. And why have they gone? Because they were unable to deal even inefficiently with the imperative, the life and death tasks of the new national economy." (pp. 420-21)

Similarly, Laski concluded, "the epoch of federalism is over." The federal government stood ready to react to the crisis, but could not depend on the states to do the same.

THE RISE OF COOPERATIVE FEDERALISM

339. W. Brooke Graves, "State Constitutional Provision for Federal-State Cooperation," *Annals of the American Academy of Political and Social Science*, 181, (September 1935): 142-48; also

340. V. O. Key, Jr., *The Administration of Federal Grants to States* (Chicago: Public Administration Service, 1937).

The solution of the 1930s, like the solution of the 1910s, was more funding and more centralized control. With these expanded programs came more interaction between the levels of government, and these were two of the first works to discuss the evolving federal-state relationship in cooperative terms. Graves, who documented cases of successful cooperation, suggested that state constitutions be rewritten when necessary to remove barriers to such cooperation and provide the needed flexibility. Key's book, the first released by the Committee on Public Administration of the Social Science Research Council, found that many of the federal requirements on states, such as the need to submit advance plans, often improved the operations of state government.

However, most of the monitoring devices were ineffective. Some, such as the audit, had limited purposes. Withdrawal power, on the other hand, was too potent to force incremental change, and too restricted to be an effective threat. Instead, federal officials often found themselves "lobbying" the states on their implementation decisions. Serious federal intervention happened only when state spoils systems led to genuine incompetence. State officials often organized to lobby federal officials on basic policies. As a result, a cooperative relationship arose.

341. *Social Security Act Amendments of 1939*, 53 Stat. 1360; also *Hatch Act Amendments*, 54 Stat. 767 (1940).

The one big concern among early optimists such as Key was that the spoils systems that prevailed at the state and local levels made true cooperation among equals difficult, if not impossible. This issue was finally addressed in these pieces of legislation. The Social Security amendments provided that "The Board shall make no certification for payment to any State unless it finds that the law of such State...includes...methods relating to the establishment and maintenance of personnel standards on a merit basis." The Hatch Act was amended to include state and local governments under restrictions against political coercion by governmental officials.

342. "Symposium on Cooperative Federalism," *Iowa Law Review*, 23, (May 1938): 455-650 [entire issue]; also

343.　　Jane Perry Clark, *The Rise of a New Federalism* (New York: Columbia University Press, 1938).

The symposium in the *Iowa Law Review* was probably the first published work to use the term "cooperative federalism," one of the labels that has become quite popular in the literature. It included articles by Graves, Clark, Frank Strong, Henry Toll, and John Cheadle. Only Cheadle was skeptical about cooperation, finding hostility to be the natural state of affairs. The others found evidence of cooperation and intentional state copying of federal legislation and regulations.

Clark's book is sometimes also cited incorrectly as the originator of the term "cooperative federalism," even though it never actually used the term. Nevertheless, her basic theme was that cooperative federal-state relations were necessary, were desirable, and were growing. She described some problems that had arisen, especially in the administration of grants-in-aid. No problems were insurmountable, however, or even particularly serious. "Grants-in-aid from the federal government to the states may be said to be fluids into which federal funds and requirements are poured with one hand while the other pours in state participation and activity." (p. 231) In short, grants-in-aid led to federal-state cooperation, and that meant progress.

344.　　Clyde F. Snider, "County and Township Government in 1935-36," *American Political Science Review*, 31, (October 1937): 884-913; also

345.　　William Anderson, *American Government* (New York: Henry Holt & Co., 1938); also "Federalism--Then and Now," *State Government*, 16, (May 1943): 107-12; also

346.　　W. Brooke Graves, ed., *Intergovernmental Relations in the United States, Annals of the American Academy of Political and Social Science*, 207, (January 1940).

The other popular term for the phenomenon, "intergovernmental relations" appeared possibly for the first times in these works.[3] Snider and Anderson emphasized the desirability of cooperation among the levels of government. Notable among the articles in the *Annals* was Joseph P. Harris' "The Future of Federal Grants-In-Aid." (pp. 14-26) Harris described the growth in centralized financing of governmental functions in every country in the industrialized world, but lamented that this was occurring without a "well-considered, consistent, national policy."

Anderson's 1943 article, which raised some controversy at the time, argued "that to debate national *versus* state powers is to raise one of the least important issues in American public life." (p. 110, italics in original) Cooperation was so complete, he claimed, that political scientists and statesmen needed to find some new autonomous role for state governments.

347.　　Kenneth C. Wheare, *Federal Government* (London: Oxford University Press, 1946).

In a theoretical work on federalism based on the pre-war experiences of Canada, Australia, Switzerland, and the United States (the book was written during the war when he could gather little current information), Wheare noted that federalism in all four republics was being changed by fiscal practices.

In all four cases, the central governments possessed supremacy in the ability to raise taxes. The regional governments had responsibility for social services and, during the depression of the 1930s, all four central governments had dramatically increased grants to the regions.

Wheare concluded that the federal principle was being modified in practice. He did not believe that it would disappear unless the states faced a string of wars or depressions. Also, while the changes were beneficial, he concluded that the concept of federalism was useful, and should be kept if practical.

348. Commission on Organization of the Executive Branch of Government, *Concluding Report, A Report to the Congress* (Washington, D.C.: USGPO, 1949); also

349. Council of State Governments, "Federal-State Relations," Senate Document 81, 81st Cong., 1st sess., 1949.

The First Hoover Commission acknowledged that grants-in-aid increased the quality, equality, and administration of state services, but expressed concern that the grant programs were unrelated, uncoordinated, and obstructive to state discretion. They recommended the increased use of block grants.

The Council prepared a study for the Commission, but when it was rejected, presumably for not being concerned enough with state autonomy, it was reprinted by the Senate. It praised centralization and cooperation. "The entire history is one of enlarging Government and enlarging points of contact between the units of Government within the Federal system." (p. 45) The Council recommended increasing the size of grants and the degree of coordination and national supervision, as well as establishing some governmental machinery for federal-state relations.

350. Joseph E. McLean, "Politics is What You Make It," *Public Affairs Pamphlet No. 181* (Washington, D.C.: Public Affairs Committee, April 1952).

The Public Affairs pamphlets were simple booklets illustrated with numerous cartoons, but also with serious information written by notable scholars. This tract on the duty of citizens to get involved in politics contained a phrase that was to become famous. Our federal system, McLean argued, was not like a layer cake. Rather, the administrative, financial, and political activities blended throughout the system like a marble cake. His point was that political involvement at the local level could make a difference in a politically interdependent world. However, the marble cake analogy described the changing federalism so well that it was soon adopted by many authors on federal relations.

351. Leonard D. White, *The States and the Nation* (Baton Rouge: Louisiana State University Press, 1953).

Not all observers saw the new trend as a solution without significant costs. In what was to become a famous challenge to the scholars of the field, White reversed his claim of 1933 that both federal and state powers were growing. In 1953, he speculated that grants-in-aid would soon make the states an irrelevant partner in the federal relationship. "(I)f the present trends continue for another quarter century, the states may be left hollow shells, operating primarily as the field districts of Federal departments and dependent upon the Federal treasury for their support." (p. 3)

352. Dwight D. Eisenhower, "Remarks at the Governor's Conference, Seattle, Washington. August 4, 1953," *Public Papers of the Presidents of the United States: Dwight D. Eisenhower, 1953* (Washington, D.C.: USGPO, 1960): 536-44; also

353. U.S. Commission on Intergovernmental Relations, *A Report to the President for Transmittal to the Congress*, 16 parts (Washington, D.C.: USGPO, June 1955); also

354. Dwight D. Eisenhower, "Address to the 1957 Governors' Conference, Williamsburg, Virginia. June 24, 1957," *Public Papers of the Presidents of the United States: Dwight D. Eisenhower, 1957* (Washington, D.C.: 1958): 486-97.

Federalism was one of the priorities of Eisenhower's administration. In 1953, he expressed his concern that a commission was needed to sort out federal and state roles.

The Kestnbaum[4] Commission, established by congress in 1953, issued sixteen reports before concluding in 1955. The reports generally supported strengthened state governments, but rejected attacks on categorical grants-in-aid because the conditions in those grants helped set national policies. There was considerable disagreement on the twenty-five member commission, however, which resulted in a minority report signed by seven members. Also, the staff studies were not always consistent with the commission findings on the general impacts of categorical grants-in-aid.

As Eisenhower made clear in 1957, he was still very concerned with the disappearing philosophy of "state's rights," and he referred anonymously to Leonard White's 1953 argument that state autonomy was in danger of disappearing.

355.. Arthur W. Macmahon, ed., *Federalism: Mature and Emergent* (Garden City, NY: Doubleday and Co., 1955); also

356.   William Anderson, *The Nation and the States: Rivals or Partners?* (Minneapolis:
        University of Minnesota Press, 1955); also *Intergovernmental Relations in
        Review* (Minneapolis: University of Minnesota Review, 1960).

Eisenhower's concerns, however, were not shared by most academic observers.
Anderson was a member of the Kestnbaum Commission, and he rushed this book into
publication before the Commission report was released. He felt that overlapping
functions and taxation in the federal system were inevitable, but that the constitution
had made the federal level dominant.

Macmahon's reprint of papers from the Bicentennial Conference on Federalism
in 1954 largely agreed. In separate articles, Roy Blough found that fiscal problems
would continue, but Edward Weidner reinforced the view that cooperation dominated
decision-making on federalism.

357.   W(illiam) Brooke Graves, *Intergovernmental Relations in the United States: An
        Annotated Chronology* (Chicago: Council of State Governments, 1958); also
        American Intergovernmental Relations (New York: Charles Scribner's Sons,
        1964).

Graves wrote some of the most extensive histories and literature reviews ever
produced on the subject. In 1964 he followed federalism back to the Greeks, devoting
separate chapters to intergovernmental relations on every major policy area. Chapter
25 offered a more detailed literature review than is practical here.

Graves concluded with six suggestions: 1) that we declare a national policy in the
area; 2) that we form a Department of Federal-State-Local Relations; 3) that the
president give an annual report on the subject; 4) that we form an intergovernmental
reference service; 5) that congress form a joint committee on the subject; and 6) that
states and local governments restructure themselves to promote cooperation.

358.   Advisory Commission on Intergovernmental Relations. Created by 73 Stat.
        703 (1959).

As already discussed, President Eisenhower was particularly concerned with
evolving federal relationships. During his terms as president, he established a number
of commissions to help define the new cooperative relationship that was emerging between the states and the federal government. The ACIR, founded by law in 1959, was
his final effort, and the new group had representatives of the public as well as the
executive and legislative branches of all three levels of government. Its job has been
to monitor the federal system, recommend changes in it, and issue reports on the
subject.

Those reports are numerous, and some are reviewed here. Among them, the
ACIR releases annual reports, fiscal analyses, and regular staff studies. Most of the
ideas reflected in the academic literature also appear in ACIR publications, and it is
common for federalism literature to cite recent ACIR studies.

359. Morton Grodzins, "American Political Parties and the American System," *Western Political Quarterly*, 13, (1960): 974-98; also "The Federal System," in President's Commission on National Goals, *Goals for Americans* (Englewood Cliffs, NJ: Prentice Hall, 1960), pp. 265-82; also *The American System: A New View of Government in the United States*, ed. by Daniel J. Elazar (Chicago: Rand McNally, 1966).

Grodzins organized the University of Chicago Federalism Workshop in 1955, which led to numerous federalism studies through the 1950s and early 1960s. In his 1960 publications, he helped popularize the "marble cake" analogy to such an extent that he is sometimes credited with its creation. In *Goals* he noted that "even in the absence of joint financing, federal-state-local collaboration is the characteristic mode of action." He dismissed the attempts of the 1950s to reduce federal influence with the argument that they failed because all levels of government gained power in the cooperation, and that the nation was best served by the opportunities for central leadership in local affairs.

The American System was to be the grand statement of his views on federalism, although it had to be completed after his death by Daniel Elazar. As Elazar noted in the Preface, Grodzins' final chapter reflected less enthusiasm for the marble cake analogy, and more respect for the independent role of the states in the federal system.

360. Daniel J. Elazar, *The American Partnership: Intergovernmental Cooperation in the Nineteenth Century United States* (Chicago: University of Chicago Press, 1962), adapted from *Intergovernmental Relations in Nineteenth Century American Federalism* [dissertation] (Chicago: University of Chicago, 1959); also

361. Harry N. Scheiber, *The Condition of American Federalism: An Historian's View*, study submitted to Committee on Government Operations, Subcommittee on Intergovernmental Relations, U.S. Senate, 89th Cong., 2d sess. (October 15, 1966).

Elazar argued that what was now termed cooperative federalism was actually nothing new. Using nineteenth-century examples from Virginia, New Hampshire, Minnesota, Colorado, and other states, he tried to show that a system of federal cooperation was quite old, and that the rough balance between states and the federal government had not shifted for 175 years, even though it had evolved through three different predominant forms.

To Scheiber, this was poor history. He argued that cooperation before the modern era was the exception, not the rule. Instead, federalism evolved through four eras: rivalistic state mercantilism 1790-1860; centralizing federalism 1860-1933; New Deal 1933-1941; and cooperative federalism 1941-1966.

362.   William H. Riker, *Federalism: Origin, Operation, Significance* (Boston: Little
        Brown and Co., 1964).

        In a legalistic and political analysis of the federal system, Riker tried to describe
the conditions that were necessary for "the federal bargain" of dividing responsibilities
so that each level of government had a set of decisions on which they did not need
to consult with the other levels. He decided that the key was a decentralized party
system, in which the political machinery could reflect the different levels of interest
that allowed two or more levels of government to control different policies in the
same territory.

363.   Roscoe C. Martin, *The Cities and the Federal System* (New York: Atherton
        Press, 1965).

        To Martin, the most interesting shift in cooperative federalism was in the rise
of the city. "It is the thesis of this study that the trends point toward the emergence of a federal system that rests upon three partners rather than two." (p. 109)
Such a system arose because of grants-in-aid, the depression, the rise of metropolitan
areas with their problems, and the inability of the states to finance the new programs. Martin's federal system was based on all three pillars, not just two, however.
Unlike White, he argued that the states were actually stronger than they were at the
beginning of the century.

364.   Nelson A. Rockefeller, *The Future of Federalism* (Cambridge: Harvard Univer-
        sity Press, 1962); also

365.   Max Ways, "Creative Federalism and the Great Society," *Fortune*, 73, (January
        1966): 121-23 passim; also

366.   Edmund S. Muskie, "The Challenge of Creative Federalism," *Congressional
        Record*, Vol. 112, part 5, 89th Cong., 2nd sess., (March 25, 1966), pp. 6833-
        45; also

367.   Richard Warner, *The Concept of Creative Federalism* [unpublished dissertation]
        (Washington, D.C.: American University, 1970).

        In the 1960s, Lyndon Johnson attempted to reform federal fiscal relations under
the label of "Creative Federalism." The most extensive history of the movement was
probably Warner's. The general tenets first appeared in 1962 when Governor
Rockefeller delivered the Godkin Lectures at Harvard University. His second lecture
was dedicated to the ability of the states to raise initiatives for urban and national
problems if freed from constitutional and administrative constraints.
        Ways reinforced the sense that vitality existed most prominently in the private
sector, but needed to be encouraged at the state level. The federal government would

become the "junior partner." Muskie noted that coordination would occur at the federal level, but that the states would have to carry the burden of cooperation and competition.

368.   U. S. Senate, "The Federal System as Seen by Federal Aid Officials," Committee Print. A Study prepared by the Subcommittee on Intergovernmental Relations of the Committee on Government Operations, U. S. Senate, 89th Cong., 1st sess., December 15, 1965.

This survey of federal aid officials came to the disturbing conclusion that the politicians' and academics' view of cooperation might not be shared by the practitioners. The federal officials described three friction points: professionals at the top vs. nonprofessionals at the bottom; professional program administrators vs. elected policy-makers; and administrators of individual aid programs vs. intergovernmental reformers. In each case, attitudinal differences led to conflicts. The subcommittee chair, Senator Muskie, suggested improvements in intergovernmental personnel, funding, and advisory boards.

369.   Daniel J. Elazar, *American Federalism: A View from the States* (New York: Thomas Y. Crowell, 1966).

Elazar noted that literature on federalism was common from the federal perspective, and was becoming more common from the local perspective. His goal was to write a book on federalism from the state perspective.
     The book turned out to be less about federalism than about the vitality and civic cultures of the states. He ranked them on their political culture (moralistic, individualistic, traditionalistic), their sectionalism (Northeast, Greater South, Greater West), and their sense of frontier. He described patterns of conflict and cooperation brought on by localism and intrasectional compacts. He concluded that the concept of statehood was still strong, and that states could still be innovative.

370.   U. S. Bureau of the Budget, "Circular No. A-85" (June 1967); also

371.   Advisory Commission on Intergovernmental Relations, *Annual Report on Operations Under OMB Circular A-85* (Washington, D.C.: USGPO, annual).

Coordination of federal grants programs remained an awkward problem that was addressed by the Budget Bureau in 1967. The circular required federal agencies to consult with general regional governments and advisory groups before implementing major regulations and interagency agreements. The administrative responsibilities rested with ACIR, which was required to issue annual reports on its A-85 activities.

372.   Terry Sanford, *Storm Over the States* (New York: McGraw Hill, 1967); also

373.   Harold Seidman, *Politics, Position, and Power* (New York: Oxford University Press, 1970); also

374.   Ira Sharkansky, *The Maligned States* (New York: McGraw Hill, 1972.

Using his experience as a governor, Sanford wrote a rallying defense of the contributions of the states, and a blunt description of federal barriers to coordination. The book is perhaps most often remembered, however, for its analogy that the grant-in-aid system created neither layer cakes nor marble cakes, but instead a picket-fence federalism. Specifically, the ties between balkanized sections of federal and state bureaucracies and legislative committees created a system of service delivery that ran "straight down like a number of pickets stuck in the ground." (p. 80) State government was not able to join them at the local level.

In a sympathetic but more irreverent review of cooperative federalism, Seidman attacked those "whose culinary tastes run to 'marble cake'" on the grounds that the system had developed without separating functions by levels of government. He described the system as "cooperative feudalism," and complained that it was unable to respond to the most urgent needs of society.

Sharkansky revived Sanford's major argument, stating that "(t)he states are maligned." He defended the cultural diversity that created the need for states. He described the financial power of the states, and recounted some policies in which states had been dynamic. He concluded that the states would remain financially strong, and would probably move more into solving urban problems as the federal government split its resources between foreign and domestic priorities.

375.   *Intergovernmental Cooperation Act*, 90 Stat. 577 (1968); also

376.   U.S. Office of Management and Budget, "Budget Circular No. A-95" (July 24, 1969) [plus five attachments]; also

377.   James Sundquist, *Making Federalism Work: A Study of Program Coordination at the Community Level* (Washington, D.C.: Brookings Institution, 1969).

By 1967, a complaint voiced by Sanford became more common. Federal grants were so dispersed and so many of them called for state actions that ranged from impossible to contradictory, that Johnson called for major simplifications in the funding processes in his 1967 budget speech. The Intergovernmental Cooperation Act, passed in 1968, was the response. It simplified procedures for the distribution of funds; it allowed area-wide planning instead of grant-by-grant planning; it provided federal technical assistance on grants; it ensured coordination with local land-use plans; it increased congressional oversight of grant programs.

The Act was implemented through Budget Circular A-95, which required states to set up clearinghouses so that information about proposed grants could be disseminated throughout the planning agencies in the area, and so that comments and reactions could be gathered.

To Sundquist, the legislation was a step in the right direction, but it missed some important causes of the problem. By surveying programs and officials in eight states (with the collaboration of David W. Davis who later dropped out of the project), he concluded that we have a "federal system under stress. Perhaps at no time in recent years has intergovernmental conflict, compounded by federal interdepartmental rivalry, been so severe."

They proposed a model that would leave administration of grants to departments, but would put federal coordination in the hands of a neutral agency, preferably in the Executive Office of the President. At the local level, one coordinating body (similar to Model Cities, but with real power) would submit a single local plan for single approval by the federal agency.

378. Richard H. Leach, *American Federalism* (New York: W. W. Norton and Co., 1970); also "Federalism: A Battery of Questions," in Daniel J. Elazar, ed., "The Federal Polity," *Publius: The Journal of Federalism*, 3, (Fall 1973): 11-47.

In sympathy with Lyndon Johnson's proposals, Leach argued in 1970 that federalism is merely a process into which the actors put the content. In 1973, he reemphasized that federalism is adaptable, and that we restrict its potential when we treat it constitutionally, rather than procedurally.

In his book, he was unsympathetic with Sanford's complaint that states are being confined, arguing that they are largely to blame, through both their structures and their politics, for their own inaction. Instead, they need to adjust to an evolving system of intergovernmental cooperation. On the separate issue of the inherent fiscal imbalance of federalism, he offered no long-term solutions, but felt that problems could be addressed through the reforms happening throughout the system.

379. Martha Derthick, *The Influence of Federal Grants: Public Assistance in Massachusetts* (Cambridge: Harvard University Press, 1970); also *Between State and Nation* (Washington, D.C.: Brookings Institution, 1974); also *Uncontrollable Spending for Social Services Grants* (Washington, D.C.: Brookings Institution, 1975).

In 1970, Derthick studied the implementation in Massachusetts of the public assistance program under the Social Security Act. She noted that federal influence led to a bureaucratized, standardized, professionalized state program. The feds also fostered the development of state agencies that could be political allies, in a manner earlier described by Sanford.

In 1974, as a senior fellow at Brookings, she studied the experience of regional planning organizations to conclude that they needed to be pragmatic in structure and function. It was useful to have centralized leadership in the federal government, for which OMB cooperation would be required. At the regional level, however, things must be organized on an ad hoc basis.

In 1975, she investigated the fiscal impact of the open-ended matching social service grants that were attached to the Social Security Act in 1962. Once federal controls were amended out of the law in 1967 and demands for services grew, federal matching funds rose uncontrollably until stopped by legislation in 1972. In analyzing what happened, Derthick described the dynamics of each agency involved, including OMB's monitoring of legislative mandates, but not of regulations. Among the major lessons, however, were that the federal government should not offer open-ended grants for vague purposes. Administrative controls should be tightened, and presidential advisors should be generalists, not program specialists.

380.   Arthur W. Macmahon, *Administering Federalism in a Democracy* (New York: Oxford University Press, 1972).

This is the third book in Roscoe Martin's series on Public Administration and Democracy. As such, much of it is structural and fundamental, reviewing the inherent relationships that make federalism work, and following fiscal relations back to the early days of property transfers.

Macmahon believed the federal courts to be the referees who can keep the system stable. Centralization under national leadership is inevitable with our fiscal relationships and growing national programs. However, Macmahon believed that local governments will remain strong, particularly if reorganized into meaningful units through regional planning.

381.   Melvin Laird, H.R. 12080, *Congressional Record*, 104, 85th Cong., 2nd sess., (April 22, 1958): 6953; also

382.   Richard M. Nixon, "Address to the Nation on Domestic Programs. August 8, 1969." *Public Papers of the Presidents of the United States: Richard M. Nixon, 1969* (Washington, D.C.: USGPO, 1970): 637-45; also

383.   Richard P. Nathan, *Congressional Record*, vol. 115, part 20, 91st Cong., 1st sess., (September 26, 1969): 27275-77; also

384.   Daniel J. Elazar, ed., "The *Publius* Symposium on the Future of American Federalism," *Publius*, 1, (Spring 1972), pp. 95-97 [symposium follows on 98-146]; also

385.   Michael Reagan, *The New Federalism* (New York: Oxford University Press, 1972).

After Creative Federalism, many of the same concerns with lack of coordination and local discretion remained. The next major attempt to change the intergovernmental relationship was initiated by President Nixon using revenue sharing under the label "New Federalism."

Revenue sharing was first introduced in an unsuccessful bill by Representative Melvin Laird in 1958. In 1969, however, in a speech written by Raymond K. Price, Jr., Nixon revived the technique as a strategy for simplifying the management of federal grants and increasing the role of all levels of government. Nathan, as Assistant Budget Director, introduced the proposal before congress under the general themes of responsible decentralization, a strong concern with basic systems, and a greater emphasis on governmental policies.

From an academic standpoint, however, the most unusual twist of the New Federalism may have been the "new federalist papers" that circulated within the White House in 1970, and that were reprinted in the *Publius* above. In January, William Safire circulated a paper entitled "New Federalist Paper No. 1" signed "Publius." It argued that states' rights had become states' duties, and that Washington should set national objectives while the states should implement the policies.

Tom Huston, author of the later disastrous "Huston Plan," responded with another semi-anonymous "Federalism: Old And New" signed by "Cato," raising constitutional objections to the first paper. Richard Nathan then offered the "New Federalism No. 3" authored by "Johannes Althusius," trying to draw a compromise between the two positions. The final entry was by "Polybius" [Wendall Hulcher], entitled "In Support of Strengthening the American Federal System."

To Michael Reagan, the difficulty with Nixon's proposal was that it substituted a system with no national priorities for one in which the national government was oppressively dominant. Reagan proposed instead a middle ground of "permissive federalism," in which the states and the federal government would work together through grants that retain instructions on issues of national priorities.

386.   *Joint Funding Simplification Act*, 88 Stat. 1604 (1974); also

387.   U.S. Office of Management and Budget, "Circular No. A-111" (1975).

Tensions were relieved somewhat by this Act. Its aim was to enable state and local governments "to use Federal assistance more effectively and efficiently" by authorizing the heads of federal agencies to adopt uniform guidelines when multi-agency guidelines conflicted, and to permit reviews by a single board. Agency heads were allowed to delegate their oversight responsibilities to other agencies when that would aid coordination.

The Act was implemented through budget circular A-111, which permitted grants from numerous agencies to be filed through a single application, with a single audit, and with a single negotiating point of contact in the federal government.

388.   Donald H. Haider, *When Governments Come to Washington: Governors, Mayors, and Intergovernmental Lobbying* (New York: Free Press, 1974).

Haider traced the development of associations of state and local chief-executives in Washington through three phases from small associations to full-fledged lobbyists. Using eight case studies, he illustrated their range of inter-group cooperation from consensus to open competition, and he described some of their bargaining tactics. He concluded that their role in the federal system is beneficial, and he encouraged their mutual cooperation and support.

389.   Jimmy Carter, "Address on Urban Policy to the United States Conference of Mayors," June 29, 1976; also "National Urban Policy, Message to the Congress. March 27, 1978," *Public Papers of the Presidents of the United States: Jimmy Carter, 1978, Book I* (Washington, D.C.: USGPO, 1979): 581-93.

The third modern entry in presidential attempts to bring cooperation and coordination to federal relations through a new label was the "New Partnership" of President Carter. His basic goal was to balance the various funding mechanisms that were available so as to satisfy his five principles: simplifying and improving programs at all levels; combining governmental resources to cooperate with private resources; providing the flexibility to give help where it is needed; increasing access to opportunity by the disadvantaged; and drawing on community and volunteer efforts.

390.   Advisory Commission on Intergovernmental Relations, *Improving Federal Grants Management*, Report A-53 (Washington, D.C.: February 1977); also *The Intergovernmental Grant System as Seen By Local, State, and Federal Officials*, Report A-54 (Washington, D.C.: USGPO, March 1977); also *Summary and Concluding Observations: The Intergovernmental Grant System: An Assessment and Proposed Policies*, Report A-62 (Washington, D.C.: USGPO, June 1978).

These are three of the more commonly cited volumes in the ACIR's 14 part study of the intergovernmental grant system, published between 1976 and 1978. Report A-53 noted the difficulties in finding structural solutions to coordination problems when federal officials have few incentives to standardize. Report A-54 surveyed grant officials at all levels. Among the findings were that the federal government influences local decision-making more than do the state governments, and federal grants receive more local attention than do state grants.

The major conclusions of the study, however, were reported in A-62. Among the more significant findings, the ACIR advised congress to choose the type of grants carefully, so as to accomplish their original objectives. They urged consolidation of many grants, and sunset legislation for many programs. They also asked that funding uncertainties for local governments be reduced.

391.   Parris N. Glendening and Mavis Mann Reeves, *Pragmatic Federalism* (Pacific Palisades, CA: Palisades Publishers, 1977).

The Glendening and Reeves text described federalism with the dual beliefs that both sovereign levels of government are strong, and that the system is pragmatic enough to make necessary adjustments in the future. They described the system as "rampant incrementalism." Furthermore, while the system has experienced some administrative decentralization, true decentralization cannot occur without state initiative.

392.   Deil S. Wright, *Federal Grants-in-Aid: Perspectives and Alternatives* (Washington, D.C.: American Enterprise Institute for Public Policy Research, 1968); also "Intergovernmental Relations: An Analytical Overview," *Annals of the American Academy of Political and Social Science*, 416, (November 1974): 1-16; also *Understanding Intergovernmental Relations* (North Scituate, MA: Duxbury Press, 1978).

Wright, who has been one of the more prolific writers on the subject in recent years, expressed his concern in 1968 that grants-in-aid were growing uncontrollably. Coordination and state control were suffering and hurting morale among state policymakers. He suggested revenue sharing and reductions or credits in federal taxes to return policy discretion to the states.

In his "Overview" in 1974, Wright noted that "intergovernmental relations" is different from federalism in the multiplicity of units, the primacy of public officials' attitudes and actions in determining policies, the informal working patterns, the prominence of administrators, and the policy emphasis. He divided federalism into five phases: conflict; cooperation; concentration; creativity; and competition.

In 1978, Wright published a general textbook on the subject, using both historical and descriptive approaches, organized around nine "features or characteristics" of governmental processes. He concluded that IGR is stable, is influenced by domestic more than international variables, and is likely to see both more diversity and more centralization in the future.

393.   George F. Break, *Financing Government in a Federal System* (Washington, D.C.: Brookings Institution, 1980).

In addition to the general literature on intergovernmental relations described in this section, there is a more technical set of studies on taxation and public finance that is beyond the scope of this chapter. Some appears in chapter eighteen on budgeting, and some more properly belongs in the literature of economic theory, and is not covered in this review at all. Among IGR literature, the most common place to find this approach has been in ACIR staff studies and in some Brookings studies-- particularly those by George Break.

This book is an updating of a 1965 "background paper" by Break that was used at a 1965 conference at the Brookings Institution and later published separately.[5] In the 1980 study, Break reviewed methods of taxation, especially of tax coordination between the branches. He reviewed the status of each of the major forms of federal grants, and speculated on the impacts of the *Serrano* and *Rodriquez* decisions on state grants to local jurisdictions. He concluded by reviewing the major proposals for fiscal reform, including tax revolt, user fees, and public choice theory, and by noting the ability of the federal system to test several alternate approaches at once.

394.   David B. Walker, *Toward a Functioning Federalism* (Boston: Little, Brown and
        Co., 1981).

To Walker, who often framed his arguments in terms used during the original constitutional debates, the U.S. has neither dual federalism nor cooperative federalism, but an increasingly overburdened and dysfunctional federalism in which intergovernmental relations are "more pervasive, more expansive, less manageable, less effective, and above all less accountable." (p. 225) He described eight overloads on the system, and advocated decongestion and disengagement as remedies.

His remedy was not reduced budgets, but increased relevance of each program to the needs being met. Instead of assigning roles so that the federal government finances, the state manages, and the locals deliver, he suggested reductions in fiscal transfers, in federal and state regulations, and in proliferation of local authorities. Each function would be divided according to appropriate needs.

395.   Martha Derthick, "American Federalism: Madison's Middle Ground in the
        1980s," *Public Administration Review*, 47, (January/February 1987): 66-74.

As a general summation, Derthick found wisdom in Madison's original argument that the states would maintain a "subordinately useful" role under a supreme national government. While tremendous pressures forced centralization in the period 1965-1980, Derthick noted that the states maintained important roles in areas that were not suited for national policy implementation.

CONTINUING CONCERNS

Federalism is schizophrenic. It rests on two contradictory principles, independence and interdependence, and the faith that each strengthens the other so long as there remains what Grodzins called "a little chaos." Furthermore, as *Texas v White* settled in 1867, it is a relationship without divorce. When things become unbalanced, there must be an arbiter to straighten them out. That role has long been played by the federal courts.

The rules have remained surprisingly stable over time. The significant variations have dealt with the emphasis on independence or interdependence, but never at the expense of abandoning the other principle. To do otherwise would be to abandon federalism as a form of government, a truly rare proposal in recent American literature.[6]

Federalism literature is left with the mechanics. Which funding mechanisms foster the balance? From where must the revenues come? To whom must the participants be accountable? It is one area in which there are few radical proposals on the table. The distribution of needs and resources will no doubt continue to be adjusted, but to virtually the entire political spectrum, the relationship itself remains sacred.

NOTES FOR CHAPTER EIGHT

1. Carl Friedrich, ed., *Politica methodice digeste of Johannes Althusius (Althaus)* (Cambridge: Harvard University Press, 1932). Friedrich reported that the only copy of the original in the United States was a photostatic copy he brought back and filed in the Widener Library of Harvard University.

2. The classic statement of the nineteenth century solution was by Justice Taney in *Abelman v Booth*, 21 How. 506 (1859).

3. Graves in 1964 in *American Intergovernmental Relations* (p. 821) speculated that the term was used for the first time in his 1940 symposium in *Annals*. These two works predate that. Deil Wright, in *Understanding Intergovernmental Relations* (p. 6) reviewed later, reported that he contacted Snider and Anderson in 1969 and 1970. Neither claimed to have invented the term, but neither could name an earlier source.

4. Named for commission chair Meyer Kestnbaum.

5. George F. Break, *Intergovernmental Fiscal Relations in the United States* (Washington, D.C.: Brookings Institution, 1967).

6. For recent exceptions, see Rexford Guy Tugwell, *A Model Constitution for a United Republic of America* (Santa Barbara: Center for the Study of Democratic Institutions, 1970); or Leland D. Baldwin, *Reframing the Constitution: An Imperative for Modern America* (Santa Barbara: Clio Press, 1972).

9
Press and Interest Group Relations

BACKGROUND

The next two chapters complete the discussions of relations between agencies and outside political groups. Within that arena, four subjects have generated a significant number of publications, but have not yet been discussed directly. First, the media have become a political force of considerable weight and impact upon bureaucratic behavior. Second, interest groups have been a subject of study in this field for half a century, and many older works on that subject have been described in earlier chapters. In this chapter, the early works are supplemented by newer studies on the same topic.

The third and fourth concerns are the basic questions to which the rest of the bureaucratic literature has tried to provide some answers. The subjects are intertwined enough that their literature is discussed together in chapter ten. First, how does government determine the popular will of the public it is supposed to serve? More specifically, what is the popular will and how can it be measured? Finally, how can bureaucracy be made responsive to a democratic environment?

AGENCY RELATIONS WITH THE PRESS

This is one of the more dramatic examples of a subject from which Public Administration has borrowed only a scattering of the available literature. The study of press relations in the governmental arena generates not only its own courses, but its own schools. A smaller selection of that literature has also been read and cited frequently by public administration audiences, and that literature is the subject here.

Notably, this review ignores all but a few studies on the press itself, as well as presidential-press relations, since both subjects have generated too much literature that is marginally relevant to public administration. It does, however, include the specialized issue of governmental secrecy, a topic that is an inherent part of government-press policies.

Finally, it should be noted that the overlap between this topic and public opinion, in the next chapter, is considerable. The press literature is often more focused on the mechanics of the media and the relations of reporters with the bureaucracy, rather than with the public. Both topics should be consulted, however, for a more representative sample of the literature.

396.   U.S. Supreme Court, *Totten v. United States*, 92 U.S. 105 (1876).

Long before literature appeared on the role of the media in government, some rules of government's limited obligations were set. During the Civil War, Lincoln contracted with Totten to conduct espionage behind Confederate lines. When enforcement of the contract was later disputed, the Supreme Court held that the case could not be heard by the Court of Claims for fear that military secrets would be inevitably revealed.

397.   Woodrow Wilson, *New Freedom* (New York: Doubleday, Page, and Co., 1913).

Military questions notwithstanding, the general thrust of American literature since colonial days has been toward open governmental operations. The sentiment peaked during the Progressive era as the abuses of secret dealings between government and industrialists were fresh in everyone's memories. As Wilson noted in a 1912 campaign speech, "Publicity is one of the purifying elements of politics. The best thing that you can do with anything that is crooked is to lift it up where people can see that it is crooked, and then it will either straighten itself out or disappear." (pp. 115-16)

398.   Leo C. Rosten, *The Washington Correspondents* (New York: Harcourt, Brace, and Co., 1937).

In the twentieth century, the press corps in Washington grew large enough that it became interesting as a subject for separate study, and Leo Rosten was one of the first to investigate their backgrounds. Using interviews, he found that Washington correspondents tended to be more educated and more heavily "Democratic" than the population. However, they were not well trained as journalists. They also preferred concrete and personal stories to those about abstract concepts, reinforcing the "crisis" and disjointed nature of the news. They also frequently had difficulty with their editors over the content of their stories.

399.   James L. McCamy, *Government Publicity* (Chicago: University of Chicago Press, 1939); also

400.   J(ohn) A(lfred) R(alph) Pimlott, *Public Relations and American Democracy* (Princeton, NJ: Princeton University Press, 1951).

As the press grew, government also expanded its use of information policy. As early as 1913, congress attempted to restrict the use of funds to publicize the achievements of those in the bureaucracy (38 Stat. 212). Such efforts continued, however, and these were some of the early attempts to describe them.

By 1937, when his information was gathered, McCamy found public relations offices to be common and highly placed in the bureaucracy. Nine agencies even had a network of regional publicity offices. Tactics varied from traditional press releases to large fairs to ten regular feature programs broadcast from government offices. The purpose was often public information rather than propaganda, and was not a threat to democracy so long as publicists remembered their duties as well as rights.

In 1951, Pimlott updated the description of expanded public relations, noting that everyone agreed that some public relations was necessary for government to work, but that the recent expansion in both "lobbying" efforts and publications unrelated to agency business had led to new controversy. He differentiated public relations from the more narrowly-focused advertising, and from legislator-focused lobbying, and concluded that public relations reflected a professionalization of a function that had always been present, but that had grown more difficult. He also concluded that the media and public relations officers had become both partners and rivals in the information process.

401.   Dwight D. Eisenhower, Executive Order 10501, "Safeguarding Official Information in the Interests of the Defense of the United States," (November 6, 1953).

In the 1950s, the issue of secrecy took on new urgency in American politics. In 1953, Eisenhower tried to arrest the growing tendency of government to classify documents having nothing to do with national security by replacing Truman's Executive Order 10290 of September 24, 1951. The new order redefined and tightened the categories and time-frames of classification decisions, and eliminated the category of "restricted" material altogether.

402.   Harold L. Cross, *The People's Right to Know--Legal Access to Public Records and Proceedings* (New York: Columbia University Press, 1953); also

403.   James R. Wiggins, *Freedom or Secrecy* (New York: Oxford University Press, 1956); also

404.   Edward A. Shils, *The Torment of Secrecy* (Glencoe, IL: Free Press, 1956).

Academics soon joined the chorus of those who felt that government secrecy was endangering democratic accountability. Cross' book was particularly gloomy on executive department secrecy. "The entrance gates to records are shut and guarded except on those occasions when official grace is moved to set them ajar for light and air." (p. 183)

Both Cross and Wiggins recounted the revolution in access to information that accompanied the beginning of the republic, and the deterioration in that access that had become rampant in the twentieth century with such new common-law concepts as the right to privacy, and especially with the delegation of more of government's authority to secretive executive agencies.

Shils argued that society should be pluralistic, which meant a balance of publicity, privacy, and secrecy. The problem of the 1930s to 1950s was that we had allowed publicity through our media to grow too large, resulting in a societal move toward greater secrecy. Secrecy, to Shils, was privacy made compulsory, or in other words, no privacy at all. We needed a coalition of the political spectrum to put our values back in order and restore a pluralistic society.

405. Douglass Cater, *The Fourth Branch of Government* (Boston: Houghton Mifflin, 1959).

Cater's book, which is by far the most frequently cited in the area of government-media relations (often incorrectly as the first), contained a general description of the business of Washington correspondents, which "has become specialized, compartmentalized, channelized, even routinized to a degree that would shock...predecessor(s) of few decades ago." He noted the tendency of correspondents to seek the sources of action--presidents rather than administrators; congress rather than presidents. Once focused, however, he noted their tendency to routinize their sources of information.

Despite their regular patterns of behavior, Cater was impressed that Washington correspondents were more willing to dig for information when necessary than was the case in other European nations, and that they played "an almost constitutional role" in U.S. government.

406. Francis E. Rourke, *Secrecy and Publicity: Dilemmas of Democracy* (Baltimore: Johns Hopkins Press, 1961).

Rourke argued that secrecy and the government's need for publicity were parts of the same governmental weapon for increasing control over society. He documented the growth of government secrecy, noting that it had been encouraged by congress, the president, and the courts. He also described the ways in which controlled publicity could coerce private actions that could never be forced by law, although he noted that the courts were becoming more concerned about the use of public "exposure" to control behavior. He concluded with no appropriate balance among secrecy, publicity, and democracy, arguing that society's best protection was to avoid apathy on the subject.

407.   Daniel J. Boorstin, *The Image, or What Happened to the American Dream* (New York: Atheneum, 1962).[1]

Underlying much of the media literature is a concern with the disjointed and incomplete picture of public events that is presented to the public through the tactic of reporting only developing crises. Boorstin followed the pseudo-events that are created by the media's practice of compressing the world into incidents that are interesting and quickly reportable. He also described the ways in which government administrators and politicians have adjusted to the practice by creating packaged events for public consumption to generate favorable publicity.

408.   Bernard C. Cohen, *The Press and Foreign Policy* (Princeton: Princeton University Press, 1963).

The second of the three almost universally cited works on government-press relations (after Cater's) is focused specifically on foreign affairs. Using the themes of the press as observer, as participant, and as catalyst, Cohen reinforced the image of reporters as both captives and occasional unwitting framers of foreign policy news. He saw the conflict between the needs for secrecy and publicity as essential, although he did suggest that the information function would be better served if the reporting was not geared toward mass audiences, who paid little attention anyway.

409.   Dan Nimmo, *Newsgathering in Washington* (New York: Atherton Press, 1964).

The third book cited by virtually all later studies is this study of the relationship of news reporters and agency officials. Nimmo found that such relations fall into three major categories: cooperative, marked by continual, informal contacts between the two sides; compatible, marked by less frequent, more formalized contacts; and competitive, marked by very formalized contact with little real communication. Compatible relations are the norm, although the likelihood of each style depends on shared views of the roles and functions of each, mutual respect for each other's status in their professions, and the type of agency.

410.   William L. Rivers, *The Opinionmakers* (Boston: Beacon Press, 1965)[2]; also *The Adversaries: Politics and the Press* (Boston: Beacon Press, 1970); also *The Other Government: Power and the Washington Media* (New York: Universe Books, 1982).

In each of his works, Rivers combined anecdotal descriptions of the Washington press corps with analytical discussions of the appropriate role of the press in democracy. He acknowledged that the press and government need and help each other, and that "information policy has been at the very center of governing the United States from the beginning." (1965, p. 1)

The cooperation that goes with such arrangements, however, seemed increasingly dangerous to him as he moved into his 1970 sequel, and added the data of the Johnson and Nixon administrations. "The power of political journalism is dangerous, but it is also necessary....The only way for a reporter to look at an official is skeptically." (pp. 252-53) He was equally harsh on the press corps, repeating Lasswell's proposal that the press corps could be cleaned up through an industry-staffed Committee on Public Communication, which could rid the industry of those "whose distinguishing characteristic is their questionable choice of vocation." (1965, p. 200)

By 1982, some of those concerns seemed more distant. He spent more time on the internal workings of Washington media. He described the way in which press "wisdom" has often framed later presidential reputations. He noted, however, that the bureaucracy still receives almost no television coverage.

411.   Ray Eldon Hiebert, ed., *The Press in Washington* (New York: Dodd, Mead, and Co., 1966).

This is a compilation of sixteen guest lectures from Hiebert's advanced journalism class at American University, including such diverse contributors as Art Buchwald and Clark Mollenhoff. Much of the content is personalized and conversational, with little analysis of how the press and Washington fit together. An exception is Mollenhoff, whose discussion of "Secrecy, Classified Information, and Executive Privilege" updated Cross' and Wiggins' earlier works on the subject.

412.   James Reston, *The Artillery of the Press* (New York: Harper and Row, 1967).

Reflecting the renewed skepticism of the Johnson era, Reston's "theme is that the rising power of the United States in world affairs, and particularly of the American President, requires, not a more compliant press, but a relentless barrage of facts and criticism, as noisy but also as accurate as artillery fire." (p. vii) His focus, in these lectures before the Council on Foreign Relations, was foreign affairs. As is common for inside accounts, Reston often seemed to be harsher on his industry than on politicians, and he used anecdotes freely as he described the role of the press in spreading information for the government, resulting in both manipulation by, and influence over the government.

413.   Ray Eldon Hiebert and Carlton E. Spitzer, eds., *The Voice of Government* (New York: John Wiley and Sons, 1968).

Recruiting highly-placed current and former officials as contributors, Hiebert and Spitzer compiled a set of readings on government's public information activities. The theme, similar to Lippmann's discussed later in this chapter, is that the press alone is not sufficient to shape public opinion. Government needs public information officers to help describe its programs to the press, congress, and affected interests. Unfortunately, two of the authors complained, such officers are often treated as stepchildren in their agencies, hindering their effectiveness.

414.   Delmer D. Dunn, *Public Officials and the Press* (Reading, MA: Addison-Wesley, 1969).

As a Political Scientist, Dunn used 75 interviews among the press corps and officials of Wisconsin state government to analyze more systematically the role of the press in providing information for public policy-makers. He noted that reporters often try to be objective, although the pressures of their jobs steer them towards disjointed, crisis coverage. As a corollary, political events receive more attention than administrative ones. Officials' views of the press depend on their recent success with it. In general, Dunn found that the press has its highest impact on government when policies are new, although it serves an important informational role at all times.

415.   Dale Minor, *The Information War* (New York: Hawthorn Books, 1970); also

416.   William J. Small, *Political Power and the Press* (New York: W. W. Norton and Co., 1972); also

417.   David Wise, *The Politics of Lying* (New York: Vintage Press, 1973).

These are three of the better-known examples from what Stephen Hess later called the "Outrage School" of journalism that flourished during the Johnson and Nixon administrations. To the extent that such a term is accurate, it may be more a reflection of the time than of these authors. Two of the books, Minor's and Wise's, used narrative descriptions of events of the era as data. Both also concluded with a point similar to Boorstin's, that what appears in the media is a set of events tailored more to the media than to reality.

Small's book is the most historically based and the most analytical. However, he also treated the press as the captive of politicians who make the news, whatever its value or honesty. Of the three books, Wise's is the most adamant in its solution. "Lying and secrecy have no place in a democracy." Minor concluded with a set of ethical dilemmas for the reporter, while Small pushed for greater research and diversity in reporting.

418.   Leon V. Sigal, *Reporters and Officials* (Lexington, MA: Lexington Books, 1973).[3]

Sigal studied the operation of the *Washington Post* and the *New York Times* to determine how national news is made. After reviewing the operations of reporters and officials, he concluded that news "could be seen as the product of the interaction of two bureaucracies--one composed of newsmen and the other of officials." Disagreeing with the mythology of individualized reporting, he saw information as coming mainly through "routine channels," and news decisions as being consensual. Furthermore, he felt that consensus is needed to adjust for the limited perspective of individual reporters, the need of government and the press to work together, and the disjointed nature of both sources and newsworthy events.

419.   David Morgan, *The Capitol Press Corps: Newsmen and the Governing of New York State* (Westport, CT: Greenwood Press, 1978).[4]

From the state level (New York), Morgan found that a triangle of distrust develops among the media, the agencies, and the legislature. Instead, all parties rely on individual relationships that develop over time. He argued that while governmental elites often ascribe great power for mischief to the press, the press actually has little power. Individual reporters can easily be cut off from sources. Also, the common complaint that the press lacks competence is probably justified. Finally, he marvelled that none of the actors felt that the public demands more information than is being offered.

420.   Stephen Hess, *The Washington Reporters* (Washington, D.C.: Brookings Institution, 1981); also *The Government-Press Connection* (Washington, D.C.: Brookings Institution, 1984).

In these books, Hess described first the journalists and then the governmental-press officers who work in Washington. He found that reporters tend to come from elite backgrounds, are more liberal than the population, and prefer "exciting" beats to more developmental matters such as economics. They receive less resistance from editors than Rosten reported in the 1930s, but the headline writers tend to give their stories a presidential flavor even when congressional sources have been used.

Press officers are "semibureaucrat/semireporter, in the bureaucracy but not truly of it, tainted by association with the press yet not of the press." They are generally more competent than their reputations indicate. However, they seldom manipulate the news because they are not skillful enough, they are given too little room to maneuver in the bureaucracy, and alternative sources of information are too easily available.

421.   Lewis M. Helm, Ray Eldon Hiebert, Michael R. Naver, and Kenneth Rabin, eds., *Informing the People* (New York: Longman Inc., 1981).

This book of readings was an attempt to update and expand the topics in the then-dated *The Voice of Government* on government communications policies. The basic theme, summarized by Scott Cutlip, was that the press and government are adversaries, but each needs the other since neither can do its job alone. The book also described new publicity tactics and the new conflicts under the Freedom of Information and Privacy Acts.

AGENCY RELATIONS WITH INTEREST GROUPS

By the nature of our government, much of our interest group activity is directed through what has recently become called "the iron triangle"--a cooperative arrangement between the groups, the agencies, and congressional committees. That literature is discussed in chapter eight under the topic of agency relations with congress. This literature is more concerned with the groups themselves and the impact of interest-group pluralism on agency operations.

422.   "Publius" [James Madison], "The Federalist No. 10," *New York Packet*, November 23, 1787.

The appreciation of interest groups began in Political Science, where the subject can be traced back as far as Aristotle.[5] In the United States, however, the standard starting place is Madison's argument in the Federalist Papers that the causes of faction are sown in the nature of men. He felt it likely that people would organize to repress each others' interests. Trying to stop their organizing would be "worse than the disease." However, factions could be controlled by a representative government that was bigger than any faction.

423.   Graham Wallas, *Human Nature in Politics* (Lincoln: University of Nebraska Press, 1908); also

424.   Arthur F. Bentley, *The Process of Government* (Chicago: University of Chicago Press, 1908).

Understanding the role of interest groups took on new urgency during the Progressive era as several authors tried to abandon the "rational man" approach to politics in favor of the study of subjective people operating within the opinion groups that were growing in strength.

The origins of the new approach are so diverse that no works can be given the label of "first." Two reinterpretations of the constitution as a product of group interests deserve mention.[6] In later Public Administration works, however, the two works listed above have become accepted as the first to approach politics as an amalgam of interest-group activities.

Of the two works, Wallas' is the more sociological. He was concerned with the two themes that political man does not operate through a series of rational decisions, but that progress is possible only if he tries to develop "methods of thought" for behaving that way. With a continually changing environment, groups help with the process of adjustment.

Bentley's work, largely shunned for some years after publication because of its abrasive and difficult style, was more directly concerned with group behavior as a useful methodology for studying politics. He used both anthropological and political theory to justify the necessity for group behavior, and he discussed the operations of interest groups within and between the branches of government.

425.   Peter Odegard, *Pressure Politics: The Story of the Anti-Saloon League* (New York: Columbia University Press, 1928); also

426.   Harwood L. Childs, *Labor and Capital in National Politics* (Columbus: Ohio State University Press, 1930).

These works are largely the opposite of the theoretical works that helped introduce the subject before 1910. Each followed a particular pressure group as it developed from a perceived lack of ability among members to protect their own interests. Odegard's study of the Anti-Saloon League was the most sophisticated study of its time on the rise and activities of an interest group during the nineteenth century. Similarly, Childs provided what still remains the definitive study of the rise of the U.S. Chamber of Commerce. However, while the complicated techniques of organizing and lobbying were described in considerable detail, both works remained descriptive and used little generalized analysis.

427.   E(dward) Pendleton Herring, *Group Representation before Congress* (Baltimore: Johns Hopkins Press, 1929); also *Public Administration and the Public Interest* (New York: McGraw Hill, 1936); also

428.   E. E. Schattsneider, *Politics, Pressures and the Tariff* (New York: Prentice-Hall, 1935).

With these works, studies of interest groups began combining the theoretical and descriptive approaches. The authors continued the Progressive tradition of treating groups with distrust, but also saw them as a possible conduit for government to read the public interest. The three books concentrated on different aspects of governmental operation, and carried different mixes of theory and description. Herring's second book was the most interested in the impact of interest groups on the bureaucracy. Schattsneider classified groups according to defensive-offensive, positive-negative, and primary-secondary types, and discovered that a group's activity could not be explained solely by its economic stake in the policies.

All three books carry the same theme, however. Interest groups arise because people have interests that are not reflected in the structure of government. The groups are healthy for the political system so long as government recognizes them as representatives of localized interests that need to be balanced, and not as representatives of the national interest.

429.   Avery Leiserson, *Administrative Regulation: A Study in Representation of Interests*, Studies in Public Administration, vol. 13, [dissertation] (University of Chicago Press, 1941); also trade edition (Chicago: University of Chicago Press, 1942).

Leiserson's work accepted the growing argument that the public interest could be measured by "the perponderant (sic) acceptance of administrative action by politically influential groups." (p. 16) In this legalistic text, he felt that "the entire range of government activities involves some form of interest representation." Agencies and groups increasingly engaged in joint consultations, although Leiserson did not favor placing groups in official roles in government. Such practices created an atmosphere of distrust, and could negate the benefits of positive government.

430.   V. O. Key, Jr., *Politics, Parties, and Pressure Groups* (New York: Thomas Y. Crowell Co., 1942); also

431.   David B. Truman, *The Governmental Process* (New York: Alfred A. Knopf, 1951).

These two general texts showed the growing acceptance of interest groups as a legitimate part of the American political process. In chapters seven and eight, Key viewed both the bureaucracy and interest groups as attempts to shape the diverse interests of society. When the two groups cooperated, for instance on the framing of regulations, the interest groups often provided a useful source of information.

Truman, who taught courses using Bentley as a text, updated Bentley's approach in this far more readable version. Interest groups were considered to be not only helpful to the political system, but of limited potential abuse because of overlapping loyalties and memberships so long as the groups are not divided along class lines. Also, politics is complicated, and the government answers to more factors than interest-group pressure. The book also described the internal workings of groups and their interactions with each part of the government, including bureaucracies, which were seen as an extension of the political decision-making process.

432.   Robert M. MacIver, *The Web of Government* (New York: Macmillan Co., 1947).

From the perspective of political theory, MacIver illustrated the distinction between states and communities by arguing that "human beings are everywhere members of groups" that are not part of the state structure. Overlapping memberships are inevitable, for no individual is totally absorbed in his group, his state, or his society. As a result, a burden of the state is an ego adjustment between the needs of the state and the needs of the individual.

433.   Samuel J. Eldersveld, "American Interest Groups: A Survey of Research and Some Implications for Theory and Method," in Henry W. Ehrmann, ed., *Interest Groups on Four Continents* (Pittsburgh: University of Pittsburgh Press, 1958), pp. 173-96.

Despite the progress made in methods of analysis in the 1950s, Eldersveld complained that a useful methodology for studying interest groups had not yet been developed. Definitions of self-interest, legitimacy, and the groups themselves needed to be refined. Data still primarily consisted of observation and personal, unstructured interviews. Until these problems were fixed, progress in research would be limited.

434.   Lester W. Milbrath, *The Washington Lobbyists* (Chicago: Rand McNally & Co., 1963).

Using the interview method attacked by Eldersveld, Milbrath tried to describe who lobbyists are and what they do. He discovered that they come from numerous backgrounds, that they do not see electoral politics as part of their job, and that they spend more time with staffs than with politicians. To be effective, lobbyists need to follow a code of conduct established by those being influenced, resulting in a remarkably clean process. Their most important contribution is to present opposing points of view so that, if lobbyists did not exist, they might have to be invented to improve the policy-making process.

435.   Harmon Zeigler, *Interest Groups in American Society* (Englewood Cliffs, NJ: Prentice-Hall, 1964). Second edition, 1972, coauthored with G. Wayne Peak.

Zeigler's book was written in the tradition of, and in defense of, Truman's 1951 work. He felt that attacks on Truman and group theory misunderstood that groups were not presented as the only force in American politics, and that they did not have to explain everything that happened. Instead, the forces that explained the operations of both groups and politics varied. However, groups had a good possibility of success if they met three conditions: 1) they drew their membership from the high-ranking social strata; 2) they espoused goals not in conflict with societal values; and 3) they were accorded legitimacy by those in a position to make authoritative decisions.

436.   Grant McConnell, *Private Power and American Democracy* (New York: Alfred A. Knopf, 1966).

By the mid-1960s, the tide of literature on interest groups turned. In one of the more complete histories of interest group-government relationships, McConnell noted that no orthodoxy exists on how private power should be handled. Empirically, how-ever, large parts of the government have come under the control of narrowly-focused, autonomous elites. These small interests protect against the tyranny of mass move-ments, but at the price of freedom and equality.

Furthermore, the problem is complicated by decentralization, since the oppor-tunity for one interest to exclude others from small governments is increased. There-fore, government needs to encourage the growth of national interests to counteract the influence of the groups.

437.   Theodore Lowi, *The End of Liberalism* (New York: W. W. Norton and Co.,
        1969).

        Lowi was even more adamant that interest-group liberalism is destructive to the
public interest through its penetration of the bureaucracy, where it is capable of
rewriting policies during implementation, making planning impractical, making it impossible to achieve justice, and weakening our ability to live by formal rules. He
argued that the representative function should be fulfilled through its constitutional
role, and that bureaucracy should be left out of the representative process.

438.   *Federal Election Campaign Act Amendments of 1974*, 88 Stat. 1263; also

439.   U.S. Supreme Court, *Buckley, et al. v Valeo*, 424 U.S. 1 (1976).

        It is now universally agreed that in 1974 the rules of interest-group representa-
tion changed in fundamental ways. The Federal Election Campaign Act of 1971 was
amended in an effort to curb abuses by private interests in the electoral process.
Specifically, the Act provided matching public funds for presidential races, and limited
contributions from individuals and groups for each candidate and in each election.
The Supreme Court, in *Buckley v Valeo*, disallowed some of the provisions of the act
as unconstitutional. Most importantly, they eliminated ceilings on independent expenditures by political committees, making it possible for individual contributions to be
funneled through single-interest groups that could speak with enormous financial
power. Almost immediately, lobbying in Washington began to be increasingly chan-
neled through these organizations.

440.   Jeffrey M. Berry, *Lobbying for the People* (Princeton, NJ: Princeton University
        Press, 1977); also *The Interest Group Society* (Boston: Little, Brown, and Co.,
        1984); also

441.   Allan J. Cigler and Burdett A. Loomis, eds., *Interest Group Politics* (Washing-
        ton, D.C.: Congressional Quarterly Press, 1983).

        At first, the scope of the change was not obvious. Berry's 1977 book, based
primarily on 1972-73 interviews, casually mentioned the Federal Election amendments
once, but concentrated instead on the independent rise of public interest groups. His
second book and the introduction to Cigler and Loomis however, agreed that the
changes in lobbying in the 1980s were fundamental. Cigler and Loomis summarized
them as: 1) a great proliferation in the number of groups; 2) centralization of headquarters around Washington, D.C.; 3) technical improvements in grass-roots lobbying;
4) a rise in single-interest groups; 5) a change in finance laws leading to political
action committees; 6) the penetration of groups into the bureaucracy, the presidency,
and congress; 7) the decline of the power of political parties; and 8) the rise of
public interest groups.

CONTINUING CONCERNS

In an interdependent world, relationships are not always what they seem. In chapter seven, literature is discussed that argues that the bureaucracy has taken on roles that were reserved for other parts of our political machinery, but that have been more successfully fulfilled by the administrative function. Both the press and interest groups are making similar contributions from outside the governmental machinery.

By tradition and the constitution, the press and government are rivals. By the heritage of the progressive era, interest groups are similarly a rival force to be controlled. Yet, government has come to rely on both for its information about the electorate, and even about itself. The information function has not been "taken over" so much as it has been performed so well by these outside groups that government administration has not invested the resources to keep its own sources competitive.

Jefferson's adage about preferring a press with no government to a government with no press may never have been a serious proposal, but it was an imaginable scenario. Today, the possibility of eliminating either body (or interest groups) is too speculative to usefully imagine what might remain. The rivals are no longer prepared to operate without each other. Should the unlikely happen, through some massive realignment in political priorities, the remaining groups would simply have to assume the roles left vacant by the departing partner.

NOTES FOR CHAPTER NINE

1. The 1961 date listed in later Harper and Row editions is the copyright, not the first date of publication.

2. An earlier version appeared in *The Washington Correspondents and Government Information* [unpublished dissertation] (Washington, D.C.: American University, 1960).

3. This is the publisher for the clothbound edition only. The paperback edition was released by D.C. Heath and Co., the parent company of Lexington Books.

4. This was the second volume in Greenwood's Contributions in Political Science series.

5. A brief history of interest-group questions can be found in Peter H. Odegard's "Introduction" to Arthur F. Bentley, *The Process of Government* (Cambridge: The Belknap Press of Harvard University Press, reprint of 1967).

6. J. Allen Smith, *Spirit of American Government* (New York: Macmillan, 1907); and Charles A. Beard, *Economic Interpretation of the Constitution of the United States* (New York: Macmillan, 1913).

10
Public Opinion and Democracy

BACKGROUND

This is a subject in which definitions are critical. In Lincoln's famous phrase, is a government *of* the people one that is *by* the people, *for* the people, or both? Does a bureaucracy represent the public interest because it measures their will and implements it, or because it is composed of a microcosm of the public itself? Are the two even compatible? At different times, each cause has been advanced, and the literature on democracy in the administrative state cannot be summarized without treating the definitions as attempted answers to the larger question of how bureaucracy can be made more democratic.

Two warnings are in order about the subjects of this chapter. First, the literature discussed here on the topic of representative bureaucracy largely excludes proposals and descriptions of the mechanics of affirmative action, which are discussed in the chapter on staffing. The same term has also been used in our literary heritage to describe the ability of the bureaucracy to represent interest groups rather than classes or races. This literature is included in chapter seven.

The second warning relates to the term public opinion. As V.O. Key described in the 1960s, the measurement of the concept was a political science activity that was eventually taken over by sociologists. Later, it was reclaimed by political scientists, but for the purposes of analyzing voter behavior. This summation is concerned solely with public administration applications, and borrows from other disciplines only when the field has been inclined to do the same.

442.   Roberto [Robert] Michels, *Political Parties: A Sociological Study of Oligar-
       chical Tendencies of Modern Democracies*, see note for English-language transla-
       tions.[1] Originally *Zur Soziologie des Parteiwesens in der modernen Demokratie;
       Untersuchengen über die oligarchischen Tendenzen des Gruppenlebens*,
       Philosophisch-soziologische Bücherei. Bd. XXI (Leipzig: Klinkhardt, 1911).

       At first, the concern was completely focused on the ability of government to
reflect the will of the majority. Michels investigated the German Social Democratic
Party and concluded that oligarchy was inevitable in large organizations, or stated in
the reverse, bureaucracy and democracy were incompatible. Under what he called the
"iron law of oligarchical tendencies," Michels felt that elites inevitably arose because
of access to knowledge, control of the means of communication, and increased political skill. Representative bureaucracy was impossible because the leaders would be
removed from their old classes by their new positions. Leaders could oppose other
factions, but a socialist revolution would result only in a new oligarchy run under the
name of socialism.

443.   A. Lawrence Lowell, *Public Opinion and Popular Government* (New York: Long-
       mans, Green and Co., 1913).

       Lowell, the president of Harvard University, was not concerned with the rise of
oligarchies so long as political parties could control the process. In this expanded
version of lectures delivered at Johns Hopkins in 1909, he recognized that party
cleavages were artificial. However, they focused political opinions on national issues
and made it possible to control abuses by special interests. To aid in implementing
their will, he advocated that experts be recruited into government. However, he
recognized that securing and retaining them would be difficult under then-present
personnel regulations.

444.   James Bryce, *Modern Democracies*, 2 vol. (New York: Macmillan, 1921).

       Bryce, who studied six major democratic systems and other smaller ones, con-
cluded that democracy had two major weaknesses. First, particularly in the United
States, it was subject to undue influence by wealthy special interests. The problem
was not manifested at the higher levels of the bureaucracy to a great extent because
of the publicity focused on those offices. It became critical at lower levels of the
bureaucracy, however, where the officers were weak and unskilled while the special
interests were still strong.
       The solution, which could be only partially effective, was responsible publicity
by the press. That solution was complicated by the second major weakness of democracies, which was the tendency of the press to become irresponsible in its basically
unregulated state.

445. Walter Lippmann, *Public Opinion* (New York: Harcourt, Brace, and Co., 1922).

In trying to coordinate governmental and administrative policies with public opinion, Lippmann argued that public opinion could not exist without adequate sources of information. Instead of informed opinion, the public too easily substituted stereotyped information.

The pictures of reality needed to be presented by someone other than decision-makers. However, since the press had its own priorities that often clouded its objectivity, he suggested special investigating units attached to each cabinet department.

446. Carl J. Friedrich and Taylor Cole, *Responsible Bureaucracy: A Study of the Swiss Civil Service* (Cambridge: Harvard University Press, 1932); also

447. Carl J. Friedrich, *Constitutional Government and Politics* (New York: Harper and Brothers, 1937)[2]; also "Public Policy and the Nature of Administrative Responsibility," in Carl J. Friedrich and Edward S. Mason, eds., *Public Policy* (Cambridge: Harvard University Press, 1940); also

448. Herman Finer, "Better Government Personnel," *Political Science Quarterly*, 51, (December 1936): 569-599; also "Administrative Responsibility in Democratic Government," *Public Administration Review*, 1, (Summer 1941): 335-50.

During the 1930s and 1940s, the field was treated to what became the running Friedrich-Finer debate on administrative accountability. Friedrich's position was based in his attack on Goodnow's politics-administration dichotomy. Instead, Friedrich argued, policy was continually being formed through many sources, including the bureaucracy. That being the case, congressional oversight through legislation was impossible, and more active oversight had proven to be dysfunctional since it was often ill-informed, and it left administrators with inadequate discretion for efficient operation.

Fortunately, Friedrich argued, the bureaucracy has slowly developed its own set of mechanics for accountability. The most promising is professionalism, or the internalized and group definitions of responsible behavior. This is supplemented by such tactics as direct citizen participation in policy formulation, a tool that bureaucracy often helped develop.

Finer felt that government had become too powerful to be given such "professional" discretion. Accountability could not be achieved without correction and punishment by outsiders up to dismissal from the service. Only once the sense of real responsibility had been achieved would efficiency be possible.

449. Henry A. Wallace and James L. McCamy, "Straw Polls and Public Administration," *Public Opinion Quarterly*, 4, (June 1940): 221-23; also

450.   Ens. David R. Truman, "Public Opinion Research as a Tool of Public
        Administration," *Public Administration Review*, 5, (Winter, 1945): 62-72.

These authors were more concerned with the precise mechanics by which public
administration could determine public opinion. To Wallace and McCamy, public opinion polls had become "just as much an essential part of the administrative process as
budgeting or personnel or organization." To Truman, "opinions are facts." Public
opinion research had four potential uses for both academics and practitioners: testing
hypotheses; testing plans for projected programs; evaluating the effectiveness of
ongoing programs; and facilitating the informational aspects of the agency.

451.   Harold D. Lasswell, *Democracy Through Public Opinion* ([Menasha, Wisconsin]:
        George Banta Publishing Co., 1941).

Lasswell was less concerned with measuring public opinion than with explaining
it and suggesting how to steer it in democratic directions. He described the tendency
of public opinion to fall prey to propaganda and uneducated opinion. The way to
fight the tendency, he felt, was to encourage open and educated exchanges of ideas.
In that spirit, one chapter was entitled "Democracy Needs a New Way to Talk."
Many of his suggestions would seem radical or even anti-democratic today. He
considered, for instance, the Instant Reply Plan, which would force anti-democratic
publications and even meetings to present opposing views. He also considered a
National Bureau of Communications Research and a democratic-values training institute for politicians. This last suggestion, applied to bureaucrats, resurfaced with such
authors as Appleby and Mosher, as described later in this chapter.

452.   Charles M. Wiltse, "The Representative Function of Bureaucracy," *American
        Political Science Review*, 35, (June 1941): 510-16.

As mentioned in chapter seven, Wiltse helped develop the argument that
bureaucracy could assist congress in fulfilling its constitutional obligation of representativeness. "(T)here exist within the administrative branch of the federal government
numerous agencies whose concern is focused upon particular industries or interest
groups, and whose function extends to recommending to Congress legislation with
respect to these interests." (p. 514) Since the representative ability of congress had
declined, this new partner was to be welcomed.

453.   J. Donald Kingsley, *Representative Bureaucracy: An Interpretation of the British
        Civil Service* (Yellow Springs, OH: Antioch Press, 1944).

The debate over representative bureaucracy continued with Long (mentioned
below) and others who are discussed in chapter seven. However, the more common
usage of the term is not related to interest-group representation, but to the class or

racial makeup of the administrative service. As such, it is the more traditional *of* the people context of democratic administration.

Both Heinz and Krislov have credited Kingsley with introducing the new term. Kingsley's study of the British civil service system found that it was staffed by members of the upper and middle classes, but not the working class, and that such a practice was potentially dangerous for its neutrality. If the Labour Party took control of the government, Kingsley doubted that the civil service could represent its interests. The reforms after Northcote-Trevelyan had more effectively isolated the upper class in the top of the bureaucracy. As a solution, he recommended that the ranks of government be opened to the working class, as was happening in the United States.

454.   Charles S. Hyneman, "Bureaucracy and the Democratic System," *Louisiana Law Review*, 6, (1945): 309-49; also *Bureaucracy in a Democracy* (New York: Harper and Brothers, 1950).

So long as the War remained in recent memories, however, most democratic concerns were about the policies of government--not its internal make-up. In 1950, Hyneman felt that: 1) the bureaucracy must be judged on how it uses its power; 2) all people with authority must exercise it within limits defined by an inclusive, informed electorate; 3) power has the potential to be turned toward unacceptable ends; and 4) elected officials must be the primary agents for directing and controlling the bureaucracy.

Most of the book filled in the details of legislative, presidential, and judicial control. Notably, Hyneman felt that the top administrators should be a team selected from a political party that could be voted out of office. He did not favor the abolition of the bipartisan Civil Service Commission, however, and he did not feel that the Bureau of the Budget had been given enough strength to coordinate policies. In general, he favored discretion but accountability for the bureaucracy rather than prior restraint and control.

455.   Paul H. Appleby, *Big Democracy* (New York: Alfred A. Knopf, 1945); also *Policy and Administration* (University: University of Alabama Press, 1949); also *Morality and Administration in Democratic Government* (Baton Rouge: LSU Press, 1952).

Appleby's approach to democratic administration was a harbinger of the New Public Administration literature that would eventually stress the integration of internal and external controls. In *Big Democracy* and *Morality*, Appleby described the political nature of public administration, and the necessity for administrators to answer to the population through the political process. Without centralized hierarchy, responsiveness could not be enforced. In *Policy and Administration*, he also offered that an organization that is considerate of its own employees through democratic internal processes is also likely to be considerate of the public, while an authoritarian organization is likely to treat the public in the same style.

456.   Ordway Tead, *Democratic Administration* (New York: Association Press, 1945).

This reprint of Tead's 1935 brochure "Creative Management" contained the newer essay "Democracy in Administration," in which Tead agreed with Appleby that democracy expressed through control of interest groups is pointless without effective and moral administration to implement the results. He concluded that "the realization of the good life can take place only as associated action expresses itself through good organization."

457.   David M. Levitan, "The Responsibility of Administrative Officials in a Democratic Society," *Political Science Quarterly*, 61, (December 1946): 562-98; also

458.   Reinhard Bendix, *Higher Civil Servants in American Society: A Study of the Social Origins, the Careers and the Power Position of Higher Federal Administrators*, Studies in Sociology Series #1 (Boulder: University of Colorado Press, 1949).

Levitan applied Kingsley's class argument on representative bureaucracy to the United States as he searched for methods to control the bureaucracy in a world without the politics-administration dichotomy. "(T)o preserve democratic government in the United States--it is essential that...the base of recruitment for all positions and branches of government...should be widened and made truly representative of American society." (pp. 582-83)

Bendix approached the subject quantitatively, measuring the social origins, the cultural patterns, and the professionalism of high-level federal administrators. He discovered that they were heterogeneous and broadly recruited from lower and middle classes. They usually worked to obtain higher education. They were often compensated at levels comparable to the private sector, but were offered low respect by the population.

459.   David Riesman (in collaboration with Reuel Denny and Nathan Glazer), *The Lonely Crowd* (New Haven: Yale University Press, 1950).

Riesman's somewhat disjointed analysis speculated on changes in American society that have impacts on both bureaucratic behavior and democratic politics. For bureaucracy, he tried to show that Americans were changing from inner-directed to outer-directed personalities, meaning that they were creating a work environment with great pressures toward conformity. In politics, however, class divisions were giving way to "veto groups," which allowed people to select the interests to which they would conform, and through which they could struggle for resources.

460.   Norton E. Long, "Bureaucracy and Constitutionalism," *American Political Science Review*, 46, (September 1952): 808-18.

As mentioned in chapter seven, Long reinforced Wiltse's notion of representative bureaucracy by recognizing that "by appropriate recruitment, structure, and processes, the bureaucracy can be made a vital part of a functioning constitutional democracy, filling out the deficiencies of Congress and the political executive." (p. 818) The bureaucracy, Long felt, could be particularly useful at representing groups that are underrepresented in congress.

461.   Avery Leiserson, "Notes on the Theory of Political Opinion Formation," *American Political Science Review*, 67, (March 1953): 171-77.

Public opinion research slipped out of favor in Political Science until its revival by the University of Michigan Survey Research Center in the late 1950s. Leiserson complained that we often treated it in mystical or even religious terminology. Instead, he felt that we needed to treat opinion formation as part of the political process by studying how public policies affect the media as well as its relations with politics, including the access it offers to political elites.

462.   Georges Langrod, "Local Government and Democracy," *Public Administration* [England], 31, (Spring 1953): 25-34; also

463.   Roscoe C. Martin, *Grass Roots* (University: University of Alabama Press, 1957).

Langrod argued before the International Political Science Association that the common assumption that local government leads to democracy might be incorrect since each has existed without the other, and since local government leads to decentralization while democracy encourages integration.
In the United States, Martin argued in a set of 1955 lectures that democracy seldom appears in private organizations or small governments. Local governments are usually too small to achieve administrative efficiency or democracy, and are often led in a personal style by generalist amateurs.

464.   Peter Blau, *The Dynamics of Bureaucracy* (Chicago: University of Chicago Press, 1955); also

465.   Harry Cohen, *The Demonics of Bureaucracy: A Study of a Government Employment Agency* [dissertation] (Urbana: University of Illinois, 1962); also trade edition as *The Demonics of Bureaucracy: Problems of Change in a Government Agency* (Ames: Iowa State University, 1965).

Most of Blau's book is more relevant to the chapter on bureaucracy, in which it is described in more detail. However, it also contained an argument that has been frequently cited since that "(b)ureaucracy and democracy are two fundamentally different analytical types of social organization." They are incompatible. However, because bureaucracy is poor at making fundamental choices and democracy is poor at implementation, they need each other, and adjust to each other.

Cohen, who collaborated on Blau's second edition in 1963, developed the argument somewhat further in *Demonics*. Studying a different part of the same employment agency that provided Blau's data, he discovered that "*(b)ureaucracy is dynamic, but in a way that may best be called demonic, referring to change (dynamics), but in a dysfunctional direction.*" (1965, p. 222) Specifically, in an effort to be adaptable, the bureaucracy places itself in a position to be pushed toward pathological behavior by clients expecting favorable treatment. This leads to complaints by others, and eventual malaise in the organization.

On the subject of democratic control, however, Cohen found that the demonics are only a trend, and that outside political forces could force the bureaucracy back into acceptable behavior.

466.   Gabriel Almond, "Public Opinion and National Security Policy," *Public Opinion Quarterly*, 20, (Summer 1956): 371-78.

Almond described the special problems of generating useful public opinion on national security policy because of its technical aspects, the need for secrecy, and the gravity of the stakes. He suggested that national security be introduced into university curricula, that military specialists be trained in media relations, that interest groups be trained in military affairs, and that military leaders be trained in politics.

467.   Paul Van Riper, *History of the United States Civil Service* (Evanston, IL: Row, Peterson and Co., 1958); also

468.   W. Lloyd Warner, Paul Van Riper, Norman Martin, and Orvis Collins, *The American Federal Executive* (New Haven: Yale University Press, 1963).

These two works were in general agreement (as indicated by the role of Van Riper in each), but they are also good examples of two extremes in possible approaches to representative bureaucracy. In 1958, Van Riper used a verbal and logical approach to define representative bureaucracy as requiring the bureaucracy to have two characteristics: a reasonable cross section of the society based on occupation, class, geography, and the like; and general ethos and attitudes that are in tune with society as a whole.

The Warner, et al., study was the ultimate in data comparison, based on 12,929 interviews with civilian and military bureaucratic leaders, and compared to an earlier empirical study of business leaders. The study concluded that civilian bureaucrats are more representative than military leaders, who are more representative than business leaders. None of the groups duplicates society's socio-economic distribution, but lower class children can enter high bureaucratic ranks. They are then likely to achieve high geographic mobility, and more likely to obtain advanced degrees than is the case for business leaders.

469.   Morris Janowitz, Deil Wright, and William Delany, *Public Administration and the Public--Perspectives Toward Government in a Metropolitan Community*, no. 36 in University of Michigan, Michigan Governmental Studies (Ann Arbor: Bureau of Government, Institute of Government Administration, University of Michigan, 1958).

The authors used public surveys in Detroit in 1953-1954 to measure the four criteria by which they believed that bureaucracies achieve democratic consent: 1) that the public has knowledge about the bureaucracy; 2) that the public believes that their self-interest is being served; 3) that the public believes the bureaucracy to operate according to certain moral principles; and 4) that the public holds the bureaucracy in sufficient prestige for it to be able to operate effectively. They found that the public was largely uninformed even about agencies with which they had contact. They also believed that a market for positive information was waiting for the local media to exploit. However, they also found more acceptance of the worth of bureaucracy among most of the public than they had expected.

470.   Angus Campbell, Philip E. Converse, Warren E. Miller, and Donald E. Stokes, *The American Voter* (New York: John Wiley and Sons, 1960); also

471.   V. O. Key, Jr., *Public Opinion and American Democracy* (New York: Alfred A. Knopf, 1961).

In 1960, several researchers from the University of Michigan Survey Research Center published a summation of some of the more comprehensive political opinion polls then taken. Along with Key, who used their work heavily in documenting his study, they argued that the public is generally uninformed on political issues. However, political activists constitute what Key called a political subculture that helps resolve conflicts and create consenses. In particular, elites work through publicly-set limits on broad goals, called funnels or dams. Within these, the elites need to seek some consistency on opinions about policies that are interrelated. Their tactic is often to be vague, although even that can achieve a quiet public consensus so long as the basic concerns of the public are not aroused.

472.   Eric Strauss, *The Ruling Servants: Bureaucracy in Russia, France--and Britain?* (New York: Frederick A. Praeger, 1961).

Basing his study in the radical theories of James Burnham (see chapter on bureaucracy), Strauss argued that bureaucracy is an outgrowth of industrialization and advanced technology and that it inevitably deteriorates through "bureaucratic degeneration" so that bureaucrats begin responding to their own interests rather than to "primary social forces." Once that happens, radical political solutions eventually follow.

473.   Norton Long, *The Polity* (Chicago: Rand McNally and Co., 1962).

In a defense of bureaucracy, Long found that the departments of administration are among the most responsible units in government. Measured by sensitivity and expert consideration of issues, he argued that the administrative machinery is uniquely qualified to respond to the public interest. They are also large enough to have a representative selection of personnel, and they are stable enough to learn from mistakes and be self-correcting.

474.   Peter Woll, *American Bureaucracy* (New York: W. W. Norton and Co., 1963).

While Woll's arguments on democracy were developed in earlier works, this is a concise and readable enough summation that it has frequently been cited in subsequent discussions of the topic. In separate chapters, Woll commented on two different aspects of the democratic contributions of bureaucracy to the policy process. First, he noted that the bureaucracy is nonelected, but is more representative of some of society's interests than is congress. Second, the bureaucracy serves as a third party in policy formulation that is often able to break the deadlock between congress and the president on legislative deliberations.

475.   Franklin P. Kilpatrick, Milton C. Cummings, Jr., and M. Kent Jennings, *The Image of the Federal Service* (Washington, D.C.: Brookings Institution, 1964); also *Source Book of a Study of Occupational Values and the Image of the Federal Service* (Washington, D.C.: Brookings Institution, 1964); also

476.   Milton C. Cummings, M. Kent Jennings, and Franklin P. Kilpatrick, "Federal and Nonfederal Employees: A Comparative Social-Occupational Analysis," *Public Administration Review*, 27, (December 1967): 393-402.

These two reports, plus the Source Book, were based on more than 2000 interviews conducted during the Spring of 1960 with both federal employees and the general public. The researchers found federal and non-federal workers to be more similar than dissimilar. Some variations were noted, and the one that has had the greatest impact on the literature is that federal employment is more open to minorities, especially Blacks. The authors were concerned, however, that the egalitarianism of the federal government might be pushed too far. Specifically, they found evidence that those of higher socio-economic status think less favorably of the federal service, and are less inclined to want to work there or to think of its functions as legitimate.

477. Roscoe C. Martin, ed., *Public Administration and Democracy: Essays in Honor of Paul H. Appleby* (Syracuse, NY: Syracuse University Press, 1965).

This set of essays in honor of one of the most respected authors on the subject of administrative democracy includes one essay compiled from Appleby's unpublished manuscripts. More relevant to this topic, however, are the excerpts from previous writings that conclude the book. Appleby's often wandering writings on the subject are also summarized in the essays by John Gaus on the limits and potential contributions of citizens as administrators, Arthur Macmahon on access to advisory mechanisms, Victor Thompson on administrative control, and Stephen Bailey and Rowland Egger on the moral responsibility of bureaucracy.

478. Walter Gellhorn, *When Americans Complain* (Cambridge: Harvard University Press, 1966).

Gellhorn argued that government has become big enough that, even though most administrators are well-intentioned, mass production techniques lead to harm in society. The most common method of correcting such harm across Western cultures is judicial. Other useful devices include the 535 "ombudsmen" in congress, the (then) Bureau of the Budget, and the General Accounting Office. Gellhorn felt, however, that an outside critic, similar to an ombudsman, was worth trying in the United States.

479. Robert A. Dahl, *Pluralist Democracy in the United States: Conflict and Consent* (Chicago: Rand McNally, 1967).[3]

In trying to control government, Dahl saw conflict as inevitable in a pluralist system that has multiple centers of power with none sovereign. Democracy is achieved by making the competition as fair as practical.

Political institutions serve two roles in this conflict. They can represent various interests. Secondly, they can reduce the intensity of conflict if there is wide agreement on their procedures for negotiation and on their ability to close negotiations through decision-making. In both cases, however, bureaucracy's role was mentioned by Dahl only in passing.

480. Hanna Finichel Pitkin, *The Concept of Representation* (Berkeley: University of California Press, 1967).

As has already been mentioned, representation is not only a term with multiple uses in the discipline, but it is an entirely independent field of study in political theory. Most of that literature is seldom cited in public administration works, although this one is an exception.

Pitkin used both linguistic and political theory approaches in an attempt to define representation. She described the Burkian-liberal interest-group model as involving independent actions in the interest of, and responsive to, the represented. This is a particularly well-suited model for the kinds of nebulous decisions often faced by legislators. The microcosm model, on the other hand, is inappropriate unless the chosen person can act in the Burkian-interest-group mode. The book did not discuss representation in the bureaucracy.

481.   V. Subramanian, "Representative Bureaucracy: A Reassessment," *American Political Science Review*, 61, (December 1967): 1010-19.

Subramanian reexamined some of the discussions of representative bureaucracy to conclude that there are problems with both definitions and logic. For one, the literature seems to assume that one can ascribe class behavior to "representatives" without testing whether they actually behave that way.

Most importantly, however, he felt that some of the essential qualifications for bureaucrats lead to the recruitment of the middle class (over 80 percent in many countries). In the United States, that could be used as evidence of a representative bureaucracy. In countries such as India, the same trend could be used as evidence that the requirements of bureaucracies are inherently contradictory with representative bureaucracy.

482.   Samuel P. Krislov, *The Negro in Federal Employment* (Minneapolis: University of Minnesota Press, 1967); also *Representative Bureaucracy* (Englewood Cliffs, NJ: Prentice-Hall, 1974).

In 1967, Krislov recounted the relationship that had developed between Blacks and the government, and described the problems that still remained. He concluded by citing the statistical evidence that government employment had been a particularly effective vehicle for Black advancement to that time.

In *Representative Bureaucracy*, Krislov took a more theoretical approach when he described the conflict of definitions between "virtual representation" of interests and attempts to create a microcosm of society in the bureaucracy. He felt that absolute representation was not possible "(s)ince government service requires skills different from those needed by society as a whole." However, through its complexity, the bureaucracy is capable of being more representative than any other segment of government.

483.   Frederick C. Mosher, *Democracy and the Public Service* (New York: Oxford University Press, 1968); also

484.   Emmette S. Redford, *Democracy in the Administrative State* (New York: Oxford University Press, 1969).

These are the first two books published in Roscoe Martin's series on Public Administration and Democracy. In the first, Mosher described the development of the public service as progressing through a number of phases, concluding with the then-current age of Government by Professionals. He was very concerned that professionals not enter the service without a broadening educational experience. In what he called the Barnard-Appleby-Bailey construct, he argued that professionalism is needed, but only if those in power have university-level training in the public responsibility of their professions.

Mosher also addressed the issue of representative bureaucracy, arguing that the representation could be done actively or passively. Considering the trouble that could be caused by attempts at active representation, he preferred the passive approach.

Redford tried to reconcile the administrative state with democracy by arguing that democratic morality rests on three tenets--individual realization, equality in claims for attention, and participation. These can be achieved because policies are made by interaction among minorities operating through political subsystems, although the process can be protected only by the effective oversight of a representative superstructure. Redford also described some of the specific protections of both citizens and workers that are needed in the democratic state.

485.   Warren G. Bennis and Philip E. Slater, *The Temporary Society* (New York: Harper and Row, 1968).

As a precursor to the New Public Administration movement, Bennis and Slater predicted that our rapidly changing society would eventually cause organizational forms to become adaptive and rapidly-changing, or "temporary." People would be evaluated according to ability rather than organizational rank, and they would come together into coalitions as needed. The social implications, especially on the family, however, would be disruptive.

486.   U.S. Commission on Civil Rights, *For ALL the People...By ALL the People: A Report on Equal Opportunity in State and Local Government Employment* (Washington, D.C.: USGPO, 1969).

This report studied the employment patterns of Blacks in state and local governments in seven metropolitan areas. Agency hiring patterns varied widely. However, while Blacks tended to be clustered in lower-paying jobs, they were employed in higher numbers, and they achieved white-collar status in greater percentages than was the case in the private sector in the same metropolitan areas.

487.   David H. Rosenbloom, *Federal Service and the Constitution: The Development of the Public Employment Relationship* (Ithaca, NY: Cornell University Press, 1971).

Rosenbloom's concern with democracy was the differential treatment offered citizens as subjects vs. employees of government. He retraced the history of American bureaucracy to determine whether employees were subject to positive discrimination, meaning extra privileges, or negative discrimination, meaning extra constraints. The record varied with the era being discussed. On balance, however, employees were subject to negative discrimination, most often through restraints on such rights as privacy, speech, and association.

488.   William A. Niskanen, Jr., *Bureaucracy and Representative Government* (Chicago: Aldine-Atherton, 1971).

Niskanen worked with the RAND Corporation and in McNamara's Pentagon before becoming disillusioned with the potential of the new tools of policy analysis. In conversations with Gordon Tullock, he developed the ideas behind the core of this book.

Using extremely detailed mathematics, he created a model to support his contention that large government inevitably finance more programs than make economic sense, and have a tendency to behave as if they are sovereign. He concluded that a better government would be a smaller government. He did not favor such brute tactics for reducing government as requiring two-thirds votes on appropriations, but did favor competitive supplies and more progressive and localized taxation.

489.   Peter Bachrach, ed., *Political Elites in a Democracy* (New York: Atherton Press, 1971).

Bachrach argued in his introduction that most of the respected writings of the day accepted that democracy is possible despite the rise of elites in modern society. In this book, he compiled a set of previously-published readings by such authors as Dahl, Lasswell, Lazersfeld, and Marcuse that both supported and attacked that position.

Bachrach stated that elite status in American society is based in authority more than in power. Furthermore, governmental elites are constrained in their authority by democratic accountability while private-sector elites are not. The answer to whether the constraints are sufficient varies with each author.

490.   U.S. Supreme Court, *Griggs v Duke Power Company*, 401 U.S. 424 (1971).

In 1971, the Supreme Court eliminated many of the barriers that had served to block representativeness in bureaucracy and elsewhere when it disallowed the practice of the Duke Power Company of Draper, North Carolina of requiring high school diplomas and two aptitude tests for common laborer positions. The effect, which was not extended to government until the Equal Employment Opportunity Act of 1972 (86 Stat. 103), is that discrimination is assumed to exist when minorities are underrepresented in relation to the available labor pool, and that selection instruments in such cases have to be specific to the task for which the applicants are hired.

Note: See also chapter 16 on staffing.

491.   Frank Marini, *Toward a New Public Administration: The Minnowbrook Perspective* (Scranton, PA: Chandler Publishing, 1971); also

492.   Dwight Waldo, *Public Administration in a Time of Turbulence* (Scranton, PA: Chandler Publishing, 1971).

In the Summer of 1968, when radical politics was at one of its high-water marks on American college campuses, Dwight Waldo arranged for a conference of "young" Public Administrators to express the ideas that became called the "New Public Administration." As Marini noted in the summation of *Toward a New Public Administration*, there was considerable diversity among the papers that were delivered. However, the general thrust was toward a "relevant" administration that is more interested in adaptability, confrontational decision-making, and client interests than toward traditional positivist and removed forms of study.

Public Administration in a Time of Turbulence is a set of papers collected from several panels organized by Waldo at the American Political Science Association convention in 1969. He also added works by Kaufman and Mosher, and a concluding essay of his own. The general goal was to "carry forward the 'Minnowbrook idea,'" although the tone of the book put that idea into a calmer perspective. Kaufman revived his tripartite division of administrative goals to describe our movement toward greater representativeness. Several authors described the heightened interest in decentralization, in public participation, and in the prescriptive, rather than descriptive, study of the field.

493.   Eugene P. Dvorin and Robert H. Simmons, *From Amoral to Humane Bureaucracy* (San Francisco: Canfield Press, 1972); also

494.   Frederick C. Thayer, *An End to Hierarchy! An End to Competition!* (New York: New Viewpoints, 1973).

Following the same general theme, Dvorin and Simmons complained that bureaucracy is unable to foster human dignity because it does not believe in it. Furthermore, the academic field has done virtually nothing to improve the situation since it has become stuck in the development of techniques rather than morality.

More generally, Thayer argued that political theory has grown beyond hierarchy, which has existed as an organizational form for millennia. Unfortunately, both hierarchy and its resulting competition are partially to blame for some of the societal crises that are arising, and they are going to be unable to solve these problems once they arise.

He argued that we need to adopt a more fluid form of organization based on collective decision-making, the integration of work and income, the end of the concept of property, and similar measures. It is possible to adopt this new "paradigm" before the crises come to fruition, or we can wait until they are at hand.

495.   Lewis C. Mainzer, *Political Bureaucracy* (Glenview, IL: Scott, Foresman, 1973).

At a time when much of the literature on bureaucratic accountability found the concept to be a contradiction of terms, Mainzer stood out as a relative optimist. He evaluated recent bureaucratic experience through the three criteria of competence, selfhood, and political responsibility to find that much of the public service falls short of the ideal. However, much of what has been accomplished is impressive, and "(i)n a world so bungled, whatever of worth has been achieved merits a restrained word of praise." (p. 151)

496.   Victor A. Thompson, *Without Sympathy or Enthusiasm: The Problem of Administrative Compassion* (University: University of Alabama Press, 1975).

Thompson also found little of use in radical proposals. His concern was why administrators so often enforce rules in inappropriate or even inhumane circumstances. The reason is that organizations are created as artificial systems based on functional rather than substantive rationality. In short, they can do no differently. Thompson then looked at various methods of possible control, including such proposals as ombudsmen and organization development. He could not get around the problem that bureaucracies work this way because it is the effective way to deliver the mass services for which they are set up.

He was particularly harsh on the "political absurdity and immaturity" of the New Public Administration, as both an attempted theft of society's resources and an effort to foster individualized rather than collective responsibility for the common culture. However, he was optimistic that the bureaucrats themselves can evolve in their roles toward increased humanity in their workplaces.

497.   Kenneth John Meier, "Representative Bureaucracy: An Empirical Analysis," *American Political Science Review*, 69, (June 1975): 526-42.

Meier set out to "critically examine the ideal of a representative bureaucracy and empirically test the existence of a representative bureaucracy in the United States." (p. 526) He found four faults in the theory of representation: 1) it assumes that political control is ineffective; 2) its definitions lack consensus; 3) it assumes without proof that socio-economic characteristics determine administrators' values; and 4) it advocates broad representation without explaining the benefit. Meier also found that the public service is broadly representative, although not by grades. Finally, he noted that he made no effort to test the distribution of values among administrators.

498.   Harry Kranz, *The Participatory Bureaucracy* (Lexington, MA: Lexington Books, 1976).

Kranz began his study with three themes that made his purposes clear: 1) a more representative bureaucracy is desirable; 2) the U.S. is lacking a representative bureaucracy at federal, state, and locals levels; and 3) a representative bureaucracy could be attained by changing the methods of selecting and promoting bureaucrats. The principal barriers that still remained to representative employment were the policies and structures of merit systems agencies, arbitrary qualifications requirements and limited recruitment, and inequitable selection techniques. It should also be mentioned that Kranz' citations are among the more complete and helpful on the subject for future research.

499.   John A. Rohr, *Ethics for Bureaucrats: An Essay on Law and Values* (New York: Marcel Dekker, 1978).

In the tradition of Appleby, Rohr argued that there are "regime values" within our constitutional system that can guide moral judgments in bureaucratic discretion, and that are most effectively described in Supreme Court decisions. Rohr described the Court's debates in several key areas to note that common values often underpin the disagreements on particular issues.

500.   Joel D. Aberbach, Robert D. Putnam, and Bert A. Rockman, *Bureaucrats and Politicians in Western Democracies* (Cambridge: Harvard University Press, 1981).

The authors investigated the socio-economic characteristics and attitudes of high-level bureaucrats and politicians in the United States, Great Britain, France, West Germany, Italy, the Netherlands, and Sweden. They found that the distinctions between the roles of the two groups have deteriorated in each country. However, attitudinal differences remain. Bureaucrats cluster more toward the middle of the political spectrum, and are more attentive to well-established interests and technical concerns. They are also more respectful of their own expertise.

Politicians are more polarized politically, and more enthusiastic about citizen participation in government. They also consider representativeness in government to be important.

On balance, the authors were optimistic about the ability of politics to control bureaucracy in the states studied. They had some reservations about the potential for democracy, however, in the United States, and especially in Italy.

501.   Bernard Rosen, *Holding Government Bureaucracies Accountable* (New York: Praeger Publishers, 1982).

Rosen's goal was largely descriptive as he led the readers through the "awesome armada" of techniques that have been developed to hold the bureaucracy accountable. The list is formidable, and often light on details. On some techniques, such as sunset legislation, Rosen was concerned that the legislative oversight capability is being spread too thin.

Rosen's coverage of personnel controls was more intensive, and led to a set of recommendations for improved accountability. Among them, he wanted to emphasize the selection of competent noncareer executives, to improve performance appraisal, to tighten responses to audits, and to provide training in ethics.

502.   Thomas J. Peters and Alan H. Waterman, Jr., *In Search of Excellence* (New York: Harper and Row, 1982).

In the 1980s, business also experienced an upsurge of interest in the general topic of accountability as Peters and Waterman popularized the notion that increased responsiveness to the public leads to increased profits, and more successful international competition. Excellent corporations, according to the authors, follow eight principles: a bias for action; staying close to the customers; autonomy and entrepreneurship; productivity through people; hands-on, value-driven production; sticking to the primary product; simple hierarchy with lean staffs; and a simultaneously loose-tight environment. Soon after the book was released, the "search for excellence" was extended into workshops and then publications in the public sector.

503.   Douglas Yates, *Bureaucratic Democracy: The Search for Democracy and Efficiency in American Government* (Cambridge: Harvard University Press, 1982); also

504.   Judith E. Gruber, *Controlling Bureaucracies: Dilemmas in Democratic Governance* (Berkeley: University of California Press, 1987).

These two works emphasized the diverse nature of bureaucratic control. Yates described the history, the behavior, and the politics of agencies to show that they fit into typologies that can be used to apply differential control to each. As general recommendations, however, he suggested that we need more openness in decision-making and more open debates, inside and outside the bureaucracy, on governmental policies.

Gruber outlined five broad approaches that have been advanced in the literature for democratic control of bureaucracies: direct participation; clientele relations; pursuit of the public interest; accountability; and self-control. She felt that we need to think about control in a differentiated fashion, and within the context of the particular bureaucracy. Most importantly, however, we need to think of control through a model of exchange (which she adapted from Charles Lindblom) rather than as an issue of authority. More could be gained if control came as part of an exchange of resources.

CONTINUING CONCERNS

It would be easy to argue that public administration has done its least effective job of discussing democratic responsiveness when it has tackled the task directly.

Many of the authors who wrote on other subjects in this part of the book measured their recommendations against some standard of the appropriate role for governmental administration in society. For the most part, they did it indirectly or even unintentionally. Often, it was included under the rubric of which arrangements would work most effectively and efficiently over time. Even in chapter four, which was named for a famous Appleby quotation, however, most of the discussions did not tackle the question of administrative responsiveness under that label.

That may be fortunate, for the terms have been part of the problem. The field is no closer to a consensus today on what accountability means than it ever was. It has only recently begun to recognize just how many ways the subject may be sliced. Does responsiveness come from representativeness or outside control? If control, by whom? If representativeness, of whom?

These are not easy questions, and the literature has clustered around options rather than answers. Interest groups seem more interesting for study than public opinion, for instance, but neither addresses the issues of those who see democracy as beginning with internal controls. Those authors equally fail to address the concerns of those who see democracy as beginning within properly trained administrators.

Some possible causes for such divergence are offered in the conclusion of this study. On the immediate question, however, one should not dismiss the possibility that the shotgun approach is best suited for a disjointed world.

NOTES FOR CHAPTER TEN

1. The book was not translated into English until 1915. The four translations published in that year were from the Italian translation *La sociologia del partito politico nella democrazia moderna Roberto Michels*; traduzione dall'originale tedesco del Dr. Alfredo Polledro riveduta e ampliata dall'autore (Torino: Unione Tipografico-Editrice Torinese, 1912). The translation from Italian to English was done by Eden and Cedar Paul. Michels wrote a special chapter on party life in wartime for the English translation. The publishers were Hearst's International Library Co. (probably the first), Free Press, Dover Publications, and Jarrold & Sons of London. All subsequent printings have been of the English translation of the Italian translation of the German.

2. Subsequent editions were entitled *Constitutional Government and Democracy*.

3. The 1972 second edition, by the same publisher, was renamed *Democracy in the United States: Promise and Performance*.

II
THE INTERNAL OPERATION
OF PUBLIC
ADMINISTRATION

11
Scientific Management

BACKGROUND[1]

Management studies did not emerge from the ashes of the first factory system described in section three merely because the old habits and training had become anachronisms. As Thomas Kuhn has suggested in a different context, we have an amazing capacity to persevere with entire frameworks of wisdom that are hopelessly irrelevant to the reality in which we live.[2]

Instead, management studies were introduced as the major weapon of the mechanical engineers, who were one of the three groups vying for control of the factory. In that battle, foremen stood in for the owners as the general managers of the floor. The artisans had long been the masters of the machine. In fact, until the first factory system, the artisans had invented and manufactured most of their own equipment. The improved energy sources that made factories possible, however, also made it practical for the third group, the mechanical engineers, to rise from the ranks of mechanics to machine-shop designers.

For a while, the three groups lived in strained harmony. Foremen ruled, artisans performed their work, and mechanical engineers designed and fixed the equipment. However, the improvement in power generation in the nineteenth century permitted the machines to grow in sophistication, capacity, and independence from the manipulation of its operators. Total production became more a factor of the technology and less a factor of the talent of the artisan.

Increasingly, the people were there to keep the machines operating, in the same way that the machines had once been there to keep the artisans productive. Of course, one can overstate the speed of the transition, but the transition itself made conflict for control of the factory floor inevitable.

The engineers argued that machines had too much potential and had become too expensive to be operated by lackluster performers. However, coercion of workers led to low morale and unionization, not production. In that environment, the most critical and most bitterly contested question tackled by scientific management reformers was the one we now commonly attribute to their successors: *How could one motivate employees?*

Workshops needed detailed planning and training programs. They also needed incentive plans that would instill higher work ethics, and that would take advantage of the capabilities of the new machines. Foremen and especially operators needed to be fitted to the peculiarities of the machines. Their individualities could be protected, but by scientific placement into the types of positions in which they could thrive, not by their freedom to mishandle equipment whose potential for production was often described in these works in patriotic terms.

By the 1870s, the mechanical engineers began to take on a professional identity. They organized into such groups as the American Society of Mechanical Engineers, and began to share knowledge and concerns on common problems. They did so, however, just as the technology forced them into open confrontation. Either the foremen or the mechanical engineers had to take control of the operations of the plant. Neither could perform their role without power over the workplace. Whichever group failed would be deprived of the resource that it needed to justify its dominance in American manufacturing.

A Note about the ASME Transactions

For the first 25 years of Scientific Management, almost everything published in the field appeared exclusively in the *Transactions* of the American Society of Mechanical Engineers. Since there is no current equivalent to this document in our field, a word of explanation is appropriate. The Society met semiannually in various cities in reduced versions of what would now be national conferences. Papers were presented, discussions were held, and Society business was conducted. A transcript of the proceedings was kept, and printed for distribution to those members who could not attend.

The *Transactions* included everything of interest--even a list of all members of the Society (until 1903).[3] However, for the purposes of this review, two things are worth noting about the distribution and availability of these proceedings. First, almost no one except the roughly 800 members of the Society were likely to see anything that appeared in the *Transactions*. Therefore, managers and foreman had to rely on their engineers (who were often adversaries) for second-hand information about these proceedings.

Second, the longer papers, including some of the more interesting ones on management, were available at the conferences, but were not actually read there. In fact, Taylor offered those who attended a brief outline of "A Piece-Rate System" in recognition of the fact that few were likely to read it in its entirety.[4]

Therefore, while both readers and those attending had access to these papers, it is not a safe assumption that any particular member read them. It is more obvious, however, that most members were aware of the verbal bantering among Scientific Management advocates after about 1891, and that most members had a stand (even if an uninformed one) on the issues.

505. Henry A. Towne, "The Engineer as Economist," *Transactions*, 7, (1886): 428-32; also

506. Henry Metcalfe, "The Shop-Order System of Accounts," *Transactions*, 7, (1886): 440-68.

This was the opening salvo in the war between the scientific and moralistic approaches to management that began the modern study of management. It mattered little that some of the issues had been raised by earlier scholars; the symbolism was more important because it erased any pretense that the issue could be resolved peacefully.

By later standards, the opening issue was simple. The two articles were nominally about accounting systems to eliminate waste. However, Towne's five-page article is better remembered and was more appreciated at the conference than Metcalfe's because Towne emphasized the significance of what he was suggesting.

"There are many good engineers;--there are also many good 'business men;'--but the two are rarely combined in one person." (p. 428) "But the remedy must not be looked for from those who are 'business men' or clerks and accountants only; it should come from those whose training and experience has given them an understanding of both sides...It should originate, therefore, from those who are also engineers...particularly mechanical engineers." (p. 429)

There was an extensive discussion session following the papers ("Discussion," pp. 469-88) that was enthusiastic, supportive, and generally on the subject of Towne's challenge to the field rather than the more detailed accounting system proposed by Metcalfe. A notable exception was a brash young engineer named Fred W. Taylor from Midvale Steel Works, who was in his first year of membership. Taylor, whose later cost-accounting system looked unmistakably similar to the one presented by Metcalfe in this paper and his 1885 book, honed in on the details in Metcalfe's paper, and politely but unfavorably compared some of it to his on-going experimental techniques at Midvale.[5]

507. Henry R. Towne, "Gain Sharing," *Transactions*, 10, (1889): 600-26.

Towne broke new ground once again, and better focused the contribution that his group could make to management. While much of the existing work of the fledgling reform movement in the factories had concentrated on accounting techniques and efficiency, Towne switched the debate to the question that was to become the focus of the still-unnamed Scientific Management movement: How could one motivate workers?

Incentive plans were neither new nor particularly effective. Profit sharing, for instance, had been practiced in France and England for 50 years, and had generated considerable foreign study.[6] Towne was unimpressed with profit sharing, however, since the rewards were too remote and too dependent on variables unrelated to individual or even collective efforts.

Instead, he presented his "gain sharing" plan, which he had tested for two years at the iron foundry at Yale and Towne Manufacturing Company. It required a new detailed accounting procedure that would allow the company to pay part of the actual gain that would occur when production standards were exceeded. As later critics would note, the bonus was essentially a piece-rate system. However, the bonus generated an individualized reward for individualized effort.

508.   Frederick A. Halsey, "The Premium Plan of Paying for Labor," *Transactions*, 12, (1891): 755-64.

Halsey attempted to improve incentive-pay systems by comparing the four basic forms of compensation. The day's-work plan contained no incentives. The piece-work plan "seldom works smoothly and never produces the results which it should." (p. 756) It also contained the logical flaw that costs of production varied according to volume, making calculation of a fair piece rate impossible. The profit-sharing plan was unrelated to worker effort, was too remote, and generated distrust since workers could not validate the calculations.

His "premium plan," however, was a refinement on Towne's gain sharing plan. Incentives would be based on the savings generated by the reduction in the actual time needed to complete a task. Performance standards would be needed to calculate time savings.

Halsey also introduced an argument that was to be repeated in numerous works, especially Taylor's, but that is continually violated in current practices. No incentive, he felt, would be better than a trifling one. Workers would recognize the hypocrisy of meaningless rewards, morale would suffer, and production would almost certainly decline.

THE TAYLOR ERA

The impact of Frederick Taylor on the field was both immediate and lasting. Those who were working on similar problems went to considerable efforts to meet him. In later years, those who disagreed with his approach, or who did not care for him personally, still felt obligated to praise his achievements.

The reason is partially related to the coattail effect of his popularity. However, some of those supporters dragged him into much of that popularity in the 1910s.

Instead, there were two more basic reasons for his popularity. First, when it mattered most, because the audience was almost exclusively mechanical engineers, he was doing what others were often only proposing. In many of the applications and difficult mechanics, he was first.

Second, he was better at what he was doing than almost any of his followers. One could argue that he was a more talented technician (especially of high-speed steel) than scientific manager. However, his highest respect came from his early works on scientific management. As an example, when he offered in 1901 to present the mechanics of elementary rate-fixing, his competitors deferred for the two years that it took him to complete the task. All anticipated (correctly) that his would be the definitive statement on the topic.

This is not an attempt to "tell the story" of Frederick Taylor. The books by Copley and Nelson do a more complete job than is appropriate here, and their data are borrowed freely.[7] The emphasis here, as throughout the book, is on the written study of the field--the material that shaped the opinions, not just of his colleagues, but also of the vast majority of the audience that did not work in Taylor's circle.

509.   Frederick Taylor, "Notes on Belting," *Transactions*, 15, (1894): 204-38; discussion followed pp. 238-59.

As he later realized, Taylor's first effort to describe his techniques at Midvale concentrated so much on findings and techniques, and so little on the novelty of his approach that the significance of what he was saying was largely lost on the engineering audience. In 1893, most American manufacturing tools were still belt-driven, not machine-driven. The machine's operators normally determined when and how much belts should be tightened.

For nine years at Midvale, Taylor and Gantt hired specialists to tighten the belts using belt clamps with special spring balances to measure the tension. The results were impressive enough--twice the average pulling power per machine and a fraction of the down-time--that the engineering audience largely missed Taylor's broader message of what could be done if specialists took over more factory tasks.

510.   Frederick Taylor, "A Piece-Rate System: A Step Toward Partial Solution of the Labor Problem," *Transactions*, 16, (1895): 856-883.

Following Towne's lead, Taylor's second paper on his experiments at Midvale much more bluntly attacked the factory system that he was trying to replace. His paper was far more detailed than Towne's, and it was based in a decade of experimentation. The paper was also recognized by at least some of the audience as having far greater significance.

Taylor had little use for piece-work incentive systems. In his typical immodest style, he stated that "(t)he system introduced by the writer, however, is directly the opposite, both in theory and in its results. It makes each workman's interests the same as that of his employer, pays a premium for his efficiency, and soon convinces each man that it is for his permanent advantage to turn out each day the best quality and maximum quantity of work." (p. 856)

His technique consisted of three elements: an elementary rate-fixing department, which would have responsibility for determining the precise method and a reasonable rate of production of each worker on each machine; a differential-rate system, that would pay workers a day-rate if they did not meet the standard, and a substantially higher piece-rate if they did; and the "best method of managing men," which was to pay men, not positions.

As pointed out by later critics, Taylor assumed that workers were motivated primarily by pay. As he put in capital letters, "MEN WILL NOT DO AN EXTRAORDINARY DAY'S WORK FOR AN ORDINARY DAY'S PAY." (p. 873) However, he reserved his moral indignation for the poor management techniques that had a corrupting effect on the morale of workers. He was convinced that workers would be inspired by the uniformity and justice in his system. As he boasted, "it promotes a most friendly feeling between the men and their employers, and so renders labor unions and strikes unnecessary." (p. 858)

511. Henry L. Gantt, "A Bonus System of Rewarding Labor," *Transactions*, 23, (1901): 341-60; also "A Graphical Daily Balance in Manufacture," *Transactions*, 24, (June 1903): 1322-31; also

512. Charles Day, "The Machine Shop Problem," *Transactions*, 24, (June 1903): 1302-20.

In these works, Gantt and Day tried to explain the mechanics of a system that they developed along with Taylor, who was sitting in the audience. Gantt described the bonus card, which the engineering department prepared for each worker, showing the best method of production, complete with instructions and the time that should be required. He emphasized the responsibility of management in the system. If the supervisor could not answer questions and actually do the work described, then the engineering department would have to clear up the confusion or change the card.

In the questions following the 1901 presentation, Halsey complained that elementary rate-fixing (determining what went on the card) was the key to Taylor's system, but that neither Gantt nor Taylor had described it in enough detail for others to try it. Day had provided more detail than the other two, but still not enough. Taylor, who had complained after his 1895 paper that the significance of elementary rate-fixing had been overlooked, said he was preparing another paper on the subject, which would be presented to the society when completed.

513. Frederick Taylor, "Shop Management," *Transactions*, 24, (June 1903): 1337-1456; later revised trade edition (New York: Harper and Brothers, 1911).[8]

The *Principles of Scientific Management* notwithstanding, this was Taylor's most sophisticated attempt to describe his management techniques. Harrington Emerson, who was soon to work for Taylor, rather extravagantly called it the "most important contribution ever presented to the Society and one of the most important ever published in the United States."

In his general introduction, Taylor lamented that managerial talents in American manufacturing were uneven and often unrelated to the success of the company. To correct this problem, he reintroduced the major points of his 1895 work, and added a proposal for functional foremanship.

He intentionally offered little new on differential rates, although he argued that the best rates would need to be 30-100% higher than the day rate to be effective. His emphasis was on the mechanics of elementary rate-setting, which he tried to describe in enough detail that they could be adopted by others in the audience. Accordingly, he presented actual worksheets as well as drawings of stop-watches, slide rules, and other devices that had been devised under his leadership by Sanford Thompson and Carl Barth.

514.   Frederick W. Taylor, "On the Art of Cutting Metals," [Presidential Address to ASME, December 1906] *Transactions*, 28, (1907): 31-281; also trade edition (New York: American Society of Mechanical Engineers, [1907(?)]).

After "Shop Management," Taylor's growing consulting responsibilities kept him increasingly isolated from engineering work. However, he tried to keep up experiments based on his high-speed steel discoveries of 1898, even if only by delegation of the actual experiments to his assistant Carl Barth.[9]

In 1906, Taylor was elected president of the American Society of Mechanical Engineers. In that same year, the Bethlehem Steel Corporation became involved in a patent-infringement suit trying to protect the Taylor-White patents on high-speed metal cutting. For his presidential address in 1906, Taylor chose to describe the results of continuing experiments on high-speed steel directed by Taylor and conducted by Barth at the Sellers Company since 1901.

515.   Louis Brandeis, *Evidence Taken by the Interstate Commerce Commission in the Matter of Proposed Advances in Freight Rates by Carriers, August to December, 1910*, Senate Doc. 725, vol. 4, 61st Cong., 3rd sess. (1911); also "Eastern Rate Case," *Interstate Commerce Commission Reports*, vol. 20, (Washington, D.C.: USGPO, 1910); partially reprinted in *Scientific Management and Railroads* (New York: Engineering Magazine, 1911); also *Business: A Profession* (Boston: Small, Bayard & Co., 1914); also *The Curse of Bigness*, ed. by Osmond K. Fraenkel (New York: The Viking Press, 1934).

Whatever Taylor's intentions for staying involved in engineering issues, his destiny was forever changed by the railroad tariff increase requests of 1910. In that year, the railroads applied for rate increases to the Interstate Commerce Commission (ICC), which was required to hold hearings before reaching a decision. Brandeis, as counsel for the trades associations that would have to pay the increased rates, per-

suaded Gantt, Gilbreth, Emerson and others to testify that the ICC should force the
railroads to adopt scientific management techniques before granting any increases.

Taylor declined to testify, misjudging the potential publicity that could come
from the hearings. However, using considerable last-minute help from Taylor, Brandeis was able to describe scientific management techniques in detail. Reflecting
Taylor's concern, Brandeis insisted that the system be considered as an entire package, and not just as a bonus system. However, the popular press' attention was most
dramatically caught by Emerson's claim that the railroads could save $1,000,000 per
day by implementing scientific management. As Thompson later reported, "the spectacular and seemingly extravagant form in which some of the testimony was given by
persons outside the group, but influenced by it, caught the popular fancy and was
responsible for the great publicity the movement suddenly attained."[10]

Brandeis continued to publicize the moral value of scientific methods in subsequent anti-trusts publications. Many of those were gathered from various progressive
magazines and speeches, and reprinted in *Business--A Profession*, and later in *The
Curse of Bigness*. Throughout his career, he maintained that the science of management would be as influential in the twentieth century as the development of the
machine had been in the nineteenth, and that efficiency was critical for the survival
of democracy.

516.   Frederick W. Taylor, *Principles of Scientific Management* [private printing] (New
        York: Harper and Brothers, February 1911);[11] also revised and expanded trade
        edition (New York: Harper and Brothers, 1911); also "The Gospel of Efficiency,"
        American Magazine;[12] also *Journal of Accountancy*;[13] also "The Principles of
        Scientific Management," in *Addresses and Discussions at the Conference on
        Scientific Management Held October 12.13.14 Nineteen Hundred and Eleven*
        (Hanover, NH: The Amos Tuck School of Administration and Finance,
        Dartmouth College, 1912).

After the Eastern Rate Case, the public demands on Taylor to defend his system in person were enormous.[14] More importantly, Progressive forces led by Brandeis kept trying to refocus scientific management in directions that were more general, more societally motivated, and therefore more politically useful.

In January 1910, Taylor responded with a popularized draft of *Principles* which
he submitted to the meetings committee of the ASME for publication. It was a work
that clearly bowed to his new constituencies. The examples had been dequantified,
expanded, and sometimes openly misrepresented. Schmidt (Henry Noll), for instance,
was openly libeled, although it mattered little since by then, Noll was dying from
advanced alcoholism. *Principles* was not a quality engineering document, and rather
than turn their former president down, the ASME held the draft for almost a year
without giving an answer on publication.

As pressures mounted in late 1910, Taylor withdrew the manuscript and paid to
have a shortened version (less than 70 pages of actual text) privately printed for
confidential distribution to ASME members. He also agreed to have an even shorter

version serialized, along with numerous pictures and an accompanying biographical article, in the progressive journal *American Magazine*. The version read by current students, however, is the expanded but still highly popularized trade edition of 1911, which contained additional anecdotal evidence, some false, and more vigorous defenses against the attacks of trade unionists.

Taylor identified four principles of scientific management: the substitution of scientific techniques for "rule of thumb" decision-making; the scientific selection of workmen; education and training of workmen for their tasks; and a sharing of responsibilities between management and labor. In describing the workings of each, he also recounted previous arguments from both his and his supporters' earlier works.

After *Principles*, Taylor's works continued to emphasize the societal role, to deemphasize the technical aspects of scientific management, and to defend his proposals against continuing labor opposition. One prime example was his presentation to a conference on scientific management held at the Amos Tuck School at Dartmouth College in October 1911. Taylor, Gantt, and Emerson all presented papers emphasizing these themes to varying degrees.

517. Frederick W. Taylor, *Hearings Before Special Committee of the House of Representatives to Investigate the Taylor and Other Systems of Shop Management Under Authority of H. Res. 90*, Vol. III, (Washington, D.C.: USGPO, 1912), pp. 1377-1508; also "Scientific Shop Management," [pamphlet] (Milwaukee: Milwaukee Federation of Labor, 1914); reprinted John R. Commons, ed. *Trade Unionism and Labor Problems, Second Series* (Boston: Ginn and Company, 1921), pp. 141-49; also

518. Robert F. Hoxie, *Scientific Management and Labor* (New York: D. Appleton, 1915).

From his early days at Midvale, Taylor met opposition to his plans, particularly from organized labor. While the attacks were occasionally printed in union pamphlets or similar sources, none of those works published before 1912 was substantive enough to receive wide readership then or now. When Taylor testified before the House committee investigating the broader causes of the Watertown Arsenal strike, however, Taylor was given a chance to confront the major arguments of the other side.

After Taylor's lengthy introduction, committee chair William Wilson asked Taylor about the tendency of supervisors to use scientific management as an excuse to drive workers into increased fatigue. He challenged that many of the scientific techniques were arbitrary, especially those not related to machine work. He noted that the percentages awarded as bonuses never seemed to be as high as the percentages of increased productivity. He also asked about the disruptive effects to unskilled workers of having the same work completed by fewer workmen.

Many of the same points were made by N. P. Alifas of the American Federation of Labor, in response to a speech by Taylor before the Milwaukee Federation of Labor in 1914. Alifas' remarks were informative in additional way, however, for they illustrated the preference of the labor opposition at the time to respond to what they could attack instead of what Taylor said.

Perhaps the most detailed statement of opposition to Taylorism came with Hoxie's report based on the investigations of the U.S. Commission on Industrial Relations in 1913-1915. Taylor had testified and helped organize witnesses for the Commission. Nevertheless, Hoxie found that the advocates of scientific management could not agree on what the technique was. Too often it became a driving system with unfair advantages for the owners, inadequate compensation for the workers, disruption of the labor force, and open opposition to unions.

Taylor died before Hoxie's report was published. To the other attacks, his answers were not new, even if some of them had been more eloquently stated by Brandeis in the ICC hearings. By the end of his life, Taylor was more clearly reaching out to organized labor in his speeches. He was a busy man, however, and his examples and even his wording on these issues changed little from those in his 1911 speeches and publications.

SCIENTIFIC MANAGEMENT AFTER TAYLOR

Taylor was an eclectic man, and the questions he raised pointed the field in a number of directions. Two of his concerns--elementary rate-fixing and differential (merit) pay--are pursued in the rest of this chapter, following discussions of Taylor's direct descendants. Cost accounting was refined in the General Accounting Office after 1921. However, it generated little literature that is read by general public administration audiences, and is not discussed in this work.

Study of the authority of foremen, as further developed by Gantt, Brandeis, and the impetus of the First World War, eventually led into the humanist literature discussed in chapter fourteen. Some also led into the studies of bureaucracy discussed in chapter thirteen, although that literature more clearly had independent origins. Finally, Gantt helped establish what would eventually be called Management Science, as discussed in chapter seventeen on decision-making.

519.   Harrington Emerson, *Efficiency as a Basis for Operation and Wages* (New York: Engineering Magazine, 1909); also *The Twelve Principles of Efficiency* (New York: Engineering Magazine, 1912).[15]

Until his presidency of ASME, Taylor had little trouble keeping his disciples in line. Barth presented his techniques to ASME only with Taylor's blessings. Halsey, Gantt, and others were careful to give credit where it was due. Starting about 1909, however, the published record began to reflect the growing independence of some of the followers. Emerson's *Efficiency* was one of the first examples.

Emerson was never an "insider" in Taylor's group. Most notably, as a consultant, Emerson was willing to give owners as much or as little of the "Taylor system" as they wished to receive. In his publications, Emerson was far broader, and many of his arguments predated those presented by Taylor in the later *Principles*. Emerson tied his advocacy of efficiency to societal needs, including the waste of natural resources through inefficiency. He described the need for both line and staff organizations in nature and in manufacturing, and offered a cha; ter on cost accounting.

In *Twelve Principles*, he summarized the same arguments through the twelve principles of efficient organizations: 1) clearly defined ideals; 2) common sense; 3) competent counsel; 4) discipline; 5) the fair deal; 6) reliable, immediate, adequate, and permanent records; 7) despatching; 8) standards and schedules; 9) standardized conditions; 10) standardized operations; 11) written standard-practice instructions; 12) efficiency reward. He used the principles to explain Germany's success over Napoleon III. He reemphasized that strenuousness and efficiency were antagonistic, and he advocated the full use of staff as well as line positions.

What Emerson lacked, however, was the "Taylor system." In both his consulting and his writings, he advocated efficiency, but he offered no systematic plans as to how it would be accomplished.

520. Frank B. Gilbreth, *Field System* (New York: Myron C. Clark Publishing Co., 1908); also *Bricklaying System* (New York: Myron C. Clark Publishing Co., 1909); also *Motion Study* (New York: D. Van Nostrand Co., 1911); also *Primer of Scientific Management* (New York: D. Van Nostrand Co., 1912); also

521. Frank B. and Lillian M(oller) Gilbreth, *Fatigue Study* (New York: Sturgis and Walton Co., 1916); also *Applied Motion Study* (New York: Sturgis and Walton Co., 1917); also "An Indictment of Stop-Watch Time Study," *Bulletin of the Taylor Society*, 6, (1921): 100-08; also

522. Lillian M. Gilbreth, *The Psychology of Management* [dissertation, University of California], also (New York: Sturgis and Walton Co., 1914).

Even among Taylor associates, the strain often showed. Gilbreth's role in Taylor's circle was particularly rocky since Gilbreth's concept of motion study was well developed when he began working with Taylor in 1907. Because of that emphasis, Gilbreth's work sometimes seemed to be the opposite of Emerson's, concentrating on techniques without the broader philosophical perspectives or purposes.

Both *Field System* and *Bricklaying System* were practical applications of the system eventually described in great detail in *Motion Study*, while *Primer of Scientific Management* was his most orthodox work during his tenure with Taylor. Near the end of Taylor's life, however, serious rifts developed between the two on some of Gilbreth's experiments with motion study, as well as the quality of his consulting work.

Gilbreth brought his wife Lillian into his practice. Her dissertation and subsequent book tried to integrate scientific management with the psychological needs for individuality and development, and helped give the subsequent writings a broader perspective of the needs of the workers, as reflected in the motivational concerns in *Fatigue Study* and *Applied Motion Study*. His complete break with Taylor was symbolized by his development of micromotion study as a potential substitute for Taylor's time studies, however, as eventually described in the Taylor Society *Bulletin*.

523. Henry L. Gantt, *Work, Wages, and Profits* (New York: The Engineering Magazine, 1911); also *Organizing for Work* (New York: Harcourt, Brace, and Howe, 1919).

Henry Gantt was another classic case of a Taylor disciple who would not stay within the limits of orthodoxy. Gantt had been hired by Taylor as an assistant in 1887, and never neglected to advertise that connection. However, by the turn of the century, the two theorists had diverged to such an extent that Gantt is sometimes considered to be the first humanist.

His earlier works showed a difference of degree rather than substance. *Work, Wages and Profits* was a compilation of old and new material dating from a 1904 speech to several chapters written explicitly for this book. Even in 1904, Gantt's concern that permanent increases in efficiency depended on the happiness of the workers extended beyond Taylor's simple assumptions on the subject. In a reprinted 1907 speech to Stevens Institute students (Taylor's *alma mater*), he noted that workers sold their time, not their labor. Enticing them out of the group rate would require a 20-100% bonus.

He described Taylor's contempt for American entrepreneurs, noting "the difference between the savage and civilized communities is largely that the civilized communities have enacted laws which tend to restrain individual greed." (p. 46) Like Lillian Gilbreth, he was also interested in techniques that would teach "industry" as well as skill.

By 1919, he was focusing more on employer attitudes than worker attitudes, arguing that if autocracy was not removed from the economic sphere, we could follow "Europe into the economic confusion and welter which seem to threaten the very existence of its civilization." (p. v) Entrepreneurs needed to operate on the principle of service, not just greed. As part of that package, they would recognize the value of engineering experts in organizing the work.

524. Morris Llewellyn Cooke, *Academic and Industrial Efficiency*, Bulletin # 5 (New York: Carnegie Foundation for the Advancement of Teaching, 1910); also "Spirit and Social Significance of Scientific Management," *Journal of Political Economy*, 21, (June 1913): 481-93; also "Scientific Management of the Public Business," *American Political Science Review*, 9, (August 1915): 488-95; also *Our Cities Awake* (New York: Doubleday and Co., 1918).

Cooke was the Taylor disciple who was most concerned with public administration applications of scientific management. He also spearheaded the reconciliation of labor and scientific management advocates during the First World War.

One of his more controversial studies was on university teaching, in which he compared the physics departments of eight universities to recommend how they could be operated more efficiently. He suggested that faculty not be burdened with administrative details that could be turned over to administrators or clerks. He opposed committee decision-making, but advocated functional foremen who could specialize in their roles. For undergraduate teaching, he advocated centralized lecture notes and more quantitative ways of measuring productivity.

In 1911, a reform mayor appointed Cooke to be director of Public Works for Philadelphia. Based on his experiences, he advocated in 1915 that cities be revitalized by a combination of effective management structures and increased cooperation by lower-level city employees. Cleaning up corruption without establishing a system in its place, he feared, would be ineffective. Systems were being established however, he noted in 1913, in both American government and in Europe.

He supported the "city manager" structure with fewer committees, more merit appointments, improved budgeting techniques, and "having the great body of employees increasingly critical in their judgments about both their own work and the work which is going on around them." (1918, p. 98)

525.   Josephine Goldmark, *Fatigue and Efficiency* (New York: Russell Sage Foundation, 1912).

As Brandeis tried to bring scientific management and progressive politics together, groups such as the National Consumers' League began using the scientific study of the effects of work on employee health to lobby for improvements in working conditions through "welfare work" legislation. One of the more direct and better-known examples was produced by Brandeis' colleague Josephine Goldmark, who described her book as an attempt to use the modern study of fatigue as the basis for labor legislation. The book provided a particularly detailed summation of existing studies of fatigue, as both a physiological and a work-related phenomenon. She described the legislation that had already been passed, she proposed amendments and additions to it, and she reprinted briefs of relevant cases in which she had been involved.

526.   Horace B. Drury, *Scientific Management: A History and Criticism* [dissertation plus trade edition] (New York: Columbia University Press, 1915).

In 1915, Drury published the first history of the entire movement, including the lives and writings of all of its major actors. He concluded that the attacks on scientific management were mainly unfounded. Like Thompson's 1917 history, he concluded that many of the difficulties came from Taylor's often-crass statements, especially about laborers.

In reality, however, "Scientific management is thus, first of all, a study of man, of his nature, of his ideals. It is based upon the principle that cheerful workmen are more profitable than sullen ones, that to fit the work to the man is better than to try to fit the man to the work, that the individual is a more satisfactory unit of study and administration than the mass." (dissertation, p. 202) Fifty years down the line, however, less enlightened disciples might neglect to split the profits fairly, and might destroy the promise of scientific management.

527.   C. Bertrand Thompson, *The Theory and Practice of Scientific Management* (Boston: Houghton Mifflin Co., 1917).

In 1917, Thompson attempted "to appraise a movement while that movement is still in its earlier and more enthusiastic stages." (p. v) He did this as a Taylor insider who found Drury's work to be short on the details that would come from an engineering background. After defining scientific management as resting on laws and principles rather than policies, he offered a sketch of Taylor's life, and a defense of scientific management against its common criticisms. He recognized that the popularity of the field had "brought forth a horde of 'efficiency experts,' untrained, incompetent, sometimes quacks and charlatans, whose operations are tending to discredit the name and purpose of the movement." (pp. 169-70) However, he felt that situation was improving.

His most valuable contribution, however, may have been a bibliography and literature review that listed hundreds of works in several languages, and that illustrated the degree to which the field had split in every imaginable direction.

JOB ANALYSIS

Taylor and other scientific management advocates showed little interest in the development of modern personnel departments.[16] They were more concerned with job design than with more passive job analysis. They were also more concerned with incentive plans than with standardized pay systems. Nevertheless, advocates of standardized personnel regulations found much of value in scientific management, and the fortunes of the two movements became mixed in the unemployment crises of the First World War.

The literature discussed here follows a disjointed path in that it traces the development of position classification in government as the marriage of an older merit reform movement with techniques and general philosophies openly borrowed from scientific management. Accordingly, there is no effort to follow scientific management through the current practices of time and motion studies. Furthermore, strictly private-sector applications of job analysis are omitted, as are most frequently-cited textbooks that only summarize the field.[17] Finally, general literature on the growth of the merit system is excluded because it is discussed separately in the chapter on staffing.

528.   U.S. Congress, Senate Resolution, 25th Cong., 2nd Sess., March 5, 1838; also Act of March 3, 1853 (10 Stat. 209); also Act of April 22, 1854 (10 Stat. 276).

The movement toward position classification is far older than the techniques that are needed to implement it in a systematic fashion. Based on petitions that were presented by clerks to halt the arbitrary assignment of salaries, the Senate called on department heads to classify clerks "in reference to the character of the labor to be performed, the care and responsibility imposed, the qualifications required, and the relative value to the public of the services of each class as compared with the others."

Little was done to accomplish this, however, until congress responded to a mixture of salary reform bills introduced for individual departments in 1851 by creating a uniform classification system for clerks in 1853 and 1854. The bills lacked an agency to enforce them, however, as well as specific procedures by which individual positions could be placed within the rankings.

529.   Charles U. Carpenter, "The Working of a Labor Department in Industrial Establishments," *Engineering Magazine*, 25, (April 1903): 1-9.

Until the twentieth century, employment departments of major corporations filled most vacancies by picking from among those standing at the front gate. Practices in government, described in the chapter on staffing, were often far worse. Other personnel matters were settled between foremen and workers.

Precisely when modern personnel departments evolved to replace some of these practices is a matter of some dispute. Ordway Tead puts the date at 1912.[18] The more common belief is that the first modern personnel department was created at the National Cash Register Company after a particularly bitter strike in 1901.

Carpenter, who was in charge of organizing that department, described his plans and the pressing need for such departments. "Whether employer and employee be organized in mutual bodies or not, one of the greatest needs of the present day is the development of some plan that will bring about a closer personnel relationship between them." (p. 2) To help in that task, personnel departments should handle wages, efficiency, working conditions, legal rights of the employees, and the nature of supervision through foreman's meetings.

530.   U.S. Civil Service Commission, "Nineteenth Report of the United States Civil Service Commission July 1, 1901 to June 30, 1902," House Doc. 20, 57th Cong., 2nd sess., (1902); also

531.   Committee on Department Methods, "Report to the President by the Com-
        mittee on Department Methods: Classification of Positions and Gradation
        of Salaries for Employees of the Executive Departments and Independent
        Establishments in Washington, January 4, 1907." (Washington, D.C.: USGPO,
        1907); also

532.   Committee on Grades and Salaries, "Report," House Doc. 648, 60th Cong.,
        2nd sess., (February 11, 1908).

     In government, the annual reports of the Civil Service Commission turned con-
siderably more contentious in 1902 when the commission began complaining that it
could not do its job adequately without being able to centralize classification. "The
underlying cause which operates against promotion regulation based upon merit is the
fact that there is no standard classification of clerical work." (p. 23) They wanted
ranking by positions, not persons. Within the grades, they wanted subdivisions (steps)
so that merit could be rewarded without making the pay scales meaningless.
     It was politically easier, however, to try to achieve uniformity without taking
classification away from the individual departments. The Keep Committee in 1907
suggested that boards of equalization be appointed by the heads of each department.
The first report of the subsequent Committee on Grades and Salaries was submitted
to congress in 1908.

533.   Edwin O. Griffenhagen, "Standardization of Public Employments," Parts I
        and II, *Municipal Research*, nos. 67 and 76 (1915, 1916); also "The Origin
        of the Modern Occupational Classification in Personnel Administration,"
        Public Personnel Studies, 2, (September 1924): 184-94.

     The first applications of centralized and systematic classification techniques in
government occurred in the city of Chicago in 1910-1911, and were implemented by
Griffenhagen, who directed the Efficiency Division of the Chicago Civil Service Commission. The above works described the evolution and expansion of his techniques as
his consulting firm later applied them in Illinois state government, and by the 1920s,
in the federal government as well as other levels in both the U.S. and Canada. Other
frequently cited works of Griffenhagen were his reports to the governments of Virginia and Massachusetts.

534.   *America's Interests After the European War, Annals of the American Academy of
        Political and Social Science*, 61, (September 1915); also *Personnel and Employ-
        ment Problems in Industrial Management, Annals of the American Academy of
        Political and Social Science*, 65, (May 1916); also

535.   Boyd Fisher, "Methods of Reducing Labor Turnover," Bulletin 196, U.S.
        Bureau of Labor Statistics (Washington, D.C.: USGPO, 1916).

Labor turnover had long been a largely ignored problem in American industry. Once the war started in Europe, however, the flow of immigrants slowed, and industry was faced with large labor shortages. In this environment, scientific management actively stepped in to try to help increase the tenure of those who were hired.

The 1915 *Annals* contained such articles as Morris Cooke's "Scientific Management as a Solution of the Unemployment Problem," and similar articles by Richard Feiss and the Gilbreths. The 1916 *Annals* and Boyd's report on unemployment reflected the rapid development of a coalition between the emerging personnel managers and those with scientific management training. To help reinforce the ties, the one article printed in both issues of the *Annals* was Ernest Hopkins' "A Functionalized Employment Department As a Factor in Industrial Efficiency."

536.   Congressional Joint Commission on the Reclassification of Salaries, *Report, March 12, 1920*, House Doc. 686, 66th Cong., 2nd sess.; also

537.   *Classification Act*, 42 Stat. 1488 (1923); also *Classification Act*, 63 Stat. 954 (1949).

Interdepartmental committees did not solve the problem of unequal salaries at the federal level. In 1919, congress established a joint committee that reported back in 1920 that the task could be accomplished only by an independent agency that had final authority over classification decisions. Logically, they concluded, only the Civil Service Commission was equipped to handle the task.

Fear of a strengthened Civil Service Commission (CSC), however, was still strong. In 1923, congress passed a classification bill that established an entirely new Personnel Classification Board (PCB) directed by representatives of the CSC, the Bureau of the Budget, and the Bureau of Efficiency. Many of the procedures were spelled out in the legislation, including equal pay for equal work, rank in position, and within-grade steps. However, enough of the procedures were left to the PCB that when its members were unable to cooperate (see below), the PCB was abolished in 1932, and the functions were turned over to the CSC.

After World War II, the duplicate work of preparing data within agencies and doing the calculations in the CSC proved to be too much of a burden. In 1949, the classification process was broken into two parts, with the CSC writing the position classification standards by which the decisions would be made, and the agencies actually grading new positions, subject to review and reversal by the CSC.

538.   Ordway Tead and Henry C. Metcalf, *Personnel Administration: Its Principles and Practices* (New York: McGraw Hill, 1920).

In this very early textbook of personnel administration, Tead and Metcalf called for personnel departments as an extension of the need for functional management within specializations. They also saw job analysis as a mixture of several factors, including the job itself (described in considerable detail since the methodology had been developed in scientific management), the qualifications needed, the standard instructions, the effects of the job on the worker, and the relation of the job to the organization.

539.   William O. Lichtner, *Time Study and Job Analysis* (New York: Ronald Press, 1921).

Lichtner's work helped illustrate the change in emphasis among time-study advocates after the First World War toward the standardized application of job analysis. Lichtner's book, which intermixed pay determination with sophisticated time-study analysis, described methods of standardizing production by using outside experts to install job analysis, while training permanent on-site experts to carry out the work.

540.   G. J. Kelday, "Job Analysis: Occupational Rating," [pamphlet] (New York: National Personnel Association, November 2, 1922).

By the 1920s, the four principal methods of analyzing jobs evolved. The first, ranking, had been used for some time. The second, often called the classification system, was most likely developed by the Bureau of Personnel Research at the Carnegie Institute of Technology. As Kelday noted in this address at the Pittsburgh conference of the National Personnel Association, the technique was being used in 6 or 7 companies by 1922.

541.   Fred Telford, "The Classification and Salary Standardization Movement in the Public Service," *Annals of the American Academy of Political and Social Science*, 113, (May 1924): 206-15; also "The Classification of Labor Positions and the Testing of Labor Applicants in the Public Service," *Public Personnel Studies*, 2, (January/February 1924): 5-11.

From the beginning of the Personnel Classification Board, there was friction over the procedures that were being used at the insistence of the Bureau of Efficiency. Telford, who worked at the Bureau of Public Personnel Administration, called for the implementation of the techniques developed in Chicago. Specifically, position classification would consist of nine steps: 1) collect facts about the job; 2) group jobs into classes; 3) write descriptions within the class; 4) write the minimum qualifications; 5) give each class a descriptive title; 6) allocate appropriate positions to the class; 7) show the lines of promotion; 8) devise a compensation schedule; and 9) group the classes into services to allow for easy political and budgetary oversight. As part of step nine, the services would be divided into grades.

542.   Merrill R. Lott, "Wage Scales With a Reason," *Management and Administration*, 9, (May 1925): 451-55; also *Wage Scales and Job Evaluation* (New York: Ronald Press, 1926).

The early methods of comparing jobs were strictly qualitative. Scientific management could quantitatively measure people within positions, but comparisons were verbal. Lott attempted for the first time to break positions into particular characteristics by which different positions could be compared on mathematical scales. The result was the first point-factor system (called point method), introduced in 1924-1925, and based on fifteen job characteristics that included skills, difficulties, responsibilities, working conditions, and market conditions. Lott and others soon began to refine the system and to reduce the number of factors.

543. Eugene Benge, "Gauging the Job's Worth," *Industrial Relations*, 3, [Parts I-III] (February, March, and April 1932): 65-69; 117-20; and 177-80; also *Job Evaluation and Merit Rating* (New York: National Foreman's Institute, n.d. [1941]); also

544. Eugene Benge, Samuel Burk, and Edward Hay, *Manual of Job Evaluation: Procedures of Job Analysis and Appraisal* (New York: Harper and Brothers, 1941).

The fourth major method of classifying jobs (ranking, classification, point rating, and factor comparison) was developed by Benge after he ran into difficulties applying Lott's system at the Philadelphia Rapid Transit Company in 1926. It was subsequently applied in large organizations by Burk and Hay.

The technique, which is too complex to describe in much detail here, consists of a set of factors which are defined in such generic ways that comparisons for rankings can be made across the class lines used in point-factor systems. The five factors used by Benge were mental requirements, skill requirements, physical requirements, responsibility, and working conditions. This method frees job analysis from some of the artificial mechanics of point-factor systems, and makes comparisons more general.

Benge first briefly described the evolution of the system at Philadelphia Rapid Transit in his articles in *Industrial Relations*. The system was thereafter refined and presented in much more detail in the two 1941 publications. It is particularly instructive to note how much more complicated Benge's system had become by the time it was proposed for the federal government in the Oliver Commission report that is discussed later.

545. Ismar Baruch, *History of Position Classification and Salary Standardization in the Federal Service (1789-1938)* (Washington, D.C.: U.S. Civil Service Commission, 1939); also

546. Committee on Position-Classification and Pay Plans in the Public Service, *Position Classification in the Public Service* (Chicago: Civil Service Assembly of the United States and Canada, 1941); also

547.   Harold Suskin, ed., *Job Evaluation and Pay Administration in the Public Sector* (Chicago: International Personnel Management Association, 1977).

Baruch was director of the Division of Classification in the CSC from the 1930s into the 1950s. During his tenure, the federal hybrid classification system with internal points was developed. In 1939 and in chapter 2 of the 1941 work, he described the efforts to bring classification into government.

In the 1941 report by a committee of the Civil Service Assembly, he defended the utility of classification plans, and devised a check-list of nineteen classification factors, including difficulty/complexity, non-supervisory responsibilities, supervisor responsibilities, and qualification standards, by which positions could be grouped into classes. The book then defined procedures for data collection, classification, and implementation of the plans. In 1977, Suskin attempted to update the 1941 "classic" in view of the structural changes that had been forced upon personnel. There were many similarities with the earlier study, reflecting Suskin's assertion that surprisingly little had changed. However, Suskin's work went into more detail on alternate forms of job analysis, and on the compensation and governmental funding issues that had changed the environment for position classification.

548.   U.S. Employment Service, Department of Labor, *Dictionary of Occupational Titles*, 2 vol. (Washington, D.C.: USGPO, 1939); also

549.   Sidney A. Fine and C.A. Heinz, "The Functional Occupational Classification Structure," *Personnel and Guidance Journal*, 37, (1958): 180-92; also

550.   Sidney A. Fine and W. Wiley, *An Introduction to Functional Job Analysis: A Scaling of Selected Tasks from the Social Welfare Field*, Methods for Manpower Analysis No. 4 (Kalamazoo, MI: The Upjohn Institute for Employment Research, September 1971).

The creation of the U.S. Employment Service in 1933 led to the need for a uniform method of describing jobs in the U.S. economy. Working through the Occupational Research Program of the 1930s, the Employment Service compiled a list of thousands of job titles and brief descriptions, which was published in 1939.[19] The list includes six-digit codes, which break the jobs into nine classes which are then further subdivided into groups.

For the third edition of the Dictionary in 1965, the Employment Service organized the Functional Occupational Classification Project, using the functional job analysis technique that was developed by Sidney A. Fine. The technique, which tries to include the potential for growth and advancement in each position, is based on worker function, work fields, work methods, work products, and the worker traits needed for each position.

551. Charles W. Lytle, *Job Evaluation Methods* (New York: Ronald Press, 1946).

Lytle was one of the last to describe job analysis techniques in categories other than the four already used in this book. He felt that the five types were the ranking or grading methods, straight-point method, weighted-in-money method (factor comparison), weighted-in-points method without the separate treatment of universal requirements, and weighted-in-points method with separate treatment of universal requirements. He also argued that job factors should be kept to four (skill, effort, responsibility, and working conditions) to simplify point methods.

552. Jay Otis and Richard Leukart, *Job Evaluation: A Basis for Sound Wage Administration* (New York: Prentice Hall, 1948); also

553. John A. Patton and Reynold S. Smith, Jr., *Job Evaluation* (Homewood IL: Richard D. Irwin, 1949).

These are two general textbooks on the subject, and most texts are not mentioned here. However, these two are particularly complete and were widely used for a number of years. Also, they each reflect the degree to which the field became concerned in the post-War era with the politics of job-evaluation implementation, and the integration of job analysis into pay plans.

In both books, there is continual appreciation of the need to bring unions into the process. Both texts are also easy to read. However, of the two, Otis and Leukart devote more attention to the pay side of the equation, while Patton and Smith's explanations of each of the major methods of job analysis might be easier for beginning students to understand.

554. Edward N. Hay, *The AMA Handbook of Wage and Salary Administration* (New York: American Management Association, 1950).

Hay was one of the early developers of the factor-comparison method of job analysis. As already noted, however, the technique was subject to continual revision as time went on. In this book, he described the four distinct versions of the method that then existed: Benge's plan; the Hay point plan; the Turner Per Cent Method; and the Hay Training-Job Method.

555. John C. Flanagan, "The Critical Incident Technique," *Psychological Bulletin*, 51, (July 1954): 327-58.

In 1941, the Aviation Psychology Program initiated a study to determine why student pilots dropped out of training. The research led to the identification of critical incidents during training. If people could be isolated by their ability to handle such incidents, the selection procedure could be made more valid. In this article, Flanagan described how the procedure had been refined to include the drafting of position descriptions that would account for the relevant critical incidents.

556.   Elizabeth Lanham, *Job Evaluation* (New York: McGraw-Hill, 1955).

          Lanham's general textbook on job evaluation provides a good overview of the topic, and includes the results of some original surveys on the extent of job evaluation use in the private sector. She found that 559 of 1265 organizations either used job evaluation in 1955, or planned to do so. Only a very small number, however, included managerial employees in such plans.

557.   U.S. House Committee on Post Office and Civil Service, Subcommittee on Position Classification *Report on Job Evaluation and Ranking in the Federal Government*, H.Rept. 91-28, 91st Cong., 1st sess., (February 27, 1969); also

558.   *Job Evaluation Policy Act of 1970*, 84 Stat. 72 (March 17, 1970); also

559.   U.S. Civil Service Commission, Job Evaluation and Pay Review Task Force, *Final Report*, 2 vol. (Washington, D.C.: USGPO, January 1972)[20]; also

560.   U. S. Civil Service Commission, "Implementation of the Factor Evaluation System and Consultation on a Proposed Classification Standards Advisory Board," Bulletin No. 511-12 (Washington, D.C.: U.S. Civil Service Commission, December 1975).

          Based on hearings in 1967, a House subcommittee on position classification issued a report in 1969 with 31 findings, including charges that the classification system was antiquated and unrelated to management concerns. Congress established the Oliver Commission (Job Evaluation and Pay Review Task Force) in 1970 to improve the quality of job analysis and resultant pay in the federal government. The task force report in 1972 repeated many of the charges, and advocated a factor-ranking evaluation system that is similar to Benge's generic concept, but with noticeably different mechanics. The task force hoped that the system would be more rational than the hybrid then used, and would serve to integrate managers into the job analysis process.
          As implemented by the Civil Service Commission beginning in 1975, the process involved panels of managers, union representatives, and experts who began by ranking 147 whole jobs, and then individual factors, to arrive at both benchmark job descriptions and a single set of mechanics that would tie the various factors to a weighted scale to help determine compensation.

561. G. G. Gordon and Ernest J. McCormick, "The Identification, Measurement, and Factor Analyses of Worker-oriented Job Variables," ONR Contract Nonr-1100(19), Report #3 (Lafayette, IN: Occupational Research Center, Purdue University, 1963); also

562. Ernest J. McCormick, Joseph W. Cunningham, and George C. Thornton, "The Prediction of Job Requirements by a Structured Job Analysis Procedure," *Personnel Psychology*, 20, (Winter 1967): 431-40; also

563. Ernest J. McCormick, P. R. Jeanneret, and R. C. Mecham, "A Study of Job Characteristics and Job Dimensions as Based on the Position Analysis Questionnaire (PAQ)," *Journal of Applied Psychology*, 56, (1972): 347-368; also

564. Ernest J. McCormick, *Job Analysis: Methods and Applications* (New York: Amacom, 1979).

In 1963, analysts at the Occupational Research Center of Purdue University published their first efforts to develop a Worker Activity Profile that permitted more detailed analysis of positions based on large numbers of job elements (in 1967, 162 job elements broken into 42 attributes). The technique eventually led to the development of the Position Analysis Questionnaire (PAQ), which analyzes jobs based on 187 worker-oriented job elements broken into six content categories, including information input, mental processes, work output, relationships with other persons, job context, and other job characteristics.

565. Erich P. Prien and William W. Ronan, "Job Analysis: A Review of Research Findings," *Personnel Psychology*, 24, (Autumn 1971): 371-96; also

566. Erich P. Prien, "The Functions of Job Analysis in Content Validation," *Personnel Psychology*, 30, (Summer 1977): 167-74.

These articles summarize the psychological research that had been done on job evaluation by the 1970s. Especially in 1977, Prien contrasted task-oriented methods with worker-oriented methods, noting that neither had achieved the necessary and sufficient reliability to be used in isolation. Therefore, Prien recommended a multi-method approach of both types.

567. Edwin A. Fleishman, "Development of a Behavior Taxonomy for Describing Human Tasks: A Correlational-Experimental Approach," *Journal of Applied Psychology*, 41, (February 1967): 1-10; also "On the Relation between Abilities, Learning, and Human Performance," *American Psychologist*, 27, (November 1972): 1017-32.

Some of the industrial psychological research into task analysis was quite detailed and difficult for untrained students to understand. Fleishman in particular tried to create task taxonomies through psychological testing by distinguishing human abilities from skills. He isolated eleven perceptual-motor factors and nine physical proficiency factors which were eventually used to devise his Task Abilities Scale (TAS).

568.   U.S. Department of Labor, Manpower Administration, *Handbook for Analyzing Jobs* (Washington, D.C.: USGPO, 1972); also

569.   E. L. Primoff, *How to Prepare and Conduct Job Element Examinations* (Washington, D.C.: U.S. Civil Service Commission, 1975); also

570.   U.S. Civil Service Commission, *Planning Your Staffing Needs: A Handbook for Personnel Workers* (Washington, D.C.: USGPO, 1977).

The U.S. Government, which has been involved in assisting the private sector with job analysis since the publication of the Dictionary of Occupational Titles (DOT) in 1939, stepped up its efforts in the 1970s. The *Handbook* is a complete revision of the earlier *Training and Reference Manual for Job Analysis*, published by the Bureau of Employment Security in 1944 and revised in 1965. It offers detailed instructions on preparing a job analysis with the results tied to DOT categories. More specialized instructions follow in the later documents, with a shift in emphasis toward human resources management concerns by 1977.

571.   Jay M. Shafritz, *Position Classification: A Behavioral Analysis for the Public Service* (New York: Praeger Publishers, 1973); also *Public Personnel Management: The Heritage of Civil Service Reform* (New York: Praeger Publishers, 1975).

Reflecting Philip Oliver's concern, stated in the foreword to Shafritz' 1973 book, "that position classification in both the public and private sectors was conceived by management as a simplistic approach to a burdensome administrative problem," Shafritz attacked personnel's excessive attachment to procedures, and argued that it should pay more attention to behavioral concerns. His proposal for job enrichment was "position management," using diverse task forces in which personnel experts would serve as facilitators, not as classifiers.

572.   U.S. Equal Employment Opportunity Commission, "Uniform Guidelines on Employee Selection Procedures," *Federal Register*, vol. 43, no. 166 (August 25, 1978): 38290-38310; also

573.   *U.S. v State of New York*. 21 FEP 1286 (1979).

After years of negotiations, in 1978 the Equal Employment Opportunity Commission, the Civil Service Commission, the Department of Justice, and the Department of Labor arrived at the joint uniform guidelines on selection procedures. The Guidelines include all aspects of employee placement, including job analysis. However, while the guidelines offer considerable detail on criterion-related, content, and construct validity, requiring accurate job analysis for each, it was left to the courts in 1979 to decide that job analysis must be based on task-oriented techniques, not worker-oriented techniques.

574. Donald Treiman, *Job Evaluation: An Analytic Review* (Washington, D.C.: National Academy of Sciences, 1979).

The EEOC asked the Committee on Occupational Classification and Analysis of the Assembly of Behavioral and Social Science of the National Academy of Sciences to analyze job evaluation to determine its impacts on the placement and compensation of women. This interim report is recommended for those needing a simple introduction to the vocabulary of job analysis. In addition to its recognition of the vulnerability of most techniques to gender discrimination, the report describes each technique in considerable detail, and includes forms by which each can be done.

575. Donald E. Klingner, "When the Traditional Job Description is Not Enough," *Personnel Journal*, 58, (April 1979): 243-48; also *Public Personnel Management: Contexts and Strategies* (Englewood Cliffs, NJ: Prentice-Hall, 1980).

Klingner felt that traditional PDs fail to give performance standards, or to tie together standards, skills, and qualifications. He suggested that governments supplement traditional grading techniques with results-oriented job descriptions (RODs). These descriptions would list the tasks, the conditions under which they are to be completed, the standards expected, the skills, knowledges, and abilities (SKAs) required, and the qualifications. While such a system could not replace traditional techniques for comparative purposes, it could tie PDs to performance expectations and organizational outputs.

MERIT PAY

While position classification was of no particular interest to Taylor and his immediate followers, merit pay was. In this section, the focus is on the mechanics of merit pay systems as they have evolved since Taylor's time. Questions of motivation are covered more completely in chapter fourteen.

576. Fritz Roethlisberger and William Dickson, *Management and the Worker* (Cambridge: Harvard University Press, 1939).

In Taylor's day, as already discussed, debates over the mechanics of merit pay (and such versions as profit-sharing) were lively. Once technicians divided into concerns over either time-motion studies or position classification, the literature faded from importance. The ability to motivate workers with pay was perhaps too obvious to deserve discussion.

The Hawthorne experiments, however, added a significant element of doubt. In the Bank Wiring Observation Room, established in 1931, fourteen men were placed under a system of piece-rate pay. As Taylor would have predicted, soldiering was rampant. More importantly, however, the workers falsified records and held back production to establish a uniform group-rate of production.

Roethlisberger and Dickson referred to this as the "logic of sentiments" to explain why talented workers would sacrifice money that was often easily available in order to maintain a sense of group cohesion.

577.   David C. McClelland, *The Achieving Society* (Princeton, NJ: Van Nostrand Reinhold, 1961).

McClelland added another factor by considering the possibility that merit pay could itself be a social variable. Specifically, merit pay appeals to those with high "*n*" factors, or achievement needs. The presence of high "*n*" factors depends on the culture and ethnic group of the individual. In addition, people with high "*n*" factors need a package of incentives beyond merit pay, including reasonably challenging goals with moderate risks and concrete feedback on their performances.

578.   Victor Vroom, *Work and Motivation* (New York: John Wiley and Sons, 1964); also

579.   Lyman W. Porter and Edward E. Lawler III, *Managerial Attitudes and Performance* (Homewood, IL: Richard D. Irwin, 1968): also

580.   Edward E. Lawler III, *Motivation in Work Organizations* (Monterey, CA: Brooks/Cole Publishing Co., 1973).

Further complicating the picture are the expectancy theories, popularized in the 1960s by Victor Vroom. According to Vroom, motivation is driven by three elements: valence, expectancy, and instrumentality. For merit pay to work, the worker must possess the valence to want bonus pay, the expectancy to believe that extra effort will lead to increased productivity, and the instrumentality to assume that increased productivity will lead to the desired reward. If any of the three belief systems do not fall into place, merit pay will not work. More likely, Vroom noticed, workers will adjust their elements to work toward general job satisfaction without increases in productivity.

Porter and Lawler further developed Vroom's contingency model to include effort, performance, rewards, and satisfaction. They also isolated intrinsic and extrinsic rewards, noting that government is seldom structured to give extrinsic rewards, and that the value of nonmonetary rewards has not been tested. Finally, Lawler in 1973 noted that their theory cannot be used to predict any individual's motivation.

581.   Edward L. Deci, "The Effect of Contingent and Noncontingent Rewards and Controls on Intrinsic Motivation," *Organizational Behavior and Human Performance*, 8, (1972): 217-29.

In laboratory experiments, Deci attempted to determine the effects of extrinsic rewards on intrinsic rewards among managers. He reported that those working on intrinsically interesting jobs lose interest when offered externally mediated rewards. More generally, the existence of external rewards tends to drive out the sense of intrinsic motivation among managers.

582.   Bobby J. Calder and Barry J. Staw, "The Integration of Intrinsic and Extrinsic Motivation," *Journal of Personality and Social Psychology*, 31, (1975): 599-605.

Calder and Staw reexamined Deci's experiments and concluded that his data did not support his conclusions. Rather, they argued that intrinsic and extrinsic rewards seem to be complementary and cumulative in their effects.

583.   Herbert H. Meyer, "The Pay for Performance Dilemma," *Organizational Dynamics*, 3, (Winter 1975): 39-50.

Meyer reviewed the research that had been conducted on the issue of pay for performance. He discovered two major reasons why merit pay systems tend to fail. First, managers are inclined to give such small differences between levels of merit that the effects are negligible. Second, managers as recipients of merit pay tend to have their self-esteem threatened since they often have unrealistically high estimates of their own worth to the organization.

584.   W. Clay Hamner, "How to Ruin Motivation with Pay," *Compensation Review*, 3, (Summer 1975): 17-27.

Hamner reviewed merit pay research, and noted that most critics believe the implementation, and not the concept, to be the cause of most failures. Among common attacks are that performance appraisal is often unrelated to productivity, and that the system operates in secrecy, leading to misunderstandings. He suggested five improvements: openness and trust should be emphasized; supervisors should be trained in rating and feedback; the mechanics of the plan should be widely explained; plans should be custom-tailored and involve the workers; and merit pay should be supplemented by other rewards.

585.   President's Panel on Federal Compensation, *Report to the President of the President's Panel on Federal Compensation* (Washington, D.C.: USGPO, December 1975); also

586.   President's Reorganization Project, "Final Staff Report," Volume 1 of *Personnel Management Project*, 3 vol. (Washington, D.C.: USGPO, December 1977); also

587.   *Civil Service Reform Act*, 92 Stat. 1111 (1978).

Despite primarily negative publicity, government studies and activities continued to advocate merit pay. The Rockefeller Panel of 1975 included merit pay among their five recommendations for compensation reform. The Campbell Commission of 1977, in recommendation #69 (pp. 159-60), advocated "a merit pay system for managerial positions below the levels included in the Executive Service...." Such a system for senior-level employees (GS-13, 14, 15), was legislated by the Civil Service Reform Act of 1978.

588.   Frederick Thayer, "The President's Management 'Reforms': Theory X Triumphant," *Public Administration Review*, 38, (July/August 1978): 309-14.

One of the first to attack the specific provisions of the Civil Service Reform Act was Thayer, whose concerns fell into two broad categories. First, he could find no evidence in the Campbell report and little evidence in the private sector that workers still respond well to pay incentives as opposed to more professional rewards. Secondly, he did not believe that existing performance appraisals measured productivity, believing instead that they stifled initiative and led to unfair punishments.

589.   Hal G. Rainey, "Perceptions of Incentives in Business and Government: Implications for Civil Service Reform," *Public Administration Review*, 39, (September/October 1979): 440-48.

Rainey investigated the different perceptions of merit pay among private-sector and governmental mid-level managers. Using surveys, he found that governmental managers have more reservations about the value of the system, and the possibility of making it work in government. He concluded that public agencies should instead stress improvements in their career development and performance appraisal systems.

590.   U.S. Office of Personnel Management, "Merit Pay Systems Design," [draft of regulations], February, 1981; also

591.   Comptroller General of the United States, *Federal Merit Pay: Important Concerns Need Attention* [FPCD-81-9] (Washington, D.C.: U.S. General Accounting Office, March 1981); also *Serious Problems Need to be Corrected Before Federal*

Merit Pay Goes into Effect [FPCD-81-73] (Washington, D.C.: U.S. General Accounting Office, September 11, 1981); also *Office of Personnel Management's Implementation of Merit Pay (decision B-203022)* (Washington, D.C.: U.S. General Accounting Office, September 1981).

Many of the same concerns were expressed at the federal level about the Merit Pay System, leading to the unusual process by which it was finally implemented. The original plan, set for implementation in October 1981, was to create merit pools using half of the comparability money and all the within-grade (step) money normally budgeted for the affected employees. Divisions of the pool would be made by peer-evaluation groups using newly-developed performance appraisal systems.

However, the General Accounting Office (GAO) launched an attack on the process soon after the Office of Personnel Management announced its initial plans. The GAO noted that the managers had little experience with merit pay or objective-based employee performance appraisals, and that many agencies were entering the process without a pretest. GAO recommended that the president delay implementation in all agencies that had not yet completed a pretest of the new performance appraisal system. Instead, the plan was implemented without pretests, but with a reduced merit pool since full comparability was guaranteed to the employees.

592. Nathan Winstanley, "Are Merit Increases Really Effective?" *Personnel Administrator*, 27, (April 1982): 37-41.

Expressing somewhat similar concerns, Winstanley argued that merit pay systems have ten requirements if they are to work properly: 1) worker trust and belief in management; 2) valid job evaluations; 3) agreed-upon tasks and criteria; 4) job specific, results-oriented criteria; 5) accurate performance appraisal; 6) appropriate administrative practices; 7) skilled feedback; 8) trained managers; 9) maintenance and information systems; and 10) follow-up research.

593. Richard E. Kopelman and Leon Reinharth, "Research Results: The Effect of Merit-Pay Practices on White Collar Performance," *Compensation Review*, 14, (Fourth Quarter 1982): 30-40.

Arguing that most of the research has been done on output or time-based merit systems, Kopelman and Reinharth focused on the judgmental merit-reward systems that are increasingly being used on professional and managerial employees. They found that these performance-based result in increased performance after a one to two year time delay. Also, increasing the range of merit increases affects performance more dramatically.

594. Jone L. Pearce and James L. Perry, "Federal Merit Pay: A Longitudinal Analysis," *Public Administration Review*, 43, (July/August 1983): 315-25.

At the federal level, however, the merit pay system for senior-level employees continued to receive harsh treatment among both practitioners and academics. In this time-series study of employee attitudes, Pearce and Perry reported the common belief that the objectives-based performance appraisal system did not work. Also, the pay caps on higher-level employees and the last-minute change in pay-out formulas helped undermine the credibility of the program. They suggested that the evaluation form should be fixed, and that the merit pay system should not be extended to lower-level employees.

595.   *Civil Service Retirement Spouse Equity Act*, 98 Stat. 3195 (1984).

Title II of this legislation established the Performance Management and Recognition System, which created more consistency in ratings and rewards in federal pay. The legislation mandated five levels of evaluation, with the rating of "fully satisfactory" in the middle. Among the features, comparability increases were guaranteed to those ranked "fully satisfactory." Those with the highest-level evaluation were also guaranteed performance awards. Committees were established to monitor the process. While the legislation regularized the rules, however, it also effectively tightened pay differentials.

596.   Gerald T. Gabris, ed., "Why Merit Pay Plans Are Not Working: A Search For Alternative Pay Plans in the Public Sector--A Symposium," *Review of Public Personnel Administration*, 7, Part I (Fall 1986): 1-89; Part II (Spring 1987): 28-91.

The theme of the two-part symposium was largely summed up in the pessimistic title. Thayer and Gabris isolated some intrinsic problems in any plan of merit pay for managers. The more common theme, however, was that experience to date has been clouded by poor performance appraisal systems and continually changing directives from above. Some, such as Golembiewski, saw hope for the system should these problems be corrected. On balance, however, the articles were not optimistic.

CONTINUING CONCERNS

Attacks on scientific management as an exclusive approach to administrative questions are too well known to be more than mentioned here. The original practitioners paid too little attention to motivation, often because of class prejudices against those of the working (and soldiering) classes. They also quantified variables that were not carefully enough defined to be subject to quantification.

In neither case, however, were they as guilty of these practices as many of those who carried on their concerns. While they paid little attention to motivation, the simple conclusions they reached on the subject (not to mention those of more recent research) have been largely ignored in currents efforts to implement merit pay in government. While they overquantified, they could not approach the rigor of industrial psychologists and others involved in strategies that Wallace Sayre long ago labelled "the triumph of techniques over purpose."[21]

Some of these developments are put into more focus in later chapters on staffing and motivation. A few thoughts are worth preserving, however, in summarizing the approach of scientific management reformers. They were moralistic reformers fighting anachronistic institutions. In that battle, history has judged them to be correct.

By seldom reading their works, we have also treated them unfairly. Their morality may be dated, but the evils they fought would still be considered worse. They may have been narrow in their understanding of the many facets of the work place, but broader than many of those who still carry their banner.

When they carried the quest for efficiency to extremes, it was moderation and not inefficiency that was needed in their place. Today, it may well be their moderation and broad perspective that is needed by those who still perform their major functions.

NOTES ON CHAPTER ELEVEN

1. Additional sources on the topics discussed in the background include two books by Daniel Nelson: *Frederick W. Taylor and the Rise of Scientific Management* (Madison: University of Wisconsin Press, 1980); also, *Managers and Workers* (Madison: University of Wisconsin Press, 1975). See also Lewis Mumford, *Technics and Civilization* (New York: Harcourt, Brace and Co., 1934).

2. Thomas Kuhn, *The Structure of Scientific Revolutions* (Chicago: University of Chicago Press, 1962).

3. The *American Political Science Review* at the time did the same thing, summarizing conference activities and listing membership.

4. Fred W. Taylor, "A Piece-Rate System, being a Step Toward Partial Solution of the Labor Problem," *Transactions of the American Society of Mechanical Engineering*, XVI, (June 1895): 856-83. It should be noted that, while the above title for the journal was correct, library references always list the more recent title *American Society of Mechanical Engineers Transactions*.

5. Henry Metcalfe, *The Cost of Manufactures and the Administration of Workshops* (New York: John Wiley and Sons, 1885).

6. Scholars of that era believed profit-sharing plans to have been introduced by Edme-Jean Leclaire in his Parisian house-painting company in 1842. In 1878, a group of business leaders formed a Société that on March 1, 1879 began publishing the *Bulletin de la Société de la Participation aux Bénéfices* through the Chaix publishing house (a profit-sharing operation) in Paris. A major description of German efforts was V. K. Böhmert's *Die Gewinnbetheiligung*, 2 vol. (Leipsic [Leipzig]: Brockhaus, 1878). In England, see Sedley Taylor, *Profit Sharing Between Capital and Labour* (London: Kegan Paul, Trench & Co., 1884).

7. Frank B. Copley, *Frederick W. Taylor: Father of Scientific Management*, 2 vol. (New York: Harper and Brothers, 1923). The Nelson books are cited in note one above.

8. The popular claim that Harper and Brothers (or even Harper and Row, which was not created until 1957) put out a 1903 version of this paper is inaccurate. The revisions from the 1903 text are generally described in the editor's preface to the 1911 trade edition.

9. See Nelson, *Taylor and Scientific Management*, pp. 86-87 and 113-14.

10. C. Bertrand Thompson, *The Theory and Practice of Scientific Management* (Boston: Houghton Mifflin Co., 1917), p. 193ff.

11. The book is extremely rare, and is identified by its blue (as opposed to red) cover, and the following notation on the title page: "THIS SPECIAL EDITION PRINTED IN FEBRUARY 1911 FOR CONFIDENTIAL CIRCULATION AMONG THE MEMBERS OF THE AMERICAN SOCIETY OF MECHANICAL ENGINEERS WITH THE COMPLIMENTS OF THE AUTHOR."

12. "The Principles of Scientific Management," *American Magazine*, 71, (March 1911): 570-81; also "The Gospel of Efficiency, II. The Principles of Scientific Management," *American Magazine*, 71, (April 1911): 785-93; also "The Gospel of Efficiency, III. The Principles of Scientific Management," 72, (May 1911): 101-13.

13. Part I is entitled "Theory and Principles of Scientific Management," *Journal of Accountancy*, 12, (June 1911): 117-24. Part II is "Principles and Methods of Scientific Management," *Journal of Accountancy*, 12, (July 1911): 181-88.

14. The context in which these versions were written is adapted from Nelson, *Taylor and Scientific Management*, pp. 168-76, and similar writings. The variations in Taylor's texts, which apparently are discussed in no previous published works, are taken from the originals.

15. Bibliographers are warned about the chronic confusion among contemporary sources on the precise date of publication of almost all books published by Engineering Magazine press. To increase their "shelf life," most of their official publication dates were listed as the year after the actual release.

16. On the merging of the welfare work movement and scientific management into personnel management, see Nelson, *Managers and Workers*, especially pp. 72-73; also Nelson, *Taylor and the Rise of Scientific Management*, especially pp. 44-45. See also Henry Eilbert, "The Development of Personnel Management in the United States," *Business History Review*, 33, (Autumn 1959): 345-64, and Robert F. Milkey, "Job Evaluation After 50 Years," *Public Personnel Review*, 21, (January 1960): 19-23.

17. For a bibliography on job analysis from 1911 to 1941, see J. E. Zerga, "Job Analysis: a Résumé and Bibliography," *Journal of Applied Psychology*, 27, (1943): 249-67.

18. Ordway Tead, "Personnel Administration," *Encyclopaedia of the Social Sciences*, vol. 12 (New York: Macmillan Company, 1934), p. 88.

19. W. H. Stead and C. L. Shartle, *Occupational Counseling Techniques* (New York: American Books, 1940).

20. Volume one was entitled *Findings and Recommendations*. Volume two was *Models of Evaluation Systems and Pay Structures*.

21. Wallace S. Sayre, "The Triumph of Techniques over Purpose," [a review of Paul Pigors and Charles A. Meyers, *Personnel Administration: A Point of View and a Method* (New York: McGraw-Hill Book Co., 1947)] *Public Administration Review*, 8, (Spring 1948): 134-37.

12
Woodrow Wilson and
Administrative Science

BACKGROUND

Wilson, Taylor, and Weber presented perspectives that have been uniquely influential over the field, regardless of whether these three authors arrived at them first, and regardless of whether the field appreciated their contributions when their works were published. Of those three, Taylor was the most peripheral to the subject of public administration. For Wilson and Weber, however, it is appropriate to discuss not just what they said, but how they arrived at their beliefs, and what their perspectives have meant to the field.

This chapter is divided into three sections. First, it describes the written and spoken works of Wilson that were relevant to public administration. The second section discusses several major studies of Woodrow Wilson's beliefs about administration, selected for their ability to explain the development and impacts (if any) of Wilson's thoughts on public administration.

The third section discusses the academic literature that followed in the same tradition as Wilson, under the modern label of administrative science. Specifically, this chapter is interested in organizational literature that used a large level of analysis, and that was written from the perspective of external observers. It ignores the concerns of individual workers which were more the focus of Taylor, and later of the Humanists. For the sake of keeping chapter lengths within reason, it also bypasses both the literature specifically about the bureaucratic form of organization, and works about the roles of managers in particular. Those topics are discussed in the next two chapters.

WORKS BY WILSON

597.   Woodrow Wilson, *Congressional Government* (Boston: Houghton Mifflin, 1885).

The focus of Wilson's first book, which became his dissertation, was to compare the American governmental system to the cabinet system used in England to demonstrate that the U.S. lacked unified authority. On public administration, Wilson was concerned that departments technically answered to the president, but in reality answered to congressional oversight and budgetary committees. In chapter 5, he also gave some hint of the politics/administration dichotomy when he suggested that political and nonpolitical offices should be treated differently. His terms were vague, however, and nonpolitical offices occasionally seemed to expand all the way to the cabinet officers.

598.   Woodrow Wilson, "Courtesy of the Senate," in *The Papers of Woodrow Wilson*, ed. by Arthur S. Link, vol. 5 (Princeton: Princeton University Press, 1968), pp. 44-48; also "Notes on Administration," *Papers of Woodrow Wilson*, vol. 5, pp. 49-50; also "The Art of Governing," *Papers of Woodrow Wilson*, vol. 5, pp. 50-54.

In 1884-1885, Wilson took a course in public administration from Professor Richard T. Ely at Johns Hopkins University.[1] While distracted by such projects as *Congressional Government*, he managed to write some preliminary drafts of papers related to administration by late 1885 or early 1886. "Courtesy of the Senate," published in the Boston *Citizen* in February 1886, noted that it was more difficult to implement civil service procedures at the municipal level than at the federal level, but that such procedures were preferable to senatorial courtesy appointments in both cases.

Soon thereafter, Wilson's drafts became more directed toward public administration as a subject of study. Both "Notes," (written in his Comparative Public Law notebook) and "The Art of Governing" emphasized the need to study the machinery of governing, claiming that the French and Germans were already doing so. "The Art of Governing," much of which was later integrated into "The Study of Administration," also listed the three phases of government.

Somewhat tentatively, however, Wilson suggested "I suppose that no great discoveries of method are to be made in administration. Constitutions are new, but administration is as old as government." (p. 50)

599.   Woodrow Wilson, "The Study of Administration," *Political Science Quarterly*, 2, (July 1887): 197-222.

Wilson was asked to deliver a speech before the Historical and Political Science Association at Cornell University on November 3, 1886. The speech, except for a revision of the last two paragraphs of part II, became the *Political Science Quarterly* article of July 1887.[2]

The article described the evolution of government through the three phases of absolute rule, constitutional government, and the administration of constitutional government. Wilson argued that politics and administration were different functions, making it practical to improve administration without harming political democracy. He issued a call to political scientists to study more effective techniques for administration.

600.   Woodrow Wilson, "Wilson Launches His Lectures on Administration at the Johns Hopkins," in *The Papers of Woodrow Wilson*, ed. by Arthur S. Link, vol. 5 (Princeton: Princeton University Press, 1968), pp. 668-69; also "Notes for Two Classroom Lectures at the Johns Hopkins," *Papers of Woodrow Wilson*, vol. 5, pp. 691-95; also "Notes for Lectures on Administration," *Papers of Woodrow Wilson*, vol. 6 (1969), pp. 484-521.

From 1888 through 1897, Wilson delivered a set of annual Winter lectures at Johns Hopkins on the subject of administration. The plan for the first three years was to move slowly from general description through more specific description to theory. As his readings continued, however, Wilson's views on the politics/administration dichotomy began to change toward the policy-making version used by the Germans and French.

By 1890, Wilson was arguing that administration, instead of standing alone as a business-*like* practice, was actually a part of public law. In the following years, the lectures evolved still further into municipal reform, ignoring their original intent.

STUDIES ABOUT WILSON'S PERSPECTIVES ON ADMINISTRATION

601.   Leonard D. White, *Introduction to the Study of Public Administration* (New York: Macmillan Co., 1926); also "Administration, Public," *Encyclopaedia of the Social Sciences*, vol. 1 (New York: Macmillan, 1930), pp. 440-50.

Wilson's lectures on municipal reform were quite popular in the Baltimore press by 1896. However, his contribution to the field of public administration was not appreciated, nor apparently widely-read by other scholars, until the 1930s. While John Mathews included Wilson's article in a 1917 reading list, the first reference to the article in another academic text is on pages 2 and 9 of White's first general textbook of the field, in which Wilson's "brilliant essay" is used to describe the politics/administration dichotomy.[3] White's later general description of the field in the *Encyclopaedia* also lists Wilson in the suggested readings without mentioning him in the text.

602.　Marshall E. Dimock, "The Study of Administration," *American Political Science Review*, 31, (February 1937): 28-40.

In describing the rise of the administrative state, Dimock made the second published reference to Wilson's article, praising its wisdom, but attacking the politics/administration dichotomy by saying that politics "runs all the way through administration," and arguing that Wilson was unrealistic in saying that the field of administration is a field of business.

603.　Lindsay Rogers, "A Professor With Style," *Political Science Quarterly*, 56, (December 1941): 507-14.

During the "managerial revolution" (see next chapter) of the 1930s, increasing numbers of people began to discover Wilson's 1887 article, and apparently to believe that it had been widely read since publication. The *Public Administration Review* sought but did not obtain permission to republish the article in its premier issue in 1940. Instead, it was reprinted by the *Political Science Quarterly* (pp. 481-506) in December 1941, along with a photostatic copy of Wilson's tentative accompanying letter and Rogers' essay. Rogers recounted the submission of Wilson's article, generally praised its insight, and described the increased interest in it in terms that could easily mislead one to believe that the interest had been there for generations.

604.　Dwight Waldo, *The Administrative State* (New York: Ronald Press, 1948).[4]

Waldo's treatment of Wilson was more matter-of-fact than Rogers', and was written with the assumption that the work had been widely read since publication, and that it had been able to give "the cue to subsequent writers" on a business-like approach to the field. His assumption reflected, and perhaps helped reinforce, a similar feeling among newer members of the field.

605.　Henry A. Turner, "Woodrow Wilson as Administrator," *Public Administration Review*, 16, (Autumn 1956): 249-57.

This article, written for the centennial of Wilson's birth, is understandably highly favorable to Wilson. It describes the evolution of his essay through the "Notes" to "The Art of Governing" to "The Study of Administration." Using the Baker papers that were then available, Turner was aware that Wilson had taught subsequent courses on the subject, although he had little information on their content.[5] Also, much of the essay was devoted to Wilson's impact on administration as president rather than as author.

606.　Fred W. Riggs, "Relearning Old Lessons: The Political Context of Development Administration," *Public Administration Review*, 25, (March 1965): 70-79.

Wilson's "The Study of Administration" contained enough thoughts that were still in transition that it is practical to find many things on which he can be interpreted in more than one way. In this article, Riggs introduced the point that parts of the article can be read to argue that politics and administration, being sequential parts of the same process, are actually inseparable. (pp. 71-72)

607. Arthur S. Link, "Woodrow Wilson and the Study of Administration," *Proceedings of the American Philosophical Society*, 112, (December 1968): 431-33; reprinted as chapter 3 in *The Higher Realism of Woodrow Wilson, and Other Essays* (Nashville: Vanderbilt University Press, 1971).

Until the publication of the Link papers beginning in 1966, and especially volumes 5 and 6 released in 1968 and 1969, it was impractical for the field to have more than a cursory view of how Wilson's ideas developed before 1887, or how his studies in administration continued to evolve in subsequent years. As those volumes were being released, Link described the origin of Wilson's interest in Ely's lectures of 1884-1885, his early drafts on the subject, and the evolution of Wilson's ideas during his Johns Hopkins lectures into the argument that administration is a part of public law.

608. Richard J. Stillman, II, "Woodrow Wilson and the Study of Administration: A New Look at an Old Essay," *American Political Science Review*, 67, (June 1973): 582-88.

Stillman attempted to tie Wilson's published record together by arguing that "The Study of Administration" is a continuation of the same concerns for methods of restoring good government that were expressed in *Congressional Government.*

609. Vincent Ostrom, *The Intellectual Crisis in American Public Administration* (University: University of Alabama Press, 1973).

Ostrom similarly tied Wilson's article to his earlier *Congressional Government* to argue that Wilson's central concern was that "the more power is divided the more irresponsible it becomes." To centralize power, Ostrom argued, Wilson wanted to create a professionally-trained, hierarchical bureaucracy that could be responsive to a unified political system. To Ostrom, such an arrangement was not in the best interest of the polity.

610. John M. Mulder, *Woodrow Wilson: The Years of Preparation* (Princeton: Princeton University Press, 1978), chapter 5.

Most of Mulder's book fits into the wide assortment of biographies that are available on Wilson. In pages 116 through 119, however, Mulder presented what may be the first modern argument that Wilson revised and largely abandoned his politics/

administration dichotomy during his lectures at Johns Hopkins University during the years 1888-1897.

611.   Paul Van Riper, "The American Administrative State: Wilson and the Founders--An Unorthodox View," *Public Administration Review*, 43, (November/ December 1983): 477-90; updated in *A Centennial History of the American Administrative State*, ed. by Ralph Clark Chandler (New York: Free Press, 1987), pp. 3-36.

Van Riper's 1983 article introduced a new set of arguments limiting Wilson's significance in the early years of the field. First, he noted that none of the early scholars of Political Science or Public Administration cited the article, even though many referred to *Congressional Government*. Secondly, he discovered that five years before Wilson's article, Dorman Eaton had published far more explicit calls for the study of public administration than previously had been realized.

612.   Jack Rabin and James S. Bowman, eds., *Politics and Administration: Woodrow Wilson and the Study of Public Administration* (New York: Marcel Dekker, 1984).

For the centennial of Wilson's essay, a national call for articles resulted in this collection of refereed essays on Wilson's contributions to the field. Arthur Link noted in the foreword that the authors had "not written uncritical tributes," and that was occasionally an understatement. Notably, Robert Miewald described the German literature that Wilson not only used, but incorrectly translated, to arrive at his dichotomy. Van Riper documented his claim that Wilson's article was largely ignored at the time, and attributed the dichotomy to Dorman Eaton and his civil service colleagues. Golembiewski described three specific problems that caused Wilson's article to confound the later study of administration. On balance, however, the book reflects the respect that the field still carried for Wilson.

ADMINISTRATIVE SCIENTISTS

613.   Johann C. Bluntschli, *Lehre vom modernen stat*, 3 vol. (Stuttgart: J.G. Cotta, 1876-1886); also

614.   Heinrich Rudolf von Gneist, *Englische verfassungsgeschichte* (Berlin: J. Springer, 1882).

It has become increasingly clear that administrative theory not only was quite active in Europe before Wilson wrote, but that American scholars were aware of the literature.[6] These two examples have been chosen because of their particular impact on Wilson (Bluntschli) and Goodnow, who claimed that "Gneist was almost the first

student of note to call attention to the importance of administrative institutions."
Bluntschli's massive work attempted to build a modern theory for the state, and
described in some detail the rise of merit-based administration in German government.
Gneist argued that attempts to transplant English parliamentary government to the
continent had inevitably failed because political theorists had not appreciated the
necessity for also adopting the English approach to administration.

615.   U.S. Senate, *Report [of] the Select committee of the United States Senate,*
        appointed under Senate resolution of March 3, 1887, to inquire into and examine
        the methods of business and work of the executive departments, etc., and the
        causes of delays in transacting the public business, etc., Senate Rept. 507, 3 v.
        in 2, 50th Cong., 1st sess., March 8, 1888; also *Additional report of the Select*
        committee... Senate Rept. 3 51st Cong., special sess., March 28, 1889.[7]

In the United States, congressional investigations had been seeking methods to
limit administrative expenditures since the founding of the government. This particularly comprehensive effort was generated in response to numerous complaints to
congress of administrative backlogs of months and even years in several departments.
After collecting data for almost a year, the Cockrell committee reported numerous instances of inefficient practices and needless, often ridiculous, duplication. They
recommended that the secretaries of War and Treasury form internal commissions to
implement cost-saving procedures and report back to congress. Numerous changes
were made, and the reports were reprinted in the 1889 document above.

616.   The Dockery-Cockrell Commission, *References to laws organizing executive*
        departments and other government establishments at the national capital, House
        Rept. 49 and Senate Rept. 41, 53rd Cong., 1st sess., September 30, 1893; also
        Organization of the executive departments and other government establishments
        at the national capital, and information concerning the persons employed therein,
        House Rept. 88 and Senate Rept. 58, 53rd Cong., 1st sess., October 9, 1893.

In attempting to carry on the work of the Cockrell committee, congress created
a joint committee to make recommendations for further savings. Most of the commission's 29 reports were in support of specific legislation, and a complete listing is
not given here.[8] However, the two reports above were especially useful as the first
compilations of the laws and the resulting structures of the national administration.

617.   Frank J. Goodnow, *Municipal Home Rule: A Study in Administration* (New
        York: Macmillan and Co., 1895); also *Politics and Administration: A Study in*
        Government (New York: Macmillan and Co., 1900).

As an administrative law theorist interested in municipal reform, Goodnow was
concerned about the frequent interference of state legislatures with the minor administrative matters of municipalities. Continuing the same theme, his goals in 1900

were to centralize state administration as had been done at the federal level, so that individual administrators could not block implementation of the laws, and to bring political parties under control.

His tactics were to centralize administration but decentralize the legislative process so that local differences could be expressed in policy-making. To accomplish both objectives, he described an explicit politics/administration dichotomy that allowed each part of the governing process to be amended separately while recognizing that changes in either part affected the whole.

618.   Henry Jones Ford, *The Rise and Growth of American Politics* (New York: Macmillan, 1898); also *The Cost of Our National Government* (New York: Columbia University Press, 1910).

The need for consistency in American government seems to have been appreciated by virtually everyone, including Ford, a Social Darwinist who eventually became a close advisor to Woodrow Wilson. However, Ford did not see the solution at first in administrative structure, or even in governmental structure. Instead, he argued that political parties had taken on the role of securing harmony between government and administration for the effective operation of government. Government itself could not do the job since disunity was inherent in a society of immigrants who were often beyond the control of government. By 1910, however, some of Ford's concerns became more practically-oriented, and he argued that continued budget deficits required administrative reforms.

619.   Committee on Department Methods, 1905-1909.[9]

In 1905, President Roosevelt formed a committee of five officials (led by Assistant Secretary of the Treasury Charles Keep) to recommend improvements in administrative methods. The team produced 22 reports, many of which were never publicly printed (Gustavus Weber in 1919 knew of one complete set), and many fulfilled the President's request that the recommendations be minor enough that legislation would not be required. More substantial recommendations that would have established a retirement system or standardized employee salaries were never legislated.

620.   Commission on Economy and Efficiency, 1912.[10]

In 1910, congress appropriated $100,000 for President Taft to organize studies on methods to fight lingering budgetary deficits (see Ford above). Taft recruited Frederick Cleveland from the New York Bureau of Municipal Research to head what became the five-member Commission on Economy and Efficiency. In 1912, they released numerous reports to the president and congress, and 35 circulars.

On a large scale, they wanted departments reorganized according to function, including the abolition and consolidation of some offices. They advocated a national executive budget, an expansion of the classified service to all non-policy-making

personnel, standardized efficiency reports, a retirement system, and new object categories for budgetary submissions. They also offered several operational suggestions,
including the increased use of window envelopes already suggested by the Keep Committee.

The Taft Commission, as it became called, became embroiled in jurisdictional
disputes between the president and congress, and ran out of authorization before some
projects were completed, most notably a proposal to consolidate the Army and Navy
into a Department of Defense.

621.   U.S. Bureau of Efficiency, *Report of the United States Bureau of Efficiency for
        the period from March 25, 1913 to October 31, 1916*, House Doc. 1793, 64th
        Cong., 2nd sess., 1917; also *Report of the United States Bureau of Efficiency for
        the period from November 1, 1916 to October 31, 1917*, House Doc. 901, 65th
        Cong., 2nd sess., 1918.

Upon completion of the Taft Commission's work, congress authorized the Civil
Service Commission (CSC) to "establish a system of efficiency ratings for the classified service," but without appropriation. In 1916, appropriations were added, the
scope was broadened to efficiency in general, and the Division of Efficiency was
moved out of the CSC to become the independent Bureau of Efficiency.

The Bureau's work was focused on narrow enough projects that reports were
often not publicly available. Histories of the Bureau can be found in Weber and
Arnold below. In addition, the Bureau issued occasional brief reports to congress (see
citation above) which are easily obtainable, and which summarize its activities.

622.   Frederick A. Cleveland, *Organized Democracy* (New York: Longmans, Green,
        and Co., 1913); also

623.   Frederick A. Cleveland and Arthur E. Buck, *The Budget and Responsible Govern-
        ment* (New York: Macmillan and Co., 1920).

Cleveland, as head of the Taft Commission and the New York Bureau for Municipal Research, advocated administrative reform for the growth of executive, and more
particularly, presidential leadership. While Cleveland and Buck agreed with Willoughby
(see below) that the constitution established congress as the primary branch, they
considered that to be poor judgment. They argued that executive government is a
requirement for democracy in modern society, and assumed that the reorganization
and budgetary movements were established to bring that about.

624.   John Mabry Mathews, *Principles of American State Administration* (New York:
        D. Appleton and Co., 1917); also "State Administrative Reorganization," *Amer-
        ican Political Science Review*, 16, (August 1922): 387-98; also

625.   F. W. Coker, "Dogmas of Administrative Reform," *American Political Science Review*, 16, (August 1922): 399-411.

Mathews wrote the first book to list Wilson's article in a reading list (p. 21), and he agreed with the argument that administrative questions were becoming more urgent than constitutional ones. He felt that executive consolidation was needed, with short ballots, and with no more than a dozen departments, each with a single head.

In the first academic attack on the executive-consolidation-through-reorganization movement, however, Coker complained that reorganization paid too little attention to the continuity of policy, noninterference by politicians, unpaid citizen input, leaving authority and responsibility with the professionals, and overextended elected officials.

626.   William Franklin Willoughby, *An Introduction to the Study of the Government of Modern States* (New York: The Century Co., 1919); also *The Reorganization of the Administrative Branch of the National Government* (Baltimore: Johns Hopkins Press, 1923); also *Principles of Public Administration* (Washington, D.C.: Brookings Institution, 1927).

Willoughby, who, like Cleveland, had been a member of the Taft commission, took the more traditional view that responsibility for administration had been intentionally placed in the hands of congress and should remain there. However, he described in 1919 that congress should rule by setting goals and conducting audits (surveillance). It should not interfere with the daily command of administration.

Instead, as he emphasized in 1923, coordination of executive functions was vital. In 1927, he elaborated that with the growing complexity of government, congress needed to make broad delegations of authority to the president for the integration of administration, even though the congress maintained constitutional jurisdiction over the area.

Internally, Willoughby distinguished housekeeping functions, which were appropriate for efficiency studies, from primary (policy-delivering) functions, which were not. He also placed heavy emphasis on trained personnel and rigorous accounting procedures.

627.   Gustavus Weber, *Organized Efforts for the Improvement of Methods of Administration in the United States* (New York: D. Appleton and Co., 1919).

In an effort to create a reference document through the auspices of the Institute of Government Research, Weber described the studies and bodies that had led to reorganization efforts at all three levels of government. Since some of the early reorganization studies of government were never easily available to the general public, Weber has provided an irreplaceable description of these efforts for modern scholars.

In addition to descriptions and exhaustive and precise citations, however, Weber also presented the Institute's position that was to be carried (under its subsequent name of Brookings Institution) into its eventual opposition to the Brownlow Committee report. Administration appropriately answered to the leadership of congress. To the extent that the president was chief administrator, he also served as an agent of congress. Therefore, reorganization studies were more useful and more likely to be implemented if conducted under congress' direction.

628.   Arthur E. Buck, *Administrative Consolidation in State Governments* (New York: National Municipal League, 1919); also *The Reorganization of State Governments in the United States* (New York: Columbia University Press, 1938).

Under the auspices of the National Municipal League, Buck in 1919 described the arguments and publications of those who wanted to improve management through executive consolidation into 12-15 departments with fixed lines of responsibility. In 1938, he expanded his description of the League's proposals in handbook fashion, supplemented by state-by-state reorganization proposals.

629.   Joint Committee on Reorganization, Created by 41 Stat. 1083 (1920); for report, see Senate Doc. 128, 68th Cong., 1st sess., 1924.

In one of the last efforts by congress to lead an administrative reorganization effort, the Joint Committee was created in December 1920. However, once Harding took office, he had a representative of the president added to the committee as chair. In 1923, Harding submitted a reorganization plan that, most notably, included a new Defense Department and Education and Welfare Department, and that transferred the General Accounting Office to the Treasury Department.

The proposal, minus the Defense Department, was submitted by the committee to congress in 1924. The report complained of too many agencies outside the cabinet departments, including many doing duplicate or uncoordinated work. Most of the proposals were never adopted.[11]

630.   Lloyd Milton Short, *The Development of National Administrative Organization in the United States* (Baltimore: Johns Hopkins Press, 1923).

In 1923, Short compiled the most extensive history of American administrative organizations and practices that then existed. Describing the development of each department separately, he echoed the Institute of Government Research's argument that congress, not the constitution and certainly not the president, had been most influential in determining administrative forms.

However, he also argued that circumstances were making the president more important with time, and that Willoughby's distinction between executive and administrative functions was getting hard to defend. Specifically, he saw the new Budget and Accounting Act as a still-unfulfilled opportunity for the president to create a planning instrument for the executive branch.

631.   *Competency and Economy in Public Expenditures, Annals of the American Academy of Political and Social Science*, 113, (May 1924).

In a review of recent reorganization efforts, former governor Frank Lowden described Illinois' experiences with the first state-level comprehensive administrative reorganization, begun in 1917. Walter F. Dodd provided a broader state-level review, discussing the complexity of the task and the constitutional barriers to be overcome.
Walter Thompson wrote of centralization within the federalist system, while John A. Fairlie discussed county and township experiences with reorganization. Edward Paxton discussed "The Trend of Reorganization in City Government."

632.   Leonard D. White, *Introduction to the Study of Public Administration* (New York: Macmillan Co., 1926); also 2nd ed., (1939).

Peri Arnold (see below) used the first two editions of this first American textbook of Public Administration to illustrate the shift from the machine approach of executive organization to the modern political approach of Public Administration. In 1926, White argued that centralization around the executive was needed, that "congress and state assemblies alike have allowed a strange tangle of authorities to grow up, without plan or principle, lacking coordination and confusing responsibility." (p. 54) To explain his proposal, he used the analogy of the Administrative Machine, staffed by experts, organized by specialties, and coordinated by the chief executive.
The 1939 edition was heavily amended to reflect the field's new concern with bureaucratic politics, centered more obviously around the chief executive. New chapters on "The Chief Executive as General Manager," and "Staff and Auxiliary Agencies" were supplemented with a new emphasis on such nontraditional organizations as independent regulatory agencies and government corporations. The new power of national administration was also explored in chapters on administrative responsibility and judicial control.

633.   James D. Mooney and Alan C. Reilly, *Onward Industry!* (New York: Harper and Brothers, 1931); revised as *The Principles of Organization* (New York: Harper and Brothers, 1939).

In one of the more orthodox examples of administrative science ever written, Mooney and Reilly divided the structure of organizations into the coordinative principle, the scalar principle, and the functional principle (with its subset, the staffing phase of functionalism). They described the principle, the process, and the effect of each, and included histories of the developments of government, the church, the military, and industry.

634.   John M. Pfiffner, *Public Administration* (New York: Ronald Press, 1935).

By 1935, voices of dissent became louder. While Pfiffner agreed that "good men will be thwarted in their best efforts by faulty organization," and while he advocated hierarchy, functional division of tasks, line-staff distinctions, and centralized house-keeping activities, he was concerned that such conclusions were too often treated as dogma. Instead, these conclusions needed to evolve as organizations changed.

635.   Harvey Walker, *Public Administration in the United States* (New York: Farrar and Rinehart, 1937).

In this fourth textbook of public administration, Walker saw his contribution in his inclusion of line as well as the staff functions described in the first three, and he included chapters on several generic governmental functions. Influenced by the newly released Brownlow Committee report, Walker emphasized centralization within both the federal system and the executive branch, describing increased centralization in each of his subject-area chapters. He argued that leadership was more effective than compulsion, and that barriers to executive leadership should be removed.

636.   The President's Committee on Administrative Management, *Report of the President's Committee, Administrative Management in the Government of the United States* (Washington, D.C.: USGPO, January 1937); also

637.   Luther Gulick and Lyndall Urwick, eds., *Papers on the Science of Administration* (New York: Institute of Public Administration, 1937).

The Brownlow Committee report, and the accompanying set of *Papers* that were used to establish a common vocabulary, are generally accepted as the high-water mark of orthodoxy in administrative science. Based on its famous plea that "the president needs help" (p. 5), the report described a set of recommendations that would centralize control around the president. Among the suggestions were increased staff and discretionary funds for the president, a more responsive and centralized personnel structure, a strengthened planning function, and more executive control over accounting procedures.

The most famous article in the *Papers* was Gulick's "Notes on the Theory of Organization" (pp. 1-45), in which POSDCORB was created to describe the functions of the chief executive. Other notable articles included a first translation of a work by Fayol, an original piece by Mooney, and a reprint of a speech by Follett.

638.   Brookings Institution, U.S. Senate, Select Committee to Investigate the Executive Agencies of the Government, *Report*, 75th Cong., 1st sess., 1937; also

639. Lewis C. Meriam and Laurence F. Schmeckebier, *Reorganization of the National Government: What Does It Involve?* (Washington, D.C.: Brookings Institution, 1939).

As the Brownlow report was being released, the Brookings Institution completed a study for Senator Byrd's committee that was in sharp contrast on a number of points. Most notably, the Brownlow Committee hoped to limit the legislative branch on fiscal management to a final audit while the Brookings report advocated GAO audits during disbursements, disallowance powers, and expanded preaudits.

Meriam and Schmeckebier similarly attacked the Brownlow-New Deal philosophy, advocating tighter economies for the bureaucracy and movements towards a balanced budget. At the base of the controversy was a more fundamental disagreement; Brookings' heritage from the Institute of Government Research days under W. F. Willoughby believed in the constitutional supremacy of congress over administration, and that was inconsistent with the operating style of the New Deal.

640. Charles S. Hyneman, "Administrative Reorganization: An Adventure into Science and Theology," *Journal of Politics*, 1, (February 1939): 62-75.

In 1938, the reorganization bill that would have implemented the Brownlow recommendations was rejected by congress, and the attacks on administrative science strengthened. Hyneman reviewed recent works by Buck, Porter and Willoughby by asking six questions, the answers to which were often obvious in the questions.

First, "is 'efficiency' acceptable as the first objective of reorganization?" Second, can administrative work be divorced from control of policy? Third, is there any evidence that single officers work better than boards? Fourth, are entire reorganization programs needed to obtain central direction of administration? Fifth, have reorganizations actually accomplished anything? Sixth, can governors realistically be made responsible for the conduct of administration?

Hyneman complained that administrative science has curious standards of evidence, and often proves its points by merely repeating them.

641. John D. Millett and Lindsay Rogers, "The Legislative Veto and the Reorganization Act of 1939," *Public Administration Review*, 1, (Winter 1941): 176-89.

After the 1938 reorganization act failed, a stripped-down version was passed in 1939. Still, as Millett and Rogers pointed out, it contained at least four new features. Future reorganizations would be put into plans, not executive orders, suggesting the facade that the president was an agent of congress. Disapproval would be by concurrent resolution, not joint resolution, raising some questions of constitutionality. The act specified rules of procedures for rejecting presidential plans. Among those procedures, plans must be rejected in total, not in pieces.

Since congress could no longer handle all the details of administration, but feared unlimited delegation to the president, Millett and Rogers speculated that the device would be used more extensively in the future.

642.   Schuyler C. Wallace, *Federal Departmentalization* (New York: Columbia University Press, 1941).

In the wake of the Brownlow Committee, and leaning heavily on Gulick's "Notes on the Theory of Organization," Wallace argued that the reason we were having so much trouble finding the proper form of governmental organization was that there is no such thing. Instead, organizational choices are political choices, and reformers need to consider both the political and the administrative implications of their suggestions. Both the Brownlow Committee and the Brookings Institution in its opposition to Brownlow did that, Wallace felt. The American Bar Association, however, showed little concern for the administrative feasibility of its suggestions.

643.   Lyndall Urwick, *The Elements of Administration* (London: Harper and Brothers, 1944).

Orthodoxy did not die peacefully. Based on lectures delivered in 1942, Urwick reinvestigated a number of administrative principles. While noting that we had not developed a *science* of management, a *technique* of administration was emerging. To ignore that emerging technique was "lunacy," comparable to economic theorists who treat labor as a commodity while it keeps acting like people.

644.   Herbert A. Simon, "The Proverbs of Administration," *Public Administration Review*, 6, (Winter 1946): 53-67.

To Simon, the problem with the principles of administration is that they are not principles, but criteria for diagnosing and describing administration situations. He felt that recent literature had realized that such principles should not be taken to extremes, but should be applied to an extent appropriate to the situation. Future analyses should develop both a vocabulary to describe organizations, and criteria by which those organizations should be evaluated.

645.   Dwight Waldo, *The Administrative State* (New York: Ronald Press, 1948).

Writing from the perspective of a political theorist analyzing the literature of Public Administration, Waldo attacked the "Gospel of Efficiency" that had arisen in administrative studies, noting that it was a distinct political philosophy that was not particularly appropriate to the purposes of government.

646.   Luther Gulick, *Administrative Reflections from World War II* (University: University of Alabama Press, 1948).

In these lectures before the Southern Regional Training Program in Public Administration in 1946, Gulick related that he had often been attacked for "chartism" and "putting the chart before the horse." Nevertheless, he felt that "the strength of a nation in time of war is directly conditioned by its management competence." Through a set of fifteen specific findings, he concluded that the governmental structure had proven adequate for the task.

647.   Henri Fayol, "Administration, industrielle et générale," #3, *Bulletin of the Société de l'Industrie Minérale*, (1916); also several reprints by Société; also *Administration industrielle et générale*, (Paris: Dunod Frères, 1925): also *General and Industrial Administration*, trans. by J.A. Coubrough (Geneva: International Management Institute, and London: Sir Isaac Pitman & Sons, Ltd., 1929); also *General and Industrial Management*, trans. by Constance Storrs (New York: Pitman Publishing Co., 1949).

Placing Fayol's work in chronological order presents a puzzle since his ideas had been fully developed in lectures by 1908 (and largely developed by 1900), but his major treatise had very small printings. The 1929 translation was also printed in small numbers because the publisher was convinced that few would read a book with the "government-like" word "administration" in the title. While White, Gulick, and Urwick knew of the work at an early date, it was essentially unobtainable in the United States in any language until it was reprinted with the intentionally incorrect word "management" in the title in 1949, and that translation is used here.

Fayol argued that of the six activities of industrial concerns, management was the one spread throughout the organization. Over time, he had found that fourteen principles of management often needed attention: division of work, authority, discipline, unity of command, unity of direction, subordination of individual interests to the general interest, remuneration, centralization, scalar chain, order, equity, stability of tenure of personnel, initiative, and esprit de corps. He also identified the following elements of administration: planning, organizing, command, co-ordination, and control.

Fayol, like Gantt in the United States, was both an engineer and a humanist in his writings. Also like Gantt, his concerns rose higher in the organization than was the case with Taylor and his other disciples. In those respects, he had an integrated management style that had become popular in the United States by the time that most Americans gained access to his work.

648.   Commission on Organization of the Executive Branch of Government, *General Management of the Executive Branch;* also *Concluding Report: A Report to the Congress* (Washington, D.C.: USGPO, 1949).[12]

The first Hoover Commission had members appointed by both executive and congressional leaders. In its opening report, the commission set the goal for its various task forces by arguing that "we must reorganize the executive branch to give it the simplicity of structure, the unity of purpose, and the clear line of executive authority that was originally intended under the Constitution." Its general recommendations advocated centralization, increased staff services, and continuing reorganization authorization for the president. Not all of the task forces followed the lead, as has been described elsewhere in this book. However, the argument by a joint body that the constitution supported executive authority over congressional supremacy was a dramatic statement of the change in philosophy in administrative reform efforts.

649.   Herman Finer, "The Hoover Commission Reports," *Political Science Quarterly*, 64, (September 1949): 405-19; also

650.   Louis W. Koenig, ed., "The Hoover Commission: A Symposium," *American Political Science Review*, 43, (October 1949): 933-1000; also

651.   Paul H. Appleby, "The Significance of the Hoover Commission Report," *Yale Review*, 39, (Autumn 1949): 1-22.

In the *APSR* symposium above, several staff members of the Hoover Commission reviewed the significance of the work. Koenig and Charles Aiken introduced the symposium with the claim that "(i)t well may prove that the Hoover Commission's most valuable work lies in carrying forward basic suggestions of the Brownlow group." (p. 937)

Finer was considerably less impressed, finding that the reports were so overladen with details that principles were often buried. Instead, the "repetitive gobbledygook" often resulted in triteness. The Commission did not know what role it wanted for the president, and it left a "yawning gap" on the subject of personnel.[13]

Appleby concluded exactly the opposite. Arguing that the Hoover Commission proposed episodic, as opposed to constant reorganization, he felt that such mundane matters as reducing duplication were beneath its scope of inquiry. The commission was concerned with policy implementation, and had done well in strengthening presidential management and the role of department heads.

652.   Herbert Emmerich, *Essays on Federal Reorganization* (University: University of Alabama Press, 1950); also *Federal Organization and Administrative Management* (University: University of Alabama Press, 1971).

In 1950, Emmerich argued that reorganization was not a surge in reformist spirit, but a continual process of adjustment by government to the needs of a changing world. He considered the Brownlow Committee report to be a great piece of administrative theory, but he felt that there were at least three countervailing tendencies to the growth in executive unity (independent commissions, government corporations, and grants-in-aid). He listed some of the unfinished business remaining after the Hoover Commission.

In his 1971 revision, he still advocated presidential leadership, especially as described in the Brownlow Committee and the First Hoover Commission. He opposed President Nixon's proposal to create super-cabinet positions, and he was very uncertain that the legislative veto in the Reorganization Act of 1939 was constitutional.

653. Commission on Organization of the Executive Branch of Government, *Final Report to the Congress* (Washington, D.C.: USGPO, 1955).

In 1953, conservative Republicans in congress created a second Hoover Commission with largely the same goals except with an added emphasis on eliminating inappropriate governmental functions, and with a staff solicited more from the private sector than had been the case with Brownlow and the First Hoover Commission. The Commission made 497 recommendations, most of which were procedural and minor. However, it also recommended that 33 independent offices answer to an official in the White House, that the Bureau of the Budget be strengthened, and that an administrative court be established outside the executive branch. Many of the minor procedural recommendations were later adopted.

654. William R. Divine, "The Second Hoover Commission Reports: An Analysis," *Public Administration Review*, 15, (Autumn 1955): 263-69; also

655. James W. Fesler, "Administrative Literature and the Second Hoover Commission Reports," *American Political Science Review*, 51, (March 1957): 135-57.

Divine described the different emphasis of the second Hoover Commission from the first, with the newer concern for eliminating nonessential services that were competitive with the private sector. From an administrative point of view, Hoover II abandoned the belief that principles can be applied irrespective of desired policies. To Fesler, the philosophy of the Commission was set when the membership was determined, and when those favoring the private sector were allowed to dominate the task forces.

656. Tom Burns and G. M. Stalker, *The Management of Innovation* (London: Tavistock Publications, 1961).

In 1961, Burns and Stalker carried the revolt against traditional administrative theory to lengths that were not to become popular for several more years. Specifically, they suggested that dynamic conditions might make traditional hierarchy obsolete. While mechanical forms of organizations offer some advantages, and might be appropriate in stable conditions, dynamic conditions require a more organic form of organization with much greater uncertainty for managers.

657.   Amitai Etzioni, *A Comparative Analysis of Complex Organizations* (New York: Free Press of Glencoe, 1961).

In a sociological study that is partially structural and partially behavioral, Etzioni argued that organizational effectiveness depends on the compatibility between the organization's goal structures and compliance structures. Specifically, those with order goals tend to have coercive compliance structures, those with economic goals tend to have utilitarian compliance structures, and those with culture goals tend to have normative compliance structures.

658.   Barry D. Karl, *Executive Reorganization and Reform in the New Deal* (Cambridge: Harvard University Press, 1963); also

659.   Richard Polenberg, *Reorganizing Roosevelt's Government* (Cambridge: Harvard University Press, 1966).

The literature of administrative science began changing in the 1950s. With the orthodoxy of 1930s tied into the abandoned New Deal, the literature began shifting to a smaller level of analysis--tackling agencies rather than governments, and to a new focus--sociological rather than political. Some of that new emphasis appears in Etzioni above. These are two histories of the older persuasion.

Karl took the broader approach, seeing the New Deal as a high-point in an executive consolidation process that began with Merriam, and that continued through the Hoover commissions. Polenberg more specifically studied the Brownlow report, seeing it as an attempt to consolidate the gains that had been added in an unorganized fashion in the early days of the Roosevelt presidency. The 1938 reform bill failed, he argued, because individual programs have constituencies while reorganization itself does not.

660.   Daniel Katz and Robert L. Kahn, *The Social Psychology of Organizations* (New York: John Wiley and Sons, 1966); also

661.   James D. Thompson, *Organizations in Action* (New York: McGraw Hill, 1967).

In the 1960s, these two books helped popularize an approach to organizations using systems analysis, a concept that can be traced back at least to Norbert Wiener's *Cybernetics* (Cambridge: M.I.T. Press, 1948), in which organizations are viewed as adapting to changes in the environment. Much of the systems literature leads to decision-making models or informal systems, both of which are discussed in later chapters. However, Katz and Kahn argued that many of the traditional theories fail because they treat organizations as closed systems, not appreciating that there is more than one way to solve environmental problems, and that adjustments to the environment are not necessarily aberrations.

Thompson used Gouldner's labels of rational-systems models versus natural-systems models to say that the first comes from a closed-system strategy while the second comes from an open-systems strategy. He then presented a number of propositions using the open-systems approach.

662. Frederick Mosher, *Governmental Reorganization* (Indianapolis: Bobbs-Merrill, 1967).

This joint project of the Inter-University Case Program (ICP) at Syracuse University and the Institute of Governmental Studies at Berkeley was an effort to focus the case-study technique, as it had developed at ICP, back toward specific hypotheses, as had been the case with the old Committee on Public Administration of the Social Science Research Council.

While this was not the first compilation of cases, it tried to test the hypothesis that reorganizations designed to change organizational behavior are more effective if the target populations participate in the process. It found in its cases that there are too many intervening variables on the purposes and effects of reorganizations for the hypothesis to be supported.

663. Warren G. Bennis and Philip E. Slater, *The Temporary Society* (New York: Harper and Row, 1968); also

664. Alvin Toffler, *Future Shock* (New York: Random House, 1970).

In a world in which the rate of change is increasing and personalities are becoming less important, Bennis and Slater predicted that organizations will become more temporary with less rigid bureaucratic structure, more interchangeability, and more mobility for their participants. Toffler called such arrangements ad-hocracies, with less emphasis on hierarchy and more on collaboration between participants in changing relationships.

665. Herbert Kaufman, "Administrative Decentralization and Political Power," *Public Administration Review*, 29, (January/February 1969): 3-15.

Noting the lack of representativeness in large bureaucracy and the increased political activism of the public, Kaufman speculated that decentralization of two types was likely to occur in federal programs. First, local constituent groups would demand more power over local decision-making, and area directors within the bureaucracy would gain more discretion. This new age would last only until new coalitions at the local level became dysfunctional, however, at which time reforms similar to the previous age would reemerge in a roughly continuous circle of reform movements.

666. Harvey C. Mansfield, Sr., "Federal Executive Reorganization: Thirty Years' Experience," *Public Administration Review*, 29, (July/August 1969): 332-45;

also "Reorganizing the Executive Branch: The Limits of Institutionalization," *Law and Contemporary Problems*, 35, (Summer 1970): 461-95; also

667.　Martin Landau, "Redundancy, Rationality, and the Problem of Duplication and Overlap," *Public Administration Review*, 29, (July/August 1969): 346-58.

Both Mansfield and Landau also found difficulties with traditional theories of organizational design.　Mansfield noted that, while the process of proposing reorganizations has some favorable features, it is not backed up with adequate theory to make it clear what should be done.　Instead, reorganizations are usually proposed for political rather than for organizational gains.

Landau focused on the traditional arguments for unity of command and against duplication and redundancy.　He noted that, from a theoretical perspective, redundancy geometrically increases the safety of the operating system while arithmetically increasing the cost.　Redundancy is a safety system that the polity can sometimes afford, and is not an unnecessary evil.

668.　Harold Seidman, *Politics, Position, and Power* (New York: Oxford University Press, 1970).

Arguing that "(r)eorganization has become almost a religion in Washington," Seidman attacked the orthodox theories advocating efficiency and opposing overlap and duplication.　He argued that more discretion would have to be given at the service delivery level through programs that were broadly enough based that they would not be dominated by individualized interests.

669.　Stanley M. Davis and Paul R. Lawrence, *Matrix* (Reading, MA: Addison-Wesley Publishing Co., 1977).

In the 1960s, the National Aeronautics and Space Administration managed massive temporary projects requiring both accountability and creative freedom through the experimental technique project management, "a *multiple command system* that includes not only a multiple command structure but also related support mechanisms and an associated organizational culture and behavior pattern."　Davis and Lawrence found the technique to be successful within the narrow range of organizations that regularly deal with competing critical sectors with tasks that are uncertain, complex, and highly interdependent, and with large economies of scale.

670.　Tyrus G. Fain, ed., *Federal Reorganization: The Executive Branch* (New York: R.R. Bowker Co., 1977).

For the most part, modern reorganization efforts in government have not resulted in the written statements of purpose produced by the Brownlow or Hoover teams. Instead, encouraged by the mechanical nature of the Reorganization Act, modern plans have been scattered through various government hearings or even sealed memos. Fain, in collaboration with Katherine C. Plant and Ross Milloy, helped overcome some of this difficulty by reprinting edited versions of the major reorganization documents from 1971 (the Ash Council) through the election of Jimmy Carter. The book includes documents on Carter's experiences with zero-base budgeting in Georgia.

671.   Peri E. Arnold, "The First Hoover Commission and the Managerial Presidency," *Journal of Politics*, 38, (February 1976): 46-70; also *Making the Managerial Presidency* (Princeton, NJ: Princeton University Press, 1986.

Arnold investigated reorganization efforts to show that, beginning with the Taft commission, virtually all such projects were aimed at strengthening the management position of the president. Progressives were enamored with executive authority, and sought to transform disorganized administration into a bureaucratic form, even if the traditional governmental design had to be ignored. In the twentieth century, 11 of 15 presidents had been involved in peace-time comprehensive reorganization.[14]
Reforms were initiated after large variations in the percentages of outlays, or after changes in control of at least one house. Arnold concluded, however, that reorganization can be overdone. Management is a tool for the president, and not his job.

672.   President's Reorganization Project, *Personnel Management Project*, 3 vol. (Washington, D.C.: USGPO, December 1977).

As part of Carter's reorganization efforts, this study headed by Civil Service Commissioner Alan Campbell led to the Civil Service Reform Act of 1978. Most of the recommendations are discussed in more detail in the chapter on staffing. However, the report advocated the abolition of CSC, the creation of an Office of Personnel Management and Merit Protection Board (later renamed), a senior executive service, merit pay, and a number of other changes designed to change personnel administration in the federal government into personnel management.

673.   Laurence Lynn, *The State and Human Services: Organizational Change in a Political Context* (Cambridge: M.I.T. Press, 1980).

Lynn studied reorganizations of human services delivery systems in six states to conclude that reorganizations can be started by anyone, but they need constituencies to overcome inertia. Reorganization is a political act, and state appointed officials have less protection from political interference than is the case at the federal level. Also, state elected officials are more interested in economy and efficiency than in effectiveness, especially in human services.

674.   Kenneth J. Meier, "Executive Reorganization of Government: Impact on
        Employment and Expenditures," *American Journal of Political Science*, 24,
        (August 1980): 396-412.

        Using a narrower focus, Meier investigated 16 state reorganizations that occur-
red since 1965 to demonstrate that, despite the promises of reformers, significant
reductions in government employment or expenditures after reorganizations are rare.

675.   James L. Garnett, *Reorganizing State Government: The Executive Branch*
        (Boulder, CO: Westview Press, 1980).

        Garnett applied statistical analysis to state reorganizations that occurred be-
tween 1914 and 1975 in an effort to develop scales by which the success or failure of
reorganizations could be determined. He also described several strategies for implementing reorganizations, and bureaucratic and client-based obstacles to administration reform.

676.   Daniel Robey, *Designing Organizations* (Homewood, IL: Richard D. Irwin,
        1982).

        In a more conceptual study, Robey set out to demonstrate the relevance of or-
ganization theory to organization design. He reviewed the historical models of organization design, and then used a sociological approach to argue that structure is an
adjustment between problem-solving processes and contingency approaches. Based on
that, he included suggestions on such topics as organizational domain, task design,
departmentalization, span of control, and team-based design.

677.   James G. March and Johan P. Olson, "Organizing Political Life: What Admin-
        istrative Reorganization Tells Us About Government," *American Political
        Science Review*, 77, (June 1983): 281-96.

        March and Olson argued that 12 efforts at administrative reform in the twentieth
century have accounted for a small percentage of changes in administration, and have
not had a major impact on administrative costs, efficiency, or control. Instead,
short-run outcomes are shaped by current crises while long-run outcomes are affected
by gradually evolving systems of meaning. Reorganization plans do serve as important
political symbols, however.

678.   President's Private Sector Survey on Cost Control, *A Report to the President*,
        2 vol. (Washington, D.C.: USGPO, January 15, 1984).

        When President Reagan took office, he commissioned a reorganization study
under the direction of J. Peter Grace that was given a charge in the cost-cutting

spirit of the second Hoover Commission. The summary report was accompanied by the reports of 36 task forces and 11 special studies.

Grace concluded that one-third of all tax revenue was consumed by waste and inefficiency. Also one-third of the taxes owed escaped collection. To help save $424 billion in three years, and $1.9 trillion per year by 2000, the commission offered 2478 specific recommendations.

Many of the recommendations were small or irrelevant to this study. On administrative matters, they advocated that an Office of Federal Management be added to overcome the lack of coordination in government on managerial functions. They also blamed congressional interference for many of the administrative wastes.

CONTINUING CONCERNS

However old administrative science may be, governmental reorganization and the need for useful predictions of its effects are considerably older. It is understandable, therefore, that the earliest public administration scholars worked on this set of questions.

The studies continue, but the academic enthusiasm of working within the system on them has faded. With the noticeable exception of the Campbell commission on civil service reform, recent reform proposals have been staffed in-house or from the private sector. Academics take notice of modern reforms, but often critically, and often justifiably so.

There are exceptions, and some of them have been cited here. Besides, academics (and other advocates of bureaucracy) have not been as welcome in governmental circles in recent years. However, there is another possible reason for the absence of Goodnows and Brownlows. Recent administrative theory has suggested that there are no lasting answers--that the whole process is political and fluid and that open systems logically change structures with time.

When one stops teaching the possibility that there are right answers, however, one need not abandon the possibility that there are answers to be avoided. When the literature abandons the search for recommendations and settles for explanatory theory, however, the price of being irrelevant to government service has effectively been paid.

NOTES FOR CHAPTER TWELVE

1. For a brief history, see Arthur S. Link, "Woodrow Wilson and the Study of Administration," *Proceedings of the American Philosophical Society*, 112, (December 1968): 431-33; reprinted as chapter 3 in *The Higher Realism of Woodrow Wilson, and Other Essays* (Nashville: Vanderbilt University Press, 1971).

2. The original wording before the revision is reprinted in Link, *The Papers of Woodrow Wilson*, vol. 5, pp. 358-59.

3. John Mabry Mathews, *Principles of American State Administration* (New York: D. Appleton and Co., 1917), p. 21. While Mathews used the dichotomy in Wilson's (as opposed to the European) style, Wilson's article is not mentioned in the text.

4. This is a condensed revision of his earlier dissertation *Theoretical Aspects of the American Literature of Public Administration*, submitted at Yale University, May 1942.

5. *Woodrow Wilson: Life and Letters, Youth 1856-1890*, and *Princeton 1890-1910* (Garden City, NY: Doubleday, Page & Co., 1927).

6. For a history, see Robert D. Miewald, "The Origins of Wilson's Thought: The German Tradition and the Organic State," in *Politics and Administration: Woodrow Wilson and American Public Administration*, ed. by Jack Rabin and James S. Bowman (New York: Marcel Dekker, 1984), pp. 17-30.

7. For an extensive history of this committee and the Dockery-Cockrell Commission, see Oscar Kraines, *Congress and the Challenge of Big Government* (New York: Bookman Associates, 1958).

8. For a complete listing, see Gustavus Weber, *Organized Efforts for the Improvement of Methods of Administration in the United States* (New York: D. Appleton and Co., 1919), pp. 71-73.

9. The precise citations for the various reports are quite lengthy, and can be found in Weber, *Organized Efforts for the Improvement of Methods*, pp. 81-83. For a history of the committee, see Oscar Kraines, "The President Versus Congress: The Keep Commission, 1905-1909, First Comprehensive Presidential Inquiry Into Administration," *Western Political Quarterly*, 23, (March 1970): 5-54.

10. Like the Keep Committee, the citations are too numerous and lengthy to be reprinted here, although the reports can be located with effort. The complete list is reprinted in Weber, *Organized Efforts for the Improvement of Methods*, pp. 94-103. An excellent summation can be found in Peri Arnold, *Making the Managerial Presidency* (Princeton, NJ: Princeton University Press, 1986), pp. 42-48.

11. For a history of the committee see Arnold, *Making the Managerial Presidency*, chapter 3.

12. Each report of the First Hoover Commission was released separately. However, McGraw-Hill later compiled them in *The Hoover Commission Report on Organization of the Executive Branch of the Government* (New York: McGraw-Hill, n.d.).

13. For a more specialized review of personnel, see James R. Watson, "The Hoover Commission Report on Personnel Management," *Public Personnel Review*, 10, (July 1949): 131-39.

14. The figure is from p. xii. On page 3, the figure is 11 of 14 presidents.

13
Max Weber and Bureaucracy

BACKGROUND

One of the recurring themes of this book is that the literature of public administration has been fragile enough that almost all the topics in it appeared earlier than is commonly assumed, and were subsequently redeveloped. The term "bureaucracy," and the specific study of organizational forms that springs from it, provide yet another example.

In 1798, the Institute of France's official dictionary of the French language contended that the term "bureaucrate" was coined during the French revolution.[1] A century later, at least one French dictionary felt the term to be of earlier German origin.[2] Martin Albrow more recently credited the term to the Physiocrat translator Vincent de Gournay, about 1745.[3]

Wherever the term originated, Max Weber's contribution to its study has become clearly more important than Wilson's to administrative science, and at least as significant as Taylor's to scientific management. Despite that, of the three authors now commonly considered to be "founders," Weber's works were the most difficult for even the specialists of the topic to locate at the time.

As was the case in the previous chapter, this summation begins with the works of Weber himself. It is followed by more recent analyses of the contents and significance of Weber's works. Finally, it discusses the works that followed in the same tradition. Specifically, it describes the study of bureaucratic organization, the behavioral patterns that arise from it, and the attempts to fix "bureaupathic behavior" through structural means. It does not describe attempts to overcome dysfunctional behavior through motivational or leadership techniques, since that literature is reserved for the next chapter.

WEBER'S WRITINGS

Of works that are central to the development of public administration, perhaps none are as difficult to compile, or even to find in original form (at least in the United States), as Weber's.[4] Part of the reason is found in the original publications; most of his sociological works were first printed in *Archiv für Sozialwissenschaft und Sozialpolitik* [*Archives for Social Science and Social Welfare*] (Tübingen: J.C.B Mohr <Paul Siebeck>, 1888-1933), of which he was associate editor. That series did not enjoy wide circulation in the United States. Secondly, as modern biographers have often attested, Weber wrote two major treatises on bureaucracy, but he also scattered other references among his voluminous other works. In addition, one of those treatises was published posthumously, and is untitled.

Finally, American scholars began to appreciate Weber too late to collect his works in original form. While German was the foreign language of choice among American administrative scholars of Wilson's day, Weber's major work on bureaucracy was not published until 1921 (after his death), and not translated into English until 1946. Weber's obtuse style discouraged those who were not fluent from reading the texts in German. Even today, only selections of his work are available in English, leading to occasional confusion on the larger context into which the selections originally fit.

679.   Max Weber, Speech to annual conference of Verein für Sozialpolitik, Vienna, 1909, reprinted in *Gesammelte Aufsaetze zur Soziologie und Sozialpolitik* (Tübingen: J.C.B. Mohr, 1924), pp. 412-16, translated in Jacob Peter Mayer, *Max Weber and German Politics*, 2nd ed. (London: Faber and Faber Ltd., 1961), Appendix I (pp. 125-31).

Weber's early pronouncements on bureaucracy were anchored in the political questions that dominated the nineteenth-century scholars, not the mechanical concerns by which Weber is currently known. From his early career, Weber feared the strength of the Prussian bureaucracy, largely because it was dominated by conservatives who were permitting the Polonization (the immigration of Polish peasants who worked for lower salaries) of Eastern Germany.

At a speech before a sociology conference in Vienna in 1909, Weber confronted his rather raucous pro-bureaucracy opposition, headed by Gustav von Schmoller, by arguing that training for effective administration had a tendency to cause a "passion for bureaucracy," which was "enough to drive one to despair." At its extreme, Germany could become like ancient Egypt, with everyone's lives dominated by government administrators.

680.   Max Weber, "Parlament und Regierung im neugeordneten Deutschland," [Parliament and Government in the Newly ordered Germany], series of articles in *Die Frankfurter Zeitung*, (Summer 1917), reprinted (München: Duncker

and Humblot, 1918), and in *Gesammelte Politische Schriften* (München: Drei masken verlag, 1921), pp. 126-260.

In these articles, Weber continued his concern with the "new despotism" of the civil service, caused by the power vacuum that Bismarck had created by developing a submissive state that had no mechanism for training leaders. "In the modern state, real power, which acts not only through parliamentary speeches nor through pronouncements of the Crown, but through everyday administration, lies necessarily and inevitably in the hands of the bureaucracy, both military and civil."[5]

681.   Hans H. Gerth and C. Wright Mills, translators and editors, *From Max Weber: Essays in Sociology* (New York: Oxford University Press, 1946), pp. 196-244; also

682.   A. M. Henderson and Talcott Parsons, translators and editors, *The Theory of Social and Economic Organization* (New York: Oxford University Press, 1947), 329-41.

While continuing his concern with the domination of life by bureaucrats, however, Weber was also interested in more rational forms of bureaucracy that could reap some of the benefits of rationality while limiting the costs. The original references appeared in a number of places, although some were not published until after Weber's death. They were finally compiled in *Wirtschaft und Gesellschaft, Grundriss der Sozialökonomik*, pt. iii, 2 vols. (Tübingen: J.C.B. Mohr, 1921), the relevant portions of which are translated in the two works listed above.

The Gerth and Mills selection was written about 1911-1913, and included Weber's most direct description of bureaucracy as defined by the six characteristics of fixed jurisdictional areas, hierarchy, written files, expert training, professional staff, and fixed rules. He described bureaucracy as the most efficient among styles of administration, as well as the one best suited to a leveling of social and economic differences in society.

The Henderson and Parsons selection, written somewhat later, integrates bureaucracy into the larger scheme of the three ideal types of authority. It is legal in that it is based on a style of authority that is legitimated through legal processes. It is rational in that it controlled on the basis of knowledge.

BOOKS ABOUT WEBER

683.   Jacob Peter Mayer, *Max Weber and German Politics* (London: Faber and Faber Ltd., 1944).

This continues to be a standard reference on the life of Weber. Mayer, who considered Weber to be "the most outstanding German political theorist of the post-

Bismarckian period," traced his rise through the age of Bismarck to the realization that charismatic leaders cause dependency and eventual disruptions in the polity. The book described Weber's admiration of the stability of the British state, and his eventual decision that only a ruthless parliamentary system could control the civil service and generate the kinds of leaders needed in post-war Germany.

684. Wolfgang J. Mommsen, *Max Weber and German Politics 1890-1920* (Chicago: University of Chicago Press, 1984), trans. by Michael S. Steinberg from *Max Weber und die deutsche Politik, 1890-1920*, 2nd ed. (Tübingen: J.C.B. Mohr <Paul Sieback>, 1974). First edition 1959.

When the first German edition of this book was released, it caused heated controversy among those who preferred to think of Weber as an early advocate of German democracy. Most notably, Mommsen tried to tie such right-wing radicals as Carl Schmitt (see later) into the Weberian tradition.

Mommsen's point was that Weber was first and foremost a nationalist and imperialist who was willing to support any cause to further the German state. Mommsen traced Weber's opposition to Polonization of Eastern Germany, his admiration of Bismarck's strength, his attacks on the weak skills of the Kaiser, and his eventual decision that democracy was the best way to train future leaders to save what Germany could from its disastrous war.

685. Reinhard Bendix, *Max Weber: An Intellectual Portrait* (New York: Doubleday and Co., 1960); also "Bureaucracy," *International Encyclopaedia of the Social Science* (New York: Macmillan and Free Press, 1968), vol. 2, pp. 129-55.

Among the biographies of Weber, Bendix's 1960 work is one of the more complete on Weber's concerns about bureaucracy. In particular, Bendix described the conflict that bureaucracy supports democracy in that it fosters equality before the law and protections against arbitrariness, but opposes democracy in that the bureaucrats become the trained experts who have little interest in being overruled by political amateurs. This last point is particularly emphasized in the *Encyclopaedia* article. Still, the system is far superior to more primitive forms of administration in which nobles could exploit their positions for their own gain. Bendix in 1960 also provided an extremely useful biography of translations of Weber keyed to the original works.

686. Karl Loewenstein, *Max Weber's Political Ideas in the Perspective of our Time* (Amherst: University of Massachusetts Press, 1966), trans. by Richard and Clara Winston from *Max Webers staatspolitische Auffassungen in der Sicht unserer Zeit* (Frankfurt am Main: Athenäum Verlag GmbH, 1965).

Of all the generally respected authors on Weber, Loewenstein was probably the most impressed with his subject. Claiming that Weber was in a different league from de Tocqueville and contemporary sociologists, Loewenstein still felt that Weber was wrong in his prediction that parliaments could control bureaucracy.

687.   David Beetham, *Max Weber and the Theory of Modern Politics* (London: Allen & Unwin, 1974).

Beetham investigated the democratic tendencies of Weber in his writings on the Russian revolutions in 1905 and 1917. He concluded that Weber was firmly committed to parliamentary democracy. Furthermore, while he was an advocate of strong leadership, he expected the leader to protect the mass against its own irrationality, and individuals against mob psychology.

STUDIES OF BUREAUCRACY

688.   John Stuart Mill, *Principles of Political Economy* (London: J. W. Parker and Son, 1848); also *On Liberty* (London: J. W. Parker and Son, 1859); also *Considerations on Representative Government* (London: Parker, son, and Bourn, 1861).

Numerous authors before Weber studied bureaucratic forms, and the term itself became popular after Balzac's novel *Les Employés* in 1836.[6] Martin Albrow (below) included an extensive discussion of the early literature. Much of that literature was brief and hostile to bureaucracy, as illustrated in the works of John Stuart Mill.

In 1848, Mill warned that concentrating the management skill and experience of the country in the hands of the bureaucracy harmed the political life of the state. In 1859, he elaborated that such concentration was inevitable when more functions were placed in government's hands, and the recruitment of experts through civil service exams only heightened the problem. In 1861, he reiterated the importance and difficulty of representative governments keeping bureaucracies under control.

689.   Ferdinand Tönnies, *Community and Society*, trans. by Charles P. Loomis (East Lansing: Michigan State University Press, 1957), originally *Gemeinschaft und Gesellschaft* (Leipzig: Pues's Verlag <R. Reisland>, 1887).

As is the case with virtually all scholars, the roots for Weber's concepts can be found in earlier works. One of those roots was Tönnies, whose *Gemeinschaft und Gesselschaft* described the evolution of western culture from a community-based, personalized system driven through natural will, to one of a societal-based, depersonalized system driven through rational will. In presenting his arguments, he developed a precursor to ideal types, and he presented (albeit briefly and indirectly) bureaucracy as a rational form of administration.

690.   Gaetano Mosca, *The Ruling Class* (New York: McGraw Hill, 1939), trans. by
       Hannah D. Kahn from *Elementi di scienza politica*, 2nd ed. (Torino: Fratelli
       Bocca, 1923); first edition (Roma: Fratelli Bocca, 1896).

While Michels (below) is better known today for the argument that a natural
elite would tend to arise in society, Mosca predated him with the argument that
society inevitably breaks into two classes--one that rules and one that is ruled. The
ruling class might be led by one individual, but is more likely to be an oligarchy
spread throughout the power structures of society. Within that structure, bureaucracy
is separate from both political structures and the private sector. The inevitable
interplay between politics and administration is beneficial for the effective operation
of both sides.

691.   Roberto [Robert] Michels, *Political Parties: A Sociological Study of Oligarchical
        Tendencies of Modern Democracies*, originally *Zur Soziologie des Parteiwesens in
        der modernen Demokratie: Untersuchengen über die oligarchischen Tendenzen des
        Gruppenlebens, Philosophisch-soziologische Bücherei*. Bd. XII (Leipzig: Klink-
        hardt, 1911).[7]

Michels, a student of Weber's, was one of the first to investigate the internal
dynamics of bureaucracies, concluding that all large organizations are subject to the
"iron law of oligarchical tendencies." Specifically, organizations require coordinating
staffs. Members of that staff inevitably gain access to information, communication
links, and political skill, subverting any original egalitarian tendencies they may have
had.

692.   Carl Schmitt, *Verfassungslehre* (München: Dunker & Humblot, 1928); also
        Legalität und Legitimität (München: Dunker & Humblot, 1932).[8]

Shortly after Weber's death, some conservative advocates of executive solutions
to Germany's problems eventually carried Weber's arguments all the way to National
Socialism. Schmitt attacked Weber's concept of legal-rational authority for a weakness that Weber had often admitted. When legitimacy is based entirely on accepted
legal procedures, it abandons all moral arguments for legitimacy. Schmitt claimed that
the loss of such moral legitimacy occurred in the Weimer republic, resulting in parliamentary suicide. He suggested that morality be returned to the social order by
increasing the role of the plebiscite-selected executive. Until the rise of the Third
Reich, he also praised the role of the bureaucracy for maintaining stability in Germany.

693.   Harold Laski, "Bureaucracy," *Encyclopaedia of the Social Sciences* (New York:
        Macmillan Co., 1930), vol. 3, pp. 70-74.

Laski described the transition of aristocratic administration into modern bureaucracy in Europe. "In the United States there is hardly a bureaucracy in the European sense of the term." He concluded with eight suggestions to prevent the corporate degeneration of the civil service into a caste with closed minds, including political supervision, publicity, and regular contact with the public.

694.   Carl J. Friedrich and Taylor Cole, *Responsible Bureaucracy: A Study of the Swiss Civil Service* (Cambridge: Harvard University Press, 1932).

Unlike Weber and Schmitt, Friedrich and Cole found "that no necessary antithesis exists between bureaucracy and responsible government." Bureaucratization was inevitable, and conflict with democratic politics was probably equally inevitable. However, giving the bureaucrats some say in their own governance would help instill them with a sense of responsibility.

695.   Carl J. Friedrich, *Constitutional Government and Politics* (New York: Harper and Brothers, 1937).[9]

In investigating the development of central administrative structures in selected countries in Europe and America, Friedrich identified six recurring elements that could be used to measure the degree of bureaucratization: centralization of control and supervision (hierarchy); differentiation of functions; qualifications for office; objectivity; precision and continuity; and secrecy (discretion). The first three are organizational while the last three are behavioral.

696.   Talcott Parsons, *The Structure of Social Action* (New York: McGraw Hill, 1937); also *Structure and Process in Modern Societies* (Glencoe, IL: Free Press, 1960).

More in the earlier tradition of Tönnies, Parsons described Weber as the culmination of social science's evolution from the simplistic utilitarian descriptions in Hobbes to the more modern positivistic and rational view that incorporates the subjective influences of morality and social constraint on people's actions. Weber's bureaucratic model of capitalism and government was offered as a highly-developed, impersonal, rationalized mechanism for achieving objectives through routinized behavior that often seems far removed from its ultimate goal.

697.   Hans H. Gerth, "The Nazi Party: Its Leadership and Composition," *American Journal of Sociology*, 45, (1940): 517-41.

As discussed later, many scholars find it unacceptable to link Weber's concepts with the eventual rise of National Socialism. That leaves observers of the 1930s-1940s with the need to find other explanations for what happened in Germany. Gerth saw the rise of Nazism as the fusion of charismatic and bureaucratic domination. The charismatic side was represented by the personal rule of the Führer. Gerth also documented the subversion of the normal bureaucratic process with changes in personnel at all levels, and with the introduction of arbitrary decision-making processes.

698. Robert K. Merton, "Bureaucratic Structure and Personality," *Social Forces*, 18, (1940): 560-68; also *Social Theory and Social Structure* (Glencoe, IL: Free Press, 1949).

In the United States, Merton popularized the sociological argument that bureaucracy contains dysfunctions expressed through a reward system that encourages conformity to precision and rules, but that does not punish those who apply rules and precise definitions to the extreme. The result is goal displacement, in which bureaucratic means replace the original ends of the organization.

In 1949, Merton developed many of these points more fully, and described the conflicts that logically arise between intellectuals and policy-makers within bureaucracies.

699. James Burnham, *The Managerial Revolution* (New York: John Day, 1941).

Burnham presented one of the more forceful, and one of the more commonly cited arguments that a social revolution was occurring in American society. Ownership was being removed from control as managers (treated as a class) were becoming the driving force in modern society. The goals of government and the private sector were merging, and would eventually result in global power centers.

700. Philip Selznick, "An Approach to a Theory of Bureaucracy," *American Sociological Review*, 8, (February 1943): 47-54.

Selznick helped summarize some of the arguments of Barnard, Roethlisberger, and Dickson, when he presented the three hypotheses that organizations create informal structures, goals are modified by internal processes, and the process of modification is effected through informal structures. Bureaucratization occurs when delegation leads to bifurcation of interests, and informal organizations are created to aid in control.

701. Marshall E. Dimock, "Bureaucracy Self-Examined," *Public Administration Review*, 4, (Summer 1944): 197-207; also *A Philosophy of Administration* (New York: Harper and Brothers, 1958).

Dimock continued Merton's concerns with the behavioral dysfunctions of organizations. In 1944, he identified at least 13 causes of bureaucratization with the increasing rigidity of rules and resistance to change. To partially counteract this tendency, he suggested increased emphasis on leadership and managerial powers rather than control.

In 1958, he restated the case more strongly, arguing that a small cadre of stalwarts, dedicated to public service, could not only avoid Burnham's fear of a managerial revolution, but that they could reverse dysfunctional aspects of organizational culture by keeping the competing forces of bureaucracy in balance.

702.   John H. Crider, *The Bureaucrat* (Philadelphia: J. B. Lippincott, 1944); also

703.   Ludwig Von Mises, *Bureaucracy* (New Haven: Yale University Press, 1944).

These more popularized attacks on the dysfunctions of bureaucracy contain less theory but more enthusiasm for their own arguments. Crider, who filled his book with examples of officious behavior, was mainly concerned that the war-time expanded bureaucracy would become permanent.

Answering "progressives" who "apologized" that bureaucratization is pervasive, Von Mises agreed that bureaucracy in government is inevitable, but he tried "to demonstrate that no profit-seeking enterprise, no matter how large, is liable to become bureaucratic provided the hands of its management are not tied by government interference." Instead, bureaucracy arises in the private sector because government subverts the ability of dollars to speak as votes in economic democracy.

704.   William Foote Whyte, ed., *Industry and Society* (New York: McGraw-Hill, 1946); also

705.   William Foote Whyte, *Human Relations in the Restaurant Industry* (New York: McGraw-Hill, 1948).

These opening two volumes of the Committee on Human Relations in Industry at the University of Chicago contain several articles that relate to the conflict that often arises between formal and informal organizations, especially over the issue of status. Whyte also reported on his study of 25 restaurants for the American Restaurant Association, especially on the conflicting demands placed on waiters/waitresses who seek recognition for their efforts while serving as conduits between customers and the kitchen staffs.

706.   Reinhard Bendix, "Bureaucracy: The Problem and Its Setting," *American Sociological Review*, 12, (October 1947): 493-501; reprinted in *Higher Civil Servants in American Society* (Boulder: University of Colorado Press, 1949).[10]

Bendix attacked the rational, neutral model of bureaucracy that gave rise to the iron rule of oligarchy on the grounds that both bureaucrats and their clients have a diversity of backgrounds and social beliefs. Employees often feel their interests to be at odds with those of their supervisors, and democratic administration is marked by diffuse supervision of those competing interests. By surveying administrators for his dissertation, he was able to document that federal administrators are heterogeneous in training and beliefs, that they are internally competitive, but that they are becoming more professional with time.

707.   Herbert A. Simon, *Administrative Behavior* (New York: The Macmillan Co., 1947).

Simon found that attempts to describe administrative organization had revealed very little about the ways that bureaucracies operate. From the structural standpoint, what few principles we had developed had little universal application and looked more like proverbs. From the behavioral standpoint, the theories of economic rationality failed to appreciate many of the influences within organizations that would be better explained through a model of administrative rationality.

708.   Philip Selznick, *TVA and the Grass Roots* [dissertation] (Berkeley: University of California Press, 1949); also *Leadership in Administration* (Evanston, IL: Row, Peterson and Company, 1957).[11]

Using the TVA as a base, Selznick was interested in delegation of authority as a mechanism for organizational control. He argued that delegation leads to increased specialization and expertise, but also to competition among units of the parent organization.

Because of the focus of the 1949 study on the TVA, the major control mechanism that was described was cooptation. In 1957, however, Selznick moved beyond that device to elaborate on the role of leadership in breaking through the dysfunctions of bureaucracy. Specifically, he advocated that leaders move beyond administrative management to institutional leadership by integrating a moral purpose into their activities that could turn organizational health into a means rather than an end. The precise recommendations are discussed in chapter fifteen.

709.   Robert K. Merton, Ailsa P. Gray, Barbara Hockey, and Hanan C. Selvin, eds., *Reader in Bureaucracy* (Glencoe, IL: Free Press, 1952).

This is a particularly useful selection of literature on bureaucracy that mixes most of the major theoretical concerns on the subject. Structural literature varied from Weber to Simon's attack on structural principles. Several authors analyzed the implications of the Nazis on bureaucratic theories. Separate sections discussed bureaucratic power, decision-making, recruitment, behavior, and field methods for further study.

710.   Kenneth Boulding, *The Organizational Revolution* (New York: Harper and Brothers, 1953).

In 1949, the Federal Council of Churches began sponsoring studies of Christian Ethics and Economic Life. As part of that effort, Boulding explained the rise of organizations as a decrease in the internal limits of organizations through both physical advances in the ability to organize, and in the forms and skills of organizing. Organizations are still constrained by both internal and external pressures. Notably, as they became large enough, internal democracy becomes more important to preserve liberty. Democracy is created not through formal structures, but through continual discussion. Tyranny arises when organizational members tire of discussion.

711.   Alvin W. Gouldner, *Patterns of Industrial Bureaucracy* (New York: Free Press, 1954).

Using Parsons' notion that authority in bureaucracy can come from either agreed-upon rules or punishment, Gouldner studied a gypsum plant in the 1940s in the mid-West. He suggested that there are three patterns of industrial bureaucracy--the "mock," in which rules were generated from outside; "representative," based on rules established by agreement, and "punishment-centered." Representative arrangements live within boundaries defined by punishment-centered relationships. Gouldner then suggested a number of hypotheses about the conditions under which new rules are brought into operation in a bureaucracy.

712.   Peter M. Blau, *The Dynamics of Bureaucracy* (Chicago: University of Chicago Press, 1955).

Blau reported the results of separate studies of interviewers in a state employment agency and field agents in a federal enforcement agency. Unlike those who argue that bureaucracy stifles creativity, Blau found that changes are often favored by the bureaucrats to resolve conflicting responsibilities, to foster organizational growth, and sometimes as a matter of organizational culture.

713.   William H. Whyte, Jr., *The Organization Man* (New York: Simon and Schuster, 1956).

In the stifling organizational environment of the 1950s, however, Whyte's critique was more widely known. He argued that managers were caught in a world in which they praised individualism and the Protestant ethic, but were continually seduced into conforming to the expectations of a beneficent organization. At a societal level, such individuals learned to accept a larger role for organizations in running their lives. Whyte suggested that the managers themselves could fight these trends, and that jobs could be restructured to encourage more individualism.

714.   C(yril) Northcote Parkinson, *Parkinson's Law and Other Studies in Administration* (Boston: Houghton Mifflin, 1957).

Some of the same pessimism about organizations was expressed in this compilation of articles, although in a humorous tone interspersed with cartoon illustrations.

The famous law that "work expands so as to fill the time available for its completion" was supplemented by tongue-in-cheek studies of such subjects as the optimal size for committees, rules for selection, and mandatory retirement.

715. Fritz Morstein Marx, *The Administrative State* (Chicago: University of Chicago Press, 1957).

In searching through the governments of the world, Morstein Marx isolated four major types of bureaucracies--guardian bureaucracy as popularized by the British; caste bureaucracy as it evolved in Germany and elsewhere, patronage bureaucracy from the United States; and the more modern merit bureaucracy. While the fourth type best fits the technological world, bureaucracy in general is more effective if it is a partner in political decision-making. The partnership requires that bureaucracy reorient itself away from dominant concerns about efficiency and toward analyzing the impacts of its decisions on society.

716. Milovan Djilas, *The New Class* (New York: Frederick A. Praeger, 1957); also *Land Without Justice* (New York: Harcourt, Brace and Co., 1957).

In the communist revolutions, one of the major goals defined by Marx has been the elimination of the class that owns the means of production, and the subsequent creation of a classless society. Djilas, who had been vice-president of Yugoslavia and president of its parliament, wrote that the leaders of the communist states have created a new class, a set of bureaucrats who rule society with oligarchical tendencies.
The argument was not new.[12] However, these books received added attention because of Djilas' former position, and because they were translated and published while Djilas was in prison on charges that he slandered Yugoslavia through earlier statements of the same thesis.

717. James G. March and Herbert A. Simon, *Organizations* (New York: John Wiley and Sons, 1958); also

718. Mason Haire, ed., *Modern Organization Theory* (New York: John Wiley and Sons, 1959).

These works provide particularly detailed reviews of administrative theory, with March and Simon summarizing the mechanical theories of scientific management, the human relations theories of the mid-century, and the more recent cognitive theories that attempt to account for learning processes within individual members of the organization. None of these approaches, they found, have been consistently backed with empirical verification of its findings.
Haire edited a set of symposium papers by academic and industrial participants in 1959 that include many approaches to integration of individuals and organizations,

structural questions, and the decision-making models then popular. Highlights include articles by Argyris on integration, W. F. Whyte on interaction theory, and Likert on linking-pins.

719.   Morris Janowitz, *The Professional Soldier: A Social and Political Portrait* (New York: The Free Press, 1960).

Janowitz investigated the changes in the military over the previous 50 years as it matured from an authoritarian organization with relatively low managerial skills to a modern bureaucracy with broader-based recruitment, greater reliance on persuasion and group consensus, and greater emphasis on managerial training.

720.   Herbert Kaufman, *The Forest Ranger: A Study in Administrative Behavior* (Baltimore: Johns Hopkins Press, 1960).

Kaufman studied another bureaucracy with atypical problems. He identified five forces that led the forest rangers towards centrifugal disintegration. However, the Forest Service counteracted these tendencies with three strategies, including advanced decision-making; detection and discouragement of deviation, and integration of the rangers into the organizational culture. The Forest Service was assisted in these strategies by technical innovations that made them possible.

721.   Carl Joachim Friedrich, "Political Leadership and the Problem of Charismatic Power," *Journal of Politics*, 23, (February 1961): 3-24.

Most of the studies discussed here analyze bureaucracy. However, Friedrich was concerned that Weber's description of charismatic authority was hopelessly confused, and needed to be abandoned. Weber did not distinguish leadership, which is differentiated by the function served, from power, which is differentiated by the source. He did not distinguish the motives of leaders, and routinized charisma was a contradiction in terms.

722.   Victor Thompson, *Modern Organization* (New York: Alfred A. Knopf, 1961); also "Bureaucracy and Innovation," *Administrative Science Quarterly*, 10, (June 1965): 1-20.

According to Thompson, *"the most symptomatic characteristic of modern bureaucracy is the growing imbalance between ability and authority."* Personal abilities are increased by specialized training while authority is constrained by traditional rules of hierarchy. The resulting confusion over status and goals leads to bureaupathic behavior. Thompson suggested that the old mechanical solidarity enforced by authority needs to be replaced with cooperation based on a mutual recognition of interdependence.

In 1965, he added that bureaucracy stifles creativity. He suggested tactics for fostering innovation, including increased professionalism, looser structures and communications, project organization, increased group processes, and other incentives.

723.   Robert Presthus, *The Organizational Society* (New York: Alfred A. Knopf, 1962).

Presthus argued that large organizations contain the dysfunction that they offer the opportunity for individual growth, but only if the individual conforms to organizational values. Differing abilities to conform lead to three organizational personalities--the upwardly-mobile, the indifferent, and the ambivalent. Organizations and society suffer because administrators take decision-making powers away from the experts who have the knowledge to make wise decisions.

724.   Peter M. Blau and W. Richard Scott, *Formal Organizations: A Comparative Approach* (San Francisco: Chandler Publishing Co., 1962).

Based on who is the prime beneficiary, Blau and Scott identified four types of organizations: mutual-benefit organizations; business concerns; service organizations; and commonweal organizations. Using their own case studies as well as examples from the literature, they argued that all four types face dilemmas: coordination vs. communication; discipline vs. professionalism; and planning vs. initiative. However, the varying importance of clients and subordinates in different organizations affect both the informal and formal organizations' ability to deal with dysfunctions.

725.   Joseph LaPalombara, ed., *Bureaucracy and Political Development* (Princeton, NJ: Princeton University Press, 1963).

In the opening article, LaPalombara searched for common threads in the presentations of twelve scholars for the Committee on Comparative Politics of the Social Science Research Council. He found that there was disagreement in the definitions of both bureaucracy and democracy. However, while Weber's model was taken as the definition of modern democracy, the premature development of merit systems did not seem to be correlated with rapid economic development in nonindustrialized societies. Rather, economic democracy needs to develop first, during which time an underdeveloped bureaucracy, or even an absolutely corrupt one, seems to serve national interests.

726.   Richard M. Cyert and James G. March, *A Behavioral Theory of the Firm* (Englewood Cliffs, NJ: Prentice Hall, 1963).

Cyert and March used four aspects of a firm's decision-making process to describe its bureaucratic limits. The quasi-resolution of conflict is a continual process that results in changing multiple goals and subgoals. The second is uncertainty avoidance, involving both control of the environment and neglect of long-term planning. The third is the problemistic search for simple solutions to immediate problems. The fourth is learning, or changing rules when old procedures no longer solve problems.

727.   Bertram M. Gross, *The Managing of Organizations*, 2 vol. (New York: Free Press of Glencoe, 1964).

    In attempting to sort through the myriad of administrative literature that then existed to derive findings that would "marry" theory with action, Gross compiled perhaps the most complete description of prior administrative theory ever written. In almost 900 pages of description followed by systems analysis, he concluded that the administrative revolution is both a threat and an opportunity. So long as expectations are reasonable, and so long as there are efforts to develop organizational democracy and to tie practice to theory, the threats of bureaucracy can be controlled while its potentials are released.

728.   Michel Crozier, *The Bureaucratic Phenomenon* (Chicago: University of Chicago Press, 1964), trans. by author from *Le phénomène bureaucratique* (Paris: Editions du Seuil, 1963).

    Crozier investigated two agencies in France to conclude that there are four elements that contribute to the stability of bureaucracies: impersonal rules; centralized decisions; strata isolation with group pressures to conform; and parallel power relations around areas of uncertainty. The centralization and impersonality of stable bureaucracies leads to the rise of vicious circles, including Merton's displacement of goals and Gouldner's conflict between control and supervision. While cultural differences affect the operations of the bureaucracy, change in such an organization must be from the top down, *en bloc*.

729.   Gordon Tullock, *The Politics of Bureaucracy* (Washington, D.C.: Public Affairs Press, 1965).

    As one of the founders of what would become the "public choice" school of thought, Tullock found bureaucracy's structural problems to be insurmountable. Describing bureaucrats in their roles as "political man," he contended that merit systems select against morality, and that large bureaucracies will eventually break apart under the increasing distortion of information created by bureaucrats furthering their own careers. The result will be "bureaucratic free enterprise."

730.   Sir Geoffrey Vickers, *The Art of Judgment* (London: Chapman and Hall, 1965); also *Towards a Sociology of Management* (New York: Basic Books, 1967).

    Vickers' basic argument is that organizations share a need for control, a concept that is misinterpreted in English-speaking countries because it is made synonymous with direction. Control is the process of continually comparing what is with what ought to be in an open-systems context. The obligation of management is to regulate contact between internal and external forces to maintain their balances and to maximize results.

731. Daniel Katz and Robert L. Kahn, *The Social Psychology of Organizations* (New York: John Wiley and Sons, 1966).

In a largely conceptual work that used open-systems theory, Katz and Kahn differentiated types of inputs and functions that are prevalent in large organizations. Many organizations cluster around one of the four functions: productive or technical; managerial; maintenance; and adaptive. The authors also used their models to define efficiency and effectiveness, to differentiate styles of leadership, and to speculate on democratic control in an organizational society.

732. Warren Bennis, *Changing Organizations* (New York: McGraw Hill, 1966); also

733. Frederick C. Thayer, *An End to Hierarchy! An End to Competition!* (New York: New Viewpoints, 1973).

As intellectual allies of the futurism school described in the previous chapter, these authors found the traditional hierarchical system to be inadequate for the changing needs of society. In his book of essays, Bennis saw bureaucracy as a form of organization that had little relevance until the industrial revolution, at which time it became indispensable. In the post-industrial society, he argued, the rigidity and social inefficiency of bureaucracy will outweigh its productive efficiency, and organization development will lead to a more fluid form.

Thayer took the point further by arguing that organization theory, and particularly hierarchy, predated and tainted democratic theory, and needs to be changed to a non-hierarchical system of small groups helping each other with organizational problems. The results would improve the quality of everything from government to office sex.

734. James D. Thompson, *Organizations in Action* (New York: McGraw Hill, 1967).

Thompson attempted to integrate the societal concerns of open-systems theory with the rationality of closed-systems studies. He described *"complex organizations as open systems, hence indeterminate and faced with uncertainty, but at the same time as subject to criteria of rationality and hence needing determinateness and certainty."* Determinateness and rationality are obtained through constraints which the organization must face, contingencies which the organization must meet, and variables which the organization can control.

735.   Paul R. Lawrence and Jay W. Lorsch, "Differentiation and Integration in Com-
        plex Organizations," *Administrative Science Quarterly*, 12, (1967): 1-47; also
        Organization and Environment (Boston: Harvard University, 1967).

The authors investigated six companies in the plastics industry to discover that
the functional departments usually have more formal structures as they face more
stable environments. Production departments, for instance, are more stable and have
more formal decision-making structures than research departments. Separately, they
reported that organizations with close matches between environment and structure are
able to maintain higher performance.

736.   Anthony Downs, *Inside Bureaucracy* (Boston: Little, Brown, and Co., 1967).

Like others using the "economic man" model, Downs based his predictions about
organizational success on the assumption that bureaucrats operate in their own self
interest. Depending upon their personal needs, he divided them into five categories:
climbers, conservers, zealots, advocates, and statesmen. Organizations try to control
them by enforcing the bureau ideology from above. However, according to the law of
counter control, compliance becomes more expensive as individual workers learn to be
more creative at avoiding the special bureaucracy created for control.

737.   Nicos P. Mouzelis, *Organisation and Bureaucracy* (Chicago: Aldine Publishing
        Co., 1968); earlier version accepted as thesis at London School of Economics.

Mouzelis provided a detailed summation of organization theory as it had developed by 1968. He noted that the scope of study switched with Weber from the impact
of bureaucracy on society to the mechanics of individual bureaucracies. He concluded
that there is a convergence taking place between the human relations school and
those who emphasize structure and procedure. It is a useful convergence driven by
sociologists, and it includes a greater appreciation of the role of conflict and power
in organizations.

738.   Laurence J. Peter and Raymond Hull, *The Peter Principle* (New York: William
        Morrow and Co., 1969); also

739.   Laurence J. Peter, *The Peter Prescription* (New York: William Morrow and Co.,
        1972).

Peter, the source of the principle that "In a Hierarchy Every Employee Tends to
Rise to His Level of Incompetence," is the second modern satirist on bureaucratic
studies to reach some level of respectability (and citability) within academic circles.
His first book was devoted to hierarcheology, or explaining how employees could reach
their levels of incompetence. The 1972 book was far more positive, suggesting 66
prescriptions by which employees could develop their own competencies, and avoid
being prematurely promoted into incompetence.

740. Jürgen Habermas, *Technik und Wissenschaft als "Ideologie"* (Frankfurt am Main: Suhrkamp, 1968); also *Legitimation Crisis* (Boston: Beacon Press, 1975), trans. by Thomas McCarthy from *Legitimitätsprobleme im Spätkapitalismus* (Frankfurt am Main: Suhrkamp, 1973).

In a far more serious vein, Habermas is a German social philosopher who considered the role of ethics and bureaucracy in society. In society, the "institutional frameworks of symbolic interaction" help shape personality structures by subjecting individuals to disapproval for deviant behavior. Societal morality is protected because personalities and morality become intertwined through a shared enforcement mechanism.

In "systems of purposive-rational action" (bureaucracy), however, the goal is to manipulate people so that they can successfully manipulate nature. The standard of success becomes technical, and is measured in skills. Punishment and rewards in bureaucracy are unrelated to society's view of the morality of the product.

741. Louis C. Gawthrop, *Bureaucratic Behavior in the Executive Branch* (New York: Free Press, 1969).

In a more traditional and mechanical analysis of bureaucracy, Gawthrop described organizations on a continuum from innovative to consolidative. Government bureaucracies tend to be consolidative and, therefore, not innovative because of four characteristics: they lack adequate means for control; they lack valid measures of effectiveness; they lack clear goals; and they have a political necessity to demonstrate immediate results.

742. Charles P. Perrow, *Organizational Analysis: A Sociological View* (Belmont, CA: Brooks/Cole Publishing Co., 1970); also *Complex Organizations* (Glenview, IL: Scott, Foresman, and Co., 1972).

In the tradition described earlier by Mouzelis, Perrow argued in 1970 that organizational studies have concentrated too much on leadership as the cause of organizational problems. Instead, Perrow analyzed the roles of structure, technology, the environment, and organizational goals. Goals are multiple, but can be differentiated as societal, output, system, product, and derived. In 1972, he restated his commitment to the institutional approach as characterized by Philip Selznick. He argued that the major task of organizations is to meld their members into a committed polity to meet their environments.

743. Martin Albrow, *Bureaucracy* (New York: Praeger Publishers, 1970).

As an early entry in the "Key Concepts in Political Science" series, Albrow's goal was to investigate the various uses of the term bureaucracy. He noted that confusion over the multiple uses of the word already existed in von Mohl's first analysis of the concept in 1846. Albrow followed the development of the literature over time, breaking it into seven modern concepts of bureaucracy as rational organization, organizational inefficiency, rule by officials, public administration, administration by officials, the organization, and modern society.

744.   Frank Marini, ed., *Toward a New Public Administration: The Minnowbrook Perspective* (Scranton, PA: Chandler Publishing Co., 1971).

Like both sociologists and economic theorists of the era, many of the participants at the Minnowbrook conference felt that organization theory had failed to focus on some of the most important variables and techniques of study. In this case, the call was for "relevance," which could be roughly translated as the normative impacts of bureaucracy within and without its organizations. Several participants also called for more client-based, non-confrontational administration, and postpositivist (perhaps phenomenological, perhaps something else) empirical techniques.

745.   George E. Berkley, *The Administrative Revolution* (Englewood Cliffs, NJ: Prentice-Hall, 1971); also

746.   Marshall W. Meyer, *Bureaucratic Structure and Authority* (New York: Harper and Row, 1972).

Authors less identified with the prescriptive approach also sometimes reported a decline in bureaucratic rigidity. Berkley's arguments were basically descriptive as he used examples from several countries to argue that "organization man" is fading from existence. In his place, numerous organizations are already finding less obtrusive ways to manage. Strategies vary from such expected techniques as Theory Y, client-based administration, and circles rather than triangles (hierarchy), to such non-traditional techniques as PPBS.

Meyer was even more empirical, reporting on a survey of 254 city, county, and state finance departments to conclude that centralized control is not an inevitable result of large bureaucracy. Instead, increasing complexity and decentralization of decision-making is common.

747.   Gary L. Wamsley and Mayer N. Zald, *The Political Economy of Public Organizations* (Lexington, MA: Lexington Books, 1973).

Wamsley and Zald offered a more formalistic attempt to describe a public administration theory, which they designated "PAT." Using the terminology of political economy, but reduced to the organizational level, they described the politics (goals and legitimacy) and the economics (products) of agencies, both internally and externally. While they did not specifically build upon it, they suggested that such a framework could be used to integrate the various approaches to the study of organizations.

748.   Chris Argyris and Donald A. Schön, *Theory in Practice* (San Francisco: Jossey-Bass, 1974); also *Organizational Learning: A Theory of Action Perspective* (Reading, MA: Addison-Wesley, 1978).

In 1974, the authors argued that individuals build interpersonal relations based on models of logic that become frames of reference and that they resist changing them to accommodate new data. They called this Model I. In 1978, they extended the analogy to administration, contending that organizations prefer single-loop learning (O-I) that will allow adjustments, but that will not call fundamental goals and assumptions into question through double-loop learning (O-II).

The most effective method for generating O-II learning is through intervention-oriented perspectives that synthesize other approaches, and that reintroduce ethics into organizational decision-making.

749.   Ralph H. Kilmann, Louis R. Pondy, and Dennis P. Slevin, *The Management of Organization Design*, 2 vol. (New York: North-Holland, 1976).

In an attempt to bring together varying theories and techniques on organization design, the University of Pittsburgh sponsored a conference in 1974 leading to this book of readings. In the introductory chapter, the editors noted that there is a five-fold typology of approaches to organization design: intuitively (as opposed to analytically); as genotypic selections (rational types); as systemic planning; as interacting processes; and as influenced by personality. Readings developed each approach.

750.   Harry Kranz, *The Participatory Bureaucracy* (Lexington, MA: Lexington Books, 1976).

Kranz traced the development of bureaucracy through ancient elitist forms to the modern concept of representative bureaucracy. He argued that Hegel's confidence that bureaucracy could be controlled by outside forces proved unwarranted. Instead, he advocated participatory bureaucracy in which racial-ethnic groups and women would be represented within the levels of the bureaucracy in proportion to their distribution in the population. He demonstrated that such a goal has not been achieved, and suggested selection procedures that could help achieve his goals.

751.   Ralph P. Hummel, *The Bureaucratic Experience* (New York: St. Martin's Press, 1977).

Hummel described his framework as consisting of three central points. First, bureaucracy is a new way of life, succeeding society as society succeeded community. Second, bureaucracy differs from society socially, culturally, psychologically, power-politically, and linguistically. Third bureaucracy creates special problems for citizens, politicians, managers, employees, and clients. However, all would be better off if they learned the differing rules of bureaucracy, and tried to work within it rather than against it.

752.   B. Guy Peters, *The Politics of Bureaucracy: A Comparative Perspective* (New York: Longman, 1978).

Peters described bureaucracy as one of the more successful bargaining agents in the polity. However, it is heavily influenced in various countries by both its political and its cultural environment. While most bureaucracies are not representative of the civic culture, they tend to be more representative than the other public elites. Besides, the background of administrators often do not affect their policy decisions. Nevertheless, he felt internal restraints to be more effective than external controls for assuring administrative accountability.

753.   Gibson Burrell and Gareth Morgan, *Sociological Paradigms and Organisational Analysis* (London: Heinemann, 1979).

To Burrell and Morgan, much of the literature that has been mentioned so far in this review is limited by being culture-bound. Instead, they felt that organization theory can be differentiated by two variables in the theorists' belief systems: the objectivity of social science; and the radical or regulatory nature of social control. The result is four basic approaches to organization theory: radical humanism (Marx, Lakăcs, Marcuse, Habermas); radical structuralism (the scientific socialism of Lenin); interpretive sociology (including phenomenology); and functionalism (including integrative theory and dysfunctional literature). Each approach leads to different assumptions about the nature and variability of organizational forms.

754.   Jeffrey Pfeffer, *Power in Organizations* (Marshfield, MA: Pitman Publishers, 1981).

Pfeffer claimed that there are four basic models of administrative decision-making: rational; bureaucratic; decision-process/ organized anarchy; and political power. While each is difficult to measure because each is used sporadically, his emphasis was on political power. He described numerous styles and examples of its use, contending that political power does not lead to performance problems in organizations. He concluded that it is both effective and normal for managers to behave as politicians.

755.   Charles Goodsell, *The Case for Bureaucracy* (Chatham, NJ: Chatham House, 1983).

In this book subtitled *A Public Administration Polemic*, Goodsell attempted to defend bureaucracy against the common attacks in the popular press and the academic literature. He argued that most citizens' contacts with government bureaucracy are successful. Agencies usually operate on a small scale staffed with employees who are largely representative of the public. Such agencies are usually able to adapt their cultures to the needs of their constituents.

Among bureaucracy's largest problems are the impossible and contradictory expectations placed upon it by politicians. This point was expanded in the 1985 second edition, which described the Reagan attack on bureaucracy, and which advocated the "Blacksburg Manifesto" by which academic and public coverage of the bureaucracy could become more balanced.

756.   Robert B. Denhardt, *Theories of Public Organization* (Monterey, CA: Brooks/ Cole, 1984).

Denhardt brought both academic and practitioner experience into his argument that the two perspectives need to work toward each other. He felt that techniques without theory lack an appreciation of the importance of public administration. Purely academic theories often lack relevance to the real world. Instead, he reviewed a collection of political, administrative, psychological, and philosophical theorists. He also suggested that theory can be built from practical experience.

757.   Edgar H. Schein, *Organizational Culture and Leadership* (San Francisco: Jossey-Bass, 1985).

Schein saw organizations as evolving through growth, midlife, and declining stages of development. The internal mechanics are set by organizational culture, consisting of basic assumptions learned over time. The culture determines how the organization defines its function and its ability to respond to the environment. The role of leadership is to shape and reform the culture.

Schein described a clinical interview process for identifying culture, but warned that data collection can be harmful to the organization. He also speculated that in accepting the need for self-actualization among employees, we have abandoned the leadership component.

CONTINUING CONCERNS

Eric Strauss once noted that it was unfortunate that Weber used the term "bureaucracy" to define his rational form of administration. The term had long been tainted and it remains so. Even among those who have made their careers studying the institution, a substantial number have willingly accepted that bureaucracy is incurably wracked with dysfunctions that require solutions as dramatic as capping its size through artificial competition.

Of course, one need not be an advocate of bureaucracy to make usable observations about it. It is helpful, however, to adopt methodologies that encourage recommendations. On that score, the study of bureaucracy is undergoing change.

Early studies saw bureaucracy as a growing source of power in the polity capable of great harm and/or benefit. Like the politics/administration dichotomy discussed in chapter 12, the goal was to isolate each of the actors to determine its impact on the entire system.

Weber's work on bureaucracy fit into that perspective. His legacy, however, did not. Focusing on his (and Wilson's) mechanical writings about bureaucracy, the discipline shifted in the 1930s to an internalized, structural approach to the subject. Bureaucracy became a subject for study by social science technicians.

The results were not encouraging as one author after another attacked the seemingly hopeless limits and inefficiency of the machine. Perhaps as a result, the internal approach has been partially abandoned. Led by such diverse groups as sociologists and "New P.A." advocates, it has become common again to study bureaucracy within its environment. The result has been to view administration as more flexible form than previously seemed to be the case, and to revive Weber's perspective that bureaucracy was merely one of the forms that could be used for administration.

NOTES FOR CHAPTER THIRTEEN

1. Académie Française, *Dictionnaire de l'Académie Française*, rev. ed., (Paris: Institut du France, 1798): supplément.

2. M. Block, *Petit Dictionnaire Politique et Social* (Paris: Perrin, 1896).

3. Martin Albrow, *Bureaucracy* (New York: Praeger Publishers, 1970).

4. For an almost complete list, see Marianne Weber, *Max Weber. Ein Lebensbild* [*Max Weber: A Biography*] (Tübingen: J. C. B. Mohr, 1926), pp. 715+.

5. Translation by J.P. Meyer from Weber, *Gesammelte Politische Schriften*, p. 139.

6. Originally released under the title *La femme supérieure*. Among first year releases was (Bruxelles [Brussels]: C. Hochhausen et Fournes, 1837). However, as was common with French political satire, the city and publisher data were questionable, and the date is known to be incorrect. The later more common title

was *Les Employés*. The book has been published under more titles in English than in French, the first being *Bureaucracy: Or a Civil Service Reformer* (Boston: Roberts Brothers, 1889).

7. See chapter ten for English-language translations.

8. For a detailed and sympathetic review of Schmitt's life and writings, see Joseph W. Bendersky, *Carl Schmitt: Theorist for the Reich* (Princeton, NJ: Princeton University Press, 1983).

9. Subsequent editions of this book, beginning with (Boston: Little Brown, 1941), were entitled *Constitutional Government and Democracy*.

10. This was a revision of his earlier dissertation at the University of Chicago.

11. Later the same year, Harper and Brothers acquired Row, Peterson and took the new name Harper and Row. The 1957 version under the name Harper and Row is more common.

12. Bruno R. [Bruno Rizzi], *La Bureaucratisation du Monde* (Paris: Hachette, 1939).

14
Employee Motivation

BACKGROUND

The goal of the next two chapters is to describe leadership and the factors of motivation that can be affected by it. The authors who are summarized include the industrial engineers, psychologists, sociologists, and social psychologists who studied motivation and concluded that leadership, punishments, and/or rewards, more than organizational structure, are the most fruitful avenues for improving employee performance.

Of course, most observers attribute some value to both structure and motivational techniques, resulting in even more overlap with the previous chapter than has been usual in this review. For that reason, these three chapters should be taken essentially as one unit. However, the motivational literature has been voluminous, and must be separated out for the sake of chapter length.

EARLY INDUSTRIAL PSYCHOLOGISTS

758.   Henry L. Gantt, *Work, Wages, and Profits* (New York: Engineering Magazine, 1910); also *Industrial Leadership* (New Haven: Yale University Press, 1916).

Gantt defies traditional labels. As part of the founding circles of both scientific management and management science, he is sometimes also considered to be the first humanist. While his training and experience were in engineering, he was the scientific management advocate who most clearly appreciated the role of psychology in the success of incentive plans.

While Taylor and Barth may have adopted the practice first, Gantt popularized the need for pushing the rewards in the "task and bonus system" high enough to clear the threshold of worker acceptance. In both books above he insisted on the mutuality of labor's and management's interests, and the need for worker morale. In that spirit, he created a separate bonus plan for the managers who could train their weakest workers so that the entire crew could reach production standards.

759.   Walter Dill Scott, *Increasing Human Efficiency in Business* (New York: Macmillan Company, 1911).

Many early industrial psychologists were allies of scientific management, and sometimes took the mechanical view of workers to cruel extremes. Scott, who is sometimes listed as a cofounder of industrial psychology, was a professor of psychology and consultant to the football program at Northwestern University. Using the arguments that "encouragement" by a coach could often make a player perform beyond "complete exhaustion," and that "overwork is not so dangerous or so common as is ordinarily supposed," he listed a number of techniques for improving human efficiency by at least 50 percent. Among the techniques were imitation, competition, loyalty, concentration, and responsibility. To keep the body in condition, Scott also recommended rest breaks and relaxation techniques.

760.   Josephine Goldmark, *Fatigue and Efficiency* (New York: Russell Sage Foundation, 1912).

As a logical counterpoint to Scott, Goldmark investigated the medical evidence on fatigue from overwork, stress, excessive speed, and similar causes as a justification for new labor legislation. Goldmark was Chairman of the Legal Defense of Labor Laws Committee of the National Consumers' League, and her detailed physiological studies emphasized the disproportionate strain placed on women and children by the working conditions in modern factories.

761.   Horatio Willis Dresser, *Human Efficiency: A Psychological Study of Modern Problems* (New York: G. P. Putnam's Sons, 1912).

Dresser also opposed the extreme position of Scott, although his focus is somewhat different. Dresser studied "human efficiency" as opposed to the more narrow industrial efficiency of "time planners." As an applied psychologist operating within the framework of William James, he saw human efficiency as a subject in applied ethics. Among his techniques were mental coordination, economy in nervous force, and efficiency of will. All were jeopardized when the body was subjected to extended excessive strain.

762.   Hugo Münsterberg, *Psychology and Industrial Efficiency* (Boston: Houghton
        Mifflin, 1913), revision of *Psychologie und Wirtschaftsleben: Ein Beitrag zur
        angewandten Experimental-Psychologie* (Leipzig: J. A. Barth, 1913).

Münsterberg is now best remembered as a pioneer of industrial psychology, which
he called "economic psychology." This was one of a number of specific subjects he
pursued once he took an interest in practical applications of psychological research.
In *Psychology and Industrial Efficiency*, he described previous research in various
industries to illustrate that there were motivational patterns to be discovered. While
he admired the approach of scientific management, he warned against some of its
abuses. By "economic psychology," however, he meant something broader than the
industrial psychology movement that has grown from his efforts. He also included
such topics as the effects of advertising, display, and product substitution.

763.   L(illian) M. Gilbreth, *The Psychology of Management* (New York: Sturgis and
        Walton, 1914); also accepted as a dissertation, University of California, 1915.

This work was controversial at the time for its innovative approach, because the
publishers identified the author as L. M. Gilbreth (to hide her gender), and because
the work was published only after a confrontation with the University of California.
It was accepted as a dissertation there, although in an attempt to stop her from
becoming the first female to receive a Ph.D. from the psychology department, the
faculty withheld a promised residency waiver. After the book was well received, and
after Ms. Gilbreth completed a year of residency at Brown University in 1915, the
degree was finally awarded.
        The book is a bridge between psychology and the scientific management work
of Taylor and her husband Frank. Like the other books described so far, the psychological theory is "applied" and primitive. However, Gilbreth described the evolution
of management from traditional through transitional to scientific forms. She argued
that scientific management among the three techniques was the only one to foster individuality, responsibility, and a "will to do."

764.   Mary Barrett Gilson, "The Relation of Home Conditions to Industrial Effi-
        ciency," *Annals of the American Academy of Political and Social Science*,
        65, (May 1916): 277-89.

In an early extension of the arguments of welfare-work advocates, Gilson argued
that home lives and industrial performance had such impacts on each other that
industrial psychologists were obligated to be concerned about the whole person. For
instance, filth at home was a special problem now that immigrants spent the day in
the factories instead of in the clean air of the fields. She particularly emphasized
the obligation of the factories to develop young girls toward their new opportunities
without neglecting the multiple responsibilities of later marriage and motherhood.

765. George F. Arps, "Work With Knowledge of Results versus Work Without Knowledge of Results," *Psychological Monographs*, 28, (1920), Monograph No. 125.

The concepts of competition and pride are inherent in Taylor's and Lillian Gilbreth's works, but are periphery to their major points. Arps tackled the subjects directly, determining that those who are asked to raise weights with their fingers do better if they are informed how they were doing, and how their efforts compare with their own previous performances. In short, the intervening variable of personal pride affects the results of fatigue studies and the workers' outputs.

766. Floyd H. Allport, "The Influence of the Group upon Association and Thought," *Journal of Experimental Psychology*, 3, (June 1920): 159-82; also *Social Psychology* (Boston: Houghton Mifflin Co., 1924).

The ultimately more important intervening variable, however, was described by Allport in 1920 when he noted that groups of upper classmen and graduate students performed better in groups. He named the influence "social facilitation," and reported that it has more impact on mechanical than on mental tasks. In 1924, he added rivalry (competition) as an additional stimulus to individual performance in a group.

767. Elton Mayo, "Revery and Industrial Fatigue," *Personnel Journal*, 3, (December 1924): 273-81.

In the 1920s, fatigue studies began to get more clinically sophisticated, but eventually ran into more troubling results. Mayo headed a team that studied the mule-spinning department of a textile mill near Philadelphia. The department was plagued by high labor turnover and low (by scientific management standards) production. Rest breaks were implemented, resulting in improvements in both. However, the preferred number and structure of breaks were determined by trial and error.

768. S[tanley] Wyatt and J. A. Fraser, assisted by F. G. L. Stock, *The Effects of Monotony in Work*, Industrial Fatigue Research Board, Report No. 56 (London: H. M. Stationery Office, 1929); also

769. S[tanley] Wyatt, assisted by L. Frost and F. G. L. Stock, *Incentives in Repetitive Work: A Practical Experiment in a Factory*, Industrial Health Research Board, Report No. 69 (London: H. M. Stationery Office, 1934).

Early fatigue studies were most advanced in London, where the government organized the Industrial Fatigue Research Board to continue research begun during the war. In 1929, the authors above reported a reduction in fatigue when workers were paid by the rate of production (instead of a flat rate), if the work was broken into discrete units, if they worked in groups, and if they had rest pauses. Those of lower intelligence were less fatigued by repetitive work.

In 1934, publishing through the renamed board, Wyatt found that workers in a candy packaging operation increased their work rate as they changed from flat rates to bonuses, and again as they changed to piece-rate. While they tended to change as a group, the effect was less pronounced on less-preferred jobs.

HAWTHORNE STUDIES

The Hawthorne experiments forever changed the face of motivation studies. This curious mix of scientific management and fatigue studies was conducted in two phases at the Western Electric assembly plant near Cicero, Illinois. From 1924 to 1927, internal research analysts used a grant from the National Research Council to try to determine optimum working conditions for production workers. From 1927 to 1934, the studies were joined by a team headed by Elton Mayo from Harvard University.

The studies literally created the humanist school of administrative thought, finally convincing the field that social leadership skills for managers were at least as important as technical knowledge. Among psychologists, the studies switched the future emphasis from fatigue to group processes, with the newer studies coming predominately from social psychologists.

The Hawthorne studies themselves, however, are worthy of some discussion in their own right, and they are the topic of this section.

770. Elton Mayo, *Democracy and Freedom: An Essay in Social Logic* (New York: Macmillan Co., 1919).

It is easy to argue that the influence of the Hawthorne studies was not due to new findings. Years before the experiments began, Mayo preached a gospel of human cooperation and group solidarity in the workplace. He sought a society in which it would be "possible for the individual to feel, as he works, that his work is socially necessary; he must be able to see beyond his group to society." (p. 37) If that was not accomplished, the disintegration of society would be inevitable.

771. George A. Pennock, "Industrial Research at Hawthorne," *Personnel Journal,* 8, (February 1930): 296-313; also

772. Mark L. Putnam, "Improving Employee Relations," *Personnel Journal,* 8, (February 1930): 314-25; also

773. Morris Simon Viteles, *Industrial Psychology* (New York: W. W. Norton and Co., 1932).

The experiments, however, carried an interest of their own. As they progressed, a series of internal reports were circulated within Western Electric. The first public descriptions of the experiments were these two papers read before the Personnel Research Federation in New York on November 15, 1929.

Pennock gave a brief synopsis of the experiments, supplemented by anecdotes from the workers. He described the frustration of early experiments on working conditions and concluded that mental attitudes were the dominant influence on productivity. Putnam proposed that productivity could be increased if employees were asked their opinions about the workplace, if those opinions were presented to supervisors through anonymous conferences, and if the comments were analyzed and classified for future improvement and research.

Soon, however, the outside world began to raise questions about the methodology of the studies. Viteles challenged the conclusion that fatigue was not involved in the findings. Mainly, however, he argued that the workers adapted to test conditions, so that the best production occurred in the longest test periods, regardless of test conditions.

774. Elton Mayo, *The Human Problems of an Industrial Civilization* (New York: Macmillan Co., 1933).

The first book-length analysis of the experiments, published in 1933, took the implications of Hawthorne beyond the physical description of the experiments. Mayo concluded that fatigue was a multi-faceted problem that was tied into anomie within society as a whole. The new administrator needed to strive toward social consolidation with workers. In the concluding pages, he even tied this into a plea for the consolidative work of the embattled League of Nations.

775. T(homas) North Whitehead, *Leadership in a Free Society* (Cambridge: Harvard University Press, 1936); also *The Industrial Worker*, 2 vol. (Cambridge: Harvard University Press, 1938).

In his 1936 book, Whitehead further developed the basic theme of the researchers at Hawthorne. There was a dangerous lack of social integration in society, aggravated by the reactions of workers against their stifling work environments. Modern industrial society had a tendency to crush the smaller social groups that held workers together, and supervisors should strive to arrest that trend.

In his 1938 work, Whitehead provided the most extensive detail then published on the Hawthorne experiments, once again tying the results to his central arguments.

776. Fritz J. Roethlisberger and William J. Dickson, *Management and the Worker* (Cambridge: Harvard University Press, 1939; also

777. Fritz J. Roethlisberger, *Management and Morale* (Cambridge: Harvard University Press, 1941).

The 1939 report, by authors from both Harvard and Western Electric, has become accepted as the official report and the most detailed description available of the progress and findings of the Hawthorne experiments. It describes the process by which an intended study of the effect of working conditions on fatigue and monotony grew through several stages into a general investigation of social relationships in the workplace. The 1939 report contains few conclusions, however.

In 1941, Roethlisberger published a set of speeches he had delivered to business groups between 1936 and 1941 on the implications of the experiments, followed by three concluding chapters. He affirmed the importance for management of developing cooperation and cohesion among workers, and described the inadequacy of both efficiency studies and "common sense" for achieving either.

778.   Mary B. Gilson, "*Management and the Worker*," [book review] *American Journal of Sociology*, 46, (July 1940): 98-101.

Gilson was a highly respected industrial psychologist, but her virulent review of Roethlisberger and Dickson's work was unable to dampen enthusiasm for the growing Hawthorne movement. She was incredulous that the researchers were surprised by their results. "Anyone even in the kindergarten stage of industrial knowledge would have recognized the impossibility of controlling variables in studying human beings." (p. 98)

She pointed out that she had described many of the same problems in 1916 (see earlier in this chapter). She attacked the ridiculous sample size, and the researchers' willingness to ignore the lack of production increase in the mica splitters' experiment, disproving their whole thesis. Finally, she suggested that the whole report was an effort to stifle unionism, and that the field should be wary of "Researches in the Obvious Financed by Big Business."

779.   Committee on Work in Industry, National Research Council, *Fatigue of Workers*, subsequently published by (New York: Reinhold Publishing Co., 1941); also

780.   George C. Homans, *The Human Group* (New York: Harcourt, Brace, and World, 1950).

The 1941 report, which was produced in large part by Mayo's student George Homans, offered a grander framework for the study of small groups. Homans expanded the framework further in 1950. At Hawthorne and other sites described in the 1950 work, Homans found that increased interaction between individuals caused them to like each other better, especially if outside contact also declined. Groups enforced their own social norms for membership, and those norms collapsed once contacts decreased.

781.   Reinhard Bendix and Lloyd N. Fisher, "The Perspectives of Elton Mayo," *Review of Economics and Statistics*, 31, (1949): 312-21.

One of the frequent attacks levied against Mayo's philosophy is that he failed to appreciate the value of competition and conflict in assuring the freedom of workers. Bendix and Fisher also added that Mayo had a tendency to draw grander conclusions than the data supported. Also, they claimed, he had failed to demonstrate any commonality of interest between workers and management.

782.   Jeanne L. Wilensky and Harold L. Wilensky, "Personnel Counselling: The Hawthorne Case," *American Journal of Sociology*, 57, (November 1951): 265-80.

Hawthorne-based literature continued, however. The Wilensky article described the counselling department that had been set up under the leadership of William Dickson. They found mixed feelings about the program among counsellors, workers, management, and the unions. However, they concluded that the program served as a goodwill agent, draining off resentment and bitterness that otherwise could go into militant unionism.

783.   Michael Argyle, "The Relay Assembly Test Room Retrospect," *Occupational Psychology*, 27, (April 1953): 98-103.

Like Gilson, Argyle could find "no valid conclusions" in the Relay Assembly Test Room experiment. Similarly, in the Bank Wiring Room, high cohesiveness and morale led to restricted output, not improved output as expected. Argyle concluded with suggestions for improving the methodology of further studies.

784.   Henry A. Landsberger, *Hawthorne Revisited* (Ithaca: Cornell University, 1958).

Landsberger presented a detailed summation of the attacks on the Hawthorne studies and philosophy. He argued that most of the attacks were on the social philosophy of Mayo, Whitehead, and Roethlisberger, and not on the experiments themselves. By focusing on *Management and the Worker*, and by ignoring the more interpretive works, Landsberger found some of the attacks to be justified and some to be misdirected. The biggest failing of the studies, he concluded, was that they were conducted with a focus and methodology that were not then appreciated.

785.   A. J. Sykes, "Economic Interest and the Hawthorne Researches: A Comment," *Human Relations*, 18, (August 1965): 253-64; also

786.   Alex Carey, "The Hawthorne Studies: A Radical Criticism," *American Sociological Review*, 32, (June 1967): 403-16.

If the early attacks were on the philosophy of Hawthorne, as Landsberger suggested, Carey wondered how studies "so nearly devoid of scientific merit, and conclusions so little supported by evidence" ever gained academic respect. Sykes analyzed the bank wiring room experiments while Carey investigated the relay assembly and mica splitting experiments. Both presented serious questions as to the conduct of the experiments and the ability of the data to support the conclusions that were drawn.

HUMANISTS

In its broadest context, humanism is an older intellectual tradition than any being discussed here. Its precise definition, however, depends on the academic discipline using it. For current purposes, humanistic works are assumed to focus on the quality of life of those in the workplace, but to lack the psychological rigor of the more recent "Behavioralism."

787.   John Ruskin, "Pre-Raphaelitism," [pamphlet] (London: Smith, Elder and Co., 1851); also

788.   [Pierre Guillaume] Frédéric Le Play, *Ouvriers européens* [*European workers*] (Paris: Impremerie impériale, 1855); 2nd ed., 6 vol. (Tours: A. Mame et fils, 1877-1879); also *Constitution essentielle de l'humanité* [*The Essential Constitution of Humanity*] (Tours: A. Mame et fils, 1881).

Once the industrial revolution was well established, numerous authors noted that there is more to human happiness than efficiency in work. Essayist and social reformer Ruskin wrote several works on fulfillment in work. His most concise statement, however, came in the introduction to a critique of painting.

> Now in order that people may be happy in their work,
> these three things are needed: They must be fit for it:
> They must not do too much of it: and they must have a
> sense of success in it--not a doubtful sense, such as
> needs some testimony of other people for its confir-
> mation, but a pure sense, or rather knowledge, that so
> much work has been done well, and fruitfully done,
> whatever the world may say or think about it. (p. 7)

From a more social perspective, Le Play publicized the cooperative code that was to provide the base for the Hawthorne studies. In a report that grew to six volumes by 1879, he described his studies of European workers conducted between 1829 and 1855. The early volumes, on agriculture and fishing villages in Northern and Eastern Europe, found peace and stability in which citizens felt like participants in the strong social code.

Moving west into industrialized regions, Le Play reported that the communities became shaken and finally disorganized. Living standards went up, but the social codes were not obeyed. Spontaneous cooperation disappeared. There were abuses of riches, science and knowledge, and power. However, Le Play felt that the English had avoided some of the pitfalls since their administration was built on local rule with traditional values.

789. Robert Owen, *The Life of Robert Owen*, 2 vol. [vols. 1 and 1A] (London: Effingham Wilson, 1857-1858).

Owen was probably most famous among the early reformers who tried to implement humanistic management principles on a grand scale. Based in his belief that people's personalities are shaped by their environment, he attempted to establish "villages of cooperation" at New Lanark in England, and at New Harmony in the United States. Workers were paid and treated well, and education was provided for their children in what were essentially collective societies. Owen also lobbied for labor legislation in England with mixed success.

790. Lev Tolstoĭ [Leo Tolstoy], *Voĭna i mir* [*War and Peace*] (Moskva [Moscow]: Tipografiia Г. Ris', 1868); (transliteration)

Humanism appeared in all social disciplines and even (or perhaps especially) in literature. In chapter four of the second epilogue of *War and Peace*, Tolstoy speculated that history is not determined by leaders. Instead, predating Barnard by 70 years, he argued that power is the collective will of the people which they expressly or tacitly transfer to their rulers by agreeing to accept their leadership to accomplish common objectives.

791. Thorstein Veblen, *The Instinct of Workmanship* (New York: B.W. Huebsch, 1914).

More in the spirit of modern analysis, Veblen argued that workmanship, like all instincts, is intelligent and teleological (goal directed). Modern society, however, has constrained that instinct in at least two ways. First, it substitutes money, through the pricing system, for the more fulfilling goals of being productive. Second, the machine age has stifled the learning process by creating predictable and tedious work environments.

792. Mary Parker Follett, *The New State* (New York: Longmans, Green and Co., 1918); also *The Creative Experience* (New York: Longmans, Green and Co., 1924); also reprinted speeches in *Business Management as a Profession* and *Psychological Foundations of Management*, both ed. by Henry C. Metcalf, both (New York: A.W. Shaw, 1927); also *Dynamic Administration: The Col-*

lected Papers of Mary Parker Follett, ed. by Henry C. Metcalf and Lyndall Urwick (New York and London: Harper and Brothers, [1942][1]).

Based in her belief that there is no inherent conflict among the interests of those within society, Follett was among the first to advocate to management that they share decision-making powers with the workforce. Her interests began in 1918 with the need for integration within the state. "Our political life is stagnating, capital and labor are virtually at war, the nations of Europe are at one another's throats--because we have not yet learned how to live together." (p. 3) She advocated the integration of interests rather than the competition of interests as the way toward greater peace.

In January 1925, she delivered the first of a series of speeches to the Bureau of Personnel Administration that marked her complete transition to concerns of the industrial community. These speeches, reprinted in 1927 but generally unavailable until 1942, popularized such phrases as "the law of the situation" and "power with, not power over" as her way of advocating that management and labor share power based on the ability of each to help solve current problems.

793.   Chester I. Barnard, *Functions of the Executive* (Cambridge: Harvard University Press, 1938); also *Organization and Management* (Cambridge: Harvard University Press, 1948).

Chester Barnard, whose 1938 book received only moderate attention among public administrators at the time, is now among the best known early humanists. The book is a reworking of eight lectures delivered before the Lowell Institute in 1937.

In his argument that cooperative systems must be both effective to their collective purposes and efficient in their distribution of resources to members, Barnard recognized a new importance for the role of individual workers. He argued that authority rises from below through the workers' zones of indifference. Informal organizations are as critical to cooperation as are formal organizations. To help foster cooperation, the functions of the executive are to help develop the three elements of the organization by providing communication lines, securing essential services, and determining organizational goals.

The 1948 book is also a reprint of earlier speeches, although on a variety of topics. Organizational themes were further developed in the areas of personnel and executive training. The book also addressed questions of democracy and a few world issues that had become critical in the 1940s.

794.   David E. Lilienthal, "Management--Responsible or Dominant?" [book review] *Public Administration Review*, 1, (Summer, 1941): 390-92.

By 1941, one of the better-known proponents of humanistic management styles was not an academic, per se, but a practitioner. In this review of James Burnham's book, *The Managerial Revolution*, Lilienthal used his experience as a director of the

Tennessee Valley Authority to disagree with Burnham's argument that exploitative management is inevitable. Instead, Lilienthal argued, management is more effective when it is non-exploitative, and when it uses the personal development of the employees.

795. Erich Fromm, *Escape from Freedom* (New York: Rinehart and Co., 1941); also *The Sane Society* (New York: Rinehart and Co., 1955).

In the age of Hitler, however, not all observers were so optimistic that the human compulsion for joining leads in healthy directions. Fromm used a psychoanalytical approach to argue that modern industrial democracy has been gained at the price of an atomized, impersonal social environment in which insecurity is rampant. As an escape, people might try blind devotion to political leaders, submission to powerful states, and/or aggression against other ethnic or political groups.

In 1955, the same general theme was applied to the impersonal work world. As an option for avoiding both capitalist managerialism (the West) and political totalitarianism (Marxism), he suggested "Humanistic Communitarian Socialism," or shared work experiences with an emphasis on developing a communal spirit.

796. Herbert A. Simon, *Administrative Behavior* (New York: Macmillan Co., 1947).

Although the focus of Simon's book is on administrative decision-making, his belief that it is "impossible for the behavior of a single, isolated individual to reach any high degree of rationality" leads to the same need for cooperation and coordination described by Barnard. The basic task of the administrator is to create environments for the workers so that rational decisions at their levels are also rational for the organization.

797. Peter Drucker, *The Practice of Management* (New York: Harper and Brothers, 1954).

Drucker focused on the three jobs of management--managing the business, the managers, and the workers--to show that they are integrated parts of one process. By separating the terms, however, he was able to differentiate strategies that would aid in the personal development of managers and workers. Among his managerial strategies is Management by Objectives, discussed in the next chapter. Among worker strategies are job engineering and general human resources management.

798. Reinhard Bendix, *Work and Authority in Industry* (New York: John Wiley and Sons, 1956).

Bendix used a historical sociological approach to study the "ideologies of management" that have arisen in four cultures representing formative and advanced industrialization in conditions of both relative autonomy and strict governmental control.

He found that different cultural settings lead to varying management ideologies. However, industrialization inevitably leads to bureaucratization and to a need to integrate the new industrial workforce into the power structure of society.

799.   Robert Townsend, *Up the Organization* (New York: Alfred A. Knopf, 1970); also *Further Up the Organization* (New York: Alfred A. Knopf, 1984).

After the mid-1950s, works on motivation became so heavily dominated with the language of social psychology that most of the literature is discussed under that section. A few works, however, remained more general in subject with less sophisticated research methodologies.

Townsend, for instance, rejected methodology in an intense effort to create a handbook for management. Using short chapters on subjects that are arranged alphabetically, he attempted to engage in "nonviolent guerrilla warfare" against the portions of the organization that no longer serve our purposes. Recommendations were often stated in the extreme, i.e, fining those who hire "assistant-to's" and firing the entire personnel department. The basic approach is humanistic and almost anti-structural.

The second edition of the book carries the new name listed above.

800.   William G. Ouchi, *Theory Z: How American Business Can Meet the Japanese Challenge* (Reading, MA: Addison-Wesley, 1981); also

801.   Richard T. Pascale and Anthony G. Athos, *The Art of Japanese Management* (New York: Simon and Schuster, 1981).

Responding to American concerns about losing markets to the Japanese, these two books tried to extract lessons from the Japanese managerial experience that could be applied to American industry. These include the assumptions that productivity is based (in Ouchi's terms) in trust between management and workers, subtlety in their relationships, and intimacy in their associations. Both books describe several steps for implementing Japanese-style management in American industry (Pascale and Athos use seven managerial "levers"), with case studies of companies in which they have been tried. Ouchi was not enthusiastic about Theory Z's chances in government, however, where rigid position descriptions make change more difficult.

802.   Thomas J. Peters and Robert H. Waterman, Jr., *In Search of Excellence* (New York: Harper and Row, 1982).

This was the first in what has become a collection of management literature on the general theme of excellence. Peters and Waterman investigated 62 companies chosen for their "excellent" performance based on six criteria. They derived eight characteristics of these companies: they have a bias for action; they are close to the customer; they encourage autonomy and entrepreneurship; they gain productivity through people; they are hands-on and value-driven; they stick "to the knitting," or jobs they know well; they have simple forms and lean staffs; and they have simultaneously loose and tight structures.

803. Craig R. Hickman and Michael A. Silva, *Creating Excellence* (New York: New American Library, 1984); also

804. Tom Peters and Nancy Austin, *A Passion for Excellence* (New York: Random House, 1985); also

805. Tom Peters, *Thriving on Chaos* (New York: Alfred A. Knopf, 1987); also

806. Robert H. Waterman, Jr., *The Renewal Factor* (New York: Bantam Books, 1987).

Among the books following the excellence theme, Hickman and Silva identified the three "deadly attitudes" of short-term orientations, shallow thinking, and quick-fix expectations. They also listed six "New Age strategies" of creating insight, sensitivity, vision, versatility, focus, and patience.

Peters followed his 1982 work with two books designed to help reinforce and implement the original message. The 1985 book emphasized MBWA (Management by Wandering Around) and the "Skunkworks" management style. In 1987, both Peters and Waterman argued that striving for excellence is not sufficient. Adaptability, described through 45 prescriptions in Peters book, is needed for survival in the economic chaos of modern times. Waterman chose the eight themes of informed opportunism; direction and empowerment; friendly facts and congenial controls; the use of "a different mirror"; teamwork, trust, politics, and power; stability in motion; attitudes and attention; and causes and commitment.

807. S. Prakash Sethi, Nobuaki Namiki, and Carl L. Swanson, *The False Promise of the Japanese Miracle* (Boston: Pitman, 1984).

Among many attacks that eventually developed on the importation of Japanese managerial techniques to the United States, this book emphasized the degree to which Japanese techniques are especially suited to the Japanese culture. American techniques need to accommodate the individualism and democracy of our culture. In addition, the authors noted, many of the techniques being advocated by others do not work all that well in Japan. The book includes several suggestions for improving American productivity, many of which mirror "excellence" and humanistic studies.

SOCIAL AND INDUSTRIAL PSYCHOLOGISTS

808.   Edward Lee Thorndike, *Animal Intelligence: Experimental Studies* (New York: Macmillan Co., 1911); also

809.   Robert S. Woodworth, *Dynamic Psychology* (New York: Columbia University Press, 1918).

One of the dominant themes that distinguishes scientific management from the later psychological study of motivation is the role of learning in worker behavior. To Taylor and Gantt, motivation is based in self-interest. To Freud and other early psychologists, it is based in instinct.

Thorndike was apparently the first to attempt to explain the role of learning in motivation, however. In his "law of effect," derived from animal behavior, he described the adjustment of behavior to what caused satisfaction in the past. Woodworth introduced the term "drive" to add the original energy that would cause the behavior that would lead to learning.

810.   Edward C. Tolman, *Purposive Behavior in Animals and Men* (New York: Appleton-Century-Crofts, 1932); also

811.   Kurt Lewin, *A Dynamic Theory of Personality* (New York: McGraw Hill, 1935); also *The Conceptual Representation and the Measurement of Psychological Forces* (Durham, NC: Duke University Press, 1938).

Tolman and Lewin popularized what became called the cognitive approach to learning by arguing that the current environment is more important than prior learning in influencing current behavior. The approach is largely complementary to stimulus-response learning theories because past experiences can affect current expectations (see Vroom below). However, the emphasis for research was shifted from the person's development to the current environment, and learning could be explained even if earlier observations were not driven by needs nor followed by relevant behavior.

812.   Arthur Kornhauser and Agnes A. Sharp, "Employee Attitudes: Suggestions From a Study in a Factory," *Personnel Journal*, 10, (April 1932): 393-404; also

813.   Robert Hoppock, *Job Satisfaction* (New York: Harper and Brothers, 1935).

These were among the earlier attacks on the core assumption of humanism--that job satisfaction leads to greater productivity. Kornhauser and Sharp found no relationship between efficiency ratings and attitudes among mill workers. Hoppock found that satisfaction was high among those who had work during the depression. However, satisfaction was so intertwined with emotional adjustment that separation of the concepts was meaningless.

814. Abraham Maslow, "A Theory of Human Motivation," *Psychological Review*, 50, (July 1943): 370-96; also *Motivation and Personality* (New York: Harper and Brothers, 1954).

Maslow's 1954 compilation of old and new essays also discussed some dysfunctions in the work place. However, he emphasized a "positive theory" of healthy human motivation through his hypothesis that individuals progress through five levels of needs towards which they can be motivated: physiological; safety; belonging; esteem; and self-actualization. The concept was not new.[2] However, Maslow popularized the notion that lower needs must be satisfied before higher needs are felt.

815. Norman R. F. Maier, *Psychology in Industry* (Boston: Houghton Mifflin, 1946); also *Frustration: The Study of Behavior without a Goal* (New York: McGraw-Hill, 1949).

Maier's emphasis was on dissatisfied employees. He disagreed with utilitarian views of motivation by arguing that two of the four types of learning are not goal-directed. Motivated behavior is variable, constructive, and goal directed. Frustrated behavior is rigid, stereotyped, compulsive, and not goal-directed. He also disagreed with the common view that such behavior springs from non-work emotional maladjustments.[3]

Motivated and frustrated behavior responds to different rules. While frustrated behavior responds slowly to rewards, for instance, punishment therapy can actually make frustration-driven behavior worse.

816. William Foote Whyte, *Human Relations in the Restaurant Industry* (New York: McGraw-Hill, 1948); also *Pattern for Industrial Peace* (New York: Harper and Brothers, 1951); also *Money and Motivation* (New York: Harper and Brothers, 1955).

Whyte became one of the early leaders of the social psychology movement in industrial studies. In 1948, his study of employee relations within restaurants helped popularize the argument that informal organizations (operated on status) can often have as much or more impact on productivity as the formal organization. In particular, waiters/waitresses are put into conflicting roles in balancing the demands of customers and cooks, especially when the cooks outrank them in status.

In 1955, Whyte pieced together an earlier book draft with several case studies contributed by himself and the joint authors listed on the title page.[4] Among the studies is a condensed version of Inland Steel Container case from his 1951 book. The major thesis is that the piece-rate incentive system fails to respond to the dual economic and social needs of the workers, and can often cause detrimental conflict between the two sets of needs. The precise solution often varies according to the social atmosphere of the plant.

817. Lester Coch and John R. P. French, Jr., "Overcoming Resistance to Change," *Human Relations*, 1, (1948): 512-32; also

818. John R. P. French, Jr., "Field Experiments: Changing Group Productivity," in James G. Miller, ed., *Experiments in Social Process: A Symposium on Social Psychology* (New York: McGraw-Hill, 1950), pp. 79-96.

In the 1940s, a set of studies at the Harwood Manufacturing Corporation in Marion, Virginia led to several publications, but never to the popularity of the Hawthorne studies. Coch and French studied scheduled changes in job methods, noting that efficiency suffers for shorter periods if worker representatives participate in decision-making, and efficiency suffers the least if the workers themselves are involved. French in 1950 reported the mixed results that democratic leadership styles seem to help efficiency, but the results vary according to the leader.

819. Ralph M. Stogdill, "Leadership, Membership, and Organization," *Psychological Bulletin*, 47, (January 1950): 1-14.

The Ohio State Leadership Studies began a movement away from the simpler assumptions of humanism. Stogdill argued that successful leadership is a function of the total organization. As such, it evolves from interrelationships within organizations striving to achieve common purposes, and different members of the organization can fulfill different roles. Motivation needs to be studied as part of organizational dynamics.

820. Daniel Katz, Nathan Maccoby, and Nancy C. Morse, *Productivity, Supervision and Morale in an Office Situation--Part I* (Ann Arbor: Survey Research Center, Institute for Social Research, University of Michigan, 1950); also

821. Daniel Katz, et al., *Productivity, Supervision and Morale among Railroad Workers* (Ann Arbor: Survey Research Center, Institute for Social Research, University of Michigan, 1951).[5]

The mechanics of successful leadership are discussed in the next chapter. In separate studies of Prudential Insurance and the C & O Railroad, however, the Survey Research Center joined the Ohio State studies in moving the field away from the assumption that happy workers are more productive. High production results from supervisors who motivate and lead workers. Worker satisfaction with both the job and the workplace is less convincingly related to production.

822.   Dorwin Cartwright and Alvin Zander, *Group Dynamics: Research and Theory* (Evanston, IL: Row, Peterson, and Co., 1953); also

823.   Morris S. Viteles, *Motivation and Morale in Industry* (New York: W. W. Norton and Co., 1953); also

824.   Conrad M. Arensberg, et. al., eds., *Research in Industrial Human Relations: A Critical Appraisal* (New York: Harper and Brothers, 1957).[6]

These three books were designed to summarize existing research on their prospective topics. Cartwright and Zander's book of readings reflected the "field theory" perspective of social psychologists since Lewin that groups contain special dynamics that explain leadership as well as other functions. The editors provided an explanatory introduction to each section.

Viteles summarized American and British experiments on motivation, including several formerly available only to subscribers. After reviewing Maier's frustration theory, Lewin's field theory, and the experiments at Hawthorne, Harwood, and elsewhere, he concluded that no one want or need can be used to explain all worker's desires. Higher-level workers emphasize self-expression while lower-level workers emphasize security.

The Arensberg reader is more specifically concerned with the human relations movement in industry. Readings include reprints and original contributions from those promoting as well as attacking the movement, and include a special section on the role of unions in the human relations movement.

825.   Arthur H. Brayfield and Walter H. Crockett, "Employee Attitudes and Employee Performance," *Psychological Bulletin*, 52, (September 1955): 396-424; also

826.   Frederick Herzberg, et al., *Job Attitudes: Review of Research and Opinion* (Pittsburgh: Psychological Service, 1957).[7]

These reviews of the literature on the relation of job satisfaction to performance played a large role in the shifting the field away from the more simplistic assumptions of humanism. Both studies found considerable support for links between satisfaction and lack of absenteeism and turnover. However, neither could strongly support a relationship between satisfaction and performance. Herzberg reported weak correlations. However, to Brayfield and Crockett, "there is little evidence in the available literature that employee attitudes bear any simple--or, for that matter, appreciable--relationship to performance on the job."

827.   Mason Haire, *Psychology in Management* (New York: McGraw-Hill, 1956).

In one of the last books praising the universal applications of the human relations approach, Haire used Walter Langer's hierarchy of physical needs, social needs, and egoistic needs to describe techniques by which managers can improve the environment for subordinates. Among the techniques are providing needed knowledge, maintaining an atmosphere of approval, and maintaining consistent discipline.

828. Chris Argyris, *Personality and Organization* (New York: Harper and Brothers, 1957); also *Integrating the Individual and the Organization* (New York: John Wiley and Sons, 1964).

Argyris was also part of the movement away from human relations to the more specific applications of organization behavior. His basic theme is that formal organizations place demands on individuals that are inconsistent with their healthy needs for activity, independence, flexibility, and superordination. To avoid tension and hostility, informal organizations arise to fulfill these needs. Organizations need not accept destructive organizations if they are willing to negotiate to change formal organization structures, directive leadership, and management controls.

In 1964, Argyris went into more detail in describing such techniques as vertical vs. horizontal job enlargement, working within the belief that motivation naturally arises when people are given tasks that adequately tax their decision-making abilities.

829. Frederick Herzberg, et al., *Job Attitudes: Review of Research and Opinion* (Pittsburgh: Psychological Service of Pittsburgh, 1957)[8]; also

830. Frederick Herzberg, Bernard Mausner, and Barbara Snyderman, *The Motivation to Work* (New York: John Wiley and Sons, 1959); also

831. Frederick Herzberg, *Work and the Nature of Man* (Cleveland: World Publishing Co., 1966); also "One More Time: How Do You Motivate Employees?" *Harvard Business Review*, 46, (January/ February 1968): 53-62.

Based on their belief that the lower-level needs described by Maslow tend to be satisfied in industrial society, Herzberg and others speculated by 1957 that job factors should be classified according to whether they are satisfiers or dissatisfiers. The idea was not entirely new.[9] However, the team surveyed 200 accountants and engineers to devise the theory that two factors affect work performance. Hygienic factors (salary, status, company policies, nature of supervision, etc.) can cause dissatisfaction. However, only motivators (the work itself, achievement, responsibility, recognition, advancement) can cause motivation once hygienic factors are satisfied.

Because of attacks on the methodology of his study, the data base was expanded in 1966. The 1968 article emphasized the value of job enrichment and the failure of KITA as motivators.

832. Leonard R. Sayles, *Behavior of Industrial Work Groups* (New York: John Wiley and Sons, 1958).

Sayles used an unusual approach to organization behavior by emphasizing the differences instead of the similarities among groups. By studying 300 work groups between 1951 and 1955, he concluded that the technology and the organization of the work helps create four types of groups: apathetic, erratic, strategic, and conservative. The typology led him to several conclusions, including that homogeneous groups grieve more, and that insulated work departments thwart the development of both extremely good and extremely bad worker-management relations.

833.   Melville Dalton, *Men Who Manage* (New York: John Wiley and Sons, 1959).

In the 1950s, Dalton worked "undercover" in three factories and a department store to discover the dynamics of the management process. While his report had no particular focus, he described the covert activities in which the employees engaged to subvert the official policies of management.

834.   Dorwin Cartwright, ed., *Studies in Social Power* (Ann Arbor: Research Center for Group Dynamics, University of Michigan, 1959).

Studies in psychology, and particularly in the Research Center for Group Dynamics, continued in the tradition of Lewin. In this collection of research reports on social power, Arthur Cohen found that power threatens those of low esteem and those in loose goal-oriented structures. Ezra Stotland reported that supportive peer groups heighten persistance toward goals, and aggression when faced with threatening power.

835.   Herbert Kaufman, *The Forest Ranger* (Baltimore: Johns Hopkins Press, 1960).

Most of the studies of motivation were conducted in the laboratory or in relatively confined industrial settings. Kaufman took an interest in motivation and control among the widely dispersed rangers of the U.S. Forest Service. He found that the Service endured more pressure toward disunity than occurs in more traditional surroundings. However, he described such techniques as authorization, direction, prohibition, financial allotments, diaries, inspection, limited recruitment, and post-entry training to maintain a motivated and focused work force.

836.   Douglas McGregor, *The Human Side of Enterprise* (New York: McGraw-Hill, 1960); also *The Professional Manager* (New York: McGraw-Hill, 1967).

McGregor may be best remembered for his 1960 summary of management theory through the labels Theory X (those assumptions behind scientific management) and Theory Y (those assumptions behind the humanists). His second book, which was finished by Warren Bennis and Caroline McGregor after his death in 1964, expanded on the incompatibilities between formal organizations and managers' emotional needs. He also stressed the transactional nature of influence that can result in improvements for both sides.

837.   Lyman W. Porter, "A Study of Perceived Need Satisfactions in Bottom and
        Middle Management Jobs," *Journal of Applied Psychology*, 45, (February 1961):
        1-10.

        Porter studied the applicability of Maslow's needs hierarchy in 64 bottom and 75
middle management jobs. He discovered that the major differences between the jobs
are in their potential for satisfying security, esteem, and actualization needs. Lower
level jobs more regularly reward lower level needs.

838.   Rensis Likert, *New Patterns of Management* (New York: McGraw-Hill, 1961);
        also *The Human Organization* (New York: McGraw-Hill, 1967).

        In 1961, Likert described four systems of management, ranging from the oppres-
sive, distrusting style of system 1 to the cooperative, integrative style of system 4.
He found that most successful organizations are led by managers leaning toward the
system 4 side of the continuum. In 1967, he further explained the system and updated
its experience through case histories from his work at the Institute for Social Research at the University of Michigan.

839.   Eliot D. Chapple and Leonard R. Sayles, *The Measure of Management* (New
        York: Macmillan Co., 1961).

        While Likert emphasized the scientific basis of his research, Chapple and Sayles
used the term more literally. They studied work flow, suspecting that the best style
of supervision is determined largely by the technology involved. They felt that both
efficiency and morale can be scientifically measured and improved, and they included
such suggestions as staff psychiatrists to aid with personnel adjustments to changing
task structures.

840.   E(ric) L. Trist, et al., *Organizational Choice* (London: Tavistock Publications,
        1963).[10]

        In 1951, researchers at the Tavistock Institute in England reported the adjust-
ment problems of informal work organizations when the ownership and technology of
coal mines changed.[11] A five-year study, reported in the 1963 book, illustrated that
sizable informal work groups in several mines, when allowed to be self-regulating,
were more capable than the formal organizations of adjusting to changes in the
technology of work.

841.   J. Stacey Adams, "Toward an Understanding of Inequity," *Journal of Abnormal
        and Social Psychology*, 67, (May 1963): 422-36; also "Injustice in Social
        Exchange," in *Advances in Experimental Social Psychology*, ed. by Leonard Ber-
        kowitz, vol. 2 (New York: Academic Press, 1965), pp. 267-99.

As an option to Maslow's needs hierarchy, and as an extension of Festinger's cognitive dissonance theory, Adams and others speculated that the worker's perception of equity in the work place is an important determinant of worker motivation.[12] Specifically, the worker arrives at a ratio of his perceived inputs and outputs from a job. If the ratio is significantly higher or lower than those of "significant others," the worker feels tension that hinders motivation. To be effective, supervisors need to lessen inequities.

842. Victor Vroom, *Work and Motivation* (New York: John Wiley and Sons, 1964); also

843. John W. Atkinson, *An Introduction to Motivation* (Princeton, NJ: Van Nostrand, 1964).

Using the psychological approach to arrive at still another theory of motivation, Vroom offered the expectancy theory that force (drive) is a product of valence (the desire for certain outcomes, tempered by instrumentality, or the subject's belief in his or her ability to perform the function) times expectancy (the belief that the function will lead to the desired outcome). The book also provided one of the more extensive summaries of the literature then published on worker motivation.

In a similar vein, Atkinson argued that "aroused motivation" is a product of the strength of the basic motive, times the expectancy of attaining the goal, times the perceived incentive value of the goal. Such a model can be used to explain the need for achievement (*n* Achievement) being studied by McClelland and others. While Atkinson's variables were similar to Vroom's, most subsequent expectancy theory work has credited Vroom with beginning the basic model.

844. M. Scott Myers, "Who Are Your Motivated Workers?" *Harvard Business Review*, 42, (January/February 1964): 73-88.

Myers' six year study at Texas Instruments helped support Herzberg's basic theory. Myers found that motivation comes from a challenging job that allows feelings of achievement, responsibility, growth, advancement, enjoyment of the work, and earned recognition. Dissatisfiers are often peripheral to the job, and are noticed more keenly when opportunities for achievement are removed.

845. Raymond E. Miles, "Human Relations or Human Resources?" *Harvard Business Review*, 43, (July/August 1965): 148-63.

Miles discovered that managers prefer to use the human relations approach on their subordinates, but they prefer to have the human resources approach used on themselves to allow the full use of their talents.

846.   Edgar H. Schein, *Organizational Psychology* (Englewood Cliffs, NJ: Prentice-Hall, 1965).

In this short textbook, Schein traced the evolution of organizational psychology from the individualistic approach of industrial psychologists to the group concerns of social psychologists. Using the systems approach, his emphasis was on organizational adaptability and the integration of healthy formal organizations with informal ones.

847.   Clayton P. Alderfer, *Differential Importance of Human Needs* [unpublished doctoral dissertation] (New Haven, Conn.: Yale University, 1966); also "A New Theory of Human Needs," *Organizational Behavior and Human Performance*, 4, (May 1969): 142-75; also

848.   Douglas T. Hall and Khalil E. Nougaim, "An Examination of Maslow's Need Hierarchy in an Organizational Setting," *Organizational Behavior and Human Performance*, 3, (February 1968): 12-35; also

849.   Edward E. Lawler III and J. Lloyd Suttle, "A Causal Correlational Test of the Need Hierarchy Concept," *Organizational Behavior and Human Performance*, 7, (April 1972): 265-87.

In experimental conditions, the needs hierarchies proposed by Maslow and others suffered amendments and conflicting evidence. Alderfer, in testing his own three-level hierarchy (existence, relatedness, and growth), found that growth needs expand when satisfied. Hall and Nougaim argued that the more any need becomes satisfied, the more important it becomes to the subject. Except for actualization needs, that finding contradicts Maslow's predictions.

Lawler and Suttle tested three hypotheses based around the concept that satisfaction of a need should make that need less important, and the next level need more important. In longitudinal attitudinal tests of 187 managers, they were unable to support the hypotheses.

850.   Anthony Downs, *Inside Bureaucracy* (Boston: Little, Brown and Co., 1967).

As mentioned in chapter seven, Downs categorized employee motives in his process of hypothesis building. Specifically, he speculated that workers can be described according to five models: climbers, conservers, zealots, advocates, and statesmen. Their expected behavior can be predicted from the assumptions of each model.

851.   Lyman W. Porter and Edward E. Lawler III, *Managerial Attitudes and Performance* (Homewood, IL: Irwin-Dorsey, 1968).

Most of the models of motivation have variations published by others. (Equity theory has perhaps the richest array of variations). The Porter-Lawler model presented in this book is an amendment to instrumentality theory presented within a broader study of managerial attitudes and performance. The authors at least partially tested a model with nine components, including the attitudes, traits and role perceptions of workers, as well as intrinsic and extrinsic rewards.

852.   Robert D. Pritchard, "Equity Theory: A Review and Critique," *Organizational Behavior and Human Performance*, 4, (May 1969): 176-211; also

853.   Karl E. Weick, Michel G. Bougon, and Geoffrey Maruyama, "The Equity Context," *Organizational Behavior and Human Performance*, 15, (February 1976): 32-65; also

854.   R. Dennis Middlemist and Richard B. Peterson, "Test of Equity Theory by Controlling for Comparison Co-Workers' Efforts," *Organizational Behavior and Human Performance*, 15, (April 1976): 335-406.

Pritchard provided one of the more complete reviews of the multiple variations of equity theory (under several names). While he considered Adams' theory to be the most complete and precise, he found that all of them are weak in explaining how "significant others" are chosen, how strategies are chosen to reduce tensions, and how individual differences calculate into the theory. Experimental support is strong when the subject is underpaid, but not when he or she is overpaid.

There have been efforts to provide more detail experimentally. Weick and his colleagues discovered that people normally compensate for inequities of low outcomes by requesting higher outcomes. Overpayment, however, seldom results in increased effort, perhaps due to the individual's ability to rationalize. Also, Dutch and American results differed, suggesting that the effect might be cultural.

Middlemist and Peterson found that people internalize the definition of the equitable "other" regardless of current coworkers. Also, they are willing to tolerate inequities so long as they can maintain a competitive edge.

855.   Abraham K. Korman, "Toward an Hypothesis of Work Behavior," *Journal of Applied Psychology*, 54, (February 1970): 31-41; also

856.   Robert L. Dipboye, "A Critical Review of Korman's Self-Consistency Theory of Work Motivation and Occupational Choice," *Organizational Behavior and Human Performance*, 18, (February 1977): 108-26.[13]

In 1970, Korman offered a cognitive consistency theory of motivation that individuals will work toward tasks consistent with their own self-image, even at the expense of tasks that would enhance their self-esteem. The theory came under attack by Dipboye in 1977 on the grounds that evidence offered by Korman could also be used to support the opposite conclusion. Subsequent responses (see note above) were lively, but failed to resolve the issue.

857.   John P. Campbell, et al., *Managerial Behavior, Performance and Effectiveness* (New York: McGraw-Hill, 1970).[14]

In an effort to sort the burgeoning theories of motivation, Campbell et al. suggested that the models can be divided into "process" theories and "content" theories. Process theories, such as Herzberg's, explain how behavior is caused, shaped, and arrested. Content theories, such as Maslow's, explain what in the individuals causes these behaviors to occur.

858.   Edward E. Lawler III, *Pay and Organizational Effectiveness: A Psychological View* (New York: McGraw Hill, 1971); also *Motivation in Work Organizations* (Monterey, CA: Brooks/Cole, 1973).

In 1971, Lawler summarized research on pay's importance, its role in motivation, and its effect on satisfaction. He found that pay is more important to lower-ranked workers, although they have less faith that pay levels are related to performance. He also presented a model of pay's effect on motivation as a way of explaining hierarchical differences.

In 1973, Lawler further refined his "facet satisfaction" theory, moving farther away from the instrumentality of the Porter-Lawler model (see under 1968 entry), and more toward the equity theories of Adams and others.

859.   Edward L. Deci, "Effects of Externally Mediated Rewards on Intrinsic Motivation," *Journal of Personality and Social Psychology*, 18, (January 1971): 105-15; also "The Effects of Contingent and Noncontingent Rewards and Controls on Intrinsic Motivation," *Organizational Behavior and Human Performance*, 8, (October 1972): 217-229; also

860.   James L. Farr, Robert J. Vance, and Robert M. McIntyre, "Further Examinations of the Relationship Between Reward Contingency and Intrinsic Motivation," *Organizational Behavior and Human Performance*, 20, (October 1977): 31-53.

Developing his cognitive evaluation theory, Deci conducted an experiment in which subjects already interested in a puzzle were paid either hourly (noncontingently) or by the puzzle (contingently) for the same activity. Once pay was stopped, those with noncontingent pay spent more time with the puzzles, leading to the conclusion that extrinsic reinforcement had diminished intrinsic motivation.

Deci's article has generated a number of responses, refutations, and additional experiments. Farr, Vance and McIntyre, who conducted their own studies, went the farthest in suggesting that not only was Deci incorrect, but even his original experiment did not support his conclusion.

861.   Gary A. Yukl and Gary P. Latham, "Consequences on Reinforcement Schedules and Incentive Magnitudes for Employee Performance: Problems Encountered in an Industrial Setting," *Journal of Applied Psychology*, 60, (August 1975): 294-98.

To test the effects of uncertainty built into industrial merit-pay systems, the experimenters paid tree planters a fixed bonus per bag of trees, or at twice the rate if they could correctly guess one coin toss, or four times the rate if they could correctly guess two coin tosses. The fixed rate bonus group outperformed both a control group and the other groups.

862.   Mahmoud A. Wahba and Lawrence G. Bridwell, "Maslow Reconsidered: A Review of Research on the Need Hierarchy Theory," *Organizational Behavior and Human Performance*, 15, (April 1976): 212-40.

Wahba and Bridwell reviewed studies of Maslow's needs hierarchy, and found that few researchers were able to support it. Cross-sectional studies showed no support for the argument that needs gratification leads to activation of the next level, except at the level of self-actualization. Longitudinal studies did not support the hierarchy at all. Therefore, the theory was unable to explain behavior in work organizations.

863.   Edwin A. Locke, "The Nature and Causes of Job Satisfaction," in *Handbook of Industrial and Organizational Psychology*, ed. by Marvin Dunnette (Chicago: Rand McNally College Publishing Co., 1976).

For the purposes of the handbook, Locke surveyed the literature (estimated at 3350 articles and dissertations) of job satisfaction and concluded that satisfaction comes from jobs that are varied, mentally challenging, and personally interesting. However, previous studies demonstrate that "there is no direct effect of satisfaction on productivity." (p. 1343)

864.   Hal G. Rainey, "Reward Preferences Among Public and Private Managers: In Search of a Service Ethic," *American Review of Public Administration*, 16, (Winter 1982): 288-302; also "Public Agencies and Private Firms: Incentive Structures, Goals, and Individual Roles," *Administration and Society*, 15, (August 1983): 207-42.

In investigating mid-level managers in two separate studies, Rainey discovered that financial and other extrinsic rewards are valued highly by public-sector employees. However, the public sector has more formalization of rules and constraints on extrinsic rewards. Therefore, it is necessary to take advantage of the public managers' higher responses on the "meaningful public service" nature of their jobs.

865.   Robert T. Golembiewksi, *Humanizing Public Organizations* (Mt. Airy, MD:
        Lomond Publications, 1985).

Golembiewski tried to demonstrate that despite structural barriers, it is possible
to implement Organization Development in the public sector. He described previous
efforts to implement OD in government, finding them about as successful as in the
private sector. He also argued that OD is essential to link democracy with administrative practices.

866.   Barbara S. Romzek, "The Effects of Public Service Recognition, Job Security
        and Staff Reductions on Organizational Involvement," *Public Administration
        Review*, 45, (March/April 1985): 282-91; also

867.   Samuel J. Yeager, Jack Rabin, and Thomas Vocino, "Feedback and Adminis-
        trative Behavior in the Public Service," *Public Administration Review*,
        45, (September/October 1985): 570-75.

Based on separate surveys of federal, state, and local government employees,
these authors were able to validate some aspects of motivational studies in the public
sector. Yeager, Rabin, and Vocino discovered that inadequate feedback mechanisms
have a negative effect on behavior, professional values, and attitudes. Romzek reaffirmed that recognition of their work has an important influence on public employees'
job involvement, especially among higher level workers. Lack of job security and
personnel reductions have much less influence.

CONTINUING CONCERNS

In their 1980 summation of motivation theory, Landy and Trumbo offered the
most troubling finding that plagues motivation theory. *"The models or theories of
work motivation are often more complex than the behavior they attempt to explain."*[15]
Experimental findings, which are far more common on this subject than on any other
regularly studied by public administrators, have served to amend, divide, and compli-
cate models into twentieth-century versions of Ptolemaic universe clocks. Those that
remain relatively simple tend not to be well tested.

There is cause for concern in the relative certainty that existed in the non-
empirical older writings on the subject, considering that the non-empirical approach
still pervades most of the subfields of public administration. Some are still concerned
that without quantification, there can be little progress.[16]

An alternative explanation may be that motivation studied in isolation is relatively
meaningless. Leadership is not only more subject to manipulation, but it also plays
such a crucial role in motivation that it may be the subject most deserving of study.
Many advocates and critics of such a position are discussed in the next chapter.

NOTES FOR CHAPTER FOURTEEN

1. While the American first printing of this book give no publication or copyright date, the simultaneous British first printing do.

2. For an earlier, similar version of the hierarchy of needs, see W. C. Langer, *Psychology and Human Living* (New York: Appleton-Century-Crofts, 1937).

3. For an older view that assumed that psychological maladjustments were carried to work, see V. E. Fisher and Joseph V. Hanna, *The Dissatisfied Worker* (New York: Macmillan Co., 1931).

4. As coauthors, the book lists Melville Dalton, Donald Roy, Leonard Sayles, Orvis Collins, Frank Miller, George Strauss, Friedrich Fuerstenberg, and Alex Bavelas.

5. Coauthors include Nathan Maccoby, Gerald Gurin, and Lucretia G. Floor. There is also considerable bibliographic confusion over the Part I listed in the title of the above work. This renamed work is Part II.

6. Other names listed as editors are Solomon Barkin, W. Ellison Chalmers, Harold L. Wilensky, James C. Worthy, and Barbara D. Dennis.

7. Coauthors include Bernard Mausner, R. O. Peterson, and Dora F. Capwell.

8. See coauthors in earlier note.

9. See for instance, R. B. Hersey, "Psychology of Workers," *Personnel Journal,* 14, (1936): 291-96.

10. Coauthors include G. W. Higgin, H. Murray, and A. B. Pollock.

11. See Eric L. Trist and K. W. Bamforth, "Some Social and Psychological Consequences of the Longwall Method of Coal-getting," *Human Relations,* 4, (1951): 3-38.

12. Leon Festinger, *A Theory of Cognitive Dissonance* (Evanston, IL: Row, Peterson, 1957).

13. Responses by Korman and Dipboye follow on pp. 127-28 and pp. 129-30.

14. Coauthors include Marvin D. Dunnette, Edward E. Lawler III, and Karl E. Weick, Jr.

15. Frank J. Landy and Don A. Trumbo, *Psychology of Work Behavior*, 2nd ed. (Homewood, Ill.: Dorsey Press, 1980), p. 373. Italics in original.

16. See, for instance, Howard E. McCurdy and Robert E. Cleary, "Why Can't We Resolve the Research Issue in Public Administration?" *Public Administration Review*, 44, (January/February 1984): 49-55. For responses, see Jay D. White, "On the Growth of Knowledge in Public Administration," *Public Administration Review*, 46, (January/February 1986): 15-24; and James L. Perry and Kenneth L. Kraemer, "Research Methodology in the Public Administration Review, 1975-1984," *Public Administration Review*, 46, (May/June 1986): 215-26.

15
Leadership

BACKGROUND

The literature on leadership is both voluminous and surprisingly recent. The rigorous study of the subject dates from the twentieth century.[1] However, there are more quantitative studies of leadership than of any other subject (including motivation and scientific management) discussed in this book.

Much of the material overlaps with humanism or social psychology in that it studies the relationships between leaders and subordinates. Therefore, the ties to the previous chapter are strong. Also, some excellent reviews of the experimental studies make it possible to discuss their general findings without reproducing an exhaustive bibliographic list. Those reviews and the other works that contributed directly to the study of the mechanics of leadership are discussed here.

One distinction appeared both early and often enough in this literature that it should be defined at the beginning. Leadership studies can be divided into trait vs. behavioral approaches, sometimes also labelled content vs. process approaches (from motivation studies), or even leader emergence vs. leader effectiveness studies.[2] Those who study the reasons why certain leaders emerge have tended to concentrate on the traits (contents) of those leaders. Studies of leadership effectiveness have tended to emphasize successful leadership behavior (processes). The distinction of these two approaches has often been used to categorize the studies of the field, and is reflected in these reviews.

LEADERSHIP STUDIES

868.   David R. Craig and W. W. Charters, *Personal Leadership in Industry* (New York: McGraw Hill, 1925).

In the early days, the trait approach to studying leadership was clearly dominant. Craig and Charters, for instance, interviewed top executives to determine their most important traits (intelligence and skill, forcefulness, teaching ability, health and nervous strength, kindliness, fairness and sensitivity). The detailed descriptions, which are surprisingly close to those later recommended by such theorists as Blake and Mouton, were followed by a self-training guide for less skilled managers.

869.   Ordway Tead, *The Art of Leadership* (New York: McGraw-Hill, 1935).

Craig and Charters argued that there is an intrinsic difference between managers and leaders, with leaders holding the top positions. Tead argued that the same distinction could be made between executives and leaders, even though both jobs are often part of the same position. While the executive has nine functions varying from control through coordination, the leader's responsibility is *"influencing people to cooperate toward some goal which they come to find desirable."* (p. 20) Strong leaders need the traits of "an abundance of red-blooded, free-flowing energy," a "strongly developed sense of a dominant purpose and direction," and integrity. He was confident that these statesmanlike characteristics could be taught to executives.

870.   Kurt Lewin and Ronald Lippitt, "An Experimental Approach to the Study of Autocracy and Democracy: A Preliminary Note," *Sociometry*, 1, (January/April 1938): 292-300; also

871.   Kurt Lewin, Ronald Lippitt, and Ralph K. White, "Patterns of Aggressive Behavior in Experimentally Created 'Social Climates'," *Journal of Social Psychology*, 10, (May 1939): 271-99.

Supporting the early belief that there is one successful leadership style, the researchers divided 11-year old boys into four clubs, submitting each to at least six weeks of autocratic control and six weeks of democratic control. Two clubs also worked under laissez-faire leadership. Productivity was highest under autocratic leadership, although it fell sharply when the leader left the room. Productivity was steady under democratic leadership, with or without the leader's presence, and lowest under laissez-faire leadership.

872.   William O. Jenkins, "A Review of Leadership Studies with Particular Reference to Military Problems," *Psychological Bulletin*, 44, (January 1947): 54-79; also

873.   Ralph M. Stogdill, "Personal Factors Associated with Leadership: A Survey of the Literature," *Journal of Psychology*, 25, (January 1948): 35-71.

Debates about whether the situation influences which leadership traits are effective emerged in the 1940s.[3] Jenkins reviewed the early empirical studies with an emphasis on those that were relevant to the military. He discovered that the methodology of prior studies was often poor, and that the situation seemed to determine which traits were appropriate. Still, leaders usually had technical competence in the group's area, shared several characteristics with the group, and were superior to group members in physique, age, education, and socio-economic status.

Stogdill's survey of 124 prior studies isolated numerous predictors of successful leadership, ranging from such behavioral characteristics as responsibility, goal direction, originality, initiative, and self confidence, to such physical traits as weight, height, and intelligence. He judged the role of the situation to be overstated in leadership studies.

874.   John K. Hemphill, *Situational Factors in Leadership*, monograph #32 (Columbus: Ohio State University Bureau of Education, 1949); also

875.   Andrew W. Halpin and B. James Winer, assisted by Janet W. Bieri, *The Leadership Behavior of the Airplane Commander* (Columbus: Ohio State University Research Foundation, 1952); also

876.   Ralph M. Stogdill and Alvin E. Coons, eds., *Leader Behavior: Its Description and Measurement*, Research Monograph 88 (Columbus: Bureau of Business Research, Ohio State University, 1957).

Perhaps the largest multidisciplinary collection of studies on effective leadership was conducted at Ohio State University beginning in 1945. That group adopted the revolutionary position that leader behaviors rather than leader traits carry the best explanatory value. Studying that variable, however, required that a scale for measuring leader behaviors be developed.

The early work on such a scale was first reported in Hemphill's early publications. It was developed into its final form in Halpin and Winer's report. In 1957, Stogdill and Coons gave a detailed description of the development of the Ohio State Leadership Studies since their beginnings in 1945.

The researchers developed questionnaires that allowed them to factor analyze leader behaviors into two critical dimensions, consideration and initiating structure. Scores for leaders were created using either the Leadership Opinion Questionnaire (LOQ) or the Leader Behavior Description Questionnaire (LBDQ), which would be administered to subordinates.

877.   Launor F. Carter and Mary Nixon, "An Investigation of the Relationship be-
        tween Four Criteria of Leadership Ability For Three Different Tasks," *Journal
        of Psychology*, 27, (January 1949): 245-61; also

878.   Graham B. Bell and Robert L. French, "Consistency of Individual Leadership
        Position in Small Groups of Varying Membership," *Journal of Abnormal and
        Social Psychology*, 45, (October 1950): 764-67.

Continuing the trait-situation debate, Carter and Nixon compared four methods
of measuring leadership ability on intellectual, clerical and mechanical tasks. The
correlations broke down, indicating that the situation dictates the requirements of
successful leadership. Bell and French identified the components of the situation as
the nature of the problem, the personal characteristics of the group, the group's
organization, and external influences. All of these, however, had minimal effects.
Bell and French, like Stogdill, offered that the impact of situational variables had
been overstated.

879.   Daniel Katz, Nathan Maccoby, and Nancy C. Morse, *Productivity Supervision
        and Morale in an Office Situation--Part I* (Ann Arbor: Survey Research Cen-
        ter, Institute for Social Research, University of Michigan, 1950); also

880.   Daniel Katz, et al., *Productivity Supervision and Morale Among Railroad Workers*
        (Ann Arbor: Survey Research Center, University of Michigan, 1951).[4]

While the Ohio State studies were still in their early stages, researchers at the
University of Michigan also pursued the behavioral approach to leadership. In separate studies of Prudential Insurance and the C & O Railroad, they discovered that
successful managers spend more time on general rather than close supervision. While
they are more employee centered, neither their personality traits nor their subordinates' intrinsic job satisfaction is significantly related to productivity. Their success comes from their willingness to accept the role of leader and to tackle problems
in motivation.

881.   George C. Homans, *The Human Group* (New York: Harcourt, Brace, and
        World, 1950).

Not all leadership studies were based in psychology. Speaking for the more
sociological Hawthorne approach, Homans described ten rules of effective leadership.
To him, leaders maintain their own position, live up to the norms of the group,
actively lead the group, and do not give orders that cannot be obeyed. They use
established channels, and do not thrust themselves on followers on social occasions.
They do not praise or blame individuals in front of the group. They take the total
situation into consideration, create conditions for group self-discipline, and listen
carefully as a tactic for understanding themselves.

882.   Philip Selznick, *Leadership in Administration* (Evanston, IL: Row, Peterson, and Co., 1957).

Selznick was also not a psychologist, although his sociological arguments agreed with the findings of the Michigan and Ohio State groups. He felt that only leadership can break through the dysfunctions of bureaucracy by moving beyond administrative management into institutional leadership. The strategy is to adopt a moral purpose for the organization through commitment, understanding, and determination. Only in this way can organizational health become a means rather than an end.

883.   T. W. Adorno, et al., *The Authoritarian Personality* (New York: Harper and Brothers, 1950);[5] also

884.   David C. McClelland, *The Personality* (New York: Dryden Press, 1951); also

885.   David C. McClelland, et. al., *The Achievement Motive* (New York: Appleton-Century-Crofts, 1953);[6] also

886.   David C. McClelland, *The Achieving Society* (New York: Van Nostrand Reinhold, 1961).

Also in the 1950s, several personality studies reached findings that are relevant to the workplace. The classic 1950 study of the authoritarian personality, financed by the American Jewish Committee to study the causes of anti-Semitism, noted that such a person has "*a hierarchical conception of human relationships*," (p. 413) and tends to be autocratic when placed in charge of others, but submissive when placed under the authority of others.
In 1951, McClelland developed a methodology for studying personalities. While his early emphasis was on the total personality, illustrated through the unidentified student "Karl," he quickly shifted his emphasis to the need for achievement, earlier labelled "*n* Achievement" by Henry Murray.[7]
By 1953, his joint research funded by the Office of Naval Research switched entirely to "*n* Achievement," housed within their "affective arousal" model of motivation. He found that the need for achievement, like all motives, is learned. As explained in 1961, such personalities vary by culture, and need challenging goals, moderate risks, and concrete feedback on their performance.

887.   Launor Carter, et al., "The Behavior of Leaders and Other Group Members," *Journal of Abnormal and Social Psychology*, 46, (October 1951): 589-95;[8] also

888.   Chris Argyris, *Executive Leadership* (New York: Harper and Brothers, 1953).

As later critics sometimes complained, early studies of leadership concentrated more on the emergence of effective leadership than on its maintenance. At the

University of Rochester, for instance, several experiments were run on small groups in which leaders were either designated or allowed to emerge. They found that leaders consistently exceed members in "diagnoses situation--makes interpretation" and "gives information on how to carry out action." Designated leaders tend to be coordinators, however, while emergent leaders tend to be more energetic.

In a case study of an unidentified leader who "turned around" an inefficient and unprofitable industrial unit, Argyris described the leader as 1) having constant close contact with his supervisors; 2) being loyal to the organization; 3) handling supervisors individually; and 4) setting realistic goals. He then speculated that leadership is essential because subordinates inevitably feel dependent on the leader, regardless of his style, in all aspects of the work except for work flow.

889.   Cecil A. Gibb, "Leadership," in Gardner Lindzey, ed., *Handbook of Social Psychology*, vol. 2 (Reading, MA: Addison-Wesley, 1954), pp. 877-920; also

890.   Richard D. Mann, "A Review of the Relationships Between Personality and Performance in Small Groups," *Psychological Bulletin*, 56, (July 1959): 241-70.

Gibb's widely cited review of the literature, written while the behavioral study of leadership was still emerging, provides an extensive window on the early studies of leadership. The article offers detailed definitions of groups, leaders, and leader behavior, along with extensive bibliographic descriptions of experiments on specific physical traits of leadership.

Mann's synopsis of studies between 1900 and 1957 described the relationship of personality to both behavior and status. The best predictors of leadership performance include intelligence, adjustment, extroversion, dominance, and interpersonal sensitivity.

891.   Edwin A. Fleishman, Edwin F. Harris, and Harold E. Burtt, *Leadership and Supervision in Industry* (Columbus: Ohio State University, 1955).

In a test of the efficacy of training the "Ohio State" approach to leadership, the authors measured the effects of a two-week seminar that was designed to encourage "consideration" (humanist) scores at the expense of "initiating structure" (production) orientations. While the effects of the seminar could be noted at the end of the course, they could not be detected in later follow-up attitudinal studies. Neither could they be detected after a later one-week refresher course.

892.   Basil S. Georgopoulos, Gerald M. Mahoney, and Nyle W. Jones, Jr., "A Path-Goal Approach to Productivity," *Journal of Applied Psychology*, 41, (December 1957): 345-53; also

893. Martin G. Evans, "The Effects of Supervisory Behavior on the Path-Goal Relationship," *Organizational Behavior and Human Performance*, 5, (May 1970): 277-98; also

894. Robert J. House, "A Path-Goal Theory of Leader-Effectiveness," *Administrative Science Quarterly*, 16, (September 1971): 321-38; also

895. Robert J. House and Terence R. Mitchell, "Path-Goal Theory of Leadership," *Journal of Contemporary Business*, 3, (Autumn 1974): 81-97.

While expectancy theory was still evolving as a motivational concept, researchers at the University of Michigan offered path-goal theory as a practical application of the concept for leadership study. The earliest empirical study appeared in 1957, although the theory did not become popular until the 1970s. In 1970, Evans offered six hypotheses, including that leaders can be effective if they make rewards contingent on performance. House offered several hypotheses, including that initiating-structure behavior increases the subordinates' instrumentality for non-routine or ambiguous tasks. However, the effect is different depending on whether the tasks are satisfying. In 1974, he also described the contingency effects of the personal characteristics of the subordinates and the working environment.

896. Robert N. McMurry, "The Case for Benevolent Autocracy," *Harvard Business Review*, 36, (January/February 1958): 82-90; also

897. Anthony Jay, *Management and Machiavelli* (New York: Holt, Rinehart, and Winston, 1967); also

898. Harlan Cleveland, *The Future Executive* (New York: Harper and Row, 1972); also

899. James MacGregor Burns, *Leadership* (New York: Harper and Row, 1978).

Non-psychological studies of leadership continued to appear and to present a variety of perspectives and values on the subject. McMurry, for instance, felt that the bottom-up approach to leadership sounds good, but is unworkable and inconsistent with the psychology of hard-driven managers. Instead, the bureaucratic personality wants regimentation--not responsibility or independence. Therefore, the Weberian model of bureaucracy is destined to work best.

Jay compared modern corporations to feudal states. Using Machiavelli's techniques, he believed that the leaders make the corporation (or state), and that the method of learning is to observe others in similar situations. Like Machiavelli, he was fond of colonialization (delegation of authority). He spent considerable time describing how to keep organizations creative, especially by delegating serious power to loyal groups operating in the organization's long-term interest.

By arguing that the executive world is becoming more complex, and that the working environment is becoming more horizontal, Cleveland felt that future executives will have to be more intellectual, more tolerant of others, more concerned with building coalitions, more optimistic, and more comfortable with complexity.

Burns used a variety of perspectives to illustrate his argument that leadership is a special form of political power that can be divided into transactional (exchange of resources) and transforming (shaping of desires) types. He was particularly concerned with the ethics of transforming leadership. "Divorced from ethics, leadership is reduced to management and politics to mere technique." (p. 389)

900.   Robert Tannenbaum and Warren H. Schmidt, "How to Choose a Leadership Pattern," *Harvard Business Review*, 36, (March/ April 1958): 95-101; also

901.   John R. P. French, Jr. and Bertram H. Raven, "The Bases of Social Power," in *Studies in Social Power*, ed. by Dorwin Cartwright (Ann Arbor: Research Center for Group Dynamics, University of Michigan, 1959), pp. 150-67.

Even within management studies, there was little consensus on definitions. Tannenbaum and Schmidt offered an eight-part typology of leadership styles based on a continuum of boss-centered to subordinate-centered decision-making. In the most autocratic form, the manager announces the decision. In the other options, the manager "sells" the decision, presents the ideas and asks for questions, presents a tentative decision, presents the problem and suggestions, defines the limits for a group decision, or permits the group to function within specified limits.

French and Raven argued that social power arises from one of five bases--reward power, coercive power, legitimate power, referent power, and expert power. Since each base defines what makes the power effective, it is necessary for leaders to understand their base so that they can predict what strategies will work.

902.   Warren G. Bennis, "Leadership Theory and Administrative Behavior: The Problem of Authority," *Administrative Science Quarterly*, 4, (December 1959): 259-301; also "Post-Bureaucratic Leadership," *Trans-Action*, 6, (July/August 1969): 44-51, 61.

In 1959, Bennis charted the basic differences between the traditional and the humanist approaches to leadership, while noting that recent authors, such as Argyris, were attempting to salvage the modern approach by dumping the more naive assumptions of early humanists. In 1969, Bennis argued that the rapidly changing world requires a style of leadership that shares power and solicits different contributions from each subordinate depending on the task at hand.

903.   Robert R. Blake and Jane S. Mouton, *The Managerial Grid* (Houston: Gulf Publishing Co., 1964); also *The New Managerial Grid* (Houston: Gulf Publishing Co., 1978).

In 1964, Blake and Mouton explained the theory behind a technique they had developed for fostering managerial development. The basic assumption is that managers perform most effectively when concerned about both production and people. As such, they revived the trait approach that can be adapted to virtually any situation. Scales for the two traits are placed on a grid. The authors then described managers at different places on the grid, and how the managers could be brought nearer to the optimal score of (9,9). The second edition, in 1978, expanded the discussion of daily applications, the origins of managerial styles, and the significance of the grid.

904.   Fred Fiedler, "Engineer the Job to Fit the Manager," *Harvard Business Review*, 43, (September/October 1965): 115-22; also *A Theory of Leadership Effectiveness* (New York: McGraw-Hill, 1967).

Fiedler followed the more popular belief that commitment to both production and people is not always the most effective approach, and he is now largely credited with developing the contingency approach to leadership.[9] Fiedler studied various groups and leadership positions in situations that varied according to leader-member relations, task structure, and the power of the leader's position. He found that people-oriented leaders (high Least Preferred Coworker scores) do best in positions that are neither extremely favorable nor unfavorable to the leader. Production-oriented leaders have the best results in the extreme positions.

905.   David G. Bowers and Stanley E. Seashore, "Predicting Organizational Effectiveness With a Four-Factor Theory of Leadership," *Administrative Science Quarterly*, 11, (September 1966): 238-63; also

906.   Edwin I. Megargee, Patricia Bogart, and Betty J. Anderson," Prediction of Leadership in a Simulated Industrial Task," *Journal of Applied Psychology*, 50, (August 1966): 292-95.

Supporting the position that leadership is a complex variable, Bowers and Seashore studied leaders in 40 life insurance agencies on the scales of support, interaction facilitation, goal emphasis, and work facilitation. They discovered that leadership is multidimensional, that differing styles have contingent success, and that subordinate behavior needs to be measured as well.

Similarly, Megargee and associates found that the value of dominance as a predictor of leader emergence depends on the situation. Dominant leaders emerge when leadership is emphasized, but not necessarily when task completion is emphasized.

907.   Abraham Korman, "'Consideration,' 'Initiating Structure' and Organizational Criteria: A Review," *Personnel Psychology*, 19, (Winter 1966): 349-61; also

908.   Peter Weissenberg and Michael J. Kavanaugh, "The Independence of Initiating Structure and Consideration: A Review of the Evidence," *Personnel Psychology*, 25, (Spring 1972): 119-30; also

909.   Chester A. Schriesheim, Robert J. House, and Steven Kerr, "Leader Initiating Structure: A Reconciliation of Discrepant Research Results and Some Empirical Tests," *Organizational Behavior and Human Performance*, 15, (April 1976): 297-321.

Scores for leader behavior based on the Ohio State technique allowed researchers to use leader questionnaires (LOQs) or subordinate questionnaires (LBDQs). Korman reviewed previous studies to discover that consideration and initiating structure were not related when LOQs were used, but were related when LBDQs were used. The two questionnaires clearly measured different things, although it was not clear whether leader or subordinate answers were more reliable.

Weissenberg and Kavanaugh uncovered the same relationship and speculated that leaders believe the two dimensions to be independent, although they do not behave that way in the work place. To make matters more confusing, the Ohio State group has revised the LBDQ several times. In 1976, Schriesheim, House, and Kerr reported that a large percentage of recent studies used versions of the Ohio State instruments that had been revised by the users.

910.   William K. Graham, "Description of Leader Behavior and Evaluation of Leaders as a Function of LPC," *Personnel Psychology*, 21, (Winter 1968): 457-64.

To determine whether a leader is people or production oriented, Fiedler used a measure of how highly they rate their least-preferred coworker (LPC). Low LPC managers are more task-oriented. Graham used the same scale, and found that neither is obviously the more effective style. Also, low LPC ratings are often as much a factor of working conditions as of personality styles.

911.   Edwin P. Hollander and James W. Julian, "Contemporary Trends in the Analysis of Leadership Processes," *Psychological Bulletin*, 71, (May 1969): 387-97; also

912.   John P. Campbell, et al., *Managerial Behavior, Performance and Effectiveness* (New York: McGraw-Hill, 1970);[10] also

913.   Ralph M. Stogdill, *Handbook of Leadership: A Survey of Theory and Research* (New York: The Free Press, 1974).

With general disagreement over terms and procedures for studying leadership, many reviews remain skeptical that much has been discovered. Hollander and Julian noted that many studies fail to appreciate the group nature of leadership and the two-way influence of leader-follower relations. Future studies needed to distinguish leadership emergence from maintenance.

Campbell, et al. summarized that little is commonly known about effective managerial performance since effectiveness is determined by a combination of personal attributes, characteristics of the job, and the organization's motivational policies. They offered some criteria for measurement of the relevant variables, a model of managerial motivation, and suggestions for further research.

Stogdill noted that person-oriented leadership is related to job satisfaction, but inconsistently related to production. Work-oriented leadership is related to production if it maintains role differentiation and specifies the manager's expectations.

914. Edwin P. Hollander, *Leaders, Groups, and Influence* (New York: Oxford University Press, 1964); also *Leadership Dynamics: A Practical Guide to Effective Relationships* (New York: The Free Press, 1978); also

915. T(homas) O(wen) Jacobs, *Leadership and Exchange in Formal Organizations* (Alexandria, VA: Human Resources Research Organization, 1970 [i.e. 1971]); also

916. Fred Dansereau, Jr., George Graen, and William J. Haga, "A Vertical Dyad Linkage Approach to Leadership Within Formal Organizations: A Longitudinal Investigation of the Role Making Process," *Organizational Behavior and Human Performance*, 13, (February 1975): 46-78.

Social exchange theory was developed to explain leadership as a "relationship between a person exerting influence and those who are influenced, and...it is best seen within the framework of group process." (1964, p. 1) Leaders emerge because their competence, fulfillment of the group's expectations, perceived motivation, and adaptability allow them the "idiosyncratic credits" to deviate from group norms without penalty. Leadership maintenance is a separate process also best studied within the group context.

Vertical dyad theory extended the exchange relationship by studying the different relationship between managers and each individual subordinate. Managers use both supervision and leadership, depending on the dyad relationship. The latitude given the subordinate in negotiating his or her role predicts the subsequent behavior of both parties.

917. Henry Mintzberg, *The Nature of Managerial Work* (New York: Harper and Row, 1973).

Mintzberg studied what managers actually do on the job. He found that they work at an unrelenting pace, spending a brief period on each task with frequent interruptions. They prefer oral communications, mostly with other managers, their subordinates, and those outside of the organization. Mintzberg identified ten managerial roles of figurehead, leader, liaison, monitor, disseminator, entrepreneur, disturbance handler, resource allocator, and negotiator.

918.   Victor Vroom and Philip W. Yetton, *Leadership Decision Making* (Pittsburgh: University of Pittsburgh Press, 1973); also

919.   Victor H. Vroom and Arthur G. Jago, *The New Leadership* (Englewood Cliffs, NJ: Prentice Hall, 1988).

Fiedler popularized the argument that different types of leaders work best in different situations. Vroom and Yetton created a normative model of decision-making that takes the contingency approach one step further. Each leader, they suggested, should choose among five basic decision styles to solve different types of problems. They offered a decision tree to aid managers in selecting the proper style.

Use of the model would result in managers being both autocratic and participative, based on their answers to seven questions, including the importance of the decision quality, the leader's relevant information, the problem's structure, the importance of subordinate acceptance, the probability of subordinate acceptance, the congruence of organizational and subordinate goals, and the likely conflict among subordinates.

In 1988, the authors reviewed six validation studies of the original model, noting that across all studies, decisions were successful 62% of the time when the model was followed, and 37% of the time when the model was violated. More importantly, however, the authors further refined the decision tree to include degrees of participation and nebulous answers, resulting in a decision tree that is too complicated to draw (although four simplified versions are offered in the book), but that is available on floppy disk for personal computers.

920.   James G. Hunt and Lars L. Larson, *Contingency Approaches to Leadership: A Symposium Held at Southern Illinois University, Carbondale* (Carbondale: Southern Illinois University Press, 1974).

This reprint of papers from the second leadership conference at Carbondale, held May 17-18, 1973, offered empirical verification by both James C. Taylor and George Farris that technology affects successful leadership styles. Robert J. House and Gary Dessler tested a path-goal model while Bernard M. Bass and Enzo R. Valenzi offered their own complex contingency model. Abraham Korman, in overviewing the literature of the subject, suggested that leadership studies need to concentrate on behavior more than personalities, and need to move toward longitudinal tests to improve their claims of validation.

921.   Bernard M. Bass, et al., "Management Styles Associated with Organizational, Task, Personal, and Interpersonal Contingencies," *Journal of Applied Psychology*, 60, (December 1975): 720-29.[11]

Supporting the argument that the styles of each leader are variable, Bass, et al. found that leaders accomplish their tasks through five basic approaches: direction, negotiation, consultation, participation, and delegation. The styles are distinct conceptually, but not empirically. Each style relates differently to varying tasks and contingencies.

922. Michael Maccoby, *The Gamesman* (New York: Simon and Schuster, 1976); also *The Leader* (New York: Simon and Schuster, 1981).

Based on psychological analyses of 250 executives in 12 corporations, Maccoby used the more simple explanation that there are four "ideal types" of executives--the craftsman, the jungle fighter, the company man, and the gamesman. He emphasized the gamesman as the new corporate type who uses team building to drive the organization toward success. In 1981, he argued that we need a new-style leader more concerned with consensus building and the moral responsibilities of leadership.

923. Victor H. Vroom and Arthur G. Jago, "On the Validity of the Vroom-Yetton Model," *Journal of Applied Psychology*, 63, (April 1978): 151-62; also

924. R. H. George Field, "A Critique of the Vroom-Yetton Model of Leadership Behavior," *Academy of Management Review*, 4, (April 1979): 249-57; also *A Test of the Vroom-Yetton Contingency Model of Leadership Behavior* [unpublished doctoral dissertation] (Toronto: University of Toronto, 1981); also "A Test of the Vroom-Yetton Normative Model of Leadership," *Journal of Applied Psychology*, 67, (October 1982): 523-32.

When originally presented, the Vroom-Yetton model (see above) was largely conceptual. In 1978, Vroom and Jago presented the first empirical test of the model by interviewing 96 managers who described 181 key decisions. They reported success in predicting the technical quality of the decision, the subordinate acceptance, and the overall effectiveness of the decision.

The most notable detractor from the theory was Field, who raised questions in 1979 about trying to validate concurrent parts of the model, and about using self-reports as data. He also felt that the model has limited utility since it deals with only one aspect of leader behavior. In 1981 and 1982, he reported on tests manipulating the decision process and situations for 276 business students. Only one of the three quality rules and three of the four acceptance rules performed as predicted. The goal congruence rule also failed.

925. Gary A. Yukl, *Leadership in Organizations* (Englewood Cliffs, NJ: Prentice-Hall, 1981).

Many literature reviews already discussed in this chapter concluded that, despite all the effort, little firm knowledge has been gained about leadership. Yukl, in his "incisive rather than comprehensive" review, disagreed. He felt that each approach to leadership studies has contributed something, even if we still need to integrate the parts. Also, he felt that leadership can be improved through proper selection, training, and situational engineering.

926.   Daniel R. Ilgen, Terence R. Mitchell, and James W. Frederickson, "Poor Performers: Supervisors' and Subordinates' Responses," *Organizational Behavior and Human Performance*, 27, (June 1981): 386-410; also

927.   Kenneth Blanchard and Spencer Johnson, *The One Minute Manager* (New York: William Morrow and Co., 1982).

Like motivation studies, most popular studies of leadership have been concerned with typical employees. In 1981, Ilgen, Mitchell, and Frederickson tested 41 work groups to determine how problem employees respond to supervision. They found that feedback from supervisors affects attitudes and beliefs more than performance. Supervisors are inclined toward the halo effect of overemphasizing unusual or recent performance in their evaluations. Also, specific feedback has more impact on subordinates than general feedback.

In their popularized list of suggestions to managers, Blanchard and Johnson were even more explicit about telling managers how to handle one minute praisings and reprimands. Both techniques involve telling subordinates that their performance is the subject, telling them explicitly what is right or wrong about the performance and how that makes the supervisor feel, reaffirming the supervisor's confidence in the subordinate, and then allowing the subject to drop.

MANAGEMENT BY OBJECTIVES

928.   Peter Drucker, *The Practice of Management* (New York: Harper and Brothers, 1954).

Within the literature on leadership, numerous techniques have been proposed for improving managerial performance. However, Management by Objectives has been among the more resilient, and was "officially" implemented in the federal government during the Nixon administration.

It is now common to trace MBOs origin to chapter 11, entitled "Management by Objectives and Self-Control," of this 1954 book.[12] Drucker's purpose was not to outline a specific strategy so much as to emphasize the point that the manager's job is to manage toward objectives rather than toward polished techniques. To accomplish that, he suggested that objectives and strategies should be agreed upon in advance.

929. "The Work of the Professional Manager," *Professional Management in General Electric*, vol. 3 (New York: The General Electric Company, 1954).

Drucker argued that MBO as a technique went back at least to the 1920s. The clearest evidence that its major components evolved in practice may be this report of a major corporate reorganization of General Electric in 1952-1954. The corporation reported that its decision to decentralize managerial decision-making required long-range goals, specific objectives, and techniques for measuring progress rather than subjective performance appraisals and personal supervision. The corporation tried to identify and measure key result areas.

930. Douglas McGregor, "An Uneasy Look at Performance Appraisal," *Harvard Business Review*, 35, (May-June 1957): 89-94; also *The Human Side of Enterprise* (New York: McGraw-Hill Book Co., 1960).

Besides Drucker, McGregor has become the second major theorist commonly cited as a founding source for MBO. McGregor's concern was with the technique's utility for performance appraisal more than corporate planning. He commented in 1957 that performance appraisal is often resisted because of its subjective judgment of personal worth. MBO, on the other hand, can establish specific criteria for judgment, can involve the subordinate in self-appraisal, and can concentrate on strengths rather than weaknesses.

In 1960, McGregor referred to the technique as Management by Integration and Self Control to criticize the growing tendency of management to treat MBO as a tactic for greater direction and control. He followed a specific example of MBO to show how it is an integral part of Theory Y.

931. Edward C. Schleh, *Management By Results: The Dynamics of Profitable Management* (New York: McGraw Hill, 1961); also

932. C. L. Hughes, *Goal Setting: Key to Individual and Organizational Effectiveness* (New York: American Management Association, 1965.

More evidence for the contention that the tactics of MBO are quite old may be that many early studies neither cited Drucker nor used his terminology in describing the concept. Schleh, citing no sources, restated the argument that managers are paid to produce results, and should be judged accordingly. Written goals for managers should blend short and long term goals for the work group, and should be stated in measurable terms. The managers should be given regular feedback, and should be given accountability before being granted authority.

Hughes, who leaned heavily on McGregor but never mentioned Drucker, sought a technique for creating goal oriented, rather than task oriented, companies. Such "self-aware" companies and individuals would participate in an eight-step goal setting process including operationalized objectives, the distribution of resources according to goals, and the measurement and evaluation of results.

933. Herbert H. Mayer, Emanuel Kay, and John R. French, "Split Roles in Performance Appraisal," *Harvard Business Review*, 43, (January/February 1965): 123-29; also

934. Anthony Raia, "Goal Setting and Self Control," *Journal of Management Studies*, 1, (February 1965): 34-53; also "A Second Look at Goals and Controls," *California Management Review*, 8, (Summer 1966): 49-58.

Early empirical studies of MBO gave mixed results. Mayer, Kay, and French compared a control group using traditional performance appraisal methods to managers working under "Work Planning and Review" at General Electric in which goals were submitted by subordinate managers for review and approval. After one year, the test group had more favorable attitudes toward their jobs and companies.

Raia's test showed similar results after one year, when declining productivity turned around, attitudes improved, and the managers became more aware of the company's goals. The follow-up study published in 1966, however, showed a number of problems developing. There was overreliance on measurable goals, quantification, and paperwork. Managers also complained that goal-setting was not tied to the reward system.

935. Joe D. Batten, *Beyond Management by Objectives* (New York: American Management Association, 1966).

Before long, the answer most often offered as to why empirical results were sometimes disappointing was that MBO has to be implemented completely and sincerely, or it will not work. Batten, using the brusk style of his earlier *Tough-Minded Management* (New York: American Management Association, 1963), suggested that establishing goals and objectives is only 30% of the task. The technique also has to be used to integrate the minds of the managers with the other corporate resources, or frustration will occur.

936. George S. Odiorne, *Management by Objectives* (New York: Pitman Publishing Co., 1965); also

937. John W. Humble, *Management by Objectives* (London: Industrial Education and Research Foundation, 1967); also *Management by Objectives in Action* (London: McGraw-Hill, 1970); also

938. Anthony P. Raia, *Managing by Objectives* (Glenview, IL: Scott Foresman and Co., 1974).

As already mentioned, Drucker's pivotal role in developing the vocabulary of MBO was not widely acknowledged in the early literature. Beginning in the mid-1960s, however, public awareness of his contribution was greatly expanded by these three popular proponents of the technique. Odiorne saw MBO as having responded to the kinds of crises that had come from "management by pressure" in the Korean War. "Management by Objectives, first used by Peter Drucker in his *Practice of Management* (1954), has since become fairly well known." (p. viii) Humble, a management consultant who credited both Drucker and McGregor with the basic concepts, saw the technique as a method of integrating managers' growth needs with those of the company. Raia's book was focused heavily on the mechanics of implementing MBO. It also contained an annotated bibliography on the subject that far exceeds the scope of this one.

939.   Judith F. Bryan and Edwin A. Locke, "Goal Setting as a Means of Increasing Motivation," *Journal of Applied Psychology*, 51, (1967): 274-77; also

940.   Edwin A. Locke, "Toward a Theory of Task Performance and Incentives," *Organizational Behavior and Human Performance*, 3, (1968): 157-89.

The psychological research on goal setting dates back to the 1920s, although much of the early research was not relevant to an organizational setting. Once MBO was developed, however, some of the studies lent empirical support for the new device. Bryan and Locke found that by the end of a second experimental task, a group with low levels of motivation, but that was given a specific goal, was performing as well as a high motivation group that had been told to do the best they could. The low motivation group also developed an equally high attitude toward the task.

The study that generated by far the most attention and efforts at validation, however, was Locke's 1968 article. In it, he offered the two hypotheses that hard goals, if accepted, lead to higher task performance levels than easy goals. Secondly, specific hard goals lead to higher performance than general or "do your best" goals, or no goals at all. For validation studies of Locke's theories, see Latham and Yukl (1975) later in this section.

941.   Walter S. Wikstrom, *Managing By--and With--Objectives* [Studies in Personnel Policy No. 212] (New York: National Industrial Conference Board, 1968).

This popular description of the MBO technique noted the variety of forms that it took in the five major companies being studied. More importantly, however, Wikstrom differentiated the appraisal aspects of MBO, tied to previous performance, from the forwardly-focused planning, organizing, motivating, and controlling aspects of the device. Each facet of MBO has limits and contributions that it can make to organizations.

942. Henry L. Tosi and Stephen J. Carroll, Jr., "Managerial Reaction to Management by Objectives," *Academy of Management Journal*, 11, (December 1968): 415-26; also

943. Stephen J. Carroll, Jr. and Henry L. Tosi, "Goal Characteristics and Personality Factors in a Management-by-Objectives Program," *Administrative Science Quarterly*, 15, (September 1970): 295-305; also *Management by Objectives: Applications and Research* (New York: Macmillan and Co., 1973).

Tosi and Carroll interviewed 50 managers involved in the Work Planning and Review program to arrive at a number of recommendations to increase the likelihood that MBO would be well received. In 1968, they discovered short-term enthusiasm for the plan, but also doubts as to whether the company was truly committed to it. In 1970, they emphasized the importance of clear goals, especially for certain personality types. Clear goals increased satisfaction and the sense that the goals are important.

In 1973, the authors warned that employees must be notified that expectations about their levels of participation are changing. The plan must be integrated with existing evaluation systems. By hindsight, it is also interesting how carefully the authors warned of the dangers of neglect or abuse of the system just as it was being implemented in the federal government.

944. George L. Morrisey, *Management by Objectives and Results* (Reading, MA: Addison-Wesley, 1970); also *Management by Objectives and Results in the Public Sector* (Reading, MA: Addison-Wesley, 1976).

Finding most of the literature on MBO to be too stuffy and laden with jargon, Morrisey set out to write an elementary book aimed at the experiences of first-line to mid-level managers in the private sector. The book was based around the five basic management functions of planning, organizing, staffing, directing, and controlling, with an emphasis on the first and last.

Soon, however, Morrisey found that his book had become popular among government managers who were now sometimes mandated to use MBO techniques (see Jun [1976]). Since some of the environmental problems were different in government, Morrisey produced the second book, complete with instructor's guide, workbook, and audiocassettes.

945. John M. Ivancevich, James H. Donnelly, and Herbert L. Lyon, "A Study of the Impact of Management by Objectives on Perceived Need Satisfaction," *Personnel Psychology*, 23, (Summer 1970): 139-51; also

946. John M. Ivancevich, "A Longitudinal Assessment of Management by Objectives," *Administrative Science Quarterly*, 17, (March 1972): 126-38.

Ivancevich was particularly interested in the role of change agents in implementation. In 1970, he and his colleagues studied two organizations that had adopted MBO--one through the personnel department and the other through top management. Using a questionnaire, he determined that there was more needs satisfaction among mid-level managers when top management initiated the practice. Lower-level managers complained that they were not involved. When the personnel department initiated MBO, lower-level managers complained of excess paperwork.

In 1972, he also reported that the effects of training to help in implementation were short-lived. Perceived job satisfaction went up shortly after adopting MBO, but returned to original levels within 20 months.

947. W. J. Reddin, *Effective Management by Objectives: The 3-D Method of MBO* (New York: McGraw-Hill, 1971); also

948. Harold Koontz, *Appraising Managers as Managers* (New York: McGraw-Hill, 1971); also

949. Paul Mali, *Managing By Objectives* (New York: Wiley-Interscience, 1972); also

950. Karl Albrecht, *Successful Management by Objectives* (Englewood Cliffs, NJ: Prentice Hall, 1978).

The literature on implementation techniques of MBO has remained exhaustive, often with suggestions on how to ease some of the common problems of implementation. Suggested techniques, however, show little consensus on what is wrong. Reddin worked as a change agent, and noticed that consultants spend more time taking out failed MBO plans than installing new ones. However, he still prescribed it, using team implementation of his 3-D theory described in his earlier *Managerial Effectiveness* (New York: McGraw-Hill, 1970).

Koontz also keyed his technique to his earlier *Principles of Management*, and based his suggestions on the argument that appraisal needs to be on both objectives and performance as managers.[13] Specific management principles for appraisal include planning, organizing, staffing, directing, and controlling.

Mali was one of the more successful MBO change agents, reporting that he had trained 15,000 people in 7500 companies on his five phase technique. While the technique is laid out so as to be easy to understand in training sessions, however, it offers no obvious changes from traditional practices.

Albrecht argued that the only serious problem with MBO is that it is often presented as a system or method or procedure. Instead, it is a philosophy, or a managerial behavior pattern. It works only with objective-oriented managers, objective-oriented workers, and a reward-centered environment.

951.   Arthur C. Beck, Jr. and Ellis D. Hillmar, *A Practical Approach to Organization Development Through MBO--Selected Readings* (Reading, MA: Addison-Wesley, 1972).

In 1970 (see above), Morrisey created a simple guidebook to help managers implement MBO. Beck and Hillmar compiled this book of readings to complement Morrisey's work, as well as to explain their experiences with MBO at the University of Richmond's Management Center. The result is a combination of selections from the "classics" on the subject, and explanations of the Morrisey/ Beck/Hillmar perspective on MBO, labelled Management by Objectives and Results (MOR) to emphasize the importance of proper implementation.

952.   Richard M. Steers and Lyman W. Porter, "The Role of Task-Goal Attributes in Employee Performance," *Psychological Bulletin*, 81, (July 1974): 434-52.

The authors looked at six factors of MBO: goal specificity; participation in goal setting; feedback; peer competition; goal difficulty; and goal acceptance. They concluded that only goal specificity and goal acceptance are positively related to performance, and even those depend on such situational variables as the nature of the goals, the environment, and individual differences.

953.   Gary P. Latham and Gary A. Yukl, "A Review of Research on the Application of Goal Setting in Organizations," *Academy of Management Journal*, 18, (December 1975): 824-45; also

954.   Anthony J. Mento, Robert P. Steel, and Ronald J. Karren, "A Meta-Analytic Study of the Effects of Goal Setting in Organizations," *Organizational Behavior and Human Decision Processes*, 39, (February 1987): 52-83.

Few articles have generated as many validation and follow-up studies as the one by Locke (1968) on the effects of goal setting on performance. The validation studies are too numerous to list in this work. However, these two literature reviews survey those validation studies and summarize their conclusions.

Mento, Steel, and Karren found strong support for the two central hypotheses, as well as for the positive effects of feedback with hard goals, as well as for goals set by subordinate participation over those that are assigned. This last hypothesis has generated fewer studies, and the setting (laboratory vs. the field) seems to be a moderating influence on all the hypotheses.

Latham and Yukl also found strong support for the basic hypotheses, although problems arise when the goals are interdependent or complex. Also, they found little evidence that goals mediate the effects of participation, monetary incentives, or performance feedback.

955.   Jong S. Jun, ed., "*A Symposium:* Management by Objectives in the Public Sector," *Public Administration Review*, 36 (January/ February 1976): 1-45.

In 1973, Nixon permitted earlier OMB experiments with MBO to be extended to the entire federal government. This symposium was one of the more extensive efforts to summarize government's experience at all levels with MBO. The symposium featured such "founders" as Drucker and Odiorne describing the potentials and the results of governmental efforts to implement MBO. Many of the articles maintained some optimism despite the federal experience with Malek and Ash. More specific applications to budget and policy-making were discussed in articles by McCaffrey and Newland.

956.   Dennis Daley, "Performance Appraisal and the Creation of Training and Development Expectations: A Weak Link in MBO-Based Appraisal Systems," *Review of Public Personnel Administration*, 8, (Fall 1987): 1-10.

The track record for MBO in government, however, remains spotty. Daley investigated the MBO performance appraisal system used for Iowa public employees in 1983 to find that the appraisal system neither helped managers develop training plans for employees, nor helped them get the training once the plans were developed.

CONTINUING CONCERNS

It is an established observation of physical scientists that theories tend to get complex and laden with nuances before a new theory comes along that is so simple and beautiful that it is able to replace that which came before. By that standard, leadership studies have not fared well.

Leadership theories began as simple and beautiful models of human behavior. However, the essence of contingency theory is complication, and few today challenge the need for contingency approaches to leadership. The two-pronged approach of Fiedler has yielded to the seven-factor theory of Vroom and Yetton, and then to the "improvements" of Vroom and Jago that can be contained only by a floppy disk.

There is one voice of dissent, and its simplicity is an unmistakable asset. The empirical support for Locke's goal setting theory is compelling, even if some of the moderating influences are not well understood. However, it is also an old enough theory in the literature of psychology that one could question whether it is a revolution of understanding, or an anachronism from the simpler age. If the former is the case, one must question why the average public administration reader has taken so long to appreciate it. If the latter is the case, it is not clear why the more complicated theories of modern psychological research seem to explain less data.

NOTES FOR CHAPTER FIFTEEN

1. According to one story, the Library of Congress contained no books on the subject as recently as 1896. See Cecil A. Gibb, "Leadership," in Gardner Lindzey, ed., *Handbook of Social Psychology*, vol. 2 (Reading, MA: Addison-Wesley, 1954), p. 877.

2. Frank J. Landy and Don A. Trumbo, *Psychology of Work Behavior*, 2nd ed. (Homewood, IL: Dorsey Press, 1980), has been used heavily in this chapter. The distinction is on page 427.

3. For an earlier argument that only the situation matters in effective leadership, see the entry for Mary Parker Follett in the previous chapter.

4. Coauthors include Nathan Maccoby, Gerald Gurin, and Lucretia G. Floor. This is the second part of the "Part I" listed in the title of the work cited above.

5. Coauthors include Else Frenkel-Brunswik, Daniel J. Levinson, and R. Nevitt Sanford. Those listed as collaborators include Betty Aron, Maria Hertz Levinson, and William Morrow.

6. The authors were David C. McClelland, John W. Atkinson, Russell A. Clark, and Edgar L. Lowell.

7. Henry A. Murray, *Explorations in Personality* (New York: Oxford University Press, 1938).

8. Coauthors include William Haythorn, Beatrice Shriver, and John Lanzetta.

9. The argument that there might be two types of successful leadership was implied in the Ohio State studies before 1950, and was explicitly described in Daniel Katz, N. Maccoby, and Nancy C. Morse, *Productivity, Supervision, and Morale in an Office Situation* (Detroit: The Darel Press, 1950). Fiedler's research evolved at about that same time.

10. Coauthors include Marvin D. Dunnette, Edward E. Lawler III, and Karl E. Weick, Jr.

11. Coauthors include Enzo R. Valenzi, Dana L. Farrow, and Robert J. Solomon.

12. Drucker maintained from the beginning that the technique began in DuPont and later in General Motors, and dated from the 1920s.

13. The book is keyed to page numbers in Harold Koontz and Cyril O'Donnell, *Principles of Management*, 4th ed. (New York: McGraw-Hill, 1968).

16
Staffing

BACKGROUND

Some aspects of personnel are discussed in other chapters, including its history in chapters one and two, position classification in chapter 11, and employee motivation in chapters 13 and 14. This chapter discusses four aspects of personnel that have not been included in other sections.

RISE OF THE MERIT SYSTEM

The deterioration of the American personnel system through the nineteenth century is so effectively summarized by Fish and Van Riper (see later in this section) that only the rise of the civil service movement is detailed here.

957. Thomas Jenckes, "Civil Service of the United States," House Report 8, 39th Congress, 2nd Session (January 31, 1867); also "Civil Service of the United States," House Report 47, 40th Congress, 2nd Session (May 25, 1868), 220 pp.; also

958. Dorman B. Eaton, *Civil Service in Great Britain* (New York: Harper and Brothers, 1879); also

959. Chester Arthur, "First Annual Message," in *A Compilation of the Messages and Papers of the Presidents: 1789-1897*, vol. 8, ed. by James D. Richardson (Washington, D.C.: Government Printing Office, 1897), pp. 37-65. Speech was December 6, 1881. Relevant pages are 60-63.

Much of the early literature of civil service reform was less than analytical, and is buried in countless journal articles produced by both reform leagues and the popular press (see especially *Good Government*, *Harper's Weekly*, and *Nation*). The three entries above, described in greater detail in chapter two, had an especially large impact on the eventual adoption of the merit system. To Representative Jenckes, the spoils system sapped the moral fibre of the republic, and could only be repaired by a merit system. The 1868 report also reprinted as appendices several earlier governmental studies that are now difficult to find in original form.

Eaton wrote a detailed history of British administration, arguing that the effort to reform the civil service was the most remarkable achievement of the last century. The book was also surprisingly popular in the United States, circulating in a paperback edition into the 1890s.[1] In chapter 28, Eaton compared the British changes to possible changes in the U.S. system.

After Garfield's assassination, President Arthur argued for a bottom-entry, promotion-based merit system. He was concerned that literacy alone was not sufficient as a test, and in describing moral responsibilities, he made one of the first published references to the need for government to operate according to good business principles. After elaborating on the details of his proposal, he assailed those who attacked the honesty, competence, and efficiency of the average civil servant, arguing that most were doing a good job.

960.   *Sundry Civil Appropriations Act*, 16 Stat. 514 (1871); also

961.   Lionel V. Murphy, "The First Federal Civil Service Commission: 1871-1875," *Public Personnel Review*, 3, (January, July, and October, 1942): 29-39; 218-31; 299-323.

In December 1870, President Grant asked congress for civil service legislation. While their action was not in direct response to his request, a sentence was attached to a sundry appropriations bill in 1871 that allowed the president to establish a commission with a $25,000 budget to promulgate civil service rules.

Grant took the act far more seriously than most congressmen anticipated, appointing a seven-member commission under the leadership of reformer George William Curtis, and accepting its proposed regulations in April, 1872. Congress still had much to gain from the spoils system, and withdrew funding in 1873. The commission finally collapsed in 1875. See the Murphy articles for the most detailed history available on the early commission.

962.   William E. Foster, *The Literature of Civil Service Reform in the United States* (Providence: Providence Press Co., 1881); also *The Civil Service Reform Movement* (Boston: Press of Rockwell and Churchill, 1881); also

963.   W[illiam] B. Wedgwood, *Civil Service Reform* (Portland: Stephen Berry, Printer, 1883).

The literature of civil service reform picked up significantly after the 1880 reorganization of the New York Civil Service Reform Association (CSRA), first formed in 1877. Foster was one of the more prolific contributors to the pamphlets that were distributed by the Association, and in 1881, he summarized the literature that had already been distributed. The second citation above was an answer to critics of reforms, with separate chapters proclaiming that reform was not undemocratic, unconstitutional, impractical, unbusiness-like, indefinite, unnecessary, destructive, or opposed to public sentiment. It also reprinted the 1881 version of the Pendleton bill.

The precise nature of the needed reform was still subject to debate, however. Wedgwood, who had long lobbied for a national university, objected that common-school-type examinations would "not test the business capacity of the applicant." He therefore suggested special training programs in schools, with graduates chosen by lots for terms of university instruction and public service that would expire after four years, or upon dismissal for cause.

964. Civil Service Reform Association, "Purposes of the Civil Service Reform Association: Publication #1" (New York: CSRA, 1881); also

965. National Civil Service Reform League, *Good Government*, 1-, (1881-); also *Proceedings of the Annual Meeting* (New York: National Civil Service Reform League, 1882-); also

966. Frank M. Stewart, *The National Civil Service Reform League* (Austin: University of Texas Press, 1929).

From its beginnings in 1877, the CSRA reprinted and distributed many speeches and pamphlets for others. In 1881, they and the newly formed National Civil Service Reform League (NCSRL) began distributing literature under their own labels. By 1885, this literature exploded through several local associations such as the Brooklyn Civil Service Reform Association. In that year, the Civil Service Reform Association of Maryland produced the first full newspaper, the *Civil Service Reformer*. These publications were largely repetitive except to the extent that they kept advocates informed on developments in other governmental jurisdictions.

While a few libraries retain a wide selection of the original pamphlets and papers, a more accessible modern source is Stewart's summation of the NCSRL. He included a short biography on each of the major early reformers. He described the strategies and goals of the organization, as well as the difficulties the organization had always encountered with internal governance. In short, it was perennially underfunded and understaffed for its mission. Nevertheless, in 1929, Stewart felt that it still had major contributions to make to American governance.

967. *Harper's Weekly*, 25, (July 8, 1881).

On July 2, 1881, President Garfield was shot, and he eventually died from wounds inflicted by Charles Guiteau. Once it became known that Guiteau was a disappointed office seeker, the press used this angle to exploit the tragedy by sensationalizing the depravity of the spoils system. The eulogies numbered in the thousands, although the *Harper's Weekly* special edition cited above is a useful summation, and contains several excerpts from the press at the time.

968. *Civil Service Act*, 22 Stat. 403 (1883).

The Civil Service Act, redrafted by Dorman Eaton and the NCSRL from the 1881 version (see Foster above) and sponsored by the always-cooperative but less than zealous Senator George Pendleton, authorized President Arthur to establish a Civil Service Commission (CSC), which he quickly did under director Dorman Eaton. The original coverage of the CSC was relatively small, including clerks in Washington D.C. and staffs of customs houses and post offices with more than fifty employees. The total coverage was about 14,000 employees.

Incumbents were "grandfathered in" to their old positions. Vacancies were filled through examinations from among those scoring highest. The rule of three had already evolved in limited practice, and soon fell into use, even though it did not become law until the Veterans' Preference Act (see below). In an effort by Dorman Eaton to keep the civil service dynamic, the law also left open the "back door" in that civil servants could be fired for almost any reason. See the separate section on employee protections later in this chapter.

969. Committee on Municipal Program, National Municipal League, "A Municipal Corporations Act" (New York: n.p., 1899)[2]; revised as "A Model City Charter and Municipal Home Rule As Prepared by the Committee on Municipal Program of the National Municipal League," (Philadelphia, n.p., 1916); also

970. The Committee of the National Assembly of Civil Service Commissions, "Model Civil Service Law" (Chicago: Press of Barnard and Miller, 1914); also "Minority Report of the National Assembly of Civil Service Commissions, submitted by Lewis H. Van Dusen," (n.p., 1914); also

971. J. J. Donovan, "The Civil Service Assembly: 1906-1956," *Public Personnel Review*, 17, (October 1956): 312-19.

After the passage of the federal law, most reform associations turned their attention to state and local jurisdictions where reform had not yet taken hold. The first organization to write a model law for local government was the National Municipal League, which proposed a strong mayor who could appoint civil service commissioners for indefinite terms (Article IV, Section 2). The mayor's power would be counterbalanced by a strong merit system, including the innovative proposal of removal only for written cause. In 1916, the model charter was amended to a city manager form, but with continuation of a strong merit system.

The most radical proposal for a complete merit system came in the hotly contested 1913 proposal of the National Assembly. Even civil service commissioners were to be chosen by scoring highest on competitive examinations conducted by three-person panels. The commission would control classification, salaries, tests for efficiency, and removal under written charges.

In the long run, however, the National Assembly may have had the most impact on personnel, as described by Donovan. Through two name changes, the association became the Civil Service Assembly, responsible for publishing, organizing, or helping organize the Bureau of Public Personnel Administration, seven volumes of studies with the NCSRL, and the periodicals *Public Personnel Studies* and *Public Personnel Review*.

972.   Henry Jones Ford, "The Results of Reform," *Annals of the American Academy of Political and Social Science*, 21, (March 1903): 221-37; also

973.   William D. Foulke, *Fighting the Spoilsmen: Reminiscences of the Civil Service Reform Movement* (New York: G.P. Putnam's Sons, 1919).

The early years of the CSC were politically rocky, as described in detail by both Fish and Van Riper below. For a more personal view, however, Foulke described his experiences as an active civil service reformer since 1885, and as the head of the CSC from 1901 until an illness in 1903.

With an obvious ax to grind, Foulke described President Cleveland's initiation of removals under secret charges, the "fixing" of the census in 1890, and the improvement of conditions under presidents Roosevelt and Taft.

Not all felt that the blame for civil service troubles lay at the hands of the spoilsmen, however. In addition to Roscoe Conkling and other representatives of political machines, serious political scientists such as Ford argued that politics had deteriorated into even worse passion and recklessness since reforms were initiated. Political party enthusiasm had originally evolved as a mechanism to reflect democratic will. Civil service and other reformers were destroying party power without replacing it with democratic alternatives. Once their reforms caused abuses, having no fresh ideas, they continued to call for even more unsuccessful reforms.

974.   Carl Fish, *The Civil Service and the Patronage* (Cambridge: Harvard University Press, 1904); also

975.   Howard Lee McBain, *De Witt Clinton and the Origin of the Spoils System in New York* [dissertation] (New York: Columbia University Press, 1907).

Once the civil service changes became relatively secure under Roosevelt's administration, it seemed appropriate to reflect back on the system that had been left behind. As described in chapter one, Fish recounted the evolution from rotation in office to the more insidious full-fledged spoils system. He bracketed the history into eras of efficiency (1789-1829), spoils (1829-1865), and reform (1865-present). He also noted the evolution of the reform efforts toward placement rather than protection against removal.

In New York, conventional wisdom held that Governor Clinton had introduced rampant spoils in the late eighteenth century. McBain argued that, while some of Clinton's practices were unprecedented, the true developers of New York's infamous spoils system were the Executive Council and John Jay, who succeeded Clinton.

976. Charles H. Keep, "Annual leave, sick leave, and hours of labor." December 24, 1906 (10 pp.); also "Classification of positions and gradation of salaries for employees of the Executive departments and independent establishments in Washington," January 4, 1907 (16 pp.); also "Superannuation of civil-service employees of the government [together with draft of a proposed bill providing for the payment of annuities to employees upon retirement]," February 18, 1908 (also issued as Senate Doc. No. 308, 60th Cong., 1st Sess. Serial No. 5265).

On June 2, 1905, President Theodore Roosevelt appointed a Committee on Department Methods under the leadership of Assistant Secretary of the Treasury Charles Keep.[3] While the reports of the committee were often short and enjoyed only limited circulation, they described many aspects of what would become the more sophisticated merit system of the future. They proposed regulations to standardize annual leave policies. They suggested a schedule of pay with salaries high enough to attract qualified candidates. They wanted to equalize salaries based on the work performed, and to provide enough grades for frequent promotions.

They also proposed a retirement pension system to begin at age 70, and to be financed entirely out of employee contributions. The pension would be the sum of 1.5% of the employee's salary for each year.

Other reports which were issued by the Keep Committee were not directly relevant to personnel.[4]

977. Harold Harper, "Constitutionality of Civil Service Legislation," *Political Science Quarterly*, 22, (December 1907): 630-44; also

978. Ben A. Arneson, "Constitutionality of Merit System Legislation," *American Political Science Review*, 13, (November 1919): 593-606.

In the early years, opponents of civil service restrictions challenged the new laws on constitutional grounds. However, Harper noted that the only successful challenge was to a New York law that mandated appointment for the top name on the list. Rules of three, on the other hand, did not usurp the executive power of appointment since appointment was not exclusively an executive function. In short, merit systems were legal so long as they were worded correctly. Arneson similarly concluded that the laws were on the most stable ground if enacted as a constitutional amendment, as in New York and Ohio. However, "in no case has a civil service law been held un-constitutional." (p. 606)

979.   Joint Commission on the Reclassification of Salaries, *Report*, U.S. Congress, House Doc. 686, 66th Cong., 2nd sess., (March 12, 1920); also

980.   Lewis Mayers, *The Federal Service: A Study of the System of Personnel Administration of the United States Government* (New York: D. Appleton and Co., 1922).

In 1919, congress organized a joint commission for the purpose of conducting a pay and classification study in government. The report of March 1920 outlined a set of classification standards and pay charts for government, but also went beyond its mandate to attack the current system for a lack of equal pay, for inconsistent leave, transfer, and employee welfare practices, and for a lack of leadership that could be cured through a rejuvenated, independent, centralized Civil Service Commission. They called for scientific selection, systematic training, advances and promotions based on measured efficiency, and a retirement system so that aged employees would no longer have to be brought to work, in some cases, in wheelchairs.

As a former "insider," Mayers also wrote about the shortcomings of the federal merit system. In a classic statement of the goals of merit reformers, he argued that "personnel administration may be defined as the recruitment of capable workers and their retention under conditions which will develop their maximum usefulness." (p. 173)

In government, the process was made more difficult by the intrusion of politics and the inherent lack of incentives for effective work. In particular, no start had been made (by 1922) on a meaningful classification system. Promotion and transfer policies virtually did not exist. Support for outside educational training was needed. The government had inadequate methods for awarding efficiency. Like the congressional committee, he felt that many of the solutions would lie in a centralized and neutral personnel agency, assisted by employees' committees as recommended in the congressional report.

981.   W[illiam] E. Mosher, "A Federal Personnel Policy," *Monthly Labor Review*, 11, (July 1920): 11-25.

Mosher also applauded the Commission for trying "to lay the foundation for a flexible policy that may be adapted to the changing and varied needs of different organizations." (p. 11) In particular, they were trying to decentralize personnel powers to those holding authority except for such centralized functions as grievances, equal pay, and worker cooperatives. The CSC would have extension agents in the agencies, but would be restricted on topics it could handle. Otherwise, "many fear that the Civil Service Commission, if endowed with greater power, will hamper administrative efficiency." (p. 15)

982. Ordway Tead and H. C. Metcalf, *Personnel Administration: Its Principles and Practice* (New York: McGraw Hill Book Co., 1920); also

983. Ordway Tead, *A Course in Personnel Administration: Syllabus and Questions* (New York: Columbia University Press, 1923); also

984. Arthur W. Proctor, *Principles of Public Personnel Administration* (New York: D. Appleton and Co., 1921).

With the strength of the merit system growing, what could reasonably be labelled the first full textbooks on industrial and public personnel administration were published. Tead and Metcalf described the operations of the ideal personnel department, employment methods, health and safety concerns, motivation, union relations, and administrative coordination. By 1923, the field exploded with numerous textbooks, listed in Rossi and Rossi below. However, the most detailed was probably Tead's, which successfully melded personnel concerns with industrial psychology and scientific management.

In the public sector, Proctor's work did not generate as much attention since there were few university courses in which it could be used. It is now all but forgotten, and Mosher and Kingsley are usually considered to have published the first public personnel textbook 15 years later.[5] Proctor's book discussed the basic structures and practices of personnel, and complained that "the present state of public employment in the national government, and in the various state and local government, is unsatisfactory to the public at large, to public employees, and to responsible administrative officers." (p. 9) He complained of high turnover and low pay. He felt that the merit system must be expanded, that the pension system must be made more serious, and that the Civil Service Commission must have a more important role in government. He also reprinted the NCSRL's draft civil service law.

985. Leonhard Felix Fuld, *Civil Service Administration* (New York: Self-published, 1921).

As merit systems became powerful enough to affect agency discretion, managers often became more skillful in avoiding them. Fuld, a former New York City Commission examiner, described the commissions as interdepartmental police forces. They were treated as outsiders by the agencies, and typical hiring agents tried all they could think of to defeat the purposes of the commissions.

986. *Classification Act of 1923*, 42 Stat. 1488; also

987. *Economy Act*, 47 Stat. 416 (1932).

The reclassification committee report described above caused considerable controversy among unions and in congress, especially with suggestions that would result in higher expenditures or a strengthened and centralized personnel authority. After more than three years of negotiation, congress finally passed the Classification Act of 1923, mandating equal pay for equal work through five pay schedules. The system of class standards and grades was established. The central authority, however, was the Personnel Classification Board, consisting of an uneasy coalition of representatives of the Civil Service Commission, the Bureau of the Budget, and the Bureau of Efficiency. In 1932, the intervening years of squabbling were put to an end when the Personnel Classification Board was abolished, and position classification was assigned to the Civil Service Commission.

988.   William H. Rossi and Diana I. P. Rossi, *Personnel Administration: A Bibliography* (Baltimore: Williams and Wilkins, 1925); also

989.   U.S. Civil Service Commission (beginning 1979 U.S. Office of Personnel Management), *Personnel Literature*, 1, (Washington, D.C.: USGPO, 1941-).

Personnel is the subfield of both Public Administration and Business Management that has probably generated the most exhaustive coverage by bibliographies. An early and particularly complete description of generic personnel is this massive compilation by Rossi and Rossi in 1925. The monthly listing of international literature in *Personnel Literature* is probably the most complete public sector source. Both sources subdivide the literature by topics.

990.   "The Personnel Problem in the Public Service," *Public Personnel Studies*, 4, (January 1926): 1-44; also

991.   Bureau of Public Personnel Administration, *The Merit System in Government: Report of the Conference Committee on the Merit System* (New York: National Municipal League, 1926).

Beginning in the 1880s, reform associations drafted laws that were occasionally adopted in various levels of government. In the 1920s, representatives of the National Municipal League, Governmental Research Conference, National Civil Service Reform League, National Assembly of Civil Service Commissions, and Bureau of Public Personnel Administration joined together to advocate a joint draft civil service law. However, their product showed little consensus. The law included a choice of six different structures for the central personnel agency, and the jurisdiction's choice could be plugged into the draft law at the appropriate places.

992.   Fred Telford, "Needed Personnel Legislation, Federal and Local," *Public Personnel Studies*, 5, (June 1927): 106-10; also

993.   "Some Trends in Public Personnel Administration," *Public Personnel Studies*, 7, (November 1929): 150-58.

These two articles in the short-lived journal of the Bureau of Public Personnel Administration reflected the common theme of merit system advocates that the flaws in the system came from neglect and underfunding.[6] Telford felt that at least $10,000 per year was needed for centralized personnel work, a figure that smaller jurisdictions could not afford. The 1929 summary described the aggressive efforts of personnel departments to compete for resources with agencies holding higher esteem in the political system.

994.   Darrell Hevenor Smith, *The United States Civil Service Commission*, Institute for Government Research Service Monograph #49 (Baltimore: Johns Hopkins Press, 1928); also

995.   U.S. Civil Service Commission, *A Brief History of the United States Civil Service* (Washington, D.C.: USGPO, 1933); also *A History of the Federal Civil Service 1789-1939* (Washington, D.C.: USGPO, 1939).

Histories have been a part of civil service literature since the 1820s, when most of the experience was European. These studies, however, marked the beginning of the self-aware historical study of the Civil Service Commission by participants in the process. Of these three studies, the third is most detailed and has been most commonly cited by subsequent researchers. It was later updated, but never enjoyed the same prestige once secondary textbooks were able to provide a broader perspective on the same subjects.

996.   Leonard D. White, *The Civil Service in the Modern State* (Chicago: University of Chicago Press, 1930).

Self-awareness extended to the international arena. Under the auspices of the International Congress of the Administrative Sciences, White described the civil service systems of many of the modern world's states. While he made no recommendations for specific countries, he reprinted excerpts from the significant laws and studies conducted within those countries.

997.   A[delbert] Bower Sageser, *The First Two Decades of the Pendleton Act: A Study of Civil Service Reform*, University Studies Vols. 34-35 (Lincoln: University of Nebraska Press, 1934-1935); also thesis version (Lincoln: University of Nebraska Press, 1935).

Using mainly CSC library materials, Sageser argued that spoils had been a triumph of democracy, but began to suffocate as the offices expanded to meet the demands of office seekers. The merit system began to grow in earnest in Cleveland's second term, and withstood serious challenges in the Bryan-McKinley race. After twenty years, the major progress was in the quality of clerks, and in their protections against political abuse.

998.   International City Management Association, *Municipal Personnel Administration* (Chicago: ICMA, 1935).

In 1934, the Institute for Training in Municipal Administration was established in ICMA to conduct correspondence courses for practitioners. The personnel booklet, restricted until 1941 to those taking the course, was specifically designed to discuss the mechanics and day-to-day operations of personnel to the exclusion of trends, experiments, and the broader political contexts of personnel. By the third and fourth editions (1942, 1947), however, the text devoted considerable attention to Brownlow's (see in next section) suggestions for personnel's role in administrative management.

999.   Herbert S. Hollander, *Spoils!* (Washington, D.C.: William Ullman, 1936).

As is described in the next section, political responsiveness was repopularized in the 1930s under the general title of personnel management. Opponents of the Roosevelt Administration often focused their attacks on the disregard for the merit system that Roosevelt often showed in creating agencies outside the merit system. As Hollander warned, "the free rein given the spoilsmen during the Administration of President Franklin D. Roosevelt has reached the proportions of a national scandal." (p. 21) Hollander described why the merit system was a good idea, why the advocates of spoils were wrong, and what Roosevelt had done to subvert the system.

1000.   *Hatch Acts*, 53 Stat. 1147 (1939); amended by 54 Stat. 767 (1940).

In response to some of these concerns, and to the investigations of the Sheppard Committee in 1938, The Hatch Acts approached the issue of political control directly by prohibiting most political activities by public employees. The original Act of 1939 extended the restrictions that already applied to classified positions (by civil service rules since 1907) to unclassified positions as well. It also tightened the definitions of the restricted political activities in which non-policy-making government employees could not engage. Employees were not to interfere with elections or attempt to affect their results. The Civil Service Commission was responsible for defining which specific activities were prohibited.

The 1940 amendments extended coverage to any state or local employees paid in part or in whole from federal funds. It also clarified that dismissal was the penalty for violating the provisions of the Act.

1001. *Ramspeck Act*, 54 Stat. 1211 (1940).

The Ramspeck Act corrected a past practice of having regulations apply to large offices and headquarters only. The act included 200,000 field officers and unskilled laborers under civil service provisions. Incumbents were required to pass minimum competency examinations. Agencies were also required to set up appeals boards with Civil Service Commission participation to hear appeals of efficiency ratings.

1002.   President's Committee on Civil Service Improvement, *Report*, House Doc. 118, 77th Cong., 1st sess. (1941); also

1003.   Gordon R. Clapp, "The Rule of Three, It Puzzles Me," *Public Administration Review*, 1, (Spring 1941): 287-93.

The Committee on Civil Service Improvement, established by President Roosevelt, advocated the extension of civil service laws, rules, and regulations to the professional, technical, scientific, and higher administrative personnel (except for policy-making positions). It also advocated an expansion of the technical and professional services, as well as the addition of civil service examiners to handle the load. Ultimately, it envisioned an expansion to investigative positions as well. The report recognized that these expansions would entail a need for more training for public servants.

In his review of the Committee report, Clapp was confused by the proposals. "It seems clear, however, that the merit system school of thought has won the day. The big argument now is what are they going to do with the victory!" (p. 289) While the development of professionalism in the higher civil service was to be applauded, Clapp was particularly concerned that the rule of three would block administrative discretion in an area in which the precise measurement of qualifications was not practical.

1004.   J. J. Donavan, "The Classification of Subject Matter Dealing with Public Personnel Administration," *Public Personnel Review*, 2, (January 1941): 36-59.

The explosion in the quantity of personnel literature left some practitioners concerned that traditional library cataloguing systems were unable to differentiate its many aspects. Donavan offered a cataloguing system for libraries subdivided by topics, and leaving room for future topics.

1005. *Veterans' Preference Act of 1944*, 58 Stat. 387; also

1006. U.S. Civil Service Commission, 58 Stat. 390 (1944).

The Veterans' Preference Act, implemented and further defined through the CSC regulations listed above, served several housekeeping as well as new purposes. It enacted the long-practiced rule of three. It mandated that educational requirements for positions could be no higher than those actually required by the job. It also legislated veterans' preference, which had been practiced in various forms since Washington's Administration. Stated simply, honorably discharged veterans would receive a five-point bonus on assembled test scores; disabled veterans would receive a ten-point bonus.

1007.　　Donald H. Davenport, Charles D. Stewart, and Hugh B. Killough, "Impact of War Upon Employment," *Public Personnel Review*, 5, (July 1944): 140-45; also

1008.　　Leonard D. White, ed., *Civil Service in Wartime* (Chicago: University of Chicago Press, 1945); also

1009.　　Frances T. Cahn, *Federal Employees in War and Peace: Selection, Placement, and Removal* (Washington, D.C.: The Brookings Institution, 1949); also

1010.　　Gladys M. Kammerer, *Impact of War on Federal Personnel Administration, 1939-1945* (Lexington: University of Kentucky Press, 1951).

The 1944 article first sensitized the field to the enormous interindustry shifts that would occur after the Second World War. White noted that the size of the civilian government workforce had quadrupled, and retrenchment seemed inevitable. Classification standards had deteriorated during the expansion. Other authors in White's reader noted that the recruitment of outside talent had been excellent.

Cahn also described the decentralization of classification, the increased recruitment and flexible eligibility requirements that had allowed the rapid buildup of technical expertise in government, and the lack of provisions for demobilization, resulting in morale problems after the war. Similarly, Kammerer applauded the survival of the merit system through active recruitment and looser employment standards, increased training, the development of mechanisms to improve employee relations, and a strengthened role for personnel administration. Weaknesses included poor promotion and transfer policies, a rigid classification/compensation schedule, an inability to control governmental growth, and general incompetence in handling control of subversive applicants.

1011.　　Paul Pigors and Charles A. Meyers, *Personnel Administration: A Point of View and a Method* (New York: McGraw-Hill Book Co., 1947); also

1012.　　Wallace S. Sayre, "The Triumph of Techniques over Purpose," *Public Administration Review*, 8, (Spring 1948): 134-37.

To increasing numbers of people, however, personnel had fallen into a trap from which escape required something more substantive than a change in procedures. The moderate approach was taken by Pigors and Meyers who, writing in the context of private-sector personnel, attempted to substitute the purposes of the human relations movement into the growing proceduralism of personnel. They suggested that technical and human elements needed to be integrated through set principles to arrive at useful techniques for managing the workforce. They also used numerous case studies to help illustrate their points.

Sayre used his book review of Pigors and Meyers to attack any hope that human relations could operate through the techniques that 1) were usually inadequate for their purposes, even though their accomplishments were eventually taken for granted; 2) were frozen into regulations for universal applications, stifling research; and 3) gradually obscured the ends they were designed to serve. Moving beyond the book review, Sayre also saw little promise in the decentralization movement then in progress, since that merely changed who made decisions under burdensome regulations.

1013.   *Classification Act of 1949*, 63 Stat. 971.

As described earlier, many difficulties with the overly complex structure of the personnel process in general, and the classification machinery in particular, were uncovered during the War. In an effort to respond, the Classification Act of 1923 was replaced in 1949 by a new piece of legislation that consolidated the five pay schedules into two. To decentralize local decisions, the classification process was also formally divided into two stages. The job classification standards, or rules by which classification decisions were to be made, remained with the CSC. However, most individual position classification decisions were delegated to the agencies under the supervision of the CSC. In addition, the Act addressed the problem of pay ceilings for the highest level executives by creating the three "supergrade" levels of GS-16, 17, and 18.

1014.   Paul Van Riper, *History of the United States Civil Service* (Evanston, IL: Row, Peterson and Co., 1958); also

1015.   Ari A. Hoogenboom, *Outlawing the Spoils: A History of the Civil Service Reform Movement: 1865-1883* [dissertation] (New York: Columbia University, 1958); also trade edition (Urbana: University of Illinois Press, 1961); also

1016.   Frederick Mosher, *Democracy and the Public Service* (New York: Oxford University Press, 1968); also

1017.   Richard E. Titlow, *Americans Import Merit: Origins of the United States Civil Service and the Influence of the British Model* (Washington, D.C.: University Press of America, 1979).

The series of superb public personnel histories, begun by Eaton and Fish, continued with Leonard White's works described in chapter one, and in these efforts. Van Riper's book, which brought the histories up to the 1950s, noted that personnel has undergone fundamental crises (1828, 1883, and to a lesser degree 1958) when its representativeness has been called into question.

Hoogenboom and Titlow concentrated on the period leading to the Pendleton Act, with Hoogenboom arguing that it was not a case of government being lobbied by a business-like reform movement. Instead, the conflict could be seen as a contest between the "Ins" and the "Outs" for control of the resources of public personnel.

Titlow described the systems that were developed early in China, Prussia, and France. The majority of the book, however, documented the degree to which our system was borrowed from the British, and the degree to which that influence began to fade once the uniquely American version of merit was established.

Mosher, in chapter three, divided the personnel movements into a series of historical periods marked by different "ideals" proposed by their advocates. These included Government by Gentlemen (1789-1828); Government by the Common Man (1828-1883); Government by the Good (1883-1906); Government by the Efficient (1906-1937); Government by Administrators (1937-1955); and Government by Professionals (1955-date).

1018.   *Postal Service and Federal Employees Salary Act of 1962*, 76 Stat. 832; also

1019.   *Pay Comparability Act of 1970*, 84 Stat. 1946.

One difficulty with the federal merit system was that, by conventional wisdom, federal salaries lagged behind those of workers doing comparable work in the private sector. In 1962, congress legislated comparability for federal white-collar workers. To help administer the process, in 1970, the responsibility for complying with comparability switched from congress to the presidency. The president was given two advisory bodies--the Federal Employee's Pay Council, comprised of employee organizations; and the Advisory Committee on Federal Pay, comprised of public representatives. The president published proposed pay scales in the Federal Register, and either house of congress could veto the proposal within 30 days.

1020.   Donald R. Harvey, *The Civil Service Commission* (New York: Praeger Publishers, 1970).

This book, written by a staff member of the CSC, was perhaps the last to express basic optimism on the ability of the Commission to adjust to future needs. It described the historical ability of the agency to take on new functions by having congress add them to its existing responsibilities. Harvey saw a slow shift in personnel functions, but felt the agency was at the lead in such changes.

1021.   Martin and Susan Tolchin, *To the Victor...* (New York: Random House, 1971); also

1022.   Robert Vaughn, *The Spoiled System: A Call for Civil Service Reform* (New York: Charterhouse, 1975); also

1023.   Jay M. Shafritz, *Public Personnel Management: The Heritage of Civil Service Reform* (New York: Praeger Publishers, 1975).

On the eve of the creation of the Campbell Commission leading to the Civil Service Reform Act, the literature on the state of the merit system continued to reflect a basic discontent with the entire system. The Tolchins documented the continued operation of the patronage system in each branch and at each level of government. They accepted the inevitability of patronage, and advocated the widest possible recruitment from society into the two-party system to compete for political resources.

Vaughn's study, reflecting its original attachment to Ralph Nader's Public Interest Research Group, described the methods commonly used to subvert or otherwise foil the requirements of civil service regulations. The report also contained an attack on the implementation of affirmative action programs. Interestingly, it also recommend a division of the positive and negative functions of personnel into separate agencies. The Civil Service Commission's largely indignant response was reprinted in an appendix.

In a more academic vein, Shafritz recounted previous reform movements to argue that they had been generated in response to larger political needs in American society. Similarly, the incongruities between the rhetoric of the merit system and the needs of the administration led to a personnel netherworld in which personnel officials became organizational "harlots," sacrificing their merit principles for the good of the organization. Shafritz felt that reform was inevitable if public unions continued to push personnel decisions into the public eye.

PERSONNEL MANAGEMENT

Unless one accepts the easy answer that personnel management is the set of provisions implemented in the Civil Service Reform Act (CSRA) of 1978, it is difficult to define what the term means. Some efforts at definition are included below, although the concept predates any recognition that it was different from personnel administration.

For the purposes of this review, personnel merit includes efforts at standardization, depoliticization of non-policy-making positions, and the motivation of workers through such "hygienic factors" as adequate pay, protections against arbitrary punishment, and worker safety. Personnel management is concerned with the repolitization of the workforce (as opposed to individual positions) and the development of career systems with professional rewards for managers.

1024.   "Methods of Selecting Employees to Fill High Grade Positions in the Public Service," *Public Personnel Studies*, 2, (March/ April 1924): 13-58; also

1025.   "Editorials," *Public Personnel Studies*, 2, (July 1924): 103-04.

Much of the difficulty in identifying the beginning of the personnel management movement is that many of its primary concerns were expressed by the founders
of the merit movement, with no sense that they were advocating inconsistent policies.
By the 1920s, however, the argument began to emerge that excessively structured
merit might be the problem, and that a broader management perspective might be the
solution. Such an argument appeared in Proctor (1921) described in the previous
section.

In 1924, the editors of *Public Personnel Studies* showed a flexibility inconsistent
with modern stereotypes of them by arguing that it was an open question whether
high-level executives should be selected by exams, and whether such exams should be
assembled or unassembled. In the July issue, they came more to the point. "In the
public service, for example, there is a tendency to regard examinations as the be-all
and end-all, and all other forms of personnel work as more or less in the nature of
frills. In industry, on the other hand, the attack on personnel problems is practically
always made from the other direction--so much so that many private employment
managers vehemently deny that they do or should give tests designed to select employees." (p. 104) They argued that if this structural emphasis was not changed, the
agencies would leave personnel experts behind.

1026.   Joseph Bush Kingsbury, "The Merit System in Chicago From 1895 to 1915:
Part 4," *Public Personnel Studies*, 4, (June 1926): 178-84.

Early reformers often reported that they were making some progress toward
more responsive personnel systems. In Part four of his history of the Chicago system, Kingsbury noted that the personnel agency switched from a negative to a positive role in the 1907-1911 period. At first, the change was to "rounded personnel
policies." Then an efficiency division was added in 1911 (with a broader focus than
at the federal level) to help the Finance Committee analyze the personnel implications
of budgetary planning.

1027.   Oliver C. Short, *The Merit System: A Monograph* (Baltimore: n.p., 1928); also
"Public Personnel Agencies," *Annals of the American Academy of Political and
Social Science*, 189, (January 1937): 104-10; also

1028.   Leonard D. White, *Trends in Public Administration* (New York: McGraw-Hill
Book Co., 1933).

Another aspect of the literature that was concerned with the political role of
government personnel related to the structure of central personnel authorities. Oliver
Short was Employment Commissioner when the State of Maryland adopted the first
politically-appointed single-headed Department of Personnel in 1920, as he described
in 1928. By 1937, however, he was convinced that neither the structure nor the

method of appointment was as important as putting the personnel agency on a par with other agency heads, and designing its powers so that it did not take discretion away from agency managers. He attacked the narrow focus of personnel officers, claiming their role was to coordinate and guide.

In chapter 18, "Trends in Personnel Management," White noted that a number of states were moving toward personnel agencies with single heads, despite the prevalent recommendations of such reform organizations as the Governmental Research Conference (1922) and National Municipal League (1923) that they should not only retain commissions, but should staff them by competitive tests.

1029.   Herman Feldman, *A Personnel Program for the Federal Civil Service*, House Doc. 773, 71st Cong., 3rd sess., (February 16, 1931).

The Welch Act of 1928 required the Personnel Classification Board to survey and report to congress on the federal government's wage policies. Feldman, reporting for the Board, said that government had no wage policy. It appropriated on a lump-sum basis, and distributed salaries through the Classification Act of 1923, which he described as a compensation schedule into which classification had been fitted. The function needed to be assigned to a central personnel authority, and made similar to the Budgeting and Accounting Act in its ability to coordinate policies and influence the president and the cabinet.

1030.   Commission of Inquiry on Public Service Personnel, *Better Government Personnel* (New York: McGraw-Hill Book Co., 1935); also

1031.   Luther Gulick, "Toward a Municipal Career Service," *Public Management*, 17, (November 1935): 331-33.

Soon, the calls for career systems also began to sound more modern. The Commission was concerned that government did not offer administrators a fair chance comparable to the private sector for a lifetime of honorable work. They should develop a career system for all who were not policy-makers, judges, or military personnel. There should be active recruitment and promotion, coordinated by active personnel offices within agencies. In fact, the new professional system should extend to state and local administrators receiving federal funds.

Gulick was even more adamant. "With its present tasks American democracy will not be fit to survive if it continues to pursue its past notorious personnel policies." (p. 333) He suggested that we "pick 'em young" and "tell 'em everything" so that solidarity and professionalism could grow in the evolving career service.

1032.   William E. Mosher and J. Donald Kingsley, *Public Personnel Administration* (New York: Harper and Brothers, 1936); later editions added O[scar] Glenn Stahl as co-author. Beginning with the fourth edition (1956), Stahl was listed as the sole author.

While this was not the first textbook on public personnel administration in the United States, it is commonly accepted as such, and it has been the most influential text in the field since its publication. It was also surprisingly advanced in its first edition in its "personnel management" approach to the subject, even if it credited others. "The basic philosophy of personnel administration as an integral part of administration as well as of the factors entering into it, are to be credited to Henry C. Metcalf and Ordway Tead, authors of *Personnel Management*." (1936, p. ix).

The problems listed on pp. 41-53 (1936) melded the concerns of merit reformers and personnel management, including low prestige, neglect of personnel by the executive, a shifting body of department heads, lack of tenure, the external position of the CSC, bureaucratic behavior, political interference, and absence of common motives. Nevertheless, the Introduction to the second edition (1941) offered that "perhaps the most significant phase of this forward movement is the wide-spread acceptance of the Civil Service Commission as a personnel agency rather than an organization set up to ward off the politician." (p. ix) The authors also reported more contact between personnel authorities and other staff and line executives.

1033.   Floyd W. Reeves and Paul T. David, *Personnel Administration in the Federal Service* (Washington, D.C.: USGPO, 1937).

The best-known call for personnel management, however, was this staff report of the Brownlow Committee (President's Committee on Administrative Management). The authors cited the negative focus of federal personnel machinery, and argued that it needed to improve its handling of such functions as transfers, promotions, centralized information, training, employee relations, and interchanges of personnel. To do so, they advocated that the CSC be replaced by a Civil Service Administration, with the presidentially-appointed single head responsible for both control and assistance.

1034.   Lewis Meriam, "Personnel Administration in the Federal Government," Pamphlet Series No. 19 (Washington, D.C.: Brookings Institution, 1937); also *Public Personnel Problems From the Standpoint of the Operating Officer* (Washington, D.C.: Brookings Institution, 1938).

Speaking for the Brookings Institution, Meriam tried to present the academic case against the proposals of the Brownlow Committee. He felt that personnel involved too many functions to be centralized in one personnel authority. Many functions, especially positive ones, belonged in operating agencies. Centralized intervention would lead to confusion and inefficiency. Central authority was appropriate for defining which positions were political, classifying positions, selecting eligible candidates, investigating removals, standardizing salaries, and administering retirement. For these functions, however, boards were better able than single executives to deliberate policies, adjudicate appeals, and discourage congressional tampering.

1035. Public Administration Service, *Personnel Administration and Procedure*, Publication No. 61 (Chicago: Public Administration Service, 1938); also *Personnel Programs for Smaller Cities*, Publication No. 73 (Chicago: Public Administration Service, 1940); also *Merit System Installation*, Publication No. 77 (Chicago: Public Administration Service, 1941).

At the state and local levels, there seemed to be little question about the need for personnel responsiveness to political needs. In 1938, the Public Administration Service described an Indiana law in which agency heads were placed on a Joint Committee on Personnel Administration, with a separate Director for administrative duties. In 1940, a pilot project of the Municipal League in Michigan called for a "merit system" as opposed to the older negative "civil service system." They argued that any personnel agency must have cooperative contacts with political authorities. The 1941 implementation manual assumed that jurisdictions would have a politically-dominated board with a director for implementation of policies.

1036. Franklin D. Roosevelt, Executive Orders 7915, 7916 (June 24, 1938); also Executive Order 8248 (September 8, 1939).

Despite congressional opposition on some of the major proposals of the Brownlow report, President Roosevelt proceeded to implement personnel management to the extent that he could. The 1938 executive orders extended the competitive service to the limits allowed by legislation. They modernized civil service rules, and required that a division of personnel supervision and management be established in each department or agency. Executive Order 7916 also reorganized the Council of Personnel Administration, and placed the CSC in charge of training. In 1939, Roosevelt created a Liaison Officer for Personnel Management on the White House staff.

1037. Henry F. Hubbard, "The Elements of a Comprehensive Personnel Program," *Public Personnel Review*, 1, (July 1940): 1-17; also

1038. Civil Service Assembly, *Recruiting Applicants for the Public Service* (Chicago: Civil Service Assembly, 1942).

Of course, personnel management was more than political responsiveness. Writing for the Civil Service Assembly (previously the National Assembly of Civil Service Commissions), Hubbard warned that "public personnel administration must be broadened in scope and its emphasis shifted from a negative police approach to a positive service philosophy." (p. 1) In addition to regulatory functions, personnel must include recruitment, training, employee relations, counseling, personnel research, and integration with line departments.

Reversing its earlier extreme view of nonpolitical merit-based personnel, the Civil Service Assembly completely changed its focus in its 1942 report. "Because the Civil Service Commission was primarily conceived as an instrument for checking some of the graver abuses of a system of party spoils, its historical emphasis has been negative." (p. 4) "But the most crying governmental need in America today is for the establishment of career systems in the public service." (p. 9) Positive recruitment required an active search for the best through centralized personnel offices.

1039.   John McDiarmid, "The Changing Role of the U.S. Civil Service Commission," *American Political Science Review*, 40, (December 1946): 1067-96.

McDiarmid described the way in which the CSC, which had recently been only the central examining agency, had become the central personnel agency of the federal government. Within the agencies, there were still disagreements over whether the CSC's function was service or control, and the situation was not helped by the patch-work pattern of legislation. However, ties with the presidency were closer than ever.

1040.   William V. Holloway, *Personnel Administration in the States*, Constitutional Studies #6 (Oklahoma City: Oklahoma State Legislative Council, 1948); also

1041.   William G. Torpey, *Public Personnel Management* (New York: D. Van Nostrand Company, 1953).

Holloway noticed that the same switch from negative to positive personnel had been occurring in the states since the 1920s. The emphasis was now on recruiting, retaining, promoting the best qualified, and dismissing the inefficient. Practices lagged behind philosophy, however, in that salaries, examinations, recruitment, tenure, and retirement systems were still inadequate.

Torpey was concerned that some personnel offices created problems because they had a limited concept of progressive personnel management. He also complained that responsibilities were sometimes unclear, and there was inconsistency and a lack of training in the field offices. Procedures were often cumbersome, and there was little contact with top management or with employees.

1042.   Commission on Organization of the Executive Branch of the Government, *Task Force Report on Federal Personnel* (Washington, D.C.: USGPO, 1949); also *Personnel Management* (Washington, D.C.: USGPO, 1949).

Spurred by the administrative confusion following the Second World War, the First Hoover Commission reports included one staff study and one full Commission report on federal personnel. Both emphasized the executive staff role of personnel, and the need to deemphasize burdensome procedures at both agency and CSC levels. Both reports placed most of the blame on overlapping and often contradictory legislation. The Task Force was also concerned about the lack of attention given to the development of a career service in government. The 29 recommendations in the final report included a decentralization of many procedures, including position classification, and a strengthening for the executive role of the CSC.

1043.   William Seal Carpenter, *The Unfinished Business of Civil Service Reform*
(Princeton, NJ: Princeton University Press, 1952).

Based on his experience in the New Jersey personnel system, Carpenter was
convinced that the president needed more power to control the use of personnel, at
least partially to restrict and define government's functions. The president needed
staff assistance on personnel, not a technician in the White House as would have been
created by the Brownlow Committee recommendations. He also felt that collective
bargaining arrangements with government employees needed to be codified with arbitration of grievances.

1044.   Commission on the Organization of the Executive Branch of the Government,
Task Force Report on Personnel and Civil Service (Washington, D.C.: USGPO,
1955); also *Personnel and Civil Service: A Report to the Congress* (Washington,
D.C.: USGPO, 1955).

The revival of the Hoover Commission (with five original members) in 1955
repeated many of the same concerns about lack of incentives for career service and
civil service prestige. Its 19 final recommendations, however, placed most of their
emphasis on the isolation of high-level non-policy executives into a Senior Civil
Service of 1500-3000 career executives holding rank in person, and entitled to extra
pay and benefits. Task Force concerns about security excesses and dual roles for the
CSC Chairman were ignored by the final Commission report.

1045.   John W. Macy, Jr., *Public Service: The Human Side of Government* (New York:
Harper and Row, 1971).

As personnel advisor to Presidents Kennedy and Johnson, Macy described
competing claims on the merit system by the president, various interest groups, public
unions, and the workers themselves. He concluded that the merit system will remain
healthy only if it is responsive to many of these demands, and that the public must
recognize the human needs of the public service.

1046.   The President's Reorganization Project, *Personnel Management Project*, 3 vol.
(Washington, D.C.: USGPO, December 1977); also

1047.   Alan K. Campbell, "Civil Service Reform: A New Commitment," *Public
Administration Review*, 38, (March/April 1978): 99-103; also

1048.   *Civil Service Reform Act of 1978*, 92 Stat. 1111; also

1049.   Alan K. Campbell, "The Politics and Substance of Civil Service Reform,"
[speech at University of Louisville] (n.c. [Louisville, Ky.]: n.p. [University of
Louisville], n.d. [1979]).

During his 1976 presidential campaign, Jimmy Carter promised to reform the civil service so as to return merit and accountability to the system. On being elected, he appointed a committee under the leadership of Alan Campbell, Chair of the CSC. The Commission with its nine task forces made 125 recommendations that became the basis for the Civil Service Reform Act of 1978.

The Act is too large and has had too much impact to be reviewed adequately here. Among the points emphasized by Campbell as he lobbied for the legislation are the division of CSC responsibilities into an Office of Personnel Management (OPM) and Merit Systems Protection Board (MSPB). Other major provisions include the Senior Executive Service (SES), the Federal Labor Relations Authority (FLRA), the merit pay system for senior-level employees, and reforms in veterans' preference. The veterans provisions were substantially amended before final passage, however.

1050.   Committee for Economic Development, *Revitalizing the Federal Personnel System* (New York: Committee for Economic Development, February 1978).

Endorsing the reform efforts then active in government, the Committee described the effort at revitalizing personnel as being comprised of four goals: 1) restoring managerial authority and responsibility for personnel; 2) enhancing performance; 3) creating a federal career executive service; and 4) reorganizing civil service administration.

1051.   Frederick C. Thayer, "The President's Management 'Reforms:' Theory X Triumphant," *Public Administration Review*, 38, (July/August 1978): 309-14.

Not all were enthusiastic about the proposed reforms, although few were as pessimistic as early as Frederick Thayer. He felt that the proponents of the bill "rely upon the twin concepts of competition and authoritarianism" (p. 313) in creating a system that speaks of professionalism, but bribes employees with carrots and sticks. He predicted that flexible rewards in the SES would lead to complacency by the winners, whistle-blowing by others, and embittered careerism by the rest.

1052.   Lloyd G. Nigro, "Attitudes of Federal Employees Toward Performance Appraisal and Merit Pay: Implications for CSRA Implementation," *Public Administration Review*, 41, (January/February 1981): 84-86; also "CSRA Performance Appraisal and Merit Pay: Growing Uncertainty in the Federal Work Force," *Public Administration Review*, 42, (July/August 1982): 371-75; also

1053.   Bruce Buchanan, "The Senior Executive Service: How Can We Tell If It Works?" *Public Administration Review*, 41, (May/ June 1981): 349-58; also

1054.   Charlotte Hurley, "Civil Service Reform: An Annotated Bibliography," *Review of Public Personnel Administration*, 2, (Summer 1982): 59-90.

Literature on the implementation of the CSRA could easily make its own chapter, and it is too specific and too voluminous to be listed here. The journals that are richest in material are the *Public Administration Review, Public Personnel Management,* and the *Review of Public Personnel Administration.* Among the earlier such works, Nigro analyzed OPM surveys of federal employees to show that they agreed with the concept of merit pay, and they were dissatisfied with the old performance appraisal systems, but they were uncertain about government's commitment to the new system. Buchanan was concerned about confusion over the purposes of the SES, and proposed four criteria against which it could be judged. For those pursuing the early evolution of the CSRA, Hurley's annotated bibliography provides a list and description of many specific aspects of the 1970s reforms.

1055.   Patricia W. Ingraham and Carolyn Ban, eds., *Legislating Bureaucratic Change: The Civil Service Reform Act of 1978* (Albany: State University of New York Press, 1984); also

1056.   Carolyn Ban and Patricia W. Ingraham, "Retaining Quality Federal Employees: Life After PACE," *Public Administration Review*, 48, (May/June 1988): 708-18.

In 1984, the editors reported on a conference on the CSRA held in Fall 1981. Participants discussed the reasons for changing the system as well as the impact it has had in selected agencies. The book concludes with an analysis of the legislative change process, including an update by Thayer on his 1978 article, an argument that change is cyclical because of shifting political coalitions, and a concern that budgetary cutbacks could cause negative outcomes.

In 1988, the authors reported on developments since the PACE examination was abandoned in the *Luevano v Devine* consent decree in 1981. They noted that affirmative action goals have been met more consistently since the decree. However, the new exams that are being developed are job specific to the extent that they no longer try to select employees based on their career potentials.

1057.   David L. Dillman, *Civil Service Reform: An Annotated Bibliography* (New York: Garland Publishing Co., 1987).

Literature on the implications of the Civil Service Reform Act has understandably been massive. In his annotated bibliography, Dillman described the literature that led up to reform and that has analyzed its results since 1978. The selection of reviewed literature is quite extensive.

EMPLOYEE PROTECTIONS

The third topic of the section is the protection of employees against arbitrary abuse.

1058.   *McAuliffe v New Bedford*, 155 Mass. 216, 220 (1892).

The Civil Service Act gave no job protections or guarantees of due process or appeals in firings except for very limited circumstances. In reform jargon, it was known as the "open back door" designed to keep the civil service dynamic and responsive. In legal parlance, it was the doctrine of privilege. As Justice Holmes described in a case of a policeman fired for holding the wrong political beliefs, "the petitioner may have a constitutional right to talk politics, but he has no constitutional right to be a policeman."

1059.   U.S. Civil Service Commission, *Fourteenth Report: 1896-1897* (Washington, D.C.: USGPO, 1897); also

1060.   *Woods v Gary, Washington Law Reporter*, 25, (1897): 591.

Soon after passage of the Pendleton Act, it became obvious that arbitrary dismissals were continuing, and perhaps even getting worse. The first assault on the open back door came with McKinley's executive order, issued as a civil service regulation in 1897. It stated that dismissals would be only for just cause, and would be accompanied by written charges filed with department head. The accused must be given notice and the right to defend himself. In *Woods v Gary*, however, the courts established that enforcement was solely by the executive, and not by the courts.

1061.   *Lloyd-LaFollette Act*, 37 Stat. 413 (1912).

As part of this sweeping legislation in 1912, congress reaffirmed in legislation that dismissals would be "only for such cause as will promote the efficiency of said service and for reasons given in writing." Like the McKinley order, however, while the accused had to be permitted to respond, no formal hearing was required.

1062.   Herman Feldman, *A Personnel Program for the Federal Civil Service*, House Doc. 773, 71st Cong., 3rd sess., (February 16, 1931).

This report for the Personnel Classification Board in response to Welch Act of 1928 was primarily concerned with issues of classification and wage policies. However, it also noted that the appeals authority was too far removed from first-line supervisors, discouraging supervisors from exercising proper authority. Powerful personnel offices were needed to deal with grievances and appeals in government, and to provide a constructive outlet for union participation.

1063.   Franklin D. Roosevelt, Executive Order 7916 (June 24, 1938).

In section 6 of this executive order described in the previous section, each department was required to establish a personnel department which included some mechanism for hearing grievances and sending recommendations for settlement to the head of department.

1064.   *Veterans' Preference Act of 1944*, 58 Stat. 387.

Until 1944, responsibility for discipline and removals remained largely with the agency. The Veterans' Preference Act, however, added to the Lloyd-LaFollette Act by requiring that the CSC investigate the sufficiency of reasons given by the removing official. In 1947, the Act was amended to make it mandatory that the corrective actions recommended by the CSC be implemented.

1065.   *Bailey v Richardson*, 182 F2d 46 (1950); 341 U.S. 918 (1951).

During the Red Scare days of the late 1940s and early 1950s, the impact of personnel protections once again became politically controversial. In this case of a woman fired for disloyalty based on departmental policies that allowed unnamed informants to give unsworn testimony before a "Loyalty Review Board," the court found that justice had probably been compromised. However, the dismissal stood because it did not violate the constitution to dismiss employees for political beliefs, activities, or affiliations.

1066.   *Board of Regents of State Colleges, et al. v Roth*, 408 U.S. 564 (1972); also

1067.   *Sugarman, et al. v Dougall, et al.*, 413 U.S. 634 (1973).

In these cases, the Supreme Court began to discard the notion that government employment is a privilege as opposed to a right. In *Roth*, while a professor was not guaranteed the right to be dismissed only for cause after one year, the court found the argument of right vs. privilege to be a "wooden concept" that is meaningless for constitutional issues. In *Sugarman*, a New York law restricting government jobs to citizens was negated for the same reason.

1068.   *Elrod, Sheriff, et al. v Burns, et al.*, 427 U.S. 347 (1976); also

1069.   *Branti v Finkel, et al.*, 445 U.S. 507 (1980).

In these cases, the court more tightly defined the jobs for which political affiliation was an acceptable basis for dismissal. In *Elrod*, non-civil-service Republicans were dismissed by the new Democratic Sheriff of Cook County, Illinois. The court argued that such dismissals in non-political positions unconstitutionally restricted political beliefs and associations. In *Branti*, the same argument was upheld for Republican Assistant District Attorneys dismissed by the Democratic Public Defender in Rockland County, New York.

1070.   "A Self-Inquiry into Merit Staffing, Report of the Merit Staffing Review Team," U.S. Civil Service Commission, for the House Committee on Post Office and Civil Service, Committee Print 94-14, 94th Cong., 2d Sess., June 8, 1976; also

1071.   "Final Report on Violations and Abuses of Merit Principles in Federal Employment Together with Minority Views," Subcommittee on Manpower and Civil Service of the House Committee on Post Office and Civil Service, Committee Print 94-28, 94th Cong., 2d sess., December 30, 1976.

Following the Nixon administration, the selective placement and punishment of employees for political purposes became a subject of considerable attention. One focus of that attention was the "Federal Political Personnel Manual" drafted by Frederick Malek and circulated among members of the White House staff in the early 1970s. A copy of the unpublished Malek Manual was reproduced in the *Final Report*, pp. 573-711, above. The Manual was an attempt to explain to politically untrained Republican officials that spoils still operated in the higher ranks of the bureaucracy, and that they could hire and fire for political reasons as successfully as had Kennedy and Johnson if they followed the suggestions offered in the Manual.

The 1976 investigations by a CSC review team under Milton Sharon and by the subcommittee staff documented the preferential hiring, the misuse of staff, and the weaknesses in enforcement mechanisms that led to the activities of the Watergate era.

1072.   Robert G. Vaughn, "Public Employees and the Right to Disobey," *Hastings Law Journal*, 29, (November 1977): 261-95; also "Statutory Protection of Whistleblowers in the Federal Executive Branch," *University of Illinois Law Review*, 1982, (1982): 615-67.

In the post-Watergate era, Vaughn was concerned about the lack of protection for whistleblowers in government. In *Hastings*, he argued that employees should be protected from discipline if they refuse to obey in good faith with reasonable belief that the order is unconstitutional or illegal in that it abridges the rights of employees or third parties, or exceeds the supervisor's authority. In 1982, he described the relevant portion of the CSRA, listing the conditions under which protections are afforded. While there were problems of interpretation, he was hopeful for the success of the statute.

1073.   *Civil Service Reform Act of 1978*, 92 Stat. 1111.

Among the portions of the CSRA relevant to employee protections, two are particularly relevant. First, the MSPB was created under the leadership of a board of three, removing the confusion of the dual positive and negative roles of the old CSC, and maintaining political insulation for appeals and protection of the merit system. Second, the whistleblower protections described in Vaughn (1982) above are designed to expose gross waste, mismanagement, or illegal conduct. For reviews of the success of these operations, see the previous section in this chapter.

PUBLIC UNIONISM

1074.   *Lloyd-LaFollette Act*, 37 Stat. 413 (1912).

Public unionism dates at least to the 1830s, although the experiences in the nineteenth century largely collapsed before the revival of public unionism under the Lloyd-LaFollette Act. This legislation reacted to earlier gag orders on postal employees, and specified that employees could not be dismissed or reduced in rank for belonging to postal organizations not advocating the right to strike.

1075.   Sterling D. Spero, *The Labor Movement in a Government Industry* (New York: George H. Doran Co., 1924); also *Government as Employer* (New York: Remsen Press, 1948).

Spero described the early development and then-current status of unionism in American government. In 1924, he concentrated on the postal service--the branch of the federal government with the longest continual history of strong unionism. In 1948, he expanded his coverage to unionism at all levels of government, describing such events as the Lloyd-LaFollette Act, the Boston police strike, the TVA, and other historical events that affected the development of public unions. His treatment is both detailed and sympathetic to unionism in general.

1076.   American Federation of Labor, *Report of Proceedings of the Fifty-First Annual Convention of American Federation of Labor* (1931): 125, 172, 310-29; also *Report of Proceedings of the Fifty-Second Annual Convention of American Federation of Labor* (1932): 83-85; also

1077.   National Federation of Federal Employees, "Why the National Federation of Federal Employees Severed Its Connection with the American Federation of Labor," [leaflet] (n.c.: NFFE, n.d. [1932]).

In 1931, the mechanical craft unions challenged the NFFE and postal unions on their endorsement of the classification act then being considered, and more generally on the classification of government services within the AFL. Once the NFFE's position was voted down 140-50, the NFFE withdrew from the AFL.

After the NFFE's withdrawal vote, AFL William Green tried to appease the NFFE, eventually offering the union everything it had originally wanted. However, NFFE's resentments were deep, and they questioned Green's ability to negotiate after the convention had already voted the opposite way.

1078.   Leonard D. White, *Whitney Councils in the British Civil Service* (Chicago: University of Chicago Press, 1933).

In Britain, cooperative worker-management councils were adopted in industry in 1918, and in government service beginning in 1919. White described the operation and structure of those bodies, from the National Whitney Council down to district and office works committees. He praised their use of consensus in the equally-balanced councils rather than majority vote, and he described their successes in the early years. He offered several lessons that he felt could be of use in the United States.

1079.   "Employee Relationship Policy," (Knoxville: Tennessee Valley Authority, August 28, 1935).

Soon after the Tennessee Valley Authority was established as a semi-autonomous government corporation in 1933, it discovered several transition problems that came from inheriting a workforce that had a history of union membership. After extensive discussions with employee representatives, the Board issued a policy in 1935 that authorized collective bargaining as well as other consultation with the fifteen AFL-affiliate unions that became members of the Tennessee Valley Trades and Labor Council.

1080.   Sterling D. Spero, "Employer and Employee in the Public Service," in Carl J. Friedrich, et al., *Problems of the American Public Service* (New York: McGraw-Hill, 1935), pp. 196-229; also

1081.   Leonard D. White, *Introduction to the Study of Public Administration*, 2nd ed. (New York: Macmillan Co., 1939), pp. 426-41 (ch. 28); also

1082.   Harvey Walker, "Employee Organizations in the National Government Service: The Period Prior to the World War," *Public Personnel Studies*, 10, (August 1941): 67-73; also "Employee Organizations in the National Government Service: The Formation of the National Federation of Federal Employees," *Public Personnel Studies*, 10, (October 1941): 130-35.

Spurred by both the encouraging environment of the TVA experiment and the general good relations between organized labor and the White House, the subject of government unionism became far more popular in the late 1930s and the early 1940s. These are among the more useful histories and status reports written at the time.

1083. "The President Indorses (sic) Resolution of Federation of Federal Employees Against Strikes in Federal Service," letter reprinted in *The Public Papers and Addresses of Franklin D. Roosevelt: 1937 Volume* (New York: Macmillan Co., 1941), pp. 324-26; also

1084. "This Is a Demonstration of What a Democracy at Work Can Do," speech reprinted in *The Public Papers and Addresses of Franklin D. Roosevelt: 1940 Volume* (New York: Macmillan Co., 1941), pp. 359-69.

Over time, President Roosevelt became more amenable to collective bargaining as well. In a letter to NFFE dated August 16, 1937, he argued that "all Government employees should realize that the process of collective bargaining, as usually understood, cannot be transplanted into the public service." (p. 325) By 1940, however, the TVA and the Trades and Labor Council had signed an agreement that Roosevelt praised at his Labor Day speech at the inauguration of the Chickamauga Dam. In this case, he felt that "collective bargaining and efficiency have proceeded hand in hand." (p. 359)

1085. Eldon L. Johnson, "General Unions in the Federal Service," *Journal of Politics*, 2, (February 1940): 23-56.

In the same spirit, Johnson investigated the history of government unionism since World War I, and found no cause for alarm. They had used legislative, administrative, educational, and political tactics to call attention to the human factors of administration. Johnson found it surprising that unions had been so poorly utilized by our political system.

1086. Civil Service Assembly, *Employee Relations in the Public Service* (Chicago: Civil Service Assembly, 1942); also

1087. National Civil Service League, *Employee Organizations in the Public Service* (New York: National Civil Service League, 1946).

Under the leadership of Gordon Clapp, who had been a major participant in the TVAs bargaining agreement, The Civil Service Assembly's study advocated that personnel departments hear the grievances of employees. He felt that loose cooperative relationships with unions were a good way to accomplish such a goal, and that unions had been reasonable when given responsibility.

Similarly, the National Civil Service League argued in 1946 that divisions of public management should be established in each agency to negotiate cooperative agreements with employee representatives on causes of grievances and the development of employee morale.

1088.   Morton R. Godine, *The Labor Problem in the Public Service* (Cambridge: Harvard University Press, 1951).

Godine was also concerned that a lack of legalized collective bargaining in an environment in which union activity was prevalent was a mistake. He suggested that government should offer collective consultation as a means of granting employees the right to share in determining the conditions of employment in exchange for an unequivocal surrender of the right to strike against government.

1089.   "Union Activity in Public Employment" [Note], *Columbia Law Review*, 55, (March 1955): 343-66.

The editors argued that some body similar to the National Labor Relations Board was needed for the public sector to handle recognition, unit determination, and "good faith bargaining" issues. They felt that one national board may not be constitutional nor needed, but that each jurisdiction could establish one without difficulty.

1090.   *Wisconsin Municipal Employment Relations Act* (1959), *Wisconsin Statutes Annotated*, sec. 111.70; also

1091.   *Wisconsin State Employment Labor Relations Act* (1959), *Wisconsin Statutes Annotated*, sec. 111.80.

The first legalized collective bargaining did not occur at the federal level, but instead was introduced in Wisconsin in 1959. While many aspects of the law, including scope of bargaining and recognition procedures, were somewhat primitive, the act did include an NLRB-style Wisconsin Employment Relations Commission to administer the new policy.

1092.   John F. Kennedy, Executive Order 10988, January 17, 1962; also

1093.   Richard M. Nixon, Executive Order 11491, October 29, 1969; also Executive Order 11616, August 26, 1971.

At the federal level, the right to bargain collectively was granted before adequate mechanisms were established to administer the policy. In 1962, President Kennedy established three forms of union recognition--informal, formal, and exclusive.

While formal recognition guaranteed the right to consultation, exclusive recognition guaranteed the right to bargain collectively.

In 1969, President Nixon phased out formal and informal recognition. He also created a Federal Labor Relations Council to conduct elections and administer the policy, along with a Federal Service Impasses Panel to help with mediation. Negotiated grievances procedures were permitted in 1969, and finally required in 1971. The 1971 order also expanded the scope of bargaining.

1094.   *Postal Reorganization Act*, 84 Stat. 719 (1970).

The strongest collective bargaining agreement in the federal government, however, was reserved for the new U.S. Postal Service. Their agreements are placed under the jurisdiction of the National Labor Relations Board with a broad scope of bargaining. Disputes are resolved through factfinding by the Federal Mediation and Conciliation Service, followed if necessary by a mutually-established arbitration board.

1095.   Harry H. Wellington and Ralph K. Winter, Jr., *The Unions and the Cities* (Washington, D.C.: Brookings Institution, 1971); also

1096.   David T. Stanley, *Managing Local Government under Union Pressure* (Washington, D.C.: Brookings Institution, 1972); also

1097.   Jack Stieber, *Public Employee Unionism: Structure, Growth, Policy* (Washington, D.C.: Brookings Institution, 1973).

In the 1970s, the Brookings Institution helped develop the study of unionism at the state and local levels, where its practice had mushroomed since the pre-1959 days when it had been practiced extra-legally. Wellington and Winter concentrated on the legislative difficulties and changing legal precedents in the field. Stanley reviewed the growing political role and strength of unions in helping influence local policies.

Stieber's emphasis was on the unions themselves as he investigated the types, structures, and practices of state and local unions. He also described their expanding use of collective bargaining, strikes, and direct political activities, and predicted that such trends would continue.

1098.   Gerald M. Pops, *Emergence of the Public Sector Arbitrator* (Lexington, MA: Lexington Books, 1976).

With the rise in collective bargaining came a similar growth in arbitration for both grievance resolution and contract settlement. Pops described the history of arbitration and surveyed arbitrators in New York to determine whether they saw their roles more as settlers of contract disputes, or as problem solvers in a larger role of interpreting collective bargaining agreements. While the latter model seemed more appropriate to the public sector, the arbitrators were pulled by the parties more toward the limited contract approach to arbitration.

1099.   Michael L. Brookshire and Michael D. Rogers, *Collective Bargaining in Public Employment* (Lexington, MA: Lexington Books, 1977).

TVA has long enjoyed the most widely respected public union experience. Brookshire and Rogers studied the TVA's structure and process, particularly on pay determination, impasse resolution, contract administration, and union security. They found that the early management philosophy had been instrumental in many of the early TVA successes. In more recent years, labor and management seemed to lean more toward bargaining than excessive cooperation. The TVA model, especially with its excessive centralization, was not likely to be useful in a public jurisdiction in which unions were fighting for basic bargaining and recognition rights.

1100.   *Civil Service Reform Act*, 92 Stat. 1111 (1978).

Until 1978, many federal practices were authorized in executive orders, but not in legislation. The CSRA legislated collective bargaining, and centralized its administration in a NLRB-style Federal Labor Relations Authority (FLRA), with its three members selected by the president. The scope of bargaining was legislated and generally increased, and a General Counsel was added to the Federal Service Impasses Panel and Federal Mediation and Conciliation Service to help with various disputes.

1101.   Roger Fisher and William Ury, *Getting to Yes: Negotiating Agreement Without Giving In* (Boston: Houghton Mifflin, 1981).[7]

The authors described the general techniques for negotiating developed by the Harvard Negotiating Project. While the project is generic and includes examples of negotiating in such areas as marriage and other aspects of everyday life, there is also a section on labor-management relations that concentrates on positive issues and efforts to find areas of mutual gains.

1102.   Federal Labor Relations Authority, "Professional Air Traffic Controllers Organization, Affiliated with MEBA, AFL-CIO," 7 FLRA 34 (October 22, 1981).

Few events dampened the spirits of unionism as much as the Professional Air Traffic Controllers' (PATCO) strike of 1981. With a history of poor labor-management relations extending back to its formation in 1968, PATCO membership voted on July 29, 1981 to reject the FAA's final offer and go on strike. After a 48 hour warning period, President Reagan fired the striking workers and replaced them with as many supervisors, retirees, and military controllers as could be found. Reagan then asked MSPB to decertify the union, which it did in late October 1981. In December, PATCO filed for bankruptcy.

1103.   Jonathan Brock, *Bargaining Beyond Impasse: Joint Resolution of Public Sector Labor Disputes* (Boston: Auburn House Publishing Co., 1982).

Brock described the Massachusetts Joint Labor-Management Committee for Municipal Police and Fire Fighters (JLMC) founded in 1977 to handle labor-management disputes. Based on five years of experience, he felt that the flexible and cooperative approach of the JLMC answers many of the problems that led to its creation, and that it has potential uses in other jurisdictions.

1104.   Sar A. Levitan and Alexandra B. Noden, *Working for the Sovereign: Employee Relations in the Federal Government* (Baltimore: Johns Hopkins University Press, 1983).

Arguing that the Reagan administration was introducing radical changes into the federal personnel system, the authors investigated the impact of the changes on unionism. They described the development of federal unionism before and after 1981, and concluded that Reagan was using private-sector analogies when they did not fit, and ignoring them when they did. Specifically, Levitan and Noden felt that compensation and workers rights can be settled by bargaining, while hiring and firing need political insulation, and cannot work safely in a private-sector mode.

1105.   Jack Rabin, et al., *Handbook on Public Personnel Administration and Labor Relations* (New York: Marcel Dekker, 1983).[8]

This reference book contains ten articles on various aspects of public personnel, and another thirteen on public labor relations. The readings are largely descriptive, with readings on the historical, legal, and social context of public unions. Kearney studied union influence on personnel management, while Gerhart summarized research on a number of hypotheses about union power. There are also specific studies of unionism in transit systems, health care, the military, and law enforcement.

1106.   Michael D. Nash and Nolan J. Argyle, "Old Mother Hubbard Revisited: Comments on the Reliability of the Collective Bargaining Literature," *Review Of Public Personnel Administration*, 4, (Spring 1984): 1-12.

Complaining that the massive accumulation of literature on impasse resolution seldom operationalizes terms or makes its axioms clear, the authors felt that the conclusions are often either tautologies or unverifiable assertions. More explicit paradigms are needed to foster research in the area.

1107.   Richard Kearney, *Labor Relations in the Public Sector* (New York: Marcel Dekker, 1984).

Kearney tried to predict the directions public unionism is likely to go in lean financial times. He noted the confusion remaining among the myriad of state and local laws, while the CSRA helped clarify the federal sector somewhat. He predicted a slowdown in public union growth in tight monetary times as well as a shift to non-monetary bargaining issues. He also expected more strikes even though impasse procedures are improving.

1108.   Jim Seroka, "The Determinants of Public Employee Union Growth," *Review of Public Personnel Administration*, 5, (Spring 1985): 5-20.

Investigating the different rates of growth or decline in public union membership, Seroka noted that the region of the country and the level of government have some impact. The most important determinant, however, is state policy and enabling legislation, which affects all levels within the state.

CONTINUING CONCERNS

Personnel provides an interesting contrast to the other great staff function of government--budgeting. Both were born in moralistic fervors to correct abuses of one of the politicians' most precious governmental resources. Both were laden with procedures that threatened to make each irrelevant to policy making from the beginning; if anything, the precision of accounting procedures made budgeting even more vulnerable. Both recognized such dangers from the beginning and tried to deal with them. Personnel did not deal with them in a timely fashion, however, if indeed it has even today.

The reason for the failure requires more research than is available in an annotated review. One suggestion is that the positive functions of budgeting require only that experts be brought into a process that will be performed regardless of their presence. The positive functions of personnel require the expenditures of substantial sums on processes that are helpful, but that are not actually required for the agency to perform its functions. Of the two staff functions, the positive side of personnel may be the only expendable quadrant. If that is the case, underfunded positive reforms and reversions to a negative emphasis in personnel is not unexpected, or even unwelcome among some specialists and potential victims of personnel management.

NOTES FOR CHAPTER SIXTEEN

1. Paul P. Van Riper, *History of the United States Civil Service* (Evanston, IL: Row, Peterson, and Co., 1958), p. 65.

2. It is far easier to locate the reprint in National Municipal League, *A Municipal Program* (New York: Macmillan and Co., 1900), pp. 187-224.

3. Other committee members included Assistant Secretary of Commerce and Labor Lawrence O. Murray, Commissioner of Corporations James Garfield, and Chief Gifford Pinchot of the Forest Service. The first two reports also included Frank Hitchcock, the First Assistant Postmaster General.

4. For a description of the complete set, see Gustavas A. Weber, *Organized Efforts for the Improvements of Methods of Administration in the United States* (New York: D. Appleton and Co., 1919).

5. See for instance, Van Riper, *History of the United States Civil Service*, p. 331.

6. The journal was published from 1923 through January/February 1931, with a one-issue revival of both the organization and journal in June 1941. It never circulated widely, and the publishers failed to hold back sufficient copies of volume one. In volume two they began asking subscribers to send back earlier issues to be used to stock public libraries. No copies of volume one were found for this review.

7. The book was edited by Bruce Patton.

8. Coeditors were Thomas Vocino, W. Bartley Hildreth, and Gerald J. Miller.

17
Decision-Making and Expertise

BACKGROUND

This chapter discusses two sets of literature. First, it describes techniques and models of decision-making, from the rational approach through incrementalism, mixed-scanning and its variants. Secondly, it discusses the role of expertise within the bureaucracy, including the relationship of specialists to generalists, and the political value of limited-access information.

The literature is closely tied to the topics of budgeting and fiscal administration described in the next chapter. The four topics have grown together rather than starting from a common point. When ancestry and commonality of techniques are cranked in, heavy overlapping with the chapters on scientific management and policy analysis is also inevitable.

MODELS OF DECISION-MAKING

1109. Roberto [Robert] Michels, *Political Parties: A Sociological Study of Oligarchical Tendencies of Modern Democracies*, see note for English-language translations.[1] Originally *Zur Soziologie des Parteiwesens in der modernen Demokratie; Untersuchengen über die oligarchischen Tendenzen des Gruppenlebens*, Philosophisch-soziologische Bücherei. Bd. XXI (Leipzig: Klinkhardt, 1911).

Decision-making literature can be categorized into two groups, both of which are discussed in this review. The first, typified by Michels, attempts to determine who makes the decisions. In his "iron law of oligarchical tendencies," Michels felt that decision-making would become concentrated in the hands of a few elites because of their access to knowledge, control of the means of communication, and increased political skill. Therefore, decision-making was inevitably oligarchical.

1110.   Wallace Clark, *The Gantt Chart: A Working Tool of Management* (New York: Ronald Press, 1922).

The second approach to decision-making studies techniques that lead to effective decisions. Charles Babbage and Frederick Taylor, discussed in previous chapters, were both early examples of what is now called the rational approach to decision-making. However, neither reached the degree of detail of Henry Gantt, whose famous Gantt Chart evolved from his consulting experience. Curiously, Gantt's writings seldom discussed the chart in much detail. However, in the spirit of scientific management, Gantt's follower Clark explained the technique in such detail that even the proper pen for drawing the charts was pictured. While Clark explained that the chart was just a technique, and not a complete course on management, he considered it "the most notable contribution to the art of management made in this generation."

1111.   Mary Parker Follett, *Dynamic Administration: The Collected Papers of Mary Parker Follett*, ed. by Henry C. Metcalf and Lyndall Urwick (New York and London: Harper and Brothers, [1942][2]); also

1112.   Chester I. Barnard, *Functions of the Executive* (Cambridge: Harvard University Press, 1938).

To early decision-making scholars, it was taken for granted that one of the crucial roles of managers was to make decisions, as often and as wisely as possible. Follett and Barnard were among the first to attack such an assumption. To Follett, the "Law of the Situation" dictates that decisions should be made collectively under the leadership of whoever is best qualified. Barnard felt that the study of management had become superficial through its emphasis on small decisions. Executives should decide those matters that fall within the three "functions" of maintaining organizational communication, securing essential services from individuals, and determining organizational goals, and little else. In addition, Barnard described the internal and external efficiency needed for organizational survival, so that the organization must produce what both its clientele and its participants need if it is to stay healthy.

1113.   Edwin O. Stene, "An Approach to a Science of Administration," *American Political Science Review*, 34, (December 1940): 1124-37.

Political Scientists such as Stene, however, were more interested in advancing Public Administration by generating and testing hypotheses. He offered several "axioms," including that coordination of both activities and performance varies with the coordination of decisions, and that the knowledge behind decisions expands with the efficiency of communication.

1114.   Herbert A. Simon, *Administrative Behavior* (New York: Macmillan and Co., 1947).

It was Simon's classic work on the subject, however, that popularized the notion that "decision-making is the heart of administration, and that the vocabulary of administrative theory must be derived from the logic and psychology of human choice." (p. xiv) Individuals face such obstacles and limited resources that their decisions can hardly be called rational at all. However, organizations create boundaries around individual rationality to accommodate the needs of the individual and the organization resulting in limited but effective rationality in organizational decision-making.

1115.   Robert Dubin, "Decision-Making by Management in Industrial Relations," *American Journal of Sociology*, 54, (January 1949): 292-97.

In a similar vein, Dubin felt that bigness makes formal organizations and rules necessary. These rules control individual behavior, making consistency, prediction, and reactions to crises possible. They also make management look inflexible and formalistic when dealing with unions, however.

1116.   Philip Selznick, *TVA and the Grass Roots* (Berkeley: University of California Press, 1949). [dissertation and trade editions]

In the way that Follett and Barnard challenged some of the fundamental assumptions of decision-making theory, Selznick was a forerunner of a new method of viewing decision-making legitimacy. Cooptation was his mechanism for recognizing the impact and vulnerability of the organization with its environment. In an early statement of open-systems theory, he argued that organizations need to share decision-making powers with outside groups in order to ensure their own survival.

1117.   A. Kaplan, A. L. Skogstad, and M. A. Girshick, "The Prediction of Social and Technological Events," *Public Opinion Quarterly*, 14, (Spring 1950): 93-110.

In a more theoretical vein, the authors searched for the conditions under which experts make accurate predictions. They discovered that the expert's confidence in his or her predictions is not correlated with future success. However, as a precursor to Delphi techniques, they found that groups predict more accurately than the same individuals alone, and that their reliability is correlated with their ability to explain their reasoning.

1118.   John McDonald, "How Businessmen Make Decisions," *Fortune*, 52, (August 1955): 84-87+.

Reflecting Simon's theme, McDonald argued that "(t)he business executive is by profession a decision-maker. Uncertainty is his opponent. Overcoming it is his mission." (p. 84) He described the dramatic growth in studying decision-making behavior, especially among the mathematical modelers at the RAND Corporation. Many businessmen, however, still feel as if they are operating on educated hunches.

1119.   William J. Gore, "Administrative Decision-Making in Federal Offices," *Public Administration Review*, 16, (Autumn 1956): 281-91; also *Administrative Decision-Making: A Heuristic Model* (New York: John Wiley and Sons, 1964); also

1120.   William J. Gore and J. W. Dyson, eds., *The Making of Decisions: A Reader in Administrative Behavior* (New York: Free Press of Glencoe, 1964).

Gore published some of the first empirical studies of decision-making in an effort to develop an explanatory model. His 1955 study of a sample of federal field offices in the state of Washington led to his argument that decisions go through four phases: perception of a problem; interpretation of alternatives in terms of agency objectives; a struggle for power to implement decisions; and formalization of the decision. His 1964 study of "heuristic" or experimental behavior in the Lawrence, Kansas Fire Department led to the amended list of perception of the problem, evaluation of the problem, estimation of the consequences of alternatives, and maneuvering for position. In both cases, he felt that formal processes fail to explain much of the decision-making, although organizational structure and decision choices help shape each other.

In the book of readings, numerous authors argued for a restricted use of rationality in explaining decisions. Other authors described strategies for making decisions, organizational constraints, and the organizational roles of decision-making.

1121.   Anthony Downs, *An Economic Theory of Democracy* (New York: Harper and Row, 1957); also *Inside Bureaucracy* (Boston: Little, Brown, and Co., 1967).

Downs popularized an approach of developing hypotheses from basic assumptions in *An Economic Theory* that he then applied to bureaucracy in 1967. Based in his assumption that all bureaucrats are motivated by self-interest, Downs postulated five rational types of bureaucrats: climbers, conservers, zealots, advocates, and statesmen. While organizations can respond rationally in an attempt to control them, the law of counter control predicts that workers will become more talented in evasion, and ensuring compliance will become more expensive.

1122.   Roland McKean, *Efficiency in Government Through Systems Analysis* (New York: John Wiley and Sons, 1958).[3]

Working at the RAND Corporation, McKean was one of the first to argue that civilian government agencies should make greater use of such systems analysis techniques as cost-benefit analysis in its decision-making techniques. He offered a brief history of quantitative analysis in government decisions and a general description of the techniques. He then developed some case studies of water resources development to show how such analysis can be done.

1123.   James G. March and Herbert A. Simon, *Organizations* (New York: John A. Wiley and Sons, 1958).

In his 1947 work, Simon stated that he was not attempting to build a theory of organizations based on decision-making. In this work, March and Simon moved closer to theory as they developed untested propositions about formal organizations in an effort to generate empirical research. Their literature review described the inadequacies of scientific management and human relations in ignoring employees as decision-makers. They studied such factors as decisions to participate, conflict, planning and motivation. They described the bounded rationality of employees inside organizations leading to satisficing rather than maximizing behavior in decision-making.

1124.   Charles Lindblom, "The Science of 'Muddling Through'," *Public Administration Review*, 19, (Spring 1959): 79-88; also *The Intelligence of Democracy: Decision Making Through Mutual Adjustment* (New York: Free Press, 1965).

By 1959, rationality in organizational decision-making was under heavy attack (see March and Simon above). Lindblom was the first, however, to argue that the more incremental method of "successive limited comparisons" (or branch) method is superior to the "rational-comprehensive" (or root) method because of its ability to simplify alternatives, to answer multiple and/or conflicting objectives, and to reflect decision-making in the real world. In 1965, he developed the concept much more fully, using his training in economic modelling to describe how reasonable policies can arise through mutual adjustments without common purposes or understandings. He applied his analysis to several circumstances that arise in government and in party politics.

1125.   Herbert A. Simon, "Theories of Decision Making in Economics and Behavioral Science," *American Economic Review*, 49, (June 1959): 253-83; also "On the Concept of Organizational Goal," *Administrative Science Quarterly*, 9, (June 1964): 1-22; also "Administrative Decision Making," *Public Administration Review*, 25, (March 1965): 31-37.

In 1959, Simon praised the melding of psychological theories of motivation and economic modelling techniques that have advanced the study of decision-making. In 1964, he tried to halt the reification of organizational goals by noting that they are not solitary, but are defined by the constraints that are necessary to gain cooperation from individuals. Goals vary according to the level of the organization, and are made more complex by decentralized decision-making.

In the 25-year retrospective issue of the *Public Administration Review*, Simon praised the recent rise of decision-making in that journal and elsewhere (especially in Cyert and March) in providing a base for organization theories.

1126.   Herbert A. Simon, *The New Science of Management Decision* (New York: Harper and Row, 1960); revised edition (Englewood Cliffs, NJ: Prentice Hall, 1977).

Based on a set of lectures he delivered at New York University in 1960, Simon speculated on the changes in programmed and non-programmed decisions that were likely to occur in the future because of the new technologies of computers and operations research that had been developed since the Second World War. He concluded that less would change than might be feared. Automation would absorb much of the routine work, but hierarchies would still be built around layers for physical production and distribution, programmed decisions, and non-programmed decisions. Human fulfillment would probably be easier in the bureaucracy of the future.

1127.   John M. Pfiffner, "Administrative Rationality," *Public Administration Review*, 20, (Summer 1960): 125-32.

In an effort to test theories of rational decision-making, one of Pfiffner's students analyzed 332 administrative decisions made in the Los Angeles area.[4] As Pfiffner reported, he discovered "that administrative rationality differs from orthodox concepts of rationality because is does take into account an additional spectrum of facts. These are the facts relative to emotions, politics, power, group dynamics, personality and mental health." (p. 126)

1128.   Richard M. Cyert and James G. March, *A Behavioral Theory of the Firm* (Englewood Cliffs, NJ: Prentice Hall, 1963).

In the private sector, Cyert and March rejected profit-motive theories in an effort to develop a behavioral theory of decision-making in a firm. In their theory, goals are determined by bargaining among active participants using side payments, and creating some inconsistency through organizational slack. Organizational expectancies are shaped by an approximate sequential consideration of alternatives, favoring the existing policy when it is acceptable. Alternatives are evaluated on few criteria, and are influenced by outside promoters, and by the biases inherent in communications. Organizational choice is determined by an adaptively rational system working to maintain stability in a world of disturbances or shocks, resulting in a system that favors standard operating procedures, and reactions rather than forecasting.

1129. Yehezkel Dror, "Muddling Through--'Science' or Inertia?" *Public Administration Review*, 24, (September 1964): 153-57; also

1130. Charles E. Lindblom, "Context for Change and Strategy: A Reply," *Public Administration Review*, 24, (September 1964): 157-58.

In a symposium on decision-making, Dror argued that Lindblom's incremental technique is oversimplified because it is adequate only in relatively continuous and satisfactory circumstances. In any circumstance, it leads to inertia. Lindblom accepted the first argument, noting that he had further refined the argument in *A Strategy of Decision* (see chapter 19 of this book). He disagreed with the inertia claim, however, arguing that rationalism leads to even more stagnation.

1131. Charles J. Hitch, *Decision-Making for Defense* (Berkeley: University of California Press, 1965).

While much of the field rejected the possibility of rational-comprehensive decision-making, the 1960s were also the age of cost-benefit analysis described in detail in the next chapter, and the economic-modelling approach to decision-making developed during the 1950s at the RAND Corporation. As one of the key participants in the process, Hitch described the historical lack of coordination, the jealousies, and the political process of acquisition in the nation's defense. He then described the mechanics of Planning-Programming-Budgeting and cost-benefit analysis. He analyzed the successes of systems analysis in the Defense Department, and the problems that could still be addressed by additional rational decision-making.

1132. Mancur Olson, *The Logic of Collective Action* (Cambridge: Harvard University Press, 1965); also

1133. William H. Riker and Peter C. Ordeshook, *An Introduction to Positive Political Theory* (Englewood Cliffs, NJ: Prentice Hall, 1973).

Rationalism was also popular in political science, and Mancur Olson helped lead the way with his argument that groups do not form merely because they satisfy the interests of all participants. Rather, some form of compulsion is necessary to gain the optimal amount of production of common goods from rational, self-interested participants. Riker and Ordeshook also considered people to be bundles of opinions and self-interested preferences, which are pursued through the selection, enforcement, realization, and evaluation of social choice. The results are choices that often lack coherence and appear arbitrary.

1134. Harold L. Wilensky, *Organizational Intelligence: Knowledge and Policy in Government and Industry* (New York: Basic Books, 1967).

Most students of administration remained pessimistic on the subject of rational decision-making however. Wilensky concentrated on the role of intelligence in filtering the information needed for rationality. He studied several failures of information to show how experts are used, how failures often occur, and how bureaucracies can be restructured to improve information flow. Hierarchy, specialization, centralization, doctrines, and the nature of the decision all cause some difficulties that can be ameliorated, but cannot be totally overcome.

1135.   James D. Thompson, *Organizations in Action* (New York: McGraw-Hill, 1967).

Thompson argued that organizations operate in indeterminate and uncertain environments, while being subject to criteria of rationality requiring determinateness and certainty. He offered numerous propositions on how organizations seek to maximize rationality by creating buffers against the environment, by expanding boundaries, and by various structural adjustments to create artificial stability.

1136.   Amitai Etzioni, "Mixed-Scanning: A 'Third' Approach to Decision Making," *Public Administration Review*, 27, (December 1967): 385-92.

By 1967, rational-comprehensive and incremental (with its variants) decision-making were commonly presented as the two theoretical options. Etzioni argued that a third model fitting in between the two presents a more realistic picture. Rationalism requires more information resources than are commonly available, while incrementalism cannot explain basic societal innovations. Mixed scanning, however, allows two "cameras"--a high-order policy-making process to set basic directions, and an incremental one to prepare for fundamental decisions and to implement them once they have been reached.

1137.   Robert J. Art, *The TFX Decision: McNamara and the Military* (Boston: Little, Brown, and Co., 1968).

The great battles between the rational-comprehensive systems analysts and what they considered to be the political turf-oriented style of decision-making occurred in the Defense Department in the 1960s. Art described the battle between the forces around Secretary McNamara who wanted a new fighter to be shared by the services, and the service secretaries, each of whom wanted a separate plane and contractor. The result was something of a tie, with two of the original three services sharing distinct versions of the F-111. However, Art and most observers at the time saw it as a victory for McNamara.

1138.   Graham T. Allison, "Conceptual Models and the Cuban Missile Crisis," *American Political Science Review*, 63, (September 1969): 689-718; also *Essence of Decision: Explaining the Cuban Missile Crisis* (Boston: Little, Brown, and Co., 1971).

In 1969, Allison analyzed the Cuban missile crisis to try to make sense of the decision-making of the two parties. He argued that analysts think in terms of conceptual models through which they try to explain and predict policy. Model I, or the rational policy model, had little value in explaining the crisis. Both Model II (Organizational Process Model) and Model III (Bureaucratic Politics Model) would have been of more predictive value to analysts. In 1971, he expanded the study into a book that generalized that both Models II and III are more realistic in describing organizational decision-making.

1139.   Edward J. Mishan, *Cost-Benefit Analysis* (London: George Allen & Unwin Ltd., 1971); revised and expanded (New York: Praeger Publishers, 1976); also

1140.   Robert Sugden and Alan H. Williams, *The Principles of Practical Cost-Benefit Analysis* (New York: Oxford University Press, 1978).

Long after the departure of the "whiz kids" from the Defense Department, systems analysis and cost-benefit analysis maintained their popularity in program evaluation, and numerous textbooks described the techniques for students. Mishan's book is particularly rich in applications, describing the technique with simple mathematics for examples ranging from underground railways to social welfare functions. Sugden and Williams also presented the technique with simple mathematics, supplemented with examples and more technical appendices. They also emphasized the oversimplicity of Pareto analysis (see chapter 19), however, and recognized the interrelationship of analysis and policy.

1141.   Michael D. Cohen, James G. March, and Johan P. Olsen, "A Garbage Can Model of Organizational Choice," *Administrative Science Quarterly*, 17, (March 1972): 1-25.

At the opposite extreme, this article described decision-making in "organized anarchies" characterized by problematic preferences, unclear technology, and fluid participation. The authors created a computer simulated garbage can model of decision-making consisting of four variables: a stream of choices; a stream of problems; a rate of flow of solutions; and a stream of energy from participants. Among the eight implications were that resolution of problems is common only when flight was severely restricted, the process is sensitive to variations in the load, and problems and decision-makers track each other through the system.

1142.   Harold A. Linstone and Murray Turoff, eds., *The Delphi Method: Techniques and Applications* (Reading, MA: Addison-Wesley, 1975); also

1143.   Andre L. Delbecq, Andrew H. Van de Ven, and David H. Gustafson, *Group Techniques for Program Planning: A Guide to Nominal Group and Delphi Processes* (Glenview, IL: Scott, Foresman and Co., 1975).

In the 1950s, researchers at the RAND Corporation developed a forecasting technique to be used under conditions of extreme uncertainty and/or disagreement among experts. The Delphi technique, named for the original RAND project which itself was named for the Greek temple at which the gods professed the future, was first published in 1964.[5] Its popularity soared in the 1970s, leading to several explanatory texts such as the ones above.

Linstone and Turoff used new and reprinted articles to explain the technique, describe applications, and warn of possible pitfalls. The Delbecq study described applications of Delphi and the newer Nominal Group Technique, similar to brainstorming with written lists of options, except that all participants are in the same room during discussions and preferential secret voting. Both studies have extensive bibliographies.

1144.   Moshe F. Rubinstein, *Patterns of Problem Solving* (Englewood Cliffs, NJ: Prentice Hall, 1975); also

1145.   Ralph L. Keeney and Howard Raiffa, *Decisions with Multiple Objectives: Preferences and Value Trade-offs* (New York: John Wiley and Sons, 1976).

Much of the literature on decision-making is detailed and mathematical enough to be beyond the scope of all except those with specialized training. Two texts that fit between the specialized and general literature are listed above.

Rubinstein offered the more theoretical of the two books, beginning with the behavioral and conceptual limits of decision-making, progressing through language translations difficulties, and moving into computer simulations. The decision techniques he described have no specific focus on public policy applications. The Keeney and Raiffa book is more clearly intended for policy analysts and others concerned with multiple objectives and/or uncertain consequences. The book describes many specific variations that might be of use in public-sector applications.

1146.   Robert Axelrod, ed., *Structure of Decision: The Cognitive Maps of Political Elites* (Princeton, NJ: Princeton University Press, 1976).

Axelrod and others used the psychological approach of cognitive mapping in an effort to explain the cause and effect relationship of decisions by political elites in five case studies. They discovered that decisions tend to be consistent with the policy-makers' belief systems. However, there is little spontaneous feedback to the belief system since the decision-makers hold more relevant beliefs than they can process. Axelrod hoped for the day when cognitive mapping could be used by decision-makers to improve the quality of their decisions.

1147.   Irving L. Janis and Leon Mann, *Decision Making: A Psychological Analysis of Conflict, Choice and Commitment* (New York: Free Press, 1977).

Janis and Mann studied the psychological causes of faulty decision-making and made recommendations for improvement. They viewed man as a reluctant decision-maker who often meets conditions leading to poor decisions, especially in group situations. They were able to suggest five techniques for consultant intervention to improve data collection and processing, ranging from psychodrama to decisional balance sheets.

1148.   George P. Huber, *Managerial Decision Making* (Glenview, IL: Scott, Foresman, 1980).

Huber described many of the techniques, such as Multiattribute Utility Analysis and decision trees, that could help rationalize individual decision-making. He recognized that problems arise in group decision processes, however. Therefore, he offered a detailed description of group techniques such as brainstorming, Delphi techniques, and nominal techniques. He concluded that such techniques can help improve the quality of decisions.

1149.   Robert J. Mowitz, *The Design of Public Decision Systems* (Baltimore: University Park Press, 1980).

Based on his experience with a PPBS style system in Pennsylvania state government, Mowitz outlined the eight conditions for a decision system that is politically responsive, research oriented, and information sensitive. Such a system identifies major substantive values, converts values into performance objectives, identifies needed resources, reviews relations of values to objectives and establishes boundaries and priorities, creates annual decision cycles with review, scans alternatives, reports outside impacts, and is institutionalized. He analyzed several policy areas to show how his system works.

1150.   Lloyd G. Nigro, ed., *Decision Making in the Public Sector* (New York: Marcel Dekker, 1984).

This book of readings includes a section of analytical techniques that begins with conflicting views by William A. Kelso and Kenneth J. Meier on the advantages of cost-benefit analysis. A. W. McEachern described the Multiattribute Utility Analysis used in the Navy. Other authors described applications of scientific analysis to such policy areas as resource scarcity, toxic waste, aging, and the reorganization of the Department of Health, Education, and Welfare.

1151.   Michael A. Murray, *Decisions: A Comparative Critique* (Marshfield, MA: Pitman Publishing Co., 1986).

Murray's theme is that we have fallen into the foolish habit of viewing problems as being discrete with specialized solutions. His goal was to integrate quantitative, political, and legal approaches to decision-making. He critiqued and described the literature of each approach, and found more common bonds than differences among them. He advocated more emphasis on integration in academic training and on-the-job experiences.

EXPERTISE IN GOVERNMENT

1152. Sir Francis L. C. Floud, K.C.B., "The Sphere of the Specialist in Public Administration," *Journal of Public Administration* (London), 1, (1923): 117-26; also

1153. Charles A. Beard, "Government by Technologists," *New Republic*, 63, (June 18, 1930): 115-20.

Literature that analyzes the role of expertise in government can be traced back at least as far as Plato, and far further if interpreted loosely. In the United States, the degree of respect for expertise has fluctuated over time.

In the early years of self-aware public administration literature, however, respect for expertise waned on both sides of the Atlantic. Floud described the traditional English suspicion of experts, and suggested that specialists should be kept in advisory, not executive, roles. Administration required adaptability, which was not a strength of the specialist.

In the United States, Beard noted that the need to regulate a technological society required a more complicated and specialized government. Once that government began to operate with a sense of certainty, as was happening in some authoritarian European states, the results were often not as positive as had been expected.

1154. Robert K. Merton, *Social Theory and Social Structure* (Glencoe, IL: Free Press, 1949).

In the mid-1950s, the ascending role of technicians and scientists in governmental policy-making caught the attention of increasing numbers of scholars, and helped shape the study of bureaucratic power. Merton discussed the role of expertise in bureaucracy in 1949, but in his chapter on the "Role of the Intellectual in Public Bureaucracy," he was rather unimpressed with the limits placed on social science intellectuals. Their assigned goals were often too imprecise, and the bureaucratic intellectuals were forced to reframe their advice so as to enter the bureaucratic power struggle, lest they be ignored.

1155.   Don K. Price, *Government and Science* (New York: New York University Press, 1954).

The literature became more respectful of expertise in the scientific prosperity of the 1960s, when Price wrote what C.P. Snow later called "much the most interesting and experienced book on the subject that I have read." Price noted that the relationship between government and science was changing in ways that were not yet well defined for either.

1156.   Harold Lasswell, "The Political Science of Science," *American Political Science Review*, 50, (December 1956): 961-79; also

1157.   James L. McCamy, *Science and Public Administration* (University: University of Alabama Press, 1960).

Lasswell, in his presidential address before the American Political Science Association in September, 1956, called for the expanded study of the evolving role of scientists in government. McCamy helped reinforce the need in 1960, noting that the scientist was seen by the average public administrator as an "infallible specialist in immutable fact," causing a change in the power relationship of government which the experts had not been trained to handle.

1158.   Amitai Etzioni, "Authority Structure and Organizational Effectiveness," *Administrative Science Quarterly*, 4, (June 1959): 43-67.

Etzioni reinforced the unique role of expertise when he argued that professionalism leads to a different style of organization. In order to keep the authority structure consistent with organizational goals, the staff is usually subordinated to the line personnel. In professional organizations, however, the staff carries out the major goal activities. Therefore, in those agencies, the line personnel should be subordinated to the staff.

1159.   Sir C(harles) P. Snow, *Science and Government* (London: Oxford University Press, 1961).[6]

Through the early 1960s, literature on the political power of scientists and technicians continued as a major theme of the literature on bureaucratic politics. In the Godkin Lectures at Harvard University in 1960, Snow described the two major personalities that dominated the science advisory machinery of the 1930s that had shaped Britain's technical posture in the Second World War. Snow praised the introduction of scientists and experts into closed decision-making processes, but warned of the dangers that are inherent in some styles of scientific advice.

1160. Samuel P. Huntington, *The Common Defense* (New York: Columbia University Press, 1961); also

1161. Robert Gilpin, *American Scientists and Nuclear Weapons Policy* (Princeton, NJ: Princeton University Press, 1962).

In the United States, Huntington studied the politics of the military process during the Truman and Eisenhower administrations. He found that the general consensus on the need to arm against the Soviets led to the important implementation decisions being made by staff agencies in the executive branch. The executive became the chief legislator, and the congress became a lobbyist for special-interest projects.

Gilpin studied the role of scientists on nuclear weapons policy. While he was content with the inevitability that scientists will play increasing roles in policy making, he was concerned about the belief of many scientists and politicians that scientists speak only in truths, and that disagreements on policies arise only because someone is fabricating evidence.

1162. Victor A. Thompson, *Modern Organization* (New York: Alfred A. Knopf, 1961).

Developing his thesis that *"the most symptomatic characteristic of modern bureaucracy is the growing imbalance between ability and authority,"* Thompson saw scientific and technical specialists as the driving force behind the rationalism that leads to bureaucracy's troubles. The specialization, centralization, departmentalization, and plodding deliberation of rational bureaucracy leads to bureaupathic behavior among those being controlled.

1163. Don K. Price, *The Scientific Estate* (Cambridge: Harvard University Press, 1965).

Developing his three observations that the scientific revolution is "moving the public and private sectors closer together," "bringing a new order of complexity into the administration of public affairs," and "upsetting our system of checks and balances" (pp. 15-16), Price felt that a scientific state was rising to join the professional, the administrative, and the political estates in setting public policies.

1164. Ralph E. Lapp, *The New Priesthood* (New York: Harper and Row, 1965).

Not all saw such developments as positive. Lapp's thesis is "that democracy faces its most severe test in preserving its traditions in an age of scientific revolution." He argued that scientists have grown in strength since Benjamin Franklin's day to merge with the power of the military, and to enter politics by supporting congressional and presidential candidates. Once the few set national policies, we will become like Plato's timocracy.

1165.   Alan Altshuler, "Rationality and Influence in the Public Service," *Public Administration Review*, 25, (September 1965): 226-33.

      Altshuler expanded the role for expertise by noting that when traditional goal-directed technically-expert rationality is not practical, two other forms of rationality still exist. One involves the evaluation of means when goals are unclear. The other involves the redefinition of problems to widen the range of options. The danger that the advice of experts will be accepted uncritically seems remote.

1166.   Daniel S. Greenberg, "The Myth of the Scientific Elite," *Public Interest*, 1, (Fall 1965): 51-62.

      Greenberg agreed that while there are many more scientists lobbying to increase their own subsidies, they have not changed the way politics is done. The scientific approach does not "mix well" in Washington; the scientists are usually too busy doing their own work to worry about controlling policy.

1167.   Harvey Sherman, *It All Depends* (University: University of Alabama Press, 1966).

      One of the more dramatic attacks on the role of expertise in bureaucracy was written by Sherman, a former director of the Port Authority of New York. He argued that organizing is more an art than a science, that what is true in one circumstance is often not true in another, and that what is true today is not necessarily true tomorrow. In such a world, expert prediction of organizational outcomes seems remote.

1168.   Harold L. Wilensky, *Organizational Intelligence* (New York: Basic Books, 1967).

      Discussions of the permanent place of expertise in bureaucracy continued, however. Wilensky argued that the administrators who have come to power in the managerial revolution work most effectively in cooperation with their sources of expert advice and information. "Intelligence failures are built into complex organizations." However, the structural fixes are often mere tinkering--including formalized sharing of information or conduits to outside advice. By analyzing several bureaucratic experiences of the 1960s, Wilensky was able to argue that those who lose the bureaucratic politics game, among both managers and technicians, are those who remain isolated.

1169.   Townsend Hoopes, *The Limits of Intervention* (New York: David McCay Co., 1969); also

1170. David Halberstam, *The Best and the Brightest* (New York: Random House, 1972).

Expertise in organizations seldom underwent the scrutiny that it received as a result of the Vietnam War. Townsend Hoopes, who had occupied several key offices in the Pentagon, concentrated on Johnson's decision to begin deescalation in 1968. Halberstam described the initial stages of involvement in the war. In both cases, the authors described a system of piecemeal planning that was driven by a virtual obsession with anticommunism, but that lacked any clear sense of long-range strategy to accomplish their goals.

1171. Guy Benveniste, *The Politics of Expertise* (Berkeley: Glendessary Press, 1972); also

1172. Allan W. Lerner, *The Politics of Decision-Making*, Volume 34, Sage Library of Social Research (Beverly Hills: Sage Publications, 1976).

Following the lead of Wilensky, these two authors viewed experts from the perspective of organizational dynamics to study the interplay between politicos (Lerner's term) and experts. Benveniste's conceptual work argued that "princes" (using a Machiavellian analogy) have entered a world of planning, and that they are caught in the paradox that they need to trust experts in order to increase their own power. He distinguished four types of planning, but concentrated on strategies by which experts can use "intentional planning" to increase their own power. He concluded that the political system cannot abolish planners because the world is too uncertain without them. However, planners can be controlled by integrating them into the political process.
Lerner ran laboratory experiments and cited social psychological research to describe the tactics used by experts at the levels of roles, personalities, problem content, and organizational and societal variables. While experts play a variety of roles (leaders, brokers, nonhostile independents) they tend to be more assertive and to assume larger roles than laymen. He also described 11 conditions under which the role of the expert tends to increase in organizational dynamics.

1173. Garry D. Brewer, *Politicians, Bureaucrats and the Consultant* (New York: Basic Books, 1973).

At the local level, both San Francisco and Pittsburgh attempted computer simulations during the 1960s to replicate local housing and urban renewal projects. Brewer interviewed over 100 participants in the two projects to discover that the goals of the simulations were unclear and that the data were inadequate to make them work. In the end, they led to political animosity and eventual cancellation. He warned against the unrealistic use of computer simulations to answer essentially political questions.

1174.   Kenneth R. Hammond, ed., *Judgment and Decision in Public Policy Formation*,
         AAAS Selected Symposium 1 (Boulder, Colorado: Westview Press, 1978).

The authors in this AAAS symposium, with additional papers added later, addressed the declining role of science and the low technological quality inherent in
political decisions. Colorado governor Richard Lamm noted how seldom he used the
scientific advice available to him, while both Lamm and Joseph F. Coates speculated
that much of the cause is in the narrow focus and egocentric behavior of academi-
cians. Still, several contributors felt it might be possible to improve the technical
quality of policy decisions through a variety of techniques, including changes in the
decision-making process, in the decision makers, and in the technical advice.

1175.   David Faust, *The Limits of Scientific Reasoning* (Minneapolis: University of
         Minnesota Press, 1984).

Faust's thesis is "simple--that human judgment is far more limited than we
have typically believed and that all individuals, scientists included, have a surprisingly
restricted capacity to manage or interpret complex information." (p. xxv) While this
makes scientists poor interpreters of policy-related information, even crude models and
simulations work somewhat better. Therefore, Faust expected computers and decision
modelling to play larger roles in the future of organizations.

CONTINUING CONCERNS

The gulf remains wide between those who prescribe economic rationality for
organizational decision-making, and those who argue that something like administrative rationality is either desireable or merely the best that can be accomplished. It
could easily be argued that the gulf should remain wide, because few would argue
against such tactics as rationality, economy, or efficiency in pursuit of the organization's goals. These tactics cannot be developed to their full potential without the
careful attention of those who believe in their potential.

The tendency of the tactics to become goals in their own right seems at times
to be overpowering, however. As in the case of Vietnam, eventual policy failures are
sometimes the only check. At other times, according to group decision-making theory,
the necessity to justify one's position before opposing theorists may temper the
enthusiasm of extremists.

NOTES FOR CHAPTER SEVENTEEN

1. The book was not translated into English until 1915. The four translations published in that year were from the Italian translation *La sociologia del partito politico nella democrazia moderna Roberto Michels*; traduzione dall' originale tedesco del Dr. Alfredo Polledro riveduta e ampliata dall'autore (Torino: Unione Tipografico-Editrice Torinese, 1912). The translation from Italian to English was done by Eden and Cedar Paul. Michels wrote a special chapter on party life in wartime for the English translation. The publishers were Hearst's International Library Co. (probably the first), Free Press, Dover Publications, and Jarrold & Sons of London.

    All subsequent printings have been of the English translation of the Italian translation of the German.

2. While the American first printing of this book give no publication or copyright date, the simultaneous British first printing do.

3. For the Operations Research Society of America, this was "Publications in Operations Research No. 3".

4. The original report was Nicholas G. Nicolaidis, *Policy-Decision and Organization Theory*, John W. Donner Memorial Fund Publication No. 11 (Los Angeles: University of Southern California Bookstore, 1960).

5. The original study was Norman C. Dalkey and Olaf Helmer, *The Use of Experts for the Estimation of Bombing Requirements--A Project Delphi Technique*, RM-727-PR (Santa Monica, Calif.: RAND Corporation, November 1951). The 1964 study was Theodore J. Gordon and Olaf Helmer, "Report on a Long Range Forecasting Study," Rand Paper P-2982 (Santa Monica, Calif.: RAND Corporation, September 1964).

6. The book was copyrighted in December 1960, but was published in 1961.

18

Budgeting and Fiscal Administration

BACKGROUND

This chapter discusses two topics that are closely tied to those in the previous chapter. The first is budgeting literature within government, or the long standing concern with the politics and structure by which government funds are dispersed. Secondly, fiscal literature is reviewed as it relates to the generation of revenue, and the balancing of revenue with expenditures.

BUDGETING IN GOVERNMENT

1176.   James A. Garfield, "National Appropriations and Misappropriations," *North American Review*, 128, (June 1879): 572-86.

Literature on the congressionally dominated appropriations process was seldom favorable. In the years leading into the reform era, future president Garfield complained about the poor methods used to implement a budget in which political parties took care of their own interests. Among the weaknesses were permanent and indefinite appropriations, the abuse of unexpended balances, deficiencies requiring supplemental appropriations, and the excessive use of contingency funds.

1177.   Ephraim D. Adams, *The Control of the Purse in the United States Government*, [Unpublished Ph.D. thesis, University of Michigan], 1894.[1]

In one of the first books to have an impact on future scholars, Adams argued that the House of Representatives had taken on more than its constitutionally permitted role in the budgeting process. He described the development of their all-powerful role, and complained that the committee system had led to lack of coordination and responsibility.

1178. Henry Carter Adams, *Science of Finance* (New York: Henry Holt and Co., 1898).

In the first textbook on the subject, Adams proposed a systematic analysis of budgets, recognizing that all public wants could be reduced to money. He argued against false economies, claiming that government protection allowed propitious forces to operate, thereby reducing the future need for protection. He proposed that government patrimony must be restrained, and that political organizations must be given a recognized and regulated role in the political process.

1179. Committee on Municipal Reform, National Municipal League, "A Municipal Corporations Act" (New York: n.p., 1899); reprinted in National Municipal League, *A Municipal Program* (New York: Macmillan and Co., 1900), pp. 187-224.

In the United States, the movement toward unified budgets first grew strong among municipal reformers. In 1899, the National Municipal League drafted a model charter that included a provision (Article III, Section 7) by which the mayor would submit an annual budget of current expenses to the city council, which could reduce or eliminate any items, but could not increase individual items nor the entire budget.

1180. *Anti-Deficiency Act*, 33 Stat. 1214, 1257 (1905).

At the federal level, the concern remained with control more than with budgetary planning. In an effort to stop the annual practice of agencies running deficiencies that had to be made up through supplemental appropriations, congress adopted an old French practice and instructed department heads or their designated representatives to create monthly allotments so that expenditures would be spread evenly over the year.

1181. Eugene E. Agger, *The Budget in the American Commonwealths*, Studies in History, Economics, and Public Law vol. XXV, No. 2 (New York: Columbia University Press, 1907).

Budgeting at the state level was not much different from the federal example. Agger found state budget practices to be inadequate as reports (auditors and comptrollers were weak) and as projects of law (legislative domination led to extravagance and waste). He proposed that some constitutional restrictions be eliminated, and that governors prepare budget estimates to allow better balance in budget requests.

1182.   Bureau of Municipal Research, *Making a Municipal Budget* (New York: Bureau of Municipal Research, 1907).

    The first real victory for reformers came in the creation of the first comprehensive line-item budget for the New York City Department of Health in 1907. The Bureau, then called the Bureau of City Betterment, had designed the plan in 1906. In 1907, they described the "classified budget" with its "service records" of everything that was purchased or completed during the year.

1183.   Commission on Economy and Efficiency, *The Need for a National Budget System*, House Document 854, U. S. Congress, House. 62 Cong., 2d sess., (1912).

    In 1911, President Taft appointed a commission on economy and efficiency to study the federal budgetary process and to recommend changes.[2] The commission recommended an annual executive budget submission by the president to cover expenditures (in functional format) and revenues. Congress would review the policy directions implicit in the budget, but department heads would be left with considerable discretion to transfer funds to aid in implementation. Also, accounting procedures would be tightened under the Treasury department. Except for the marginally relevant creation of the Division of Efficiency in the Civil Service Commission, the procedures were not implemented.

1184.   Frank J. Goodnow, "The Limit of Budgetary Control," *American Political Science Review*, 7, (February 1913): 68-77; also

1185.   Charles D. Norton, "Constitutional Provision for a Budget," *Proceedings: Academy of Political Science of the City of New York*, 5, (October 1914): 189-92.

    As had been the case with merit system laws (see chapter 16), questions arose as to the legality and constitutionality of some budget proposals. Reflecting his belief in the politics/administration dichotomy, Goodnow saw a need for constitutional change only if the constitution or statutes clearly divided the budget as a policy-making device from the executive and administrative functions of policy execution. Most authors agreed more with Norton, however, who proposed complete, constitutional change. "Our federal, state, and municipal charters and courts have surrounded government executives with fantastic regulations which, if applied in private business, would certainly wreck any enterprise dependent for its existence on yearly profits."

1186.   A. R. Hatton, ed., "Public Budgets," *Annals of the American Academy of Political and Social Science*, 62, (November 1915).

    This was a particularly useful collection of articles from some of the most widely-known names in the reform movement. Frederick Cleveland, who had headed the Taft commission, proposed that budgets should consist of a plan that balanced resources and expenditures, a system for accountability, and the actual revenues, expenditures, and financial conditions of the government. Bruère proposed that the budget could be used for administrative planning and control. Ford described our budget's deterioration from the original English model. Separate authors (notably Charles Beard) described the experience in several states, while others described municipal reform experiences.

1187.   Bureau of Municipal Research, "Responsible Government," *Municipal Research* no. 69 (January 1916): 57-67; also "Budget Legislation in Two States," *Municipal Research* no. 70 (February 1916); also "Three Proposed Constitutional Amendments for Control of the Purse," *Municipal Research* no. 73 (May 1916); also "The Elements of State Budget Making," *Municipal Research* no. 80 (December 1916).

In 1916, numerous proposals for reform arose in various states, pushed in large part by the bureau movement. In January, budgets at all levels were described as a prerequisite for responsible government. Specific analyses of proposals in New Jersey (no. 70 above), New York (nos. 70 and 73), and Maryland (nos. 73 and 80) occupied much of the Bureau's time.

1188.   "Report of Commission on Economy and Efficiency of the State of Maryland," *Senate Journal* [Maryland], (January 28, 1916): 129-32; also

1189.   Article III, Section 52. *Constitution of Maryland*, regulating the making of appropriations by the General Assembly of Maryland. Amendment adopted November 7, 1916.

Maryland was the first state to ratify a constitutional amendment creating an executive budget process. In 1915, certified public accountant Harvey S. Chase announced that the state was running a deficit of almost $1.5 million. The Democratic Party initiated a study under the leadership of Frank J. Goodnow. The group's report, reprinted in the *Senate Journal*, proposed a constitutional amendment for an executive budget. With a few amendments, it was adopted in November, 1916.

1190.   Governor's Conference, *Proceedings*, 9, (1916): 25-58; also

1191.   [Fred Wilbur Powell], "The Recent Movement for State Budget Reform, 1911-1917," *Municipal Research*, 91, (November 1917); later Ph.D. thesis (New York: Columbia University Press, 1918).

The spread of the Maryland example was steady but slow. In December 1916, governors from 23 states met at an annual conference in Washington, D.C.. Overwhelmingly, they approved the concept of an executive budget, and several initiated such proposals in their 1917 legislative sessions.

As Powell described, however, progress was slow. While there were many proposals as he was writing, he felt that the movement toward executive budgets could be crippled by the half-way measures that were often being adopted.

1192.   William F. Willoughby, Westel W. Willoughby, and Samuel M. Lindsay, *The System of Financial Administration of Great Britain* (New York: D. Appleton and Co., 1917); also

1193.   Rene Stourm, *The Budget*, trans. Thaddeus Plazinski (New York: D. Appleton and Co., 1917); originally *Le budget (Cours de finances)* (Paris: Guillaumin, 1889). Translation was of 7th ed. (Paris: F. Alcan, 1913).

In 1917, the Institute for Government Research entered the foray with its first Study in Administration, a comparison of the strongly centralized British system of finances with the hopelessly disorganized American approach. This was supplemented by the widely-circulated translation of Stourm's work, which Charles Beard argued offered a closer parallel to the American system of government. Both works strongly supported centralized budgets prepared solely by the executive.

1194.   Charles Wallace Collins, *A National Budget System* (New York: Macmillan Co., 1917).

Speaking for the business community, Collins contended that the U.S. system was more cumbersome and less democratic than the British, French, Japanese, or Swiss systems. Executive budgets with planning needed no constitutional amendment, he argued.

1195.   William Franklin Willoughby, *The Problem of a National Budget* (New York: D. Appleton and Co., 1918); also *The Movement For Budgetary Reform in the States* (New York: D. Appleton and Co., 1918).

The Bureau for Government Research continued to refine its proposals. Willoughby felt that for administrative and budgetary purposes, information should be available from the five standpoints of funds, organizational units, activities, character of expenditures, and objects of expenditures. One method would be chosen for the basic report, with the others indexed through supporting analyses.

In a separate work, he described the experiences of 31 states in creating budgetary reform. He recounted that the movement toward a unified executive budget began at the municipal level for reasons of democracy, coordination, efficiency, and economy. He described and reprinted budgetary regulations from the 31 states. While none met his requirements for perfect scientific budgeting, each represented progress toward the ultimate goal. Both books contained extensive bibliographies.

1196.   Harold G. Villard and Westel W. Willoughby, *The Canadian Budgetary System* (New York: D. Appleton and Co., 1918).

This third study of the Institute for Government Research used the Canadian experience to argue that the British system could not be transported effectively into countries with different governmental systems, standards, and customs, or with great expanses requiring public works systems. Instead, the system needed to be tailored to the conditions in each country.

1197.   Edward A. Fitzpatrick, *Budget Making in a Democracy: A New View of the Budget* (New York: Macmillan Co., 1918).

The consensus that often seemed to dominate the literature was not reflected in congress. Based on his experiences in Wisconsin, Fitzpatrick wrote a book that became a symbol for a generation of those who were concerned about the growth in executive power through budgeting. Fitzpatrick argued that truly executive budgets created autocracy, and had been created in England during a crisis. The function of the administration and executive was "preliminary, preparatory, advisory" while the function of the legislature was determining and conclusive. Agency proposals should be collected by the executive, and passed on with comments, but without amendments. Congress should allow minority party input in analyzing the proposals.

1198.   Henry Campbell Black, "A National Budget System," *The Constitutional Review*, 4, (January 1920): 38-45; also

1199.   Frederick A. Cleveland and Arthur Eugene Buck, *The Budget and Responsible Government* (New York: Macmillan Co., 1920).

Most of the political spectrum stood for reform, however. The right-wing, pro-business National Association for Constitutional Government endorsed Representative Good's bill for an executive budget, arguing that a strengthened presidential role could stop congressional pork-barreling.
Cleveland and Buck, from the Progressive tradition, argued that legislative budgets had led to the rise of bossism in America. Only an executive budget could lead to accountability and responsibility.

1200.   Luther H. Gulick, *Evolution of the Budget in Massachusetts*, Ph.D. thesis (New York: Columbia University Press, 1920); also trade edition (New York: Macmillan Co., 1920).

The transition to executive budgets did not always go smoothly. Gulick described the evolution of Massachusetts' budget from legislative control to an executive budget. Once the switch was made in 1918, however, Governor Coolidge created a crisis of "irresponsibility" by assigning the details for his budget submission to the legislature. His 1920 submission was vastly improved, however.

1201. Arthur E. Buck, Budget Making: *A Handbook on the Forms and Procedures of Budget Making With Special Reference to States* (New York: D. Appleton and Co., 1921); also *Public Budgeting* (New York: Harper and Brothers, 1929).

For those ready to make the change to executive budgets, the bureaus were ready to help. Buck, working in 1921 through the auspices of both the Bureau of Municipal Research and the new National Institute of Public Administration, provided detailed descriptions of the procedures and forms that should be used for devising, authorizing, and implementing budgets as financial plans. In 1929, he described the practices and the reforms that had been adopted in the various states.

1202. *Budget and Accounting Act of 1921*, 42 Stat. 20.

After the War, the joint drive toward expenditure and tax reduction led to the Budget and Accounting Act. The Bureau of the Budget was created to help the president compile unified budget requests. As a political compromise, however, it was placed in the Treasury Department. Auditing of accounts was moved from the Treasury Department to the new General Accounting Office that answered to congress.

1203. Charles G. Dawes, *The First Year of the Budget of the United States* (New York: Harper and Brothers, 1923).

Dawes served as the first Director of the Bureau of the Budget, and his restricted view of its functions shaped the Bureau's role for the next decade. His diary of the first year reflected a clear distinction between policy and administration, and the Bureau's purpose was to stretch dollars through "correct business principles in routine business administration." "(O)ne must remember that the Bureau of the Budget is concerned only with the humbler and routine business of government. Unlike cabinet officers, it is concerned with no questions of policy, save that of economy and efficiency." (p. xi)

1204. Clyde L. King, ed., "Competency and Economy in Public Expenditures," *Annals of the American Academy of Social and Political Science*, 113, (May 1924).

In 1924, the *Annals* updated its report of 1915 (#62, see above) to reflect the virtual revolution in executive budgets since that time. Most of the authors, notably Seidemann, were pleased with the changes. Almost all had some reservations, however. Upson described the continued growth in expenditures that came from concentrating on general programs rather than activities and accomplishments. Other authors described transition problems as plans were implemented in states in which they did not always fit political realities.

1205.   Robert Emmett Taylor, *Municipal Budget Making* (Chicago: University of Chicago Press, 1925).

Local budgeting often lagged behind in the revolution of reform. Taylor's survey of 75 municipalities showed inadequate budget staffs and practices. As a solution, he proposed administrative organizations with strict financial accountability and planning through budgeting. While he realized that budgets would not stop municipal corruption, they would restrict the rampant maladministration.

1206.   William Franklin Willoughby, *The National Budget System* (Baltimore: Johns Hopkins Press, 1927).

At the federal level, however, the reformers were pleased. Willoughby felt that the 1921 bill had improved presidential planning, deficiency budgeting, coordination, and accountability. Following extensive descriptions of budgeting history and procedure, he suggested that the Bureau be moved directly under the president and be given more functions, and that the appropriations process be improved.

1207.   Arthur E. Buck, *The Budget in Governments of Today* (New York: Macmillan Co., 1934).

Buck suggested that the U.S. still faced considerable problems because of such structural difficulties as federalism, separation of powers, bicameralism, and the possibility of divided control by parties. He proposed that executive authority for budget formulation and execution be strengthened, that the budget form be amended, that the executive and legislative machinery be reorganized, and that legislative audit and review be strengthened.

1208.   Jacob Wilner Sundelson, "Budgetary Principles," *Political Science Quarterly*, 50, (June 1935): 236-63; also *Budgetary Methods in National and State Governments*, New York State Tax Commission Special Report No. 14 (Albany: J. B. Lyon Co., Printers, 1938).

In 1935, Sundelson noted that reform literature concentrated so heavily on structural changes, that little was written on either budgeting theory or the fiscal implications of the budget. The Europeans, especially Gaston Jèze, had taken the subject much further.[3]

In 1938, however, he also updated the descriptions of budgeting practices for the states, the federal government, and several foreign governments. He advocated single-year appropriations, centralized budget planning, executive budgets, and streamlined procedures for legislative deliberations.

1209. Verne B. Lewis, "Appendix A: Budgetary Administration in the Department of Agriculture," in John M. Gaus and Leon Wolcott, *Public Administration and the United States Department of Agriculture* (Chicago: Public Administration Service, 1940); pp. 403-60.

In the 1940s, a rudimentary form of program budgeting arose in the Department of Agriculture. As Lewis described, the development was an inevitable consequence of size, as those at the top concentrated on program aspects of the budget while those at the bottom were more concerned with detail. Over time, the actual submissions to congress contained less detail. While Lewis accepted this development, he was concerned about the lack of attention to the asset side of the ledger in budgeting.

1210. V. O. Key, Jr., "The Lack of a Budgeting Theory," *American Political Science Review*, 34, (December 1940): 1137-44; also

1211. Harold D. Smith, "The Budget as an Instrument of Legislative Control and Executive Management," *Public Administration Review*, 4, (Summer 1944): 181-88; also

1212. Verne B. Lewis, "Toward a Theory of Budgeting," *Public Administration Review*, 12, (Winter 1952): 42-54.

Like Sundelson, Key lamented that budgeting studies were proceeding with little progress toward developing theory. Fiscal theories were arising, but the studies of expenditures were content to rely on descriptions. Capitalistic governmental budgeting needed to proceed in the same vein as socialistic authors and a few public works studies by developing generalized explanations and hypotheses that could be tested.

Both Smith and Lewis attempted rudimentary theories of budgeting. Considering that the budget was the best means of both legislative control and executive management, Smith suggested that eight principals could be applied to budgeting including executive programming, executive responsibility, reporting, adequate tools, multiple procedures, executive discretion, flexibility in timing, and two-way budget organization. The specifics of each were explained in the article.

Lewis worked from three propositions: that budget analysis is a comparison of the relative merits of alternate uses of funds, that incremental analysis is necessary due to the diminishing utility of funds, and that the comparison of merits is based on relative effectiveness in achieving a common objective. Based on these, he suggested the use of alternative budget submissions with justifications and estimates that would work at various funding levels.

1213. Robert A. Walker, "The Relation of Budgeting to Program Planning," *Public Administration Review*, 4, (Spring 1944): 97-107; also

1214.   Fritz Morstein Marx, "The Bureau of the Budget: Its Evolution and Present
         Rôle, I," *American Political Science Review*, 39, (August 1945): 653-84; also
         "The Bureau of the Budget: Its Evolution and Present Rôle, II," *American
         Political Science Review*, 39, (October 1945): 869-98; also

1215.   Robert E. Merriam, "The Bureau of the Budget as Part of the President's
         Staff," *Annals of the American Academy of Political and Social Science*,
         307, (September 1956): 15-23.

Through the 1940s and 1950s, much of the literature discussed the expanding
size and role of the Bureau of the Budget. Walker described how planners had suffered because they were concerned with budgets only on capital budgets and public
works. Planners and budgeters needed each other, he suggested.

Marx recounted the rise of the Bureau from its earlier technical role under
Dawes, through Secretary of Commerce Herbert Hoover's suggestion in 1924 that it
be moved under the President, to its more recent functions of the executive budget,
central clearance, and administrative studies. Merriam as Assistant Director of the
Bureau described its major role as presidential advisor, providing the presidency with
more facts to increase its power.

1216.   Commission on Organization of Executive Branch of the Government, *Bud-
         geting and Accounting* (Washington, D.C.: USGPO, February 1949); also
         General Management of the Executive Branch (Washington, D.C.: USGPO,
         1949); also

1217.   Commission on Organization of the Executive Branch of Government, *Bud-
         get and Accounting* (Washington, D.C.: USGPO, 1955).

The First Hoover Commission in 1949 is best remembered for its recommendation that the Government adopt "a budget based upon functions, activities, and
projects." The performance budget would be divided by programs and subdivided into
smaller programs to help describe the functions being fulfilled. The Commission also
suggested closer cooperation between the Bureau and the departments to aid in planning for efficiency. Performance budgeting was legislated in the Budget and Accounting Procedures Act of 1950.[4]

The task force in 1949 also suggested that the Bureau be returned to the
Treasury Department. The overall task force failed to endorse the proposal, however,
and praise for a presidentially-driven budget system increased in the second Hoover
commission report in 1955.

The 1949 commission was heavily split on accounting procedures to be used.
In 1955, however, the task force recommended the phasing in of accrual accounting,
and the adoption of cost accounting techniques then used in business. A requirement
for such cost accounting techniques was legislated in 1956.[5]

1218.   Vincent J. Browne, *The Control of the Public Budget* (Washington, D.C.: Public
         Affairs Press, 1949).

      Browne's thesis "that our present budget system works in a most unbusiness-
like fashion and that, for the most part, this has been true throughout the history of
our Republic," (p. 5) was not new. Neither was his argument that there was too much
congressional interference for the budget to be a successful planning document. His
history of budgetary politics was extensive, however, and is still useful for modern
students.

1219.   Frederick C. Mosher, *Program Budgeting: Theory and Practice* (Chicago: Public
         Administration Service, 1954).

      After the first Hoover report, the Defense Department attempted to imple-
ment performance or program budgeting. Mosher analyzed that experience within the
context of factors such as the uncertain environment, time constraints, organizational
restrictions, and interpersonal elements that complicated traditional budgeting. He
concluded that program budgeting, involving a greater emphasis on planning, was most
effective if it combined the "factorial" method of standardizing requirements from the
top, with the "field" system of allowing requests to filter up from below. The second
method was more useful when the organizational boundaries varied from logical program definitions.

1220.   Arthur Smithies, *The Budgetary Process in the United States* (New York:
         McGraw-Hill 1955).

      Smithies also proposed a program approach to satisfy his three principles that
all options which satisfy a particular objective should be considered, that expenditures
and revenues should be considered in balance, and the economy and efficiency should
be maximized. Program budgeting combined with greater congressional accountability
(but not control) would satisfy all three.

1221.   Jesse Burkhead, *Government Budgeting* (New York: John Wiley and Sons,
         1956).

      As a textbook, Burkhead's treatise on government budgeting touched on all
relevant topics, including the growth of BOB in the politics of the budgeting process,
the role of fiscal policy in the economy, and special concerns on revenue estimating,
public enterprises, and balanced budgets. Burkhead also saw performance budgeting
as one of the more exciting revolutions in budgeting, however, and described several
applications that had been made of the concept.

1222.   John Kenneth Galbraith, *The Affluent Society* (Boston: Houghton Mifflin,
         1958); also

1223.   Anthony Downs, "Why the Government Budget is too Small in a Democracy,"
         World Politics, 12, (July 1960): 541-63.

Authors such as Hayek had long argued that the overall size of governmental
budgets needed to be kept small to protect democracy. The authors above, however,
argued that governmental budgets were inevitably too small. Galbraith described the
inevitable preference that consumers would hold for private goods over public goods,
resulting in an underfunding of the public sector. Downs emphasized the lack of
information available to voters on governmental projects. Their resulting lack of
support through ignorance would only get worse as the economy became more complex.

1224.   Charles J. Hitch and Ronald N. McKean, *The Economics of Defense in the
         Nuclear Age*, RAND Report R-346 (Santa Monica, Cal.: RAND Corporation,
         March 1960)[6]; also trade edition (Cambridge: Harvard University Press,
         1960).

The rational approach to budgeting finally reached its peak in the Planning
Programming Budgeting System (PPBS) that was first proposed in this RAND Corporation study of Department of Defense budgeting. The authors, the first of whom
eventually implemented the package as Assistant Secretary of Defense, saw the technique as a way of regulating the impact of the defense budget on the economy, and
of making rational choices in awkward circumstances. They proposed a set of program categories and described the mechanics of the five-year plan and cost/benefit
analysis.

1225.   Aaron B. Wildavsky, *The Politics of the Budgetary Process* (Boston: Little,
         Brown, and Co., 1964); also *Budgeting* (Boston: Little, Brown, and Co., 1975);
         also *The New Politics of the Budgetary Process* (Glenview, IL: Scott Foresman,
         1988).

Just as rationalism was being implemented into the federal government, however, Wildavsky revived the incremental approach by popularizing the political analysis
of budgeting. In 1964, he produced a study that served as both a theoretical framework to explain budgeting as a political document, and an instruction manual for new
budget analysts. Based in his findings that the most successful budget officials were
the best politicians, and that "the largest determining factor of the size and content
of this year's budget is last year's budget," he discounted most reform proposals as
unconstitutional or simply impossible.
     In 1975, he undertook the more formidable task "to collect in one place exist-
ing knowledge on budgeting." (p. xi) Based on cross-cultural studies, he concluded
that the form of budgeting was determined by the predictability of the environment
and by the country's wealth. In the incremental style of the predictable and wealthy

U.S. budget, he felt that rational budgeting was not possible, although congressional reforms to help balance the budget would be helpful.

By 1988, however, the world of budgeting had become more complicated. Wildavsky described the collapse of the consensus on basic goals that had made incrementalism possible. In the new dissensus, entitlements drove out discretionary spending, lobby groups attacked each others' programs, and "gimmicks" such as Gramm-Rudman-Hollings were doomed to failure. For budgeting to work, fundamental political realignments would be needed.

1226.   Joseph P. Harris, *Congressional Control of Administration* (Washington, D.C.: Brookings Institution, 1964); also

1227.   Richard F. Fenno, Jr., *The Power of the Purse* (Boston: Little, Brown, and Co., 1966).

Continuing the political approach to budgeting, Harris complained that congress had overemphasized the control aspect in its budgeting decisions, but that it had allowed such powerful oversight tools as the audit to be used ineffectively. Fenno was less concerned about the control process, arguing that appropriations committees served as a bridge between agency and congressional needs. He felt that trust between the committees and agencies was important, and that the two bodies should be working towards the same goals.

1228.   Aaron Wildavsky and Arthur Hammond, "Comprehensive Versus Incremental Budgeting in the Department of Agriculture," *Administrative Science Quarterly*, 10, (December 1965): 321-46.

The authors interviewed several practitioners after the zero-base budgeting experiment in the Department of Agriculture. Most felt that the technique could not be practiced in the real world. The practitioners felt that the process may have been helpful in that it had a "Hawthorne effect" on the budget analysts in the agency. They did not feel that it had helped them personally, however.

1229.   David Novick, ed., *Program Budgeting: Program Analysis and the Federal Budget* (Washington, D.C.: USGPO, 1965); also trade edition (Cambridge: Harvard University Press, 1965); also

1230.   Fremont J. Lyden and Ernest G. Miller, eds., *Planning Programming Budgeting: A Systems Approach to Management* (Chicago: Markham Publishing Co., 1968); also 2nd ed. (1972).

In 1965, President Johnson ordered that systems analysis become a part of the budgeting process for all federal agencies. These collections of readings attempted to summarize the background for a movement that had gained considerable strength in a few years. Novick's book contained articles (notably one by Smithies) describing the strengths and promises of program budgeting. It also contained actual and potential applications for various federal programs, and included problems that still needed to be overcome.

Lyden and Miller collected previously-published articles that followed from early program budgeting proposals through the implementation of PPBS. Because experience grew rapidly in the late 1960s, an almost completely revised list of readings appeared in the second edition in 1972.

1231.   "Planning-Programming-Budgeting: A Symposium," *Public Administration Review*, 26, (December 1966): 243-310; also

1232.   "Planning-Programming-Budgeting System Reexamined: Development, Analysis, and Criticism," *Public Administration Review*, 29, (March/April 1969): 111-202.

Similarly, these symposia traced the development of PPBS in government. The first symposium, which *PAR* editor Dwight Waldo explained fell together somewhat by accident, occurred while most of government was still implementing the technique. Perhaps the best remembered article, by Alan Schick, saw PPBS as a logical third step in the development of government budgeting.[7] Wildavsky explained that economists had been better than political scientists at selling their conceptual tools.

In the 1969 "update," there was more emphasis on the application of PPBS at state and local levels, with separate articles on each. Schick and Wildavsky both had new articles, with Wildavsky concerned that PPBS had become such a burden that its demise could possible also sink any efforts at policy analysis, which was still helpful.

1233.   Charles L. Schultze, *The Politics and Economics of Public Spending* (Washington, D.C.: Brookings Institution, 1968).

Schultze compared the analytical needs of PPBS with the political needs of incremental budgeting to conclude that a mixture of the two was practical in the real world. As long as it was not carried to the extremes of zero-base budgeting, PPB introduced efficiency partisans into the political process, and made the agency heads better able to shape their programs.

1234.   Peter A. Pyhrr, "Zero-Base Budgeting," *Harvard Business Review*, 48, (November/December 1970): 111-21; also *Zero-Base Budgeting: A Practical Management Tool for Evaluating Expenses* (New York: Wiley Interscience, 1973).

Pyhrr popularized what Schultze considered to be the more extreme zero-base technique as a tactic for reexamining the "base" figure of current expenditures in each budget cycle. Each budget request would include a "decision package" with justifications, costs, alternatives, measures of performance, the consequences of failing to perform the function, and optional levels of funding for each function. These would be ranked and consolidated as they moved up the budgetary hierarchy. He also described some implementation successes and problems that had arisen in his tenure at Texas Instruments (both citations above) and the state of Georgia (1973 above).

1235.   Leonard Merewitz and Stephen H. Sosnick, *The Budget's New Clothes* (Chicago: Markham Publishing Co., 1971).

Soon the literature on rational budgeting turned sour. Reacting against "an overabundance of laudatory and superficial discussions of PPB," (p. vii) the authors analyzed the five elements of PPB to determine its potential utility. They found that several elements were expensive to implement while the data gained often could not be used, or bypassed the need for more fundamental administrative reorganization. They also described the possible internal contradictions in benefit/cost analysis. In case studies of the California Water Project and the supersonic transport, they found that benefit/cost analysis had little impact.

1236.   Allen Schick, *Budget Innovation in the States* (Washington, D.C.: Brookings Institution, 1971); also "A Death in the Bureaucracy: The Demise of Federal PPB," *Public Administration Review*, 33, (March/April 1973): 146-56; also "The Road from ZBB," *Public Administration Review*, 38, (March/April 1978): 177-80.

In 1971, Schick described the difficulties that had led to limited success for program budgeting and PPBS at the state level. Traditional members of the "budgetocracy," who gained their power through emphases on control, line items, object codes, organizations rather than programs, and crisis decision-making, had helped to hold back program budgeting or to subvert it to their purposes once it was established.
        Also in 1971, the federal requirement to submit PPB-style program justifications was eliminated. Schick argued in 1973 that the "death" came from overly rapid and broad implementation without adequate expertise among budgeting officials or their analysts, and without adequate support from above. Similarly, when President Carter implemented zero-base budgeting (ZBB), Schick noted in 1978 that it resulted in the most incremental budget ever. Implementation of ZBB went smoothly because it did not change the data or structure of budgeting. Instead, the agencies submitted too many decision packages to be analyzed.

1237.   S. Kenneth Howard and Gloria A. Grazzle, eds., *Whatever Happened to State Budgeting?* (Lexington, KY: Council of State Governments, 1972); also

1238.   S. Kenneth Howard, *Changing State Budgeting* (Lexington, KY: Council of
          State Governments, 1973).

Not all authors were as pessimistic about state budgeting as was Schick.
Howard and Grazzle's 1972 collection of 51 articles included many of the "classics"
described earlier. Several of the others were reprinted from seminars sponsored by
the National Association of State Budget Officers. The focus was much more on
operational details, and on reforms that were practical to implement.

In 1973, Howard produced a training manual for the National Association of
State Budget Officers. The general theme was that states were moving toward rationalistic budgeting. While some reforms such as program budgeting had run into political road blocks, others had met with more success. To the extent that rationalistic
reforms succeeded, they could strengthen the executive role and lead to greater
program effectiveness and efficiency.

1239.   Robert D. Lee, Jr. and Ronald W. Johnson, *Public Budgeting Systems* (Balti-
          more: University Park Press, 1973).

Lee and Johnson also described the evolution of budgeting toward a more
programmed-oriented process with increasing demands that agencies justify their
programs. They had little enthusiasm for some of the reform techniques of recent
years, arguing that the long-term trend was toward developing program data and link-
ing it with resource data. They speculated that budgeting would continue to become
more rational, and that less money would be spent for the purpose of maintaining old
bureaucracies that were no longer producing.

1240.   *Congressional Budget and Impoundment Control Act*, 88 Stat. 297 (1974).

During the Nixon administration, many in congress became concerned that,
with or without analytical techniques, the budgeting process was out of control. In
an effort to regain congress' role in a budgeting process that was both hopelessly
complex and subverted by Nixon's impoundments, this legislation created budget committees for both houses as well as a Congressional Budget Office for expert analyses.
The beginning of the fiscal year was changed to October 1 to allow time for the
budget committees to consider concurrent resolutions that would establish spending
targets based on revenue projections and fiscal policies.

1241.   Louis Fisher, *Presidential Spending Power* (Princeton, NJ: Princeton Univer-
          sity Press, 1975).

Fisher described the development of presidential budgeting, and such devices
as lump-sum appropriations, reprogramming and transfers of funds, timing delays, and
impoundments to explain the context in which the Congressional Budget and Impoundment Control Act was passed. He felt that recent abuses in impoundments and presi-

dential control were unprecedented in degree if not in content. Instead of tighter controls with less executive discretion, however, he felt that more rigorous confirmation hearings and better editing of important information for congress' consideration was needed.

1242.   Charles H. Levine, "Organizational Decline and Cutback Management," *Public Administration Review*, 38, (July/August 1978): 316-25; also "More on Cutback Management: Hard Questions for Hard Times," *Public Administration Review*, 39, (March/April 1979): 179-83.

By the late 1970s, governments were facing retrenchment to degrees that had not been seen in recent times. Levine suggested in 1978 that cutbacks could be categorized into four types, and that organizational responses were different depending on the type of cutback, and on whether the goal was to resist or smooth out the effects. In 1979, he described nine common problems that managers encountered in deciding how to cut back programs, and suggested that more study of cutback management was needed.

1243.   James P. Pfiffner, *The President, the Budget, and Congress: Impoundment and the 1974 Budget Act* (Boulder, CO: Westview Press, 1979).

Pfiffner described the Budget and Impoundment Act as a turning point in a century-long development of an executive-dominated budgetary process. Congress acted because it believed President Nixon to be moving into a fifth stage of impoundment practices that usurped congress' constitutional "power of the purse." Pfiffner recounted congress' and the White House's positions through court cases, and described the politics of passing the legislation in 1974.

1244.   Allen Schick, *Congress and Money: Budgeting, Spending and Taxing* (Washington, D.C.: Urban Institute Press, 1980).

With the increased role of congress in budgeting after 1974, Schick studied the changes that had occurred in congressional behavior. He described the breakdown in conflict-resolving processes between 1966 and 1973, leading to the reforms of 1974. After describing more recent experiences, he concluded that the Act was often attacked for things it was never designed to do. On the goals of creating a legislatively-driven budget process and managing conflict within the process, however, the reforms of 1974 had worked reasonably well.

1245.   Mark S. Kamlet and David C. Mowery, "The Budgetary Base in Federal Resource Allocation," *American Journal of Political Science*, 24, (November 1980); 804-21.

The authors argued that the base figure accepted by OMB was both changable and subject to political attention. It helped coordinate fiscal and budgetary policies, resulting in a top-down decision-making influence that helped counter the bottom-up influence of incrementalism. Incrementalism was still the correct theory for most budgeting, however.

1246.   U.S. Supreme Court, *INS v Chadha, et al.*, 462 U.S. 919 (1983); also

1247.   Louis Fisher, "Chadha's Impact on the Budget Process," *Public Budgeting and Finance*, 3, (Winter 1983): 103-07.

In 1983, the Supreme Court declared legislative vetoes, or decisions to over-rule administrative decisions by something other than new legislation, to be a violation of constitutional separation of powers. Fisher speculated that this would not affect the "rescission" section of the Congressional Budget and Impoundment Control Act since it required action by both houses. However, the provision that allowed one house to overrule a "deferral" was effectively dead. Fortunately, congress had fallen into the practice of ruling on deferrals through regular legislation.

1248.   Jack Rabin and Thomas D. Lynch, eds., *Public Budgeting and Financial Management* (New York: Marcel Dekker, 1983).

Using the encyclopedic approach of the Marcel Dekker handbook series, this compilation of 25 articles attempted to cover every facet of budgeting and financial management. While a couple of articles used a cross-cultural approach, most emphasized budgeting in the United States. Different authors summarized trends on such diverse topics as revenue forecasting, risk management in pension systems, and the increasing use of computers in budgeting. Among the findings, Swan predicted a greater use of contingency approaches; Grafton and Permaloff considered Wildavsky's explanations to be outdated, and budget reforms to have been ineffective.

1249.   Gregory B. Mills and John L. Palmer, eds., *Federal Budget Policy in the 1980s* (Washington, D.C.: Urban Institute Press, 1984).

This set of readings brought together varied viewpoints on the changes in federal budgeting under the Reagan administration. Among the articles, both Heclo and Reishauer discussed Reagan's frustrations in trying to reduce spending in conditions of dispersed budgetary power. Heclo described the way in which OMB had begun paying more attention to congressional politics than the agencies. As a result, however, OMB's information base in the agencies was fading. Reishauer discussed the "fiscalization of the public policy debate."

The use of comments following the articles permitted debate. Wholey argued that cuts in the Employment and Training Administration were based on merit, for instance, while Lynn and Behn disagreed. Gramlich discussed the impacts of large debts, while Shepsle and Weingast were concerned about parochial interests in the congressional process.

1250.   Howard E. Shuman, *Politics and the Budget: The Struggle Between the President and the Congress* (Englewood Cliffs, NJ: Prentice-Hall, Inc., 1984).

As a congressional aide, Shuman approached budgeting as a political struggle between presidents, who had been made too strong by the 1974 reforms, and a congress which was divided between those with interests in power, and those who were driven by policy. He was concerned that special interests too strongly shaped the opinions of different parts of congress, and that only public debate would force congress toward the pursuit of the public interest.

1251.   Irene S. Rubin, *Shrinking the Federal Government: The Effect of Cutbacks on Five Federal Agencies* (New York: Longman, Inc., 1985).

Rubin investigated the effects of Reagan's cuts in the Employment and Training Administration, Community Planning and Development, the Bureau of Health Planning, the Urban Mass Transportation Administration, and the Office of Personnel Management. She found that cuts were determined outside the agencies, resulting in great difficulties for planning or managing the agencies' functions. Agency officials did as they were told, including the cutting of their own functions. The result, however, was great confusion and the interruption of services.

1252.   Louis Fisher, "Ten Years of the Budget Act: Still Searching for Controls," *Public Budgeting and Finance*, 5, (Autumn 1985): 3-28.

Looking back, Fisher argued that seldom had a piece of legislation missed the mark so badly without substantial amendment or repeal. He described eight goals of the legislation, and described the limited success or outright failures in meeting them. In the early years, there had been great difficulties controlling spending. More recently, budget resolutions had grown too complex. Fisher suggested that the budget resolutions could be abandoned without harming the rest of the process.

FISCAL ADMINISTRATION

Deciding how much money to spend is only half the picture for both households and governments. Such decisions make little sense without considering how much income is available. That so much of our literature speaks only to appropriations says much about the world of abundance in which budgeting theory evolved. Obviously, there is also a set of literature that discusses both income and expenditure, and still another that is concerned solely with methods of generating revenue. To the extent that these works were not included in the previous section, they are discussed here.

1253.   *Magna Charta*, June 15, 1215.

Like budgeting, the history of taxation literature can be carried back as far as one chooses to search. In the twelfth article of the bill of restrictions agreed to by King John at Runneymede was the statement "no soutage or aid should be imposed in the Kingdom unless by the common council of the realm, except for the purpose of ransoming the King's person, making his first-born son a knight, and marrying his eldest daughter once, and the aids for this purpose shall be reasonable in amount."

1254.   Paul Leroy-Beaulieu, *Traité de la science des finances*, 2 vol. (Paris: Guillaumin et Cie., 1876).

It is understandable that studies of fiscal policies began in Europe, where taxation was substantial at a time when the U.S. government was still funded by excises and tariffs. Among the European works, this one had the most impact on later Americans. Richard Ely described it as less profound and less historically accurate than German works, but more comprehensive and much easier to read. Leroy-Beaulieu followed the mainstream argument of European political economists in arguing that taxation removed investment funds from the private sector, and therefore should be minimized to the greatest degree possible.

1255.   Henry C. Adams, *Public Debts: An Essay in the Science of Finance* (New York: D. Appleton and Co., 1887).

Before his more famous *Science of Finance*, Adams expressed concern about irresponsible borrowing by American and world governments. While there were legitimate reasons for borrowing, including temporary deficits or emergencies for the national government, and public works that fostered industry at the state and municipal level, debts inherently limited capital for the private sector while not substantially helping "widow and orphan" investors. Especially at the municipal level, corruption had been fostered by a mixing of public and private sectors through pointless public investments.

1256.   Richard T. Ely, *Taxation in American States and Cities* (New York: Thomas Y. Crowell and Co., 1888).

In a strict continuation of the European tradition, Ely argued that indirect taxes were a burden on the poor, obstructed trade, and led to monopoly. Taxes should have equality of sacrifice, certainty, convenience, economy of administration, and should be focused on few items to minimize interference with business. At the local level, that required real estate taxes. Also, natural monopolies (utilities) could be used to shift some common burdens on the private sector. States could logically use income taxes.

1257.   *Sundry Civil Appropriations Act*, 35 Stat. 945 (1909).

Apart from the question of raising revenue, a second major theme of the literature was to find ways to balance revenues against expenditures. One early tactic of government was the Anti-Deficiency Act, discussed in the previous section. This provision required the Secretary of the Treasury to advise congress when appropriations exceeded revenues, and to suggest methods to raise revenues or lower expenditures. The provision was never used, however.

1258.   Merlin Harold Hunter, *Outlines of Public Finance* (New York: D. Appleton and Co., 1921); revised as Merlin Harold Hunter and Harry Kenneth Allen, *Principals of Public Finance* (New York: Harper and Brothers, 1940); also

1259.   Harley Leist Lutz, *Public Finance* (New York: D. Appleton and Co., 1924); also

1260.   Jens P. Jensen, *Problems of Public Finance* (New York: Thomas Y. Crowell Co., 1924).

After the First World War, expenditures grew so rapidly that the fiscal literature reflected in these works changed in three basic ways. First, the beneficial impact of government was generally accepted, even though Hunter argued that government expenditures replaced rather than supplemented private funds. Second, concerns about impeding commerce were replaced with the goal of balancing the impacts of taxation at all levels. In particular, the property tax played a reduced role and was difficult to defend because it had been riddled with unfair administration in most jurisdictions.
    Finally, these studies were far more detailed on the mechanics of tax implementation and the administration of public funds and debt services. There were lengthy analyses of the shifting of tax burdens, and the integration of taxes at different levels of government.

1261.   Edwin R. A. Seligman, *Studies in Public Finance* (New York: Macmillan Co., 1925); also "The Social Theory of Fiscal Science, I," *Political Science Quarterly*, 41, (June 1926): 193-218; also "The Social Theory of Fiscal Science, II," *Political Science Quarterly*, 41, (September 1926): 354-83.

Seligman was one of the earliest and most prolific writers on public finance, with publications going back to 1895.[8] In 1925, his new compilation of speeches and previously-published articles included the argument that municipalities would have to reform land taxes and increase income taxes, but that sales taxes were an unfair anachronism. He also expressed concerns for balancing spending and revenues.

His more theoretical work in 1926 defined collective vs. individual wants, with public groups satisfying more fundamental wants. Society was universal, fundamental, and compulsive, and "fiscal science is a social discipline."

1262.   A(rthur) C. Pigou, *A Study in Public Finance* (London: Macmillan and Co., 1928).

The most influential theoretical work of the period was Pigou's description of the welfare economics perspective. Pigou recognized differing levels of wants and willingness to sacrifice. He therefore proposed equal marginal sacrifices with money distributed to equalize the marginal return for satisfaction on each outlay. Spending would be set to balance marginal satisfaction with the marginal loss in taxes. Commodities would be taxed at different rates to reduce production in equal proportions.

1263.   Committee of the President's Conference on Unemployment, *Business Cycles and Unemployment* (New York: McGraw-Hill, 1923).

In response to the economic slump of 1921, President Harding asked Herbert Hoover to chair a committee to determine whether the effects of business cycles could be moderated. The committee recommended methods for lessening corporate waste, speculation, etc. during inflation, and the deferment of public works projects until they were needed to fight depressions.

1264.   Clyde L. King, *Public Finance* (New York: Macmillan Co., 1935).

King's concerns were more structural in explaining the mechanics of taxing and spending at the increased levels of the Great Depression. He found increases in social spending to be necessary and not as burdensome as lingering war debts. However, reducing the federal debt could be difficult or even catastophic since the states were not solvent, and taxes such as sales taxes tended to suppress commerce. He ended with a plea for the kind of coordinated budgeting that became a reality a few years later.

1265.   John Maynard Keynes, *The General Theory of Employment, Interest, and Money* (London: Macmillan, 1936).

The impact of Keynes on government fiscal policy was so monumental as to defy adequate treatment in this format. Simply stated, he offered that the economy was not self-correcting through investments during economic fluctuations. However, the government's fiscal policies could stabilize the economy through either deficit or surplus spending, depending on the requirements of the time.

1266.   Gerhard Colm, "Theory of Public Expenditures," *Annals of the American Academy of Political and Social Science*, 183, (January 1936): 1-11.

Colm also argued that public expenditures were large enough that they had to be considered for their impact on the economic system, and not just from a fiscal point of view. The two traditions on that question were the cameralists (Lorenz von Stein), who saw state activities as part of the economic system, and the classicalists (Jean Baptiste Say), who saw government as a disruption in the market place. Colm rejected the argument that government expenditures were non-productive, but was influenced by Wagner's argument that the public sector grew faster than the private sector.[9]

1267.   David McCord Wright, "The Economic Limit and Economic Burden of an Internally Held National Debt," *Quarterly Journal of Economics*, 55, (November 1940): 116-29; also

1268.   Henry C. Simons, "On Debt Policy," *Journal of Political Economy*, 52, (December 1944): 356-61.

Keynes' recommendations that fiscal policies be tied to the needs of the economy rather than to the debt posture of the government led to a number of adjustments in the way debt was viewed by economists. Wright attempted to find a middle ground in the "new economics" argument that internally-held debt imposed no long-term burden on citizens since they essentially owed the money to themselves.
Not all were convinced even by moderate versions of the "new economics" however. Simons contributed an early attack on the fiscal policies inherent in Keynes by arguing that money creation would stimulate the economy more effectively than deficit finance, and that money destruction would be more effective in slowing the economy than a fiscal policy of running surpluses.

1269.   Amos H. Hawley, "Metropolitan Population and Municipal Government Expenditures in Central Cities," *Journal of Social Issues*, 7, (Nos. 1 and 2, 1951): 100-08; also

1270.   Harvey Brazer, *City Expenditures in the United States*, Occasional Paper 66 (New York: National Bureau of Economic Research, 1959); also

1271.   Roy W. Bahl, *Metropolitan City Expenditures: A Comparative Analysis* (Lexington: University of Kentucky Press, 1969).

Hawley and Brazer introduced a concern that became crucial during the municipal fiscal crises of the 1960s. Both attempted to explain municipal spending patterns by the social characteristics of the metropolitan area. The authors noted that central city per capita expenditures were lower if smaller portions of the metropolitan area were within the city itself, and that expenditures in most categories were higher for more densely populated cities. Hawley found a positive correlation between per capita income and expenditures. Brazer found that intergovernmental revenue significantly affected expenditures.

The implications of the perspective, as stated by Hawley, was that urban fiscal planning needed to be conducted on a metropolitan-wide basis. In 1969, Bahl replicated the research and found the same basic patterns.

1272.   Harold M. Graves and C. Harry Kahn, "The Stability of State and Local Tax Yields," *American Economic Review*, 42, (March 1952): 87-102.

While the federal government had long relied on taxes with yields that fluctuated widely with economic conditions, the states had long been assumed to have a stable tax yield. Graves and Kahn studied the taxes to find that state income taxes were flexible, but were offset by local property taxes during times of deflation. The balanced result was that state and local governments as a unit had more stable tax yields than did the federal government.

1273.   James M. Buchanan, *Public Principles of Public Debt* (Homewood, IL: Richard D. Irwin, 1958).

Buchanan attacked the debt policies of the "new economics" by arguing that the real burden of a public debt was shifted to future generations, that public and private debt were largely analogous, and that external and internal debt were fundamentally equivalent. While significant debt retirement did not seem practical in his day, his revival of a "vulgar" view of the debt required new calculations on whether it could be afforded.

1274.   Richard A. Musgrave, *The Theory of Public Finance* (New York: McGraw-Hill, 1959).

Musgrave produced one of the more comprehensive summations of the economic theories of public finance. While he took few stands in his effort to remain neutral, he described in great detail the competing theories on the allocation, distribution, and stabilizing influence of various taxes.

1275.   Otto Eckstein, *Public Finance* (Englewood Cliffs, NJ: Prentice-Hall, 1964).

This book was a logical opposite to Musgrave's "advanced and difficult treatise." As an introductory text, it described the basic issues and goals of budgeting, tax distribution, and debt management, written so as to be understandable to new students.

1276.   Frederick C. Mosher and Orville F. Poland, *The Costs of American Govern-ments* (New York: Dodd, Mead, & Co., 1964).

Amid the moralizing that was common on government budgets, the authors attempted to describe what tax dollars were buying, and for how much. They found that real expenditures rose during times of national crises. Federal budgets usually ran deficits during crises and surpluses during peace, and had little apparent effect on the economy. The national debt was declining by most comparative measurements.

1277.   David G. Davies, "The Secular Income Elasticity and Revenue Stability of Motor Fuel Taxes," *National Tax Journal*, 18, (December 1965): 380-87; also

1278.   Robert M. Rafuse, Jr., "Cyclical Behavior of State-Local Finances," in Richard A. Musgrave, ed., *Essays in Fiscal Federalism* (Washington, D.C.: Brookings Institution, 1965), pp. 63-121.[10]

Davies investigated the motor fuel tax, which was often adopted by states because of its stability in economic cycles. Of 45 states studied during the time frame 1945-1962, only five showed stability on the tax. In the other states, the tax was productive, but was moderately unstable in 15 states and very unstable in 26.
      Rafuse more generally reviewed the perversity hypothesis that state and local governments follow and confound the effects of cycles. Instead, he discovered that these governments had been marked by steady growth since the Second World War, regardless of the appropriateness or impact of such policies.

1279.   Alan Campbell and Seymour Sacks, *Metropolitan America: Fiscal Patterns and Government Systems* (New York: Free Press, 1967); also

1280.   Advisory Commission on Intergovernmental Relations, *City Financial Emer-gencies: The Intergovernmental Dimension* (Washington, D.C.: ACIR, 1967).

In 1967, both the ACIR and Campbell and Sacks pointed out the imbalance in intergovernmental revenue. Metropolitan areas raised more taxes and had more expenditures in proportion to their populations than was the case for nonmetropolitan areas. However, state fiscal transfers were skewed against metropolitan areas. The "winners" were the suburbs that enjoyed higher levels of financing without many of the inner-city expenditures, while the losers were the inner-cities. Furthermore, the imbalance was growing worse with time.

1281.   Ira Sharkansky, *The Politics of Taxing and Spending* (Indianapolis: Bobbs-Merrill, 1969).

While metropolitan experts studied the levels of tax burdens, Sharkansky studied the methods by which such decisions were made. He found that fiscal policy-makers had no rational methods for determining tax levels, and that they were subject to a variety of political influences. To adjust, they used a combination of contained specialization (to limit political interference) and incrementalism (to limit the uncertainties of the process).

1282. Robert Bish, *The Public Economy of Metropolitan Areas* (Chicago: Markham Publishing Co., 1971).

Bish used public choice theory to analyze the public economies in the Miami-Dade and Los Angeles County areas. He concluded that smaller units of government have been more effective at responding to desires for varying levels of governmental services.

1283. Wallace C. Oates, *Fiscal Federalism* (New York: Harcourt-Brace-Jovanovich, 1972).

Oates set out to investigate the implications of economic theory for federalism. Using a broad definition of federally-shared powers, he identified 58 nations in which some form of federalism was being used. In general, he found that the assumptions behind fiscal federalism were both economically and politically workable.

1284. William V. Williams, Robert M. Anderson, David O. Froehle, and Kaye L. Lamb, "The Stability, Growth and Stabilizing Influence of State Taxes," *National Tax Journal*, 26, (June 1973): 267-74.

The authors measured the yield stability, the yield growth, and the counter-cyclical stabilizing influence of seven taxes across all states. The individual income tax was less stabilizing than was commonly assumed. The alcohol and tobacco taxes were very unstable.

1285. Donald Phares, *State-Local Tax Equity: An Empirical Analysis of the Fifty States* (Lexington, MA: Lexington Books, 1973).

Phares measured the tax burden in all fifty states to discover that total tax burden, editing out the local property tax, was basically proportional or even slightly regressive. The local property tax was so regressive, however, that it pulled most states into a regressive tax structure. Phares suggested changes to reduce the reliance on regressive property taxes.

1286. Richard A. Musgrave and Peggy B. Musgrave, *Public Finance in Theory and Practice* (New York: McGraw Hill, 1973).

The Musgraves produced one of the more detailed texts written on budgeting and fiscal policy. The general theme is that both expenditures and revenues are caught in a bind between the historical decentralization of American culture and the rise of federal coordination in the twentieth century. The desirable mix is not clear as the political culture is based in the autonomy of its parts, but the growing government is having such a substantial fiscal impact that some coordination is needed.

1287.   Joseph A. Pechman and Benjamin A. Okner, *Who Bears the Tax Burden* (Washington, D.C.: The Brookings Institution, 1974); also

1288.   Henry J. Aaron, *Who Pays the Property Tax? A New View* (Washington, D.C.: The Brookings Institution, 1975).

In the 1970s, the Brookings Institution surveyed 72,000 households to determine the impact of the tax burden on American families. Except for high burdens for the very rich and very poor, the tax burden was found to be proportional, having no appreciable effect on income distribution.

Aaron looked more specifically at the impact of the property tax. He argued that revaluation of property should be undertaken with greater accuracy and frequency than in the past. Also, circuit breaker ceilings are unfair because they reward those with the most net worth. Instead, income support payments and deferred payments should be used.

1289.   Roy W. Bahl and Walter Vogt, *Fiscal Centralization and Tax Burdens* (Cambridge: Ballinger Publishing Co., 1975).

Through case studies of nine metropolitan areas, the authors investigated the effects of fiscal centralization through state or regional revenue collection. They found that such plans help create equity and efficiency if regional financing relies more on income than property taxation. The results on educational expenditures are less clear. On balance, however, the authors expected fiscal centralization to grow in importance.

1290.   Gerald E. Auten and Edward H. Robb, "A General Model for State Tax Revenue," *National Tax Journal*, 29, (December 1976): 422-35; also

1291.   Jude Wanniski, "Taxes, Revenues, and the 'Laffer Curve'," *The Public Interest*, 50, (Winter 1978): 3-16.

Based on the Laffer curve which had gained popularity in presidential politics, and which predicted that government taxation could rise to such a level that increased tax rates would result in lowered revenues, Auten and Robb studied the revenue results of recent state tax increases. They discovered that states are on the lower end of such a curve in that a rise of one percent in taxes produces a return approaching one percent.

Wanniski's article is more theoretical, tracing the concept behind the curve back to David Hume, and describing its utility as a powerful analytical tool.

1292. James M. Buchanan and Richard E. Wagner, *Democracy in Deficit: The Political Legacy of Lord Keynes* (New York: Academic Press, 1977).

By the late 1970s, a new strain of literature developed to attack the continuing federal deficits. Before Keynesian economics, Buchanan and Wagner argued, governments responded to economic conditions without trying to change them. The result was balanced budgets in all except wartime and depressions. Keynesian assumptions, when combined with self-interested politics, led to a natural bias toward deficit finance. Specifically, expenditures gain votes while taxes cost votes. Such a tendency needs to be constrained in a return to balanced budgets.

1293. "Proposition 13," *Constitution, State of California*, Article 13A, ¾1 et seq. (1978); also

1294. Jack Citrin, "Do People Want Something for Nothing: Public Opinion on Taxes and Government Spending," *National Tax Journal*, 32, (Supplement, June 1979): 113-29; also

1295. Deborah Matz, "The Tax and Expenditure Limitation Movement," in Roy Bahl, ed. *Urban Government Finances: Emerging Trends* (Beverly Hills: Sage Publications, 1981), pp. 127-53.

On June 6, 1978, the voters of California overwhelmingly passed "Proposition 13," reducing property taxes to no more than one percent of market value, and capping assessed value at a two percent annual rise from the 1975-1976 base. The result was popularly seen as a "tax revolt," and similar measures soon spread to other states.

Matz studied the provisions that were adopted in other states, and was unable to find a single cause for them. Voters who approved the measures expressed little desire to see either specific expenditures or revenues lowered. Citrin argued that the tax revolts were against the visible taxes--particularly local property and federal income taxes. He also argued that vested interest played a role, in that homeowners were much more likely to support Proposition 13 than were renters.

1296. Charles H. Levine and Irene Rubin, eds., *Fiscal Stress and Public Policy* (Beverly Hills: Sage Publications, 1980).

This collection of twelve essays, divided into three sections, attempted to cover the basic issues in fiscal stress. The first section investigated the motives that set the levels of public funding, with explanations varying from a declining economy to bureaucratic demand. The second section looked at the impacts of scarcity on the budgetary process, with most authors expecting few changes. The third section discussed longer-term implications of fiscal stress for public policy.

1297.   Richard Rose, *Understanding Big Government: The Programmed Approach* (Beverly Hills, CA: Sage, 1984).

Rose looked at four common complaints about big government: that it is less effective; that its programs contradict each other; that it fosters ineffective programs; and that it is expensive. He argued that there is little support for the first three accusations. Furthermore, while paying for big government is a strain, it is one that most citizens are willing to bear.

1298.   John L. Mikesell, "The Cyclical Sensitivity of State and Local Taxes," *Public Budgeting and Finance*, 4, (Spring 1984): 32-39.

Mikesell argued that states are vulnerable to fiscal disruptions due to their relative lack of access to capital markets, and due to the balanced budget requirements that remain a part of many state constitutions.

1299.   Carol W. Lewis and A. Grayson Walker III, *Casebook in Public Budgeting and Financial Management* (Englewood Cliffs, NJ: Prentice Hall, 1984).

Believing that the administrative world is too complex for informed analysis and decision-making to solve problems, the authors presented a set of 36 cases for their students to analyze by applying general rules to specific problems. The cases, contributed by others, involve most aspects of budgeting and finance, and vary from those in which the students are active participants to those in which students are mainly observers.

1300.   Roy W. Bahl, *Financing State and Local Government in the 1980s* (New York: Oxford University Press, 1984).

In describing the shift in state and local financing since the 1970s, Bahl pointed out that the federal government has assumed a larger proportion of the revenue generation, giving it more power. Also, states have become more significant in the distribution of money to the cities. The cities are left in a delicate position, especially in the older cities in declining portions of the country. In the South, cities are in much the same position that Eastern cities were in the 1960s, and could be headed for similar difficulties.

1301.   *Balanced Budget and Emergency Deficit Control Act of 1985*, 99 Stat. 1038; also

1302.   U.S. Supreme Court, *Bowsher v Synar*, 106 S.Ct. 3181 (1986).

In an effort to attack steadily rising deficits at the federal level, Congress passed the Gramm-Rudman-Hollings bill in 1985. It provided for five sequential across-the-board reductions to eliminate the federal deficit if congress was unable to meet specified targets through the normal budgetary process. Entitlements and several other programs were either exempted or restricted in potential cuts, and the Comptroller General was to receive reports from OMB and CBO, and initiate the cuts.

In *Bowsher*, the section of the Gramm-Rudman-Hollings bill that allowed the Comptroller General (an agent of congress) to intervene in spending decisions was struck down. The court declared that the constitution "does not contemplate an active role for Congress in the supervision of officers charged with the execution of the laws it enacts." Instead, "once Congress makes its choice in enacting legislation, its participation ends. Congress can thereafter control the execution of its enactment only indirectly--by passing new legislation."

1303. Robert Eisner, *How Real is the Federal Deficit?* (New York: The Free Press, 1986).

As deficits continued to rise, Eisner claimed that our methods of accounting were poor. The U.S. has no capital budget, and does not take account of such effects as inflation and varied interest rates. Eisner accepted many of the "new economics" perspectives that deficits are someone else's surpluses, and he argued that our deficits tend to be both smaller and less harmful than are commonly assumed.

1304. James M. Buchanan, Charles K. Rowley, and Robert D. Tollison, eds., *Deficits* (New York: Basil Blackwell, 1987).

This collection of articles grew out of conference at the Center for Study of Public Choice at George Mason University in 1985. Anderson described changes in congressional procedures that made deficit spending inevitable after about 1970. Others attacked changes made by Keynes, or in the name of Keynes, that abandoned the classical theories that held that balanced budgets were essential for growth. Two concluding articles considered arguments for constitutional amendments for balanced budgets.

CONTINUING CONCERNS

It is conventional wisdom that the authors in public administration used to address a simpler world in which there were more obvious solutions. It is beside the point that the simpler world was seldom simple, and that the more obvious solutions were seldom obvious. So far, progression in time has indeed brought increasing complexity.

In most cases, however, the conventional wisdom brings to mind the authors of forty or fifty years ago. That is not the case with budgeting and finance. The simple world for budgeting was the 1960s and early 1970s. The problems of that era may have been dramatic, but the mechanics of the process and the rough directions for appropriate reform were easy to understand.

The 1970s and the 1980s have revolutionized the fiscal world. Placid taxpayers have rebelled. Rich nations and cities have become poor, while many poor have flourished. In some regions, a reversal of the first revolution is already well established.

In such a world, established theories have not fared well. Incrementalism has been abandoned by its author; fiscal studies are often more descriptive than explanatory; and it is possible to yearn, as some did in 1936, for a "General Theory" to reunite the world of public finance.

NOTES FOR CHAPTER EIGHTEEN

1. Subsequently released as "The Control of the Purse in the United States Government," *Kansas University Quarterly*, 2, (1894): 175-236; and as *The Control of the Purse in the United States Government* (Lawrence, KS: Self-published, n.d. [1894]).

2. The members were Frederick A. Cleveland, chairman; Frank J. Goodnow; William F. Willoughby; Walter W. Warwick; and Merritt O. Chance.

3. Among Gaston Jèze's more cited works were *Traité de science des finances* (Paris: V. Giard & E. Brière, 1910), and *Cours de finances publiques* (Paris: M. Giard, 1924).

4. 64 Stat. 832 (1950).

5. 70 Stat. 782 (1956).

6. The RAND version also listed Stephen Enke, Alain Enthoven, Malcolm W. Haag, C.B. McGuire, and Albert Wohlstetter as contributors.

7. "The Road to PPB: The Stages of Budget Reform," pp. 243-58.

8. *Essays in Taxation*, a book of articles first published in 1895, was revised and expanded continuously through the 1920s.

9. Adolph Wagner, *Grundlegung der politischen ökonomie*, Part I, vol. ii (Leipzig: C. F. Winter, 1892-94).

10. The article was based on the author's unpublished dissertation *State and Local Fiscal Behavior Over the Postwar Cycles* (Princeton, NJ: Princeton University, 1964).

19
Policy Analysis

BACKGROUND

The subject of policy analysis logically fits between the first and second parts of the book because its topics are partially within, and partially outside the organization. It is placed here, however, for both chronological reasons (it is among the most recent subfields to have taken an identifiable form) and because it feeds into the main theme of the conclusion.

The subject area is the set of literature referred to in chapter five of Waldo's *Enterprise of Public Administration*.[1] His semantic distinction is used to separate literature in which politics is called policy and administration is called implementation, from the traditional literature of the field. This chapter attempts to answer a question that Waldo left open--is the new literature qualitatively different from older literature that uses the traditional terminology for the same subjects?

Because of the central themes that have developed, separate sections of the chapter are devoted to policy determination, implementation, and evaluation.

POLICY DETERMINATION

1305. Vilfredo Pareto, *Mind and Society: A General Treatise on Sociology*, ed. by Arthur Livingston, trans. by Andrew Bongiorno and Arthur Livingston (New York: Harcourt Brace & Co., 1935). Originally *Trattato di sociologia generale*, 2 vol. (Firenze: G. Barbèra, 1916).

One of the more central and obvious questions that has plagued policy makers since the beginning of the polity has been the question of when policies should be adopted. The difficulty has been that almost all policies involve some sacrifice in return for some gain. While philosophers have pondered the issue since the beginning of recorded documents, the early theorist who had the most impact on future research was Pareto, who introduced his "Doctine of Maximum Satisfaction," or "Pareto's Optimality." Under this rather simple formula, policies should be adopted if they benefit at least one person, but harm no one.

1306. Arthur C. Pigou, *The Economics of Welfare* (London: Macmillan and Co., 1920).

Another theorist who tackled the same issue is the welfare economist Pigou, who noted that we have a tendency to discount the future too heavily in welfare decisions for present gain. Marxists discount the future completely, which is worse. Our goal should be to maximize the real value of social income based on proper discounting.

1307. Nicholas Kaldor, "Welfare Propositions of Economics and Interpersonal Comparisons of Utility," *Economic Journal*, 49, (September 1939): 549-52; also

1308. J. R. Hicks, "The Foundations of Welfare Economics," *Economic Journal*, 49, (December 1939): 696-712; also "The Rehabilitation of Consumer Surplus," *Review of Economic Studies*, 8, (1940-41): 108-16.

Unfortunately, in the real world, virtually every interesting social policy harms someone. However, the "Kaldor-Hicks Criterion" introduced the less restrictive policy decision device that those who are helped by a policy can share some of their gain to compensate those who lose. This is possible because of a social surplus that allows a benefit after the winners have distributed adequate compensation to the losers in any policy area.

1309. I(an) M.D. Little, *A Critique of Welfare Economics* (Oxford: Clarendon Press, 1950).

Little refined the Kaldor-Hicks criterion still further by arguing that policies should be adopted if they cause a good redistribution of wealth, and if the potential losers cannot profitably bribe the potential gainers to oppose it.

1310. Carl J. Friedrich and Edward S. Mason, eds., *Public Policy* (Cambridge: Harvard University Press, 1940).

In 1940, the newly created Graduate School of Public Administration at Harvard University began what was intended to be an annual series of policy studies in focused areas, with the studies coming from research seminars at the University. The first year's issue focused on the general area of industrial organization and control, although its most famous article, by Friedrich, continued the Friedrich-Finer debate on administrative responsibility.

1311.   Daniel Lerner and Harold D. Lasswell, eds., *The Policy Sciences* (Stanford, CA: Stanford University Press, 1951).

This book of readings is more evangelical in that the authors saw systematic analysis as a way to avoid the irrational behavior of recent world history. It is also more theoretical in that its focus is on methods of applying systematic analysis to aspects of the social sciences. While the "foreword" argued that both quantitative and historical approaches are of use, the articles focused mostly on modelling and quantification as techniques.

1312.   George A. Shipman, "The Policy Process: An Emerging Perspective," *Western Political Quarterly*, 12, (June 1959): 535-47.

Reinforcing the growing schism between systems analysts and those of a more traditional perspective, Shipman argued that policy studies were growing in the rigor of their theory and analysis, but that public administration in general was still far from mature.

1313.   Charles Lindblom, "The Science of Muddling Through," *Public Administration Review*, 19, (Spring 1959): 79-88; also *The Policy-Making Process* (Englewood Cliffs, NJ: Prentice Hall, 1968).

With Lindblom, the split between "theory and analysis" took a new turn. While political scientists had long been describing and analyzing the institutions and procedures that made policies, Lindblom initiated the study of the dynamics of the process. In 1959, he introduced the argument that policies are made by the "branch" or incremental process as opposed to the "root" or rational-comprehensive process. In 1968, he described in more detail a process that is complex and "systemic, with no clear-cut beginning or end."

1314.   Morton Kroll, "Hypotheses and Designs for the Study of Public Policies in the United States," *Midwest Journal of Political Science*, 6, (November 1962): 363-83.

Kroll wrestled with the difficulty that systematic analysis of policy is impractical unless the policy is separated from its mileau or program. He suggested that policy be studied as a merging of three elements: a pattern of values; ethical systems; and institutional arrangements. He also subdivided the internal factors into power arrangements, the historical dimension, involvement and role of personalities and leaders, informal and formal prescriptions, and organizational instruments.

1315.   William W. Boyer, *Bureaucracy on Trial: Policy Making By Government Agencies* (Indianapolis: Bobbs-Merrill, 1964).

Boyer divided the policy making process in agencies into five stages: decision-making, programming, communicating, controlling, and reappraisal. The point of bureaucracy is to minimize and control conflict within the steps. However, to insure democracy, the agencies also have to encourage outside participation in each step. The legislature has a crucial role in monitoring the process and assuring public participation.

1316.   Sir Geoffrey Vickers, *The Art of Judgment: A Study of Policy Making* (London: Chapman and Hall, 1965).

Vickers was concerned with the interrelationship between facts and values as expressed through decision-making. He argued that the policy-maker's job is to "appreciate" the situation, or bring together values about policies with judgments about criteria and measurements of success. Innovation occurs when the values begin to diverge.

1317.   Thomas R. Dye, *Politics, Economics, and the Public: Policy Outcomes in the American States* (Chicago: Rand McNally, 1966); also *Understanding Public Policy* (Englewood Cliffs, NJ: Prentice-Hall, 1972); also *Policy Analysis: What Governments Do, Why They Do It, and What Difference it Makes* (University: University of Alabama Press, 1976).

In trying to explain levels of state expenditures, Dye reported in 1966 that economic variables such as the degrees of urbanization, industrialization, wealth, and education, explain the policy outputs of states much more significantly than do political variables such as party competition, governmental structure, and voter participation. In 1972, he described six models by which policy making can be studied. He also suggested that impact analysis can be used to evaluate policies, although most social indicators of impact tend to be of a liberal nature. In 1976, he restated the need to develop a policy science since departments do such a poor job of analyzing their own program areas.

1318.   Fremont J. Lyden, George A. Shipman and Robert W. Wilkinson, Jr., "Decision Flow Analysis: A Methodology for Studying the Policy Making Process," in Preston P. LeBreton, ed., *Comparative Administrative Theory* (Seattle: University of Washington Press, 1968), pp. 155-68.

The authors expressed concern that methods for analyzing policies are still far too subjective. To help begin to standardize the process, they suggested a decision flow analysis based on the stimuli, responses, and consequences that provide the stimuli for subsequent decisions.

1319.   Yehezkel Dror, *Public Policymaking Reexamined* (San Francisco: Chandler
          Publishing Co., 1968); also *Ventures in Policy Sciences* (New York: American
          Elsevier, 1971); *Design for Policy Sciences* (New York: American Elsevier,
          1971).

In his "trilogy in policy sciences," Dror sought to help develop a policy science
as a solution to the widening gap between available methods for policy making and
the way policy is actually made. *Design for Policy Sciences* is the general introduction. In *Public Policymaking Reexamined*, he suggested models for optimal decision
making that could help create metapolicymaking with learning feedback, systematic
analysis, and explicit evaluation. *Ventures* provides a bridge between theoretical
models and practical applications.

1320.   Theodore Lowi, *The End of Liberalism* (New York: W. W. Norton and Co.,
          1969).

To Lowi, the problem is not in the techniques used to make decisions, but in
the process of "interest group liberalism." The tendency has arisen for regulated and
other special interests to dominate policy making in their areas at the expense of the
public interest. He suggested "juridical democracy" as a solution.

1321.   L. L. Wade and R. L. Curry, Jr., *A Logic of Public Policy: Aspects of Political
          Economy* (Belmont, CA: Wadsworth Publishing Co., 1970).

The authors used economic analysis to "develop a normative theory of public
choice." They developed a model of policy making that integrates community preferences, production possibilities, and budgetary constraints. Based on that, they made
suggestions "of the first magnitude" for improving governmental performance in the
United States.

1322.   Charles O. Jones, *An Introduction to the Study of Public Policy* (Belmont, CA:
          Wadsworth, 1970).

In his introductory text, Jones argued that policy will become the new approach to studying American government, just as structural approaches, functional
approaches, and others were once new. He divided the policy process into five systems, involving problem identification, formulation, legitimation, application, and
evaluation. He then used examples to follow policies through the five systems.

1323.   Graham Allison, *Essence of Decision: Explaining the Cuban Missile Crisis*
          (Boston: Little, Brown, and Co., 1971).

Allison used the Cuban missile crisis to demonstrate that Model I, or the rational policy model most often used to analyze policies, had little explanatory value.

Both Model II (Organizational Process) and Model III (Bureaucratic Politics) had more value, suggesting that policies often need to be explained through a number of conceptual models.

1324.   Robert H. Simmons, Bruce W. Davis, Ralph J. K. Chapman, and Daniel D. Sager, "Policy Flow Analysis: A Conceptual Model for Comparative Public Policy Research," *Western Political Quarterly*, 27, (September 1974): 457-68.

The authors argued that recent crises in the institutions of democracy show a reawakened sensitivity to the importance of value choices. They suggested a heuristic model with both natural and rational systems attributes that can describe the changed roles in executive-legislative-judicial relationships. The model can be used to explain methods by which value choices are made.

1325.   Peter Woll, *Public Policy* (Cambridge: Winthrop Publishers, 1974); also

1326.   James E. Anderson, *Public Policy-Making* (New York: Praeger, 1975).

Both Woll and Anderson studied the major actors in the decision-making process. While Woll's book is largely descriptive, Anderson isolated a number of decision criteria by which the actors can be studied, including values, political party affiliation, constituency interests, deference, public opinion, and decision rules. Based on these, three styles of decision-making can arise: bargaining, persuasion, and command.

1327.   Hugh Heclo, "Issue Networks and the Executive Establishment," in Anthony King, ed., *The New American Political System* (Washington, D.C.: American Enterprise Institute, 1978), pp. 87-124.

Heclo was concerned that static lists of participants in policy-making often are not realistic. Instead of "iron triangles," policies are made by "issue networks" consisting of both specialized and knowledgeable "intramural" players, and more widely dispersed temporary participants. The result is a series of floating audiences in which participants blend with those in the environment.

1328.   Edith Stokey and Richard Zeckhauser, *A Primer for Policy Analysis* (New York: W. W. Norton and Co., 1978).

Most sophisticated modelling in public administration applies to the decision-making described in chapter seventeen, or the policy analysis described later in this chapter. Stokey and Zeckhauser, however, used modelling to describe policy making. Using the framework that all policy making should go through the five steps of establishing the context, laying out the alternatives, predicting the consequences,

valuing the outcomes, and making a choice, the authors described the internal mechanics by which each of these steps should be completed.

1329.　Aaron Wildavsky, *Speaking Truth to Power* (Boston: Little, Brown, and Co., 1979).

　　　Wildavsky reflected on his experiences in policy analysis to argue that the
technique is more useful for making recommendations to decision-makers than for
explaining how decisions are made. All analysis is a combination of dogmatism and
skepticism that can help organizations to become self-evaluating. While policy analysis fits into no traditional academic discipline, it is a craft with several structural
characteristics described in the book.

1330.　Laurence E. Lynn, Jr. *Managing Public Policy* (Boston: Little, Brown, and Co., 1987).

　　　Lynn focused on the ability of public managers to make policy by introducing
his "model of public executive autonomy." He studied the political, organizational, and
personality constraints on an administrator's discretion. He then outlined strategies
by which public executives can increase their impacts on policies.

1331.　Robert B. Reich, ed., *The Power of Public Ideas* (Cambridge: Ballinger Publications, 1988).

　　　This book of essays has as a central focus the goal of refuting those economists (micromotives leading to macromotions) and political pluralists who see policy
as an amalgum of individual self-interests. Gary Orren attacked self-interest theory
in general, and Steven Kelman attacked public choice specifically as the authors
argued that large numbers of policies seem to be altruistic rather than driven by self-
interest. Instead, the readings suggest, policy formation comes from a mixture of
several motives, and cannot be explained by simple models.

POLICY IMPLEMENTATION

1332.　Stephen K. Bailey and Edith K. Mosher, *ESEA: The Office of Education Ad-
ministers a Law* (Syracuse, NY: Syracuse University Press, 1968); also

1333.　Jerome T. Murphy, "Title I of ESEA: The Politics of Implementing Federal
Education Reform," *Harvard Educational Review*, 41, (1971): 35-63.

　　　Policy analysts commonly divide the policy process into three stages corre-
sponding with decision making, implementation, and evaluation. One of the first areas

to be subject to implementation studies, however, produced mixed reports. Bailey and Mosher noted that the federal education structure was poorly equipped for the massive 1965 legislation that financed educational assistance for low-income schools. However, the structure rallied well. Bailey and Mosher suggested that a Department of Education was needed to coordinate future programs.

Murphy was less optimistic. While he uncovered such problems as the reformers not being the implementers, inadequate staffing, low monitoring, local control, and little interest by the poor, the major problem was that the federal system encouraged "evasion and dilution of federal reform."

1334.   Gary Orfield, *The Reconstruction of Southern Education* (New York: John A. Wiley and Sons, 1969).

Orfield was also concerned with education--in this case, the implementation of the Civil Rights Act of 1964 in Southern education. He found that because of the institutions of federalism, and because the bulk of the administrative machinery of education is at the state and local levels, federal intervention can be only temporary and marginally successful. The "general practice is to accept whatever can be obtained through negotiation," (p. ix) making the implementation of federal programs difficult.

1335.   Daniel Patrick Moynihan, *Maximum Feasible Misunderstanding: Community Action in the War on Poverty* (New York: Free Press, 1969).

Moynihan tried to explain implementation problems in the anti-poverty programs of the 1960s. He argued that the "maximum feasible participation" requirement of the Economic Opportunity Act of 1964 was not adequately explained by its drafters. Once the provision was implemented by those operating under unclear guidelines, the purposes of the legislation became subverted by both bad faith and general confusion at the local level.

1336.   James Sundquist and David Davis, *Making Federalism Work* (Washington, D.C.: Brookings Institution, 1969).

Sundquist and Davis similarly complained that the "little chaos" inherent in the federal system was growing beyond control. Massive new experimental programs implemented at the local level and monitored by a myriad of federal officials were resulting in uneven implementation and confusion. The authors suggested the creation of regional federal coordinators, answerable to the White House, who could monitor the implementation of federal programs as a whole.

1337.   Harry Lambright, "The Minnowbrook Perspective and the Future of Public
         Affairs: Public Administration *Is* Public-Policy Making," in Frank Marini, ed.,
         Toward a New Public Administration: The Minnowbrook Perspective (Scranton,
         PA: Chandler Publishing Co., 1971), pp. 332-45.

Perhaps no group was as appreciative of the importance of implementation
techniques as the "New Public Administration" movement of the 1960s. In summarizing the views of the conference, Lambright pronounced the politics/administration
dichotomy dead. He argued that administrators make policies by their actions, and he
felt that the participants at the conference wanted increased citizen participation
during implementation. Also, schools of public administration would have to adjust
their training better to prepare administrators for their roles.

1338.   Douglas R. Bunker, "Policy Sciences Perspectives on Implementation Pro-
         cesses," *Policy Sciences*, 3, (March 1972): 71-80.

Bardach (below) identified Bunker's 1970 AAAS paper (revised for *Policy
Sciences*) as the first attempt to conceptualize the implementation process. Bunker
argued that implementation is a process of amassing assent. To measure the minimum
effective coalition for implementation, each potential actor can be located in a three-
dimension space by vectors of issue salience, power resources, and agreement.

1339.   Harvey Sapolsky, *The Polaris System Development* (Cambridge: Harvard
         University Press, 1972).

In one of the few truly optimistic studies of implementation, Sapolsky studied
the development of the Polaris missile system with support services and 41 submarines.
He found that the Navy used four bureaucratic strategies to increase their chances for
successful implementation: differentiation; co-optation; moderation; and managerial
innovation. They were also helped by a lucky convergence of technology and political
consensus.

1340.   Martha Derthick, *New Towns In-Town* (Washington, D.C.: Urban Institute,
         1972).

Derthick's focus is on a plan to turn federal lands within metropolitan areas
into model communities to revive the economic vitality of the area. In studying the
reasons why the implementation of the program failed, she described an inherent
conflict between federal idealism and local political realities. She was more optimistic
than observers such as Orfield, however, in that she felt that both the idealism and
the realities need to be expressed, and that the federal system is designed to do that.

1341.   Jeffrey L. Pressman and Aaron Wildavsky, *Implementation* (Berkeley: Univer-
         sity of California Press, 1973).

In the 1960s, a group of students and faculty at the University of California, Berkeley, undertook a series of studies known as the Oakland Project. Their best-known effort is a study of the implementation of the Economic Development Administration program in Oakland, California. They discovered that the program suffered from contradictory legislative mandates, antagonistic federal agencies, and less than reliable local businesses. They suggested that the program could have been simplified by a clearer federal understanding of the Oakland economy, and by wage subsidies to local businesses. In any circumstances, however, implementation remained an extraordinarily difficult task.

1342.   Frank Levy, Arnold J. Meltzner, and Aaron Wildavsky, *Urban Outcomes: Schools, Streets, and Libraries* (Berkeley: University of California Press, 1974).

The members of the Oakland Project next investigated spending patterns on selected government services to discover a "U" curve in the distribution of resources. In wealthy neighborhoods, high local resources were supplemented by citizen funds. Poorer constitutents often received federal anti-poverty resources, leaving those in the middle with lower services. Complicating the picture were the actions of self-protecting administrators and the unintended consequences of programs that often fit together in unanticipated ways.

1343.   Raymond E. Wolfinger, *The Politics of Progress* (Englewood Cliffs, NJ: Prentice Hall, 1974).

At the local level, Wolfinger investigated the ability of mayors to implement policies within their own cities. He concluded that the mayoral position is not well suited for implementing policies because of the typically short tenure and lack of party support. Mayor Richard Lee of New Haven, who provided the data for Wolfinger's case study, was an exception with long tenure, a strong political machine, and success in implementing policies.

1344.   Jeffrey L. Pressman, *Federal Programs and City Politics* (Berkeley: University of California Press, 1975).

Also as part of the Oakland Project, Pressman compared the political leaders at the federal and local levels, arguing that their differing objectives lead to mutual distrust. He suggested that programs be geared towards results rather than planning, and that they be designed to increase the power base and responsibility of local officials.

1345.   Beryl Radin, *Implementation, Change, and the Federal Bureaucracy* (New York: Columbia University Press, 1975).

Radin investigated the law, structures, and constituencies by which HEW implemented school desegregation policies from 1964 to 1968. She found that HEW officials encountered uncertainties, conflicts, and new "customers" who had not been anticipated and were not used wisely. She suggested that greater use of bargaining, interdependence, and sympathetic local and regional officials would have been helpful.

1346.   Michael Lipsky, "Toward a Theory of Street-Level Bureaucracy," in Willis Hawley, et al., *Theoretical Perspectives on Urban Politics* (Englewood Cliffs, NJ: Prentice Hall, 1976);[2] also "Standing the Study of Implementation on its Head," in Walter Dean Burnham and Martha Wagner Weinberg, *American Politics and Public Policy* (Cambridge: M.I.T. Press, 1978).

One of the unsettled questions of implementation is whether local interference in centrally-planned programs constitutes obstruction or democracy at work. Among those who see bottom-level discretion to be necessary for democratic administration, Michael Lipsky is perhaps the best known. In these articles, he argued that the emphasis of political study should be shifted to local levels, and more specifically to street-level implementation within the local levels.

1347.   Eugene Bardach, *The Implementation Game: What Happens After a Bill Becomes a Law* (Cambridge: M.I.T. Press, 1977).

Bardach investigated a mental health reform effort in California, as well as other case studies, in an effort to arrive at recommendations for effective implementation. Suggestions include starting with a sensible theory, writing a good scenario for implementation, and using strategies to "fix" the game. Ultimately, Bardach felt that implementation goes reasonably well considering that liberal reformers often expect too much from government.

1348.   Kai N. Lee, Review of Eugene Bardach, *The Implementation Game*, *Policy Sciences*, 10, (December 1978): 225-27.

The major justification for implementation studies, and for policy studies more generally, is that they offer lessons about effective government that we cannot learn by more traditional approaches. Lee, who considered Bardach's book to be one of the better of the slim lot of implementation studies, complained that the literature of the "Berkeley Know-Nothing School" failed to appreciate earlier efforts that stretched back over six decades. While those earlier studies were disappointing, the new literature made little improvement.

1349.   Richard R. Nelson and Douglas Yates, eds., *Innovation and Implementation in Public Organizations* (Lexington, MA: Lexington Books, 1978).

The authors compiled nine case studies of innovation to determine what lessons could be learned about implementation problems of innovative programs. Among the studies, an effort to establish neighborhood team policing in six cities seemed to indicate that early public participation leads to success. Other studies succeeded without such participation, however.

1350.   Richard Elmore, "Organizational Models of Social Program Implementation," *Public Policy*, 26, (Spring 1978): 185-228.

Elmore emphasized the lack of conceptual consensus in implementation studies by describing four models of organizations, each of which sees implementation as performing different roles. The systems management model views implementation as an ordered, goal-directed activity. The bureaucratic process model sees implementation as including controlled discretion and changing routines. The organizational development model sees implementation as an effort by bureaucrats to shape and "claim" policies. The conflict and bargaining model sees implementation as bargaining to solve temporary problems.

1351.   Carl E. Van Horn, *Policy Implementation in the Federal System* (Lexington, MA: Lexington Books, 1979).

Van Horn studied three programs of the 1970s that were intended to return power to the states: general revenue sharing; CETA; and the Housing and Community Development Act. Implementation experiences varied widely, leading Van Horn to speculate that part of the difficulty with implementation is the congressional practice of passing legislation with unclear, unstated, or contradictory goals.

1352.   Walter Williams, *The Implementation Perspective* (Berkeley: University of California Press, 1980); also

1353.   Walter Williams, ed., *Studying Implementation: Methodological and Administrative Issues* (Chatham, NJ: Chatham House, 1982).[3]

Williams investigated the methodology of implementation studies to discover that they have a "healthy eclecticism" that leans heavily on open-ended interviews with principle actors in case studies. The studies are not laden with strict methodologies, and borrow from several academic disciplines as they seem useful.

In 1982, Williams compiled six essays from researchers using a variety of approaches to answer different types of questions. Elmore described "*backward mapping*" as bottom-up planning, while Yin provided a history of eleven "exemplary" implementation studies. Several other authors provided studies of techniques and/or cases.

1354.   Daniel A. Mazmanian and Paul A. Sabatier, *Implementation and Public Policy* (Glenview, IL: Scott, Foresman and Co., 1983).

The authors investigated five programs to support their contention that six conditions lead to successful implementation. Stated briefly, the legislation needs to be clear, and to delegate responsibilities, resources, and instructions to competent administrators. Implementation is still difficult, but can be improved through the use of the authors' "checklist."

1355.   Martin A. Levin, "Effective Implementation and Its Limits," in Donald J. Calista, ed., *Bureaucracy and Governmental Reform* (Greenwich, CT: JAI Press, 1986), pp. 215-41.

Levin studied effective implementation to determine what made it possible. He found that the most important factors are talented executives, a favorable context, and private interest groups. However, the factors are limited because the conditions often cannot be replicated, nor would we want them to be. In addition, factors that lead to effective implementation do not always lead to good policies.

POLICY EVALUATION

The final category is the evaluation of policies that are in place. At least as much as with the other categories, determining where the literature begins is a subjective judgment. Evaluation in some form has been practiced since the first governments implemented policies. Evaluation "research" can been traced back to the 1800s in health delivery systems. The literature below, however, is selected because the mainstream of current evaluation research cites it with some regularity.

1356.   Valentine F. Ridgway, "Dysfunctional Consequences of Performance Measurements," *Administrative Science Quarterly*, 1, (September 1956): 240-47.

Ridgway warned that an excessive concentration on performance measurements to determine success can entice administrators to skew their efforts to achieve those results. As a consequence, efforts can become imbalanced. Ridgway defined some potential difficulties with single, multiple, and composite performance measurements.

1357.   David Braybrooke and Charles E. Lindblom, *A Strategy of Decision* (New York: Free Press of Glencoe, 1963).

Braybrooke and Lindblom also saw problems with such evaluation techniques as rational-deductive and welfare function decision-making because people seldom have the time or the information to use them in the real world. Instead, they suggested that policies are evaluated by disjointed incrementalism, involving the consideration of a limited number of options that change current policies only marginally.

1358.   Edward A. Suchman, *Evaluative Research* (New York: Russell Sage Foundation, 1967).

This general introductory text described the historical development of evaluative research as well as the common options and problems that are encountered in doing it. Suchman argued that methodologies need to be tightened as society begins to demand more from public services.

1359.   Joseph S. Wholey, et al., *Federal Evaluation Policy: Analyzing the Effects of Public Programs* (Washington, D.C.: Urban Institute Press, 1971).[4]

The Urban Institute undertook a study of evaluation in fifteen sample programs administered by four different federal agencies. They studied four types of evaluation: program impact evaluation; program strategy evaluation; project evaluation; and project rating. Based on their findings, they made 72 specific recommendations that are designed to insure funding and responsibility for evaluation, and to specify the purposes of programs as completely as possible.

1360.   Francis G. Caro, ed., *Readings in Evaluation Research* (New York: Russell Sage Foundation, 1971); also

1361.   Albert C. Hyde and Jay M. Shafritz, eds., *Program Evaluation in the Public Sector* (New York: Praeger Publishing Co., 1979).

It is to the advantage of modern students that evaluation studies have been compiled into more sets of readers of both historical and recent research than is the case for most other topics discussed in this book. Caro's major conclusion was that evaluation has become essential and will continue. However, barriers to implementation vary from the inability to keep competent researchers employed in such jobs to professional jealousies between administrators and evaluators. The book concluded with methodological suggestions (notably by Donald Campbell) and case studies in which evaluation was conducted. The introduction to the Hyde and Shafritz reader warned of the dangers of "high noon" evaluation studies that are tied to sunset legislation, and that give administrators legitimate reasons to fear the results of evaluators.

1362.   Alice Rivlin, *Systematic Thinking for Social Action* (Washington, D.C.: Brookings Institution, 1971).

Rivlin gave a set of four lectures at the University of California in 1970, and they are reprinted here. Using anti-poverty programs as her focus, she argued that evaluators had made progress in identifying and measuring social problems, and in measuring the benefits and costs of social programs. However, there was still little ability to compare the costs and benefits of different social action programs, or to produce more effective health, education, and other social services. She then suggested experimental techniques by which the answers to lingering questions could be answered.

1363.   Carol H. Weiss, *Evaluating Action Programs* (Boston: Allyn and Bacon, 1972); also *Evaluation Research* (Englewood Cliffs, NJ: Prentice-Hall, 1972).

The theme of Weiss' *Evaluation Research* "is that evaluation uses the methods and tools of social research but applies them in an action context that is intrinsically inhospitable to them." Arguing that traditional research methods do not prepare students for the action context of evaluation, her text concentrates on such real-life problems as defining objectives for programs that have never had them defined, and gathering data in hostile environments.

Evaluating Action Programs is a book of the classic and recent readings by the "treeful of owls" that developed the field. Weiss' opening article described seven common problems faced by evaluators. Her concluding article suggested that the negative results often obtained in evaluation studies "represents a fundamental critique of current approaches to social programming."

1364.   Alvin W. Drake, Ralph L. Keeney, and Philip M. Morse, eds., *Analysis of Public Systems* (Cambridge: M.I.T. Press, 1972).

This set of readings by researchers at M.I.T. and the New York City-Rand Institute was designed to apply formal modelling to the improvement of the delivery of public services. The list of articles begins with general descriptions of the Rand project, and extends through several applications that have been made, concluding with sophisticated mathematical modelling techniques for program analysis.

1365.   Thomas J. Cook and Frank P. Scioli, Jr., "A Research Strategy for Analyzing the Impacts of Public Policy," *Administrative Science Quarterly*, (September 1972): 328-39.

The authors used air pollution control to demonstrate their multivariate factorial design for evaluating policy results. The article is largely conceptual in that the authors' data collection techniques were limited. However, they suggested that the model could be used to analyze complicated and conflicting policy areas.

1366.   Aaron Wildavsky, "The Self-Evaluating Organization," *Public Administration Review*, 32, (September/October 1972): 509-20.

Wildavsky argued that evaluation is contradictory with the interests of organizations that must justify their existence in a hostile political environment. Evaluation would require incentives for uncovering negative information, and could operate effectively only under conditions of considerable trust.

1367. Harry P. Hatry, Richard E. Winnie, and Donald M. Fisk, *Practical Program Evaluation for State and Local Government Officials* (Washington, D.C.: Urban Institute, 1973); also

1368. Harry Hatry, Louis Blair, Donald Fisk, and Wayne Kimmel, *Program Analysis for State and Local Governments* (Washington, D.C.: Urban Institute, 1976).

The purpose of the Urban Institute studies was to offer specific information for states and large metropolitan governments on formal evaluation procedures. In 1973, they recommended "effectiveness status monitoring" for major policy areas and selected individual evaluation for specific programs. The book contains numerous exhibits and specific procedures. The 1976 book was more conceptual, and less geared toward practical suggestions. Both books contain case studies to show evaluation in action.

1369. Paul Wortman, "Evaluation Research: A Psychological Perspective," *American Psychologist*, 30, (May 1975): 562-75.

Wortman saw evaluation research as a complex set of feedback processes monitoring social change. He was concerned that the emphasis is usually on immediate fixes, and he described possible pitfalls with internal, external, conclusion, and construct validity.

1370. Edward S. Quade, *Analysis for Public Decisions* (New York: American Elsevier, 1975).

Quade's approach to policy analysis is somewhat less activist that Weiss', among others, in that he was careful to separate the roles of analyst and those actually recommending policies. He argued that evaluation should be expanded, and that analysts need to appreciate that the costs of objects do not always establish their political value However, his text treats analysis as an evaluative process more than one for policy advocates.

1371. Fred A. Kramer, "Policy Analysis as Ideology," *Public Administration Review*, 35, (September/October 1975): 509-17.

Kramer was even more concerned than Quade that too many analysts fail to appreciate the limits of their techniques. He argued that those doing economic modelling are particularly prone to assuming their activities to be value-free, and their recommendations to be based on scientific fact. He asked that the background assumptions of analysis be made explicit.

1372.   Peter Rossi, Howard Freeman, and Sonia Wright, *Evaluation: A Systematic Approach* (Beverly Hills, CA: Sage Publishing Co., 1979).

      This popular text of evaluation has been used in hundreds of courses, and is in a third edition at this writing. The authors offer step-by-step instructions for evaluation that emphasize the need to tailor evaluation to the situation at hand. They explain preferred and alternative methods of both data gathering and research design.

1373.   David Nachmias, *Public Policy Evaluation: Approaches and Methods* (New York: St. Martin's Press, 1979); also

1374.   David Nachmias, ed., *The Practice of Policy Evaluation* (New York: St. Martin's Press, 1980.

      Rather than concentrate on the measured results of public programs, Nichmias' 1979 textbook went more directly to the causal model inherent in all policy that certain activities will lead to predictable results. His book concentrated on building the causal models and finding methods to test them. In 1980, he supplemented the text with reprints of 21 evaluation studies, and concluded that evaluation would be used more widely if it could standardize its methodology, become institutionalized, integrate itself with policy making, and include utilization plans in its reports.

1375.   Susan Welch and John C. Comer, *Quantitative Methods for Public Administration* (Homewood, IL: Dorsey Press, 1983).

      Some policy analysts, most notably Carol Weiss, have argued that traditional research methods courses do not prepare people for the activist responsibilities of policy evaluation. Welch and Comer wrote this introductory research methods text to overcome that problem. The text ends with instructions on how the techniques that have been introduced could be used in cost/benefit analysis, PPBS, and other techniques of evaluation in agencies.

1376.   Joseph S. Wholey, *Evaluation and Effective Public Management* (Boston: Little, Brown, and Co., 1983); also

1377.   Joseph S. Wholey, Mark A. Abramson, and Christopher Bellavita, eds., *Performance and Credibility: Developing Excellence in Public and Nonprofit Organizations* (Lexington, MA: Lexington Books, 1986).

In the way that Welch and Comer integrated evaluation into traditional research methods, Wholey sought to integrate evaluation into results-oriented, as opposed to process-oriented, management. He described a set of seven levels through which agencies could climb to create results-oriented management.

In 1986, the authors laid out four key leadership functions, including specifying objectives, assessing performance, stimulating performance, and communicating results. Their central premise was that evaluators have the talents to help managers perform those functions.

1378.   Eleanor Chelimsky, ed., *Program Evaluation: Patterns and Directions* (Washington, D.C.: ASPA, 1985).

This set of articles in the *Public Administration Review* Classics series begins with a summation article by Chelimsky that summarizes the origins, definitions, audiences, and structures of evaluation in government. She describes six types of evaluations and the common problems they have encountered. She concludes with a relatively optimistic agenda for the future.

CONTINUING CONCERNS

Policy studies can reasonably be judged by two criteria. Is there any new potential in approaching administration from the angle of the policies it produces and implements? If so, has anything new been discovered? The answers to both are subject to more animated disputes in the literature than have been seen in most areas of public administration for some time.

To start, it is not clear what new potential is being sought. Implementation studies are often content with increased understanding while evaluators often seek to make qualitative judgments and effect new policies. Distractors sometimes see these goals as the same ones that led to the creation of Public Administration as a discipline.

It is also not clear what has been discovered. Analyzing government from the perspective of policy brings different parts of the process into focus, but it is reasonable to ask what is gained by the new perspective. Analysts have reached more consensus on why implementation is difficult than how it can be made easier. The evaluation literature often bemoans its own failure to reach any consensus on methodology.

Ultimately, the contribution of policy literature may be that it has returned to the "big questions" about what government is meant to accomplish, and what impact it is having on society. In a field that sometimes belabors operational issues, an occasional question about fundamental purposes can be a welcome sign.

NOTES FOR CHAPTER NINETEEN

1. Novato, CA: Chandler and Sharp Publishers, 1980.

2. Coauthors include Michael Lipsky, Stanley B. Greenberg, J. David Greenstone, Ira Katznelson, Karen Orren, Paul E. Peterson, Martin Shefter, and Douglas Yates.

3. The text identifies Richard F. Elmore, John Stuart Hall, Richard Jung, Michael Kirst, Susan A. MacManus, Betty Jane Narver, Richard P. Nathan, and Robert K. Yin as coauthors.

4. Coauthors include John W. Scanlon, Hugh G. Duffy, James S. Fudumoto, and Leona M. Vogt.

Concluding Observations

Works that have no specific research questions can support no formal conclusions. They can, however, uncover potentially interesting patterns, and two such patterns have emerged in these descriptions that are useful in reexamining some of our common beliefs about the nature of our discipline.

First, the conventional wisdom among those who have written on the subject is that the collective memory of our literature is cyclical. Works are pushed from our attention by newer studies, only to reappear when the old questions again become important. As Herbert Kaufman stated in his classic description of the cyclical nature of administrative questions:

> But if the hypothesized cycle of values is at all valid, then
> strange as it may seem to this generation of reformers, innovat-
> ors of tomorrow will defend many of the very institutions (as
> transformed in the course of current controversies) under attack
> today. And many a forgotten tome and obscure article on public
> administration, long gathering dust on unpatronized shelves and
> in unopened files, will be resurrected and praised for its pre-
> science, only to subside again into temporary limbo when another
> turn of the wheel ends its brief moment of revived relevance.[1]

This study has been able to support only part of that observation. The cyclical nature of administrative questions has been demonstrated in several chapters in this book as old values have resurfaced to dominate recent literature.

The cyclical revival of the literature, however, is a relatively rare event. In fact, there are at least two aspects of Kaufman's prediction that have little support in this study. First, classical literature is seldom read by modern students, whatever its relevance. In many library collections, it cannot even be found. A more cynical summation, but one that seems better able to catch the flavor of social science research, would be Peter Odegard's lament in the 1967 reprint of Arthur Bentley's *The Process of Government*, that "like other classics it is more often cited than read."[2]

Admittedly, Bentley wrote one of the more obtuse works to have achieved "classic" status, and reading it has seldom been considered a joy. However, the second flaw in Kaufman's observation affects a far wider range of literature. Not only have few read Bentley and many of the other classics; few remember that many of the formative studies of Public Administration were ever written.

There are exceptions. Each subfield within public administration has its standard list of founders that are politely cited in the opening chapters of texts on the topic. A few of those authors--Wilson, Weber, Barnard for instance--are often integrated into classroom readings, occasionally receiving even more attention than they did at the time of publication.

However, it is perplexing that one fruitful technique for identifying the older selections in this annotated bibliography has been to peruse the citations of those founding works, discovering that the "original" authors often identified earlier sources for the same ideas. In other cases, particularly for non-American works before 1887, the chain of citations was completely broken, and the works were sometimes found by sheer accident. In yet other cases, the works are still nominally remembered, but the authors would be dismayed by the arguments now attributed to them.

It is practical for major works, or even entire academic traditions, to become "lost."[3] The tendency seems pervasive, but obviously not universal. A few studies have survived millennia without the benefit of either mechanical printing or religious sponsorship. If there is a consistent way in which these works have achieved immortality, however, it has not been discovered here.

There is a second and more temporal conclusion that can be drawn from this bibliographic study, although it is more normative than empirical. Judging by its literature, Public Administration has long been in an identity crisis, not sure of its purposes, it academic friends, or its proper focus. Beginning at least with Kaufman, much of the field has been uncomfortable with the course charted by Waldo in *The Administrative State*.

The end of the Second World War was an important turning point for Public Administration, because it ushered in two important changes that were to reform the conduct and focus of most of the social sciences. First, wartime successes gave the academic world, and by extension the social sciences, a heightened respect for scientific methodology. To be fair, each social science discipline had long had advocates for studying social institutions as a mechanical interaction of human machines. The proponents of Scientific Management were of particular relevance to public and private administration, and were among the most advanced early practitioners of such research.

However, during the War, the physical sciences were able to accomplish technological feats that were unimaginable before the unique marriage of emigré talent and massive accumulations of money. It mattered little that the results were so threatening to humanity, or that the circumstances of wartime science were ones that no one would want to replicate. The methodology had worked. The door was open to those in each social science discipline who had long argued that people were most effectively studied as rational animals operating within larger social machines.

Such a trend of scientific distance from the subject was reinforced by a second development of the post-War era. For the first time in the memory of most scholars, there was no crisis. The services of public administrators and other social science academics were no longer convincingly needed by society.

The social sciences had bowed to outside pressure for their services longer than the memories of many of its practitioners--far longer than for the physical sciences. The American field of Public Administration had been created in the midst of the administrative explosion of municipal reform and Progressivism. Except for a period in the 1920s, a series of calamities then helped keep the academic discipline alive.

But in the 1950s, there was no depression. Neither was there anything to compare with the urgency of the war machine's calls for assistance from those who might not know how to operate it, but who might have better educated guesses than most.

For once, academics had breathing room. They could choose their purposes, and increasing numbers chose to study things merely because they were interesting. Unfortunately, mere interest has proven to be a weak organizing force for a subject with no academic discipline as a base.

The high-water mark of the pre-war approach was probably Waldo's attempt, first drafted in 1942, to use the past to chart likely courses for the future. Waldo described an ideological consensus in the field that true democracy and true efficiency were reconcilable. The belief was "so fundamental that, by definition, it could hardly be denied by an American writer on public administration."[4] Those who disagreed, Beck and Sullivan, for instance, were simply not in the field. An equal aspect of the ideology was that democracy could not be achieved unless government was able to provide the needed services that society could not obtain elsewhere.[5]

These are interesting beliefs to have been held by a virtual consensus of the field. There was a consistency to these beliefs that is missing today. It is not clear, for instance, why one would choose to devote a career to the study or practice of public administration unless one believed in what it was trying to do. Early academics were believers.

Today, many who practice and teach under the rubric of Public Administration are not believers. In fact, the basic issues of democratic administration and the role of bureaucracy in society seem to have lost fascination for many post-War Public Administration academics, although not necessarily for some in other academic disciplines, or in the electorate. The typical study of the last forty years has failed to address, or even to show much awareness of the major questions of the administrative state.

There have always been exceptions, of course, notably Appleby, Waldo, Roscoe Martin, and others mentioned in chapters four, ten, and nineteen. There also seems to be a revival of interest in the subject, encompassing the spectrum from the "hostile witnesses" for privatization and public choice to the more sympathetic views of Rohr, Goodsell, and others who follow the Blacksburg Manifesto.

However, the typical post-War study has taken on a different look. It has a sophistication that was not typical before the 1950s. General commentaries have lost ground to methodological "experiments." Legalistic prescriptions have faded before models of rational decision-making. The field has become more quantitative, but less prescriptive and, if debates over our purposes are an indicator, less significant. We are more respectable, but we generate less self-esteem.

What is being proposed is not a reactionary return to pre-scientific moralizing. In fact, one thing that is clear from this review is that the field has never been dominated by such literature in the time-frame that we normally consider Public Administration to have existed. At the height of the rankest moralizing of the early twentieth century, there were also methodological studies whose combined rigor and utility to management have not been rivaled in years, and perhaps not in generations. Such diversity is the blessing of a field that welcomes intrusions by virtually any academic disicipline.

What is being proposed is a return to a civic culture for the academic study of Public Administration. Not being defined by a traditional discipline, we have been held together by a recognition that all works--macro and micro; quantitative and qualitative; theoretical and applied--are justified by their potential impacts on institutions that affect our daily lives.

The impacts might be immediate or remote. The studies might be openly prescriptive or entirely conceptual. As both the social theorists and the mechanical engineers of the pre-War era understood, however, the study of governmental mechanics has not operated well as a Liberal Art.

Public Administration is applied knowledge, created of operational necessity, and dedicated to the training of administrators, the shaping of their institutions, and the prescriptive analysis of their results. To stay healthy, it must meld a series of academic disciplines, a variety of methodologies, and an amalgum of prescriptive and descriptive intentions. It withers when it becomes dominated by either evangelists or analysts.

In the spirit of this study, the prescription for diversity (or perhaps chaos) is not new. It was partially suggested by Harlow Person in the *Bulletin of the Taylor Society* in 1919.[6] He explained the difference between management and administration, using a distinction that was somewhat different than the one we use today.

Administration included the moral, the social, and the political aspects of running an enterprise. As one of the most respected mechanical engineers in an age when engineers were the final authority on administrative matters, he suggested that such topics were subject to scientific scrutiny under only the most limited of circumstances. More typically, their analysis was verbal, general, and ethically oriented. Only management was subject to technical analysis.

The point was made even more succinctly by Morris Llewellyn Cooke, one of the more determined advocates for adapting scientific management for use in the government. After stating his case, he often tempered his argument with a warning that retains its timeliness.[7]

> We need to be constantly reminded that the machinery of government is not the object of government.

NOTES FOR CONCLUDING OBSERVATIONS

1. Herbert Kaufmann, "Administrative Decentralization and Political Power," *Public Administration Review*, 29, (January/February 1969): 12.

2. Peter H. Odegard, "Introduction," in Arthur F. Bentley, *The Process of Government* (Cambridge: The Belknap Press of Harvard University Press, [1908] reprint of 1967), p. xiii.

3. Dan Martin, "Déjà vu: French Antecedents to American Public Administration," *Public Administration Review*, 47, (July/August 1987): 297-303.

4. Dwight Waldo, *The Administrative State* (New York: Ronald Press, 1948), p. 207.

5. Ibid, p. 74.

6. Harlow S. Person, "Scientific Management," *Bulletin of the Taylor Society*, 4, (October 1919): 8-14.

7. Morris Llewellyn Cooke, "Scientific Management of the Public Business," *American Political Science Review*, 9, (August 1915): 491.

Index of Synopses

Listings Keyed to Citation Numbers

Subject Index

Listings Keyed to Citation Numbers